GROC'S CANDID GUIDE TO THE IONIAN ISLANDS
including
CORFU, PAXOS & ANTIPAXOS, CEPHALONIA, ITHACA & ZAKYNTHOS
with Excursion details to
MEGANISI & MOGONSI
as well as
ATHENS CITY & THE MAINLAND PORTS
of
IGOUMENITSA, PARGA, PREVEZA, ASTAKOS, PATRAS & KILLINI
for the package, villa, back-packer & ferry-boating holiday maker, whether travelling by air, car, coach or train

by
Geoffrey O'Connell

Willowbridge Publishers
introduce to readers of GROC's Candid Guides

TRAVELSURANCE

A comprehensive holiday insurance plan that 'gives cover that many other policies do not reach' . . .

In addition to the more usual cover offered by other policies the **TRAVELSURANCE HOLIDAY PLAN** includes (where medically necessary):

(1) Fly-home repatriation by air ambulance.

(2) Inter-island travel costs for pregnant women.

Additionally personal accident and medical & emergency expenses EVEN while hiring a bicycle, scooter or car.

An example premium per person for Greece for 10 - 17 days is £13.40. Cover is arranged with Lloyds Underwriters.

For an application form please complete the section below and forward

---

To Willowbridge Enterprises, Willowbridge, Stoke Rd, Bletchley, Milton Keynes, Bucks.

Please forward me   *(block capitals please)*

Mr/Mrs/Miss . . . . Age . . . .

of . . . .

. . . .

a **TRAVELSURANCE** application form.

Date of commencement of holiday . . . . Duration . . . .

Signature . . . . Date . . . .

Printed in Great Britain by A. Wheaton & Co., Ltd., Exeter

CONTENTS

ROUTE TWO: Kalamaki, Laganas & Keri.
ROUTE THREE: Lithakia, Agalas, Ag Nikolaos, Kampi, Anafonitria, Volimes, Korynth, Orthones, Katastari, Alikes, Pigadakia, Kato & Meso Geraki, Planos & Tsilivi Beach.
ROUTE FOUR: Inland villages & Machairado.

ILLUSTRATIONS

Please do not forget that prices are given as a guide only especially restaurant and accommodation costs which are subject to fluctuation, almost always upwards. In the last year or so transport costs, especially ferry-boat fees have also escalated dramatically but the increased value of other currencies to the Greek drachmae has compensated, to some extent, for these seemingly inexorably rising charges.

The series is entering its fourth year of publication and I would appreciate continuing to hear from holidaymakers and travellers who have any additions or corrections to bring to my attention. As in the past, all correspondence (except that addressed 'Dear filth' or similar endearments) will be answered.

I hope readers will excuse the odd errors that creep (well gallop) into the welter of detailed information included in the body text. We manage, in order to keep the volumes as up to date as possible, to cut the period down from inception to publication to some five months which does result in the occasional slip up . . .

INTRODUCTION

This volume marks a milestone in the popular and proven series of GROCs Candid Greek Island Guides as it is the first new edition of the original guide. The rationale, the *raison d'etre* behind their production is to treat each island grouping on an individual and comprehensive basis, rather than attempt overall coverage of the 100 or so islands usually described in one volume. This obviates attempting to do justice to, say, Paxos in amongst an aggregation of many other, often disparate, islands.

Due to the vast distances involved very few, if any, vacationers can possibly visit more than number of islands in any one particular group, even if spending as much as four weeks in Greece.

It is important for package and villa holiday-makers to have an unbiased and relevant description of their planned holiday surroundings, rather than the usual extravagant hyperbole of the glossy sales brochure. It is vital for back-packers and ferry-boat travellers to have detailed and accurate information at their finger tips, on arrival. With these differing requirements in mind, factual, 'straight-from-the-shoulder' location reports have been combined with detailed plans of the major port, town and/or city of each island in the Ionian group as well as topographical island maps.

Amongst the guides on offer there are a number of books dealing with Ancient and Modern Greece, its mythology and history; there are a number of thumb-nail travel guides and there are some worthy if skimpy and or rather out-of-date guide books. Unfortunately they do not necessarily assuage the various travellers differing requirements which include speedy and accurate identification of one's position on· arrival; the location of accommodation and the whereabouts of banks, post office and tourist offices. Additional requisites are a swift and easy to read resumé of the town's main locations, cafes, tavernas and restaurants; detailed local bus and ferry timetables as well as a full island narrative. Once the traveller has settled in, then and only then can they start to feel at ease, making their own finds and discoveries.

I have chosen to omit lengthy accounts of the relevant, fabulous Greek mythology and history. These aspects of Greece are, for the serious student, very ably related by authors far more erudite than myself. Moreover, most islands have a semi-official tourist guide translated into English, and for that matter, French, German and Scandinavian, which are well worth the 150 to 300 drachmae (drs) they cost. They are usually extremely informative and rather well produced, with excellent colour photographs. Admittedly the English translation might seem a little quaint (try to read Greek, let alone translate it), and the maps are often unreliable.

Each new edition is revised but follows the now well tried formula. Part One deals with the preliminaries and describes in detail the different aspects of travelling and enjoying to the full the unforgettable experience of a Greek Island holiday. Part Two gives a full and thoroughly redrafted account of Athens, still the hub for Greek island travel, and the relevant mainland ports for connections to the Ionian islands, which for once is not Piraeus port. Part Three introduces the Ionian islands, followed by a detailed description of each island, the layout being designed to facilitate quick and easy reference.

The exchange rate has fluctuated quite violently in recent years and up-to-date information must be sought prior to departure. For instance at the time of writing the final draft, the rate to the English pound (£) was hovering about 218 drs and to the American dollar ($) some 153 drs but prices are subject to fluctuation, usually upward. Annual price increases vary between some 10-20% but fortunately the drachma devalues by approximately the same amount.

Recommendations and personalities are almost always based on personal observation and experience occasionally emphasised by the discerning comments of readers or colleagues and may well not only change from year to year but be subject to different interpretation by other observers.

For 1985 and future years some of the accommodation and eating places that are recommended in the Candid Guides may display a specially produced decal, to help readers identify the various establishments.

Enjoy yourselves and *Ya Sou* (welcome).

ACKNOWLEDGMENTS

Every year the list of those to be formally thanked grows and this edition shows no dimunition in their number which has forced the original brief entry from the inside front cover to an inside page.

There are those numerous friends and confidants we meet on passage and who, in the main, remain unnamed.

Rosemary who accompanies me, adding her often unwanted, uninformed comments and asides (and may well not be taken again!), requires especial thanks for unrelieved, unstinting (well amost unstinting) support despite being dragged from this or that sun-kissed beach.

Although receiving reward, other than in heaven, some of those who assisted me in the production of this edition require specific acknowledgment for effort far beyond the siren call of vulgar remuneration! These worthies include Linda Fehrenbach, Graham Bishop, Ted Spittles, Elizabeth, and Barbara of **The Monitor.**

Lastly I must admonish Richard Joseph for ever encouraging and cajoling me to scribble.

Geoffrey O'Connell 1986

PART ONE

1 Packing, insurance, medical matters, climatic conditions, conversion tables & a starter course in Greek

Leisure nourishes the body and the mind is also fed thereby: on the other hand, immoderate labour exhausts both. Ovid.

Vacationing anywhere on an organised tour allows a certain amount of latitude regarding the amount of luggage packed, as this method of holiday does not preclude taking fairly substantial suitcases. On the other hand, ferry-boating and back-packing restricts the amount a traveller is able to carry and the means of conveyance. The usual method is to utilise backpacks and/or roll-bags, both of which are more suitable than suitcases for this mode of travel. The choice between roll-bags and backpacks does not only depend on which are the most commodious, for at the height of the season it can be advantageous to be distinguishable from the hordes of other backpackers. To promote the chances of being offered a room, the selection of roll-bags may help disassociation from the more hippy of 'genus rucksacker'. If roll-bags are selected they should include shoulder straps which help alleviate the discomfort experienced when searching out accommodation on hot afternoons with arms just stretching and stretching and stretching. In the highly populous, oversubscribed months of July and August, it is advisable to pack a thin, foam bedroll and lightweight sleeping bag, just in case accommodation cannot be located on the occasional night.

Unless camping out, I do not think a sweater is necessary between the months of May and September. A desert jacket or lightweight anorak is a better proposition and a stout pair of sandals or training shoes are mandatory, especially if very much walking is contemplated. Leave out the evening suit and cocktail dresses, as the Greeks are very informal, instead take loose-fitting, casual clothes, and do not forget sunglasses and a floppy hat.

Should there be any doubt about the electric supply (and you shave) include a pack of disposable razors. Ladies might consider acquiring one of the small gas cylinder, portable hair-curlers. Take along a supply of toilet rolls. They are useful for tasks other than that with which they are usually associated, including mopping up spilt liquid, wiping off plates, and blowing one's nose. Do not forget some washing powder, clothes pegs, string for a line, and a few wire hangers to hook up washing.

If travelling to any extent, it is advisable to pack a few plastic, sealed-lid, liquid containers, a plate and a cup, as well as a knife and fork, condiments, an all-purpose cutting/slicing/carving knife and a combination bottle and tin opener. These all facilitate economical dining whilst on the move as food and drink, when available on ferry-boats and trains, can be comparatively expensive. Camping out will require these elementary items to be augmented with simple cooking equipment.

Mosquito coils can be bought in Greece but a preferable gadget is a small, 2 prong electric heater on which a wafer thin tablet is placed. This device can be purchased locally for some 500 drs and comes complete with a pack of the capsules. One trade name is *Doker Mat* and almost every room has a suitable electric point. The odourless vapour given off, harmless to humans, certainly sorts out the mosquitoes. Mark you we did hear of a tourist who purchased one and swore by its efficacy not even aware it was necessary to place a tablet in position. . .

Consider packing a pair of tweezers, some plasters, calamine lotion, after-sun and insect cream, as well as a bottle of aspirin in addition to any pharmaceuticals usually required. It is worth noting that sun oil and small packets of soap powder are now cheaper in Greece than much of Europe whilst, shampoo and toothpaste cost about the same. Including a small phial of disinfectant has merit, but it is best not to leave the liquid in the original glass bottle. Should it break, the disinfectant and glass mingled with clothing can prove not only messy but also leaves a distinctive and lingering odour. Kaolin and morphine is a very reliable stomach settler. Greek chemists dispense medicines and prescriptions that only a doctor would be able to mete out in many other Western European countries, so, prior to summoning a doctor, try the local pharmacy.

Insurance & medical matters

While touching upon medical matters, a national of an EEC country, should extend their states National Health cover. United Kingdom residents should contact the local *Department of Health and Social Security* requesting form number *E111 UK*. When completed, and returned, this will result in a *Certificate of Entitlement to Benefits in Kind during a stay in a Member State*. Well, that's super! In short, it entitles a person to medical treatment in other EEC countries. Do not only rely on this prop, but seriously consider taking out a holiday insurance policy, covering loss of baggage and money, personal accident and medical expenses, cancellation of the holiday and personal liability. Check the exclusion clauses carefully. It is no good imagining one is covered for 'this or that' only to discover the insurance company has craftily excluded claims under a particular section. Should you intend to hire a scooter ensure this form of 'activity' is comprehensively insured. Rather than rely on the rather inadequate standard insurance cover offered by many tour companies, it is best to approach a specialist insurance broker. For instance, bearing in mind the rather rudimentary treatment offered by the average Greek island hospital, it is almost obligatory to include *Fly-Home Medicare* cover in any policy. A couple of illustrative homilies might reinforce the argument. Firstly the Greek hospital system expects the patients family to minister and feed the inmate out of hours. This can result in holiday companions having to camp out in the ward for the duration of any internment. Perhaps more thought-provoking is the home-spun belief that a patient is best left the first night to survive, if it is God's will, and to pass on if it is not! A number of years hearing of the unfortunate experiences of friends and readers, who failed to act on the advice given herein, as well as the inordinate difficulties I have experienced in arranging cover for myself, has prompted me to offer readers an all embracing travel insurance scheme. Details are to be found on Page iii. **DON'T DELAY, ACT NOW.**

Most rooms do not have rubbish containers so include some plastic bin liners which are very useful for packing food as well as storing dirty washing. A universal sink plug is almost a necessity. Many Greek sinks do not have one, but as the water usually drains away very slowly this could be considered an academic point.

Take along a pack of cards, and enough paperback reading to while away sunbathing sojourns and long journeys. Playing cards are subject to a government tax, which makes their price exorbitant and books are expensive but some shops and lodgings operate a book-swop scheme.

Many flights, buses, ferry-boats and train journeys start off early in the morning so a small battery-operated alarm clock may well help to save sleepless, fretful nights. A small hand or wrist compass can be an enormous help orientating in towns and if room and weight allow, a torch is a useful addition to the inventory.

Do not forget your passport which is absolutely essential to (1) enter Greece, (2) book into most hotels, pensions or camp-sites, (3) change money and (4) hire a scooter or car.

In the larger, more popular tourist orientated resorts Diners and American Express (Amex) credit cards are accepted. Personal cheques may be changed as long as accompanied by a Eurocheque bank card. Americans can use an Amex credit card at their overseas offices to change personal cheques up to $1000. They may, by prior arrangement, have cable transfers made to overseas banks, allowing 24 hrs from the moment their home bank receives specific instructions. It is wise to detail credit card, traveller's cheques and airline ticket numbers and keep the list separately from the aforementioned items, in case they should be mislaid. This is a piece of advice I always give but rarely, if ever, carry out myself.

Visitors are only allowed to import 3000 drs of Greek currency (in notes) and the balance required must be in traveller's cheques and/or foreign currency. It used to be 1500 drs but the decline in the value of the Greek drachma has resulted in the readjustment. With only 3000 drs in hand it is often necessary to change currency quite quickly. One problem, to bear in mind, is that arrival may be at the weekend, or the banks will be on strike, which in recent summers has become quite a common occurrence.

Imported spirits are comparatively expensive (except on some of the duty free Dodecanese islands) but the duty free allowance, that can be taken into Greece, is up to one and a half litres of alcohol. So if a whisky or gin drinker, and partial to an evening sundowner, acquire a bottle or two before arrival. Cigars are difficult to buy on the islands, so it may well be advantageous to take along the 75 that can be imported. Note the above only applies to fellow members of the EEC. Allowances for travellers from other countries are 1 litre of alcohol and 50 cigars.

Camera buffs should take as much film as possible as it is more costly in Greece than in most Western European countries.

Officially, the Ionian Pelagos has some 3000 hours of sunshine per year, out of an approximate, possible 4250. The Ionian islands do not have to ensure the fairly constant northerly *Meltemi* wind, which blows strongly in the Aegean during the summer months. The prevailing Ionian summer breeze is the north westerly *Maestros*. The months of July and August are usually dry and very hot for 24 hours a day, although subject to occasional showers, sometimes accompanied by thunder and lightning. So pack an umbrella if space allows. The sea in April is perhaps a little cool for swimming, but May and June are marvellous months, as are September and October.

For the statistically minded

The monthly average temperatures for the Ionian are

		Jan	Feb	Mar	Apr	May	June	July	Aug	Sept	Oct	Nov	Dec
Average monthly air	C°	10	10	12	15	19	24	27	26	23	19	15	12
temperature.	F°	50	50	54	59	66	75	81	79	73	66	59	54
Sea surface temperature	C°	15	15	15	16	18	21	24	25	24	21	19	18
(at 1400 hrs).	F°	59	59	59	61	64	70	75	77	75	70	66	64
Average days of rain		14	12	7	4	3	1	—	1	2	5	8	14

The best time of the year to holiday

The above chart indicates that the best months are May, June, September and October, July and August probably being too hot. Additionally, the most crowded months when accommodation is at a premium, are also July and August and the first two weeks of September. Taking everything into account, it does not need an Einstein to work out the most favourable period to take a vacation.

Conversion tables & equivalents

Units	Approximate Conversion	Equivalent
Miles to kilometres	Divide by 5, multiply by 8	5 miles = 8 km
Kilometres to miles	Divide by 8, multiply by 5	
Feet to metres	Divide by 10, multiply by 3	10 ft = 3 m
Metres to feet	Divide by 3, multiply by 10	

Inches to centimetres	Divide by 2, multiply by 5	1 inch = 2.5 cm
Centimetres to inches	Divide by 5, multiply by 2	
Fahrenheit to centigrade	Deduct 32, divide by 9 and multiply by 5	77°F = 25°C
Centigrade to fahrenheit	Divide by 5, multiply by 9 and add 32	
Gallons to litres	Divide by 2, multiply by 9	2 gal = 9 litres
Litres to gallons	Divide by 9, multiply by 2	

Note: 1 pint = 0.6 of a litre and 1 litre = 1.8 pints.

Pounds (weight) to kilos	Divide by 11, multiply by 5	5 kg = 11 lb
Kilos to pounds	Divide by 5, multiply by 11	

Note: 16 oz = 1 lb; 1000 g = 1 kg and 100 g = 3.5 oz.

Tyre pressures
Pounds per square inch to kilogrammes per square centimetre.

lb/sq. in.	kg/cm	lb/sq. in.	kg/cm
10	0.7	26	1.8
15	1.1	28	2.0
20	1.4	30	2.1
24	1.7	40	2.8

The Greeks use the metric system but most unreasonably sell liquid (i.e. wine, spirits and beer) by weight. Take my word for it, a 640 g bottle of wine is approximately 0.7 of a litre or 1.1 pints. Proprietory wines such as *Demestika* are sold in bottles holding as much as 950 g, which is 1000 ml or 1¾ pints and represents very good value.

Electric points in the larger towns, smarter hotels and holiday resorts are 220 volts AC and will power any American or British appliance. Older buildings in out of the way places might still have 110 DC supply. Remote pensions may not have any electricity, other than that supplied by a generator and even then the rooms might not be wired up. More correctly they may well be wired but not connected.

Greek time is 2 hours ahead of GMT, as it is during British Summer Time and 7 hours ahead of United States Eastern Time. That is except for a short period when the Greek clocks are corrected for their Winter at the end of September, some weeks ahead of United Kingdom alteration.

Basics & essentials of the language

These notes and subsequent 'Useful Greek' at the relevant chapter endings are not, nor could be, intended to substitute for a formal phrase book, or two. Accent marks have been omitted.

Whilst in the United Kingdom it is worth noting that the British Broadcasting Co, Marylebone High St, London W1M 4AA have produced an excellent book, *Greek Language and People*, accompanied by a cassette and a record.

For the less committed a very useful pocket sized phrase book that I always have to hand is *The Greek Travelmate* by Richard Drew Publishing, Glasgow at a cost of £1.00.

The alphabet		Sounds like
Capitals	**Lower case**	
A	α	Alpha
B	β	Veeta
Γ	γ	Ghama
Δ	δ	Dhelta
E	ε	Epsilon
Z	ζ	Zeeta
H	η	Eeta
Θ	θ	Theeta
I	ι	Yiota
K	κ	Kapa
Λ	λ	Lamtha
M	μ	Mee
N	ν	Nee
Ξ	ξ	Ksee
O	ο	Omikron
Π	π	Pee
P	ρ	Roh
Σ	σ	Sighma
T	τ	Taf
Υ	υ	Eepsilon
Φ	φ	Fee
X	χ	Chi
Ψ	ψ	Psi
Ω	ω	Omegha

Groupings

αι	'e' as in let
αυ	'av/af' as in have/haff
ει/οι	'ee' as in seen
εν	'ev/ef' as in ever/effort
ον	'oo' as in toot
γγ	'ng' as in ring
γκ	At the beginning of a word 'g' as in go
γχ	'nks' as in rinks
μπ	'b' as in beer
ντ	At the beginning of a word 'd' as in deer
	In the middle of a word 'nd' as in send
τζ	'ds' as in deeds

Useful Greek

English	Greek	Sounds like
Hello/goodbye	Γεια σου	Yia soo (informal singular said with a smile)
Good morning/day	Καλημερα	Kalimera
Good afternoon/evening	Καληοπερα	Kalispera (formal)
Good night	Καληνχτα	Kalinikta
See you later	Θα σε δω αργοτερα	Tha se thoargotera
See you tomorrow	Θα σε δω αυριο	Tha se tho avrio
Yes	Ναι	Ne (accompanied by a downwards and sideways nod of the head)
No	Οχι	Ochi (accompanied by an upward movement of the head, heavenwards and with a closing of the eyes)
Please	Παραχαλω	Parakalo
Thank you	(Σας) Ευχαριστω	(sas) Efkaristo

No, thanks	Οχι ευχαριοτιεδ	Ochi, efkaristies
Thank you very much	Ευχαριοτωπολυ	Efkaristo poli
After which the reply may well be	Παραχαλω	Thank you (and please)
Do you speak English?	Μιλατε Αγγλικα	Milahteh anglikah
How do you say...	Πωδ λενε...	Pos lene...
... in Greek?	...στα Ελληνικα	...sta Ellinika
What is this called?	Πωδ το λενε	Pos to lene
I do not understand	Δεν καταλαβαινω	Then katahlavehno
Could you speak more slowly (slower?)	Μπορετε να μηλατε πιο αργα	Borete na melatee peo seegha (arga)
Could you write it down	Μπορειτε νο μον το γραψετε	Boreete na moo to grapsete

NUMBERS

One	Ενα	enna
Two	Δυο	thio
Three	Τρια	triah
Four	Τεσσερα	tessehra
Five	Πεντε	pendhe
Six	Εξι	exhee
Seven	Επτα	eptah
Eight	Οκτω	ockto
Nine	Εννεα	ennea
Ten	Δεκα	thecca
Eleven	Εντεκα	endekha
Twelve	Δωδεκα	thiodhehka
Thirteen	Δεκατρια	thehka triah
Fourteen	Δεκατεσσερα	thehka tessehra
Fifteen	Δεκαπεντε	thehka pendhe
Sixteen	Δεκαεζι	theaexhee
Seventeen	Δεκαεπτα	thehkaeptah
Eighteen	Δεκαοκτω	thehkaockto
Nineteen	Δεκαεννεα	thehkaennea
Twenty	Εικοσι	eckossee
Twenty-one	Εικοσι ενα	eckossee enna
Twenty-two	Εικοσι δυο	eckossee thio
Thirty	Τριαντα	treandah
Forty	Σαραντα	sarandah
Fifty	Πενηντα	penindah
Sixty	Εζηντα	exhindah
Seventy	Εβδομηντα	evthomendah
Eighty	Ογδοντα	ogthondah
Ninety	Ενενητα	eneendah
One hundred	Εκατο	eckato
One hundred and one	Εκατον ενα	eckaton enna
Two hundred	Διακοσια	theeakossia
One thousand	Χιλια	kheelia
Two thousand	Δυοχιλιαδεζ	thio kheelia

2 Getting to & from the Ionian, Athens & the mainland ports

If all the year were playing holidays, to sport would be as tedious as to work. *William Shakespeare*

To start this chapter off, a word of introductory warning. Whatever form of travel is utilised, do not pack any money or travellers cheques in luggage that will have to be stowed away. The year before last, almost unbelievably, we met a young lady who had at the last moment, prior to checking-in the airport, stuffed some drachmae notes in a zipped side pocket of one of her suitcases. On arrival in Greece, surprise, surprise she was minus the money.

BY AIR
Scheduled flights
The choice of airline access to the Ionian islands rests between direct flight to Corfu or via Athens East (international) airport, transferring by bus to Athens West (domestic) airport and then, by Olympic Airways, on to the islands of Corfu, Cephalonia, Zakynthos or mainland Preveza for Lefkas. Note both international and domestic Olympic flights use the West airport.

From the United Kingdom
Heathrow to Athens (3¾ hours): daily, non-stop British Airways, Olympic and others.
Heathrow to Corfu (3 hours). Twice weekly direct, Olympic, and via Athens daily, Olympic.
Scheduled air-fare options include: 1st class return, economy, special economy and APEX (Advanced Purchase Excursion Fare), which is the cheapest scheduled fare.

Charter flights, package tours
Some package tour operators keep a number of seats available on each flight for, what is in effect, a charter flight. A nominal charge is made for accommodation (which need not be taken up), the cost being included in the return air-fare. These seats are substantially

cheaper than the scheduled APEX fares. Apart from the relatively low price, the normal two week holiday period can be extended by a further week or weeks for a small surcharge. There is a wide variety of United Kingdom departure airports, including Birmingham, Gatwick, Manchester and Luton, arriving at Athens or Corfu. As one correspondent has pointed out, the frequency of charter flights tails off dramatically between October and March as does the choice of airport departure points. Do not forget this when contemplating an out-of-season holiday.

To ascertain what is on offer, scan the travel section of the Sunday papers, as well as the weekly magazine *Time Out* and, possibly, *Private Eye*. There are many varied package tours with a number of the large tour operators and the smaller, more personal, companies, offering a bewildering array of multi-centre, fly-drive, budget-bed, self catering and personally tailored holidays, in addition to the more usual hotel accommodation.

Exceptionally reasonable charter flights, with the necessary accommodation vouchers, are available through *Owners Abroad Ltd*, Ilford, who also have offices in Manchester, Birmingham, and Glasgow. Example fares and routes for 1986 include:

Two week return fares		**Low season**	**Mid-season**	**High season**
Corfu leaving Luton	From	£108.75	£122.75	£133.75
Monday				
Athens: leaving Gatwick	From	£105.75	£124.75	£137.75
Thursday, Friday, Sunday				
: leaving Manchester	From	£118.75	£135.75	£149.75
Thursday, Sunday				

These rates are subject to surcharges and airport taxes. The fares for three or four weeks are those above plus £20 and for five to six weeks, an additional 50 per cent is charged. Note that the extra weeks allowed for charter flights to Greece are restricted to six, not twelve weeks.

Perhaps the least expensive flights available are **Courier Flights** from *INFLIGHT COURIER, 7 - 9 Heath Rd, The Quadrant, Weybridge, Surrey KT13 8SX. Tel (0932) 57455/56*. These scheduled seats start off at about £69 return for the low season period BUT passengers can only take a maximum of 10 kg of hand-luggage. One holdall measuring no more than 1 ft x 2 ft — no other baggage.

Olympic Airways subsidiary, *Allsun Holidays* has taken up the challenge and offers selected island-hopping-holidays which include valid accommodation vouchers. This innovation does include the Ionian with a flight to Corfu. Olympic Airways has joined the charter flight fray with their *Love-A Fare* service. (Yes love-a-fare!), the London to Athens return fare costing £159 and Corfu £154. The booking must be made at least one month in advance and allows a maximum of four weeks stay. There are Olympic offices in London as well as Manchester, Birmingham and Glasgow.

Companies offering interesting and slightly off-beat holidays include the *Aegina Club Ltd*, and *Ramblers Holidays*. *Aegina* have a wide range of holidays including tours, three different locations in up to three weeks, and additionally will tailor a programme to fit in with client's requirements. *Ramblers*, as would be imagined, include in their programme walking holidays based on a number of locations with half-board accommodation. More conventional offerings in well equipped villas, houses and apartments are available from the genteel *Greek Islands Club* who place at the holiday-makers disposal a wide variety of Ionian islands, including Paxos, Cephalonia, Ithaca and Zakynthos. Their brochure is a joy in itself and includes details of sailing and wind-surfing adjuncts to the holiday. Another rather interesting if exclusive travel company is *Cricketer Holidays* who offer taverna and villa accommodation on the island of Lefkas.

Students

Students under 26 years of age (oh to be 26 again) should consider contacting *World-Wide Student Travel* who market a number of inexpensive charter flights. Students of any age or scholars under 22 years of age (whatever mode of travel is planned) should take their *International Student Identity Card* (ISIC). This will ensure discounts are available whenever they are applicable, not only in respect of travel but also for entry to museums, archaeological sites and some forms of entertainment.

If under 26 years of age, but not a student, it may be worthwhile applying for membership of *The Federation of International Youth Travel Organization* (FIYTO) which guarantees youth discounts from some ferry and tour operators.

Scheduled flights
From the United States of America
Scheduled Olympic flights include departures from:
Atlanta (via John F Kennedy (JFK) airport, New York (N.Y.)): daily
Boston (via JFK or La Guardia, N.Y.): daily
Chicago (via JFK): daily
Dallas (via JFK): daily
Houston (via JFK): daily
Los Angeles (via JFK): daily
Miami (via JFK; 15 hours): daily
Minneapolis (via JFK): daily
New York (JFK approximately 10½ hours); daily direct
Norfolk (via JFK): daily except Saturday
Philadelphia (via JFK; about 11 hours): daily
Rochester (via JFK): daily
San Francisco (via JFK; about 14½ hours): daily
Seattle (via JFK or London): daily
Tampa (via JFK): daily
Washington DC (via JFK or La Guardia): daily
Note that flights via New York's John F Kennedy airport involve a change of plane from, or to, a domestic American airline.

USA domestic airlines, including TWA also run a number of flights to Greece and the choice of air fares is bewildering including economy, first class return, super APEX, APEX, GIT, excursion, ABC, OTC, ITC, and others, wherein part package costs are incorporated.

Charter/standby flights & secondary airlines
As in the United Kingdom, scanning the Sunday national papers' travel section, including the *New York Times*, will disclose various companies offering package tours and charter flights. Another way to make the journey is to take a standby flight to London and then fly, train or bus on to Greece. Alternatively, there are a number of inexpensive, secondary airline companies offering flights to London and the major Western European capitals.

Useful agencies, especially for students, include *Let's Go Travel Services*.

From Canada
Scheduled Olympic flights include departures from:
Montreal: twice weekly direct
or (via Amsterdam, JFK and or La Guardia, N.Y.): daily except Mondays
Toronto: twice weekly (via Montreal)
or (via Amsterdam, JFK and/or La Guardia N.Y.): daily except Monday and Friday
Winnipeg (via Amsterdam): Thursday and Sunday only

As for the USA, the above flights involve a change of airline and there is a choice of domestic and package flights and a wide range of differing fares.

Student agencies include *Canadian Universities Travel Service*.

From Australia
There are Australian airline scheduled flights from Adelaide, Brisbane, Melbourne and Sydney to Athens. Regular as well as excursion fares and affinity groups.

From New Zealand
There are no scheduled flights.
Various connections are available as well as regular and affinity fares.

From South Africa
Scheduled Olympic flights include departures from:
Cape Town (via Johannesburg): Fridays and Saturdays only
Durban (via Johannesburg): Fridays and Saturdays only
Johannesburg: direct, Thursday, Friday, Saturday (up to the 2nd September) and Sunday.
Flights via Johannesburg involve a change of plane from, or to, a domestic airline.
South African airline flights from Johannesburg to Athens on regular, excursion and affinity fares.

From Ireland
Scheduled Olympic flights from:
Dublin: daily via London which involves a change of airline
Irish airline flights from Dublin.

Note that when flying from Ireland, Australia, New Zealand, South Africa, Canada and the USA there are sometimes advantages in travelling via London or other European capitals on stop-over and taking inexpensive connection flights to Greece.

Scandinavia including
From Denmark
Scheduled Olympic flights from:
Copenhagen (via Frankfurt): daily involving a change of aircraft as well as non-stop flights on Tuesday, Wednesday, Friday and Sunday.

From Sweden
Scheduled Olympic flights from:
Stockholm (via Frankfurt): daily involving a change of aircraft.

From Norway
Scheduled Olympic flights from:
Oslo (via Frankfurt): daily involving a change of aircraft. Contact SAS Airlines for Olympic Airways.

All the Scandinavian countries have a large choice of domestic and package flights with a selection of offerings.

AIRPORTS
United Kingdom
Do not forget if staying in Greece longer than two weeks, the long-stay car parking fees are fairly expensive. The difficulty is that most charter flights leave and arrive at rather unsociable hours, so friends and family may not be too keen to act as a taxi service.

Athens
Hellinikon airport is split into two parts, West (Olympic domestic and international flights)

and East (foreign airlines). There are coaches to make the connection between the two airports, and Olympic buses to Athens centre as well as the city buses. At the domestic or Western airport, the city buses pull in alongside the terminal building. Across the road is a pleasant cafe/restaurant but the service becomes fairly chaotic when packed out. To the left of the cafe (facing) is a newspaper kiosk and further on, across a side road, a Post Office is hidden in the depths of the first building.

The Eastern airport is outwardly quite smart but can, in reality, become an expensive, very cramped and uncomfortable location if there are long delays. These can occur when, for instance, the air traffic controllers strike elsewhere in Europe. Remember when leaving Greece to have enough money and some food left for an enforced stay, as flight departures are consistently overdue and food and drink in the airport are costly. There are simply no facilities for an overnight sleep and the bench seats are very soon taken up. You have been warned.

BY TRAIN
From the United Kingdom & European countries
Recommended only for train buffs and masochists but one of the alternative routes to be considered where a visitor intends to stay in Greece in excess of 6 weeks. The quickest journey of the three major scheduled overland routes takes about 60 hours, and a second-class return fare costs in the region of £215.00. One advantage is that you can break the journey along the route (a little difficult on an airline flight), and another is that it is possible to travel out on one route and back by an alternative track (if you will excuse the pun). It is important to take along basic provisions, toilet paper, and to wear old clothes.

A recent return to the 'day of the train' reinforced my general opinion and introductory remarks in respect of this particular method of travel, bringing sharply back into focus the disadvantages and rejoinders. The list of points to bear in mind, drawbacks and faults should be enough to deter any but the most determined.

Try not to have a query involving the overseas information desk at Victoria Station. The facility is undermanned and the wait to get to a counter averages ¾hr. The staff are very willing but it is of interest that they overcome the intricacies of the official British Rail European timetable ("it's all Greek to me guvnor") by overtly referring to the (infinitely) more manageable Thomas Cook publication. The channel crossing is often on craft that would not be pressed into service if we declared war on the Isle of Wight, the journey is too short for any cabins to be available, the duty free goods on offer are very limited and there are inordinate delays between train, boat and train.

The French trains that ply between the coast and Paris are of an excellent standard. Changing trains at the 'black hole' of the Gare de Nord, Paris sharply focuses travellers attention on a whole sub-culture of human beings who exist in and around a number of European railway stations. My favourite example of this little known branch of the human race is the 'bag-shuffler' — usually a middle-aged lady. The genus is initially recognisable by the multitudinous paper and plastic bags festooned about the person. Once at rest the contents are constantly and interminably shuffled from one bag to another, and back again, the ritual being accompanied by low muttering.

French railway stations which are heated to a gentle simmering have perfected a waiting room seating arrangement that precludes any but a drunk, contortionist stretching out for a nap. In common with most other railway stations food and drink are expensive and credit cards impossible to use even at the swanky station restaurants.

The Metro connection between the Gare de Nord and the Gare de Lyon is not straightforward and involves a walk. The Gare de Lyon springs a minor trap for the unwary in that the inter-continental trains depart from platforms reached by a long walk up the far left platform (facing the trains). Incidentally some of the French trains now resemble childrens rocket drawings.

The stations toilet facilities are miniscule and, other than use of the mens urinal and washbasin, are charged. Ladies have to pay about 2 Francs (F), a private closet costs 6F and a shower 12F. And do not imagine you will be able to sneak in for a crafty stand-up wash — the toilets are intently watched over.

Although it may appear to be an optional extra, it is mandatory to purchase a couchette ticket for the journey as will become apparent. It is also necessary to pack food and drink at least for the French part of the journey as usually there are no refreshment services. In Italy most trains are met at the various station stops by trolley pushing vendors of (expensive) sustenance.

Venice station is signed *St Lucia* and is most conveniently sited bang on the edge of a main canal waterfront with shops and restaurants to the left. Some of the cake shops sell slabs of pizza pie for about 800 Lira (L) which furnishes good stand-by nourishment. The scheduled stop-over here will have to be adjusted for any (inevitable) delay in arrival. Venice (on the outward journey) is the watershed where Greek and the occasional Yugoslavian carriages are coupled up and passengers can be guaranteed to encounter a number of nasties. These compartments are seedier and dirtier than their European counterparts, and the lavatories vary between bad to unspeakable. Faults include toilets that won't flush (sometimes appearing to fill up), Greek toilet paper (which apart from other deficiencies lacks body and through which fingers break), no toilet paper at all, no soap in the dispenser, no coat hooks, water taps that don't and the whole rather grimy.

From Venice the term 'Express' should be ignored as the train's progress becomes slower and slower and slower with long unscheduled stops and quite inordinate delays at the Yugoslavian frontiers. For the Yugoslavian part of the journey it is necessary to lock oneself into the couchette as some of the locals have an annoying habit of entering a compartment and determinedly looting tourists luggage. It is inadvisable to leave the train at Belgrade for a stop-over as the rooms offered to tourists are extremely expensive and it is almost impossible to renegotiate a couchette for the remainder of the onward journey. There are trolley attendants at the major Yugoslavian railway stations but the contents of the rolls proffered are of an interesting nature resembling biltong or hard-tak burgers. Certainly when poked by the enthusiastic vendors I'm sure their fingers buckle. Another item on offer are large cheese curd pies and a railway employee wanders round twice a day with a very large aluminium teapot ostensibly containing coffee. Nobody appears to be interested in payment in Yugoslavian dinars, but American dollars or English pounds sterling almost cause a purr of satisfaction. Fortunately the carriage retainer usually keeps a stache of alcoholic drinks for sale. An aside is that the Yugoslavians are obsessed by wheel-tapping and at all and every stop, almost at the drop of a sleeper, will appear and perform. Much of the journey after Belgrade is on a single line track and should, for instance, a cow break into a trot the animal might well overtake the train. At the frontier one is reminded of the rigours of the Eastern States and passengers are subjected to rigorous and lengthy baggage and papers check by a swamp of officials which include stern faced, unsmiling, gun-toting police.

In stark contrast the friendly Greek frontier town of Idomeni is a tonic. Even late at night the stations' bank is open as is the station taverna/snack-bar with a scattering of tables on the platform and a buzz of brightly lit noise and activity.

To avoid the Yugoslavian experience a very pleasant alternative is to take the train the length of Italy to Brindisi port and catch an international ferry-boat to the mainland Greek ports of Igoumenitsa or Patras. From Patras a bus or the train can be used to make the connection with Athens.

Brindisi (Italy) contains several traps for the unwary. Unfortunately the railway station and quay for the Italy-Greek ferry-boats are some 200 m apart, which on a hot day...

The railway station has no formal ticket office or barrier. It is only necessary to dismount, turn left along the platform, left again, along the concrete wall supporting the first floor

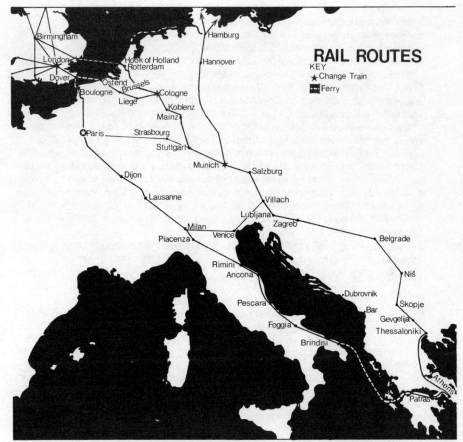

RAIL ROUTES
KEY
★ Change Train
🚢 Ferry

Birmingham
London
Dover
Boulogne
Ostend
Brussels
Liege
Hook of Holland
Rotterdam
Hamburg
Hannover
Cologne
Koblenz
Mainz
Paris
Strasbourg
Stuttgart
Dijon
Munich ★
Salzburg
Lausanne
Villach
Ljubljana
Zagreb
Milan
Venice
Belgrade
Piacenza
Rimini
Ancona
Niš
Dubrovnik
Pescara
Bar
Skopje
Gevgelija
Foggia
Thessaloniki
Brindisi
Athens
Patras

One   European railway routes

concourse (which stretches over and above the platforms), across the railway lines and left again along the sterile dockland street to the ferry-boat complex. The road, hemmed in by a prefabricated wall on the right, curves parallel to the seawall on the left from which it is separated by a high chain link fence, a number of railway lines and a tarmacadam quay. But, before leaving the station, stop, for all the ticket offices and necessary officials are situated in the referred to upper storey buildings and in the 'Main St'. My favourite tour office is across the road from the station, alongside a bank on the corner formed by the 'Main St.' and the 'ferry-boat' street. The staff are very helpful and most informative. Diagonally across the bottom of this end of the 'Main St' is a small tree edged square which, as it is well endowed with park benches, makes for an unofficial waiting room with travellers and back-packers occupying most of the available space. Do not forget when booking rail tickets to ask for Brindisi Maritime, the town railway station is some kilometres inland.

15

The international ferry-boats on this route are, in the main, luxurious, beautifully appointed and expensive. Possible trappings include a sea-water swimming pool, ladies hairdresser and beauty salon, a number of restaurants and a self service cafeteria, a coffee bar and a disco. Unfortunately the self-service meals are also outrageously expensive with, for instance, a meal for two of veal and potatoes, a spinach pie, lettuce salad and a ½ bottle of emasculated retsina costing about 1500 drs. Coffee 80 drs. Moral, try not to eat on board. A splendid 2 berth cabin with a generous en suite bathroom will set a traveller back some 4000 drs. Prices everywhere are in American dollars and the change desk even when on the Greece to Italy leg, will not change currency into Italian lira. . .?

Travellers under 26 years of age can take advantage of British Rail's Inter-Rail pass while Americans and Canadians may obtain a Eurorail pass prior to reaching Europe by applying to *Victoria Travel Centre*. There is also the Transalpino ticket available from their London office and all these offers hold out a substantial discount on standard train and ferry fares, but are subject to various terms and conditions. Certainly it must be borne in mind that the Greek railway system is not extensive and unless travelling in other European countries, a concessionary pass might not represent much of a saving. On the other hand discounts in respect of the Greek railways may include travel on the state railway buses (OSE).

Other cut-price student outfits offering train, coach and flights include *London Student Travel* and *Eurotrain.* Examples of the tickets, costs and conditions include:

Inter-Rail ticket	Under 26 years of age, valid one month, for use in 21 countries and also allows half-fare travel in the UK, on Sealink and B+I ships as well as P&O ferries via Southampton and Le Havre	from	£119

		Single	**Return**
Transalpino ticket	Under 26, valid for two months, allows stop-over en route to the destination. London to Athens via Brindisi or Yugoslavia	from £88.35	£169.60

Timetables & routes (Illustration 1)

This paragraph caused me as much work as whole chapters on other subjects. *British Rail*, whose timetable I had the greatest difficulty deciphering, and *Thomas Cook*, whose timetable I could understand, were both helpful.

Choice of routes include:

(1) London (Victoria Station), Dover (Western Docks), (jetfoil), Ostend, Brussels, Liege, Aachen, Cologne (change train, ¾ hr delay), Mainz, Mannheim, Ulm, Munich (change train ¾ hr delay), Salzburg, Jesenice, Ljubljana, Zagreb, Belgrade (Beograd), Skopje, Gevgelija, Idomeni, Thessaloniki to Athens.

An example: of the journey is as follows:

Departure: 1300 hrs, afternoon sea crossing, evening on the train, late night change of train at Cologne, night on the train, morning change of train at Munich, all day and night on the train arriving Athens very late some 2½ days later at 2314 hrs.

(2) London (Charing Cross/Waterloo East stations), Dover Hoverport, (hovercraft), Boulogne Hoverpoint, Paris (de Nord), change train (and station) to Paris (de Lyon), Strasbourg, Munich, Salzburg, Ljubljana, Zagreb, Belgrade (change train, 1¼ hrs delay), Thessaloniki to Athens.

An example:

Departure: 0955 hrs and arrive 2½ days later at 2315 hrs.

Second class single fares from £112.60 and return fare from £215.30.

(3) London (Victoria), Folkestone Harbour, (ferry-boat), Calais, Paris (de Nord), change train (and station) to Paris (de Lyon), Venice, Ljubljana, Zagreb, Belgrade, Thessaloniki to Athens.

An example:
Departure: 1415 hrs and arrive 2¾ days later at 0840 hrs.

(4) London (Liverpool St.), Harwich (Parkeston Quay), ferry-boat, Hook of Holland, Rotterdam, Eindhoven, Venlo, Cologne (change train), Mainz, Mannheim, Stuttgart, Ulm, Munich, Salzburg, Jesenice, Ljubljana, Zagreb, Belgrade, Nis, Skopje, Gevgelija, Idomeni, Thessaloniki to Athens.

An example:
Departure: 1940 hrs, night ferry crossing, change train at Cologne between 1048 and 1330 hrs, first and second nights on the train and arrive at Athens middle of the day at 1440 hrs.

An alternative is to take the more pleasurable train journey through Italy and make a ferry-boat connection to Greece.

(5) London (Victoria), Folkestone Harbour, Calais, Boulogne, Amiens, Paris (de Nord), change train and station to Paris (de Lyon), Dijon, Vallorbe, Lausanne, Brig, Domodossala, Milan (Central), Bologna, Rimini, Ancona, Pescara, Bari to Brindisi.

(5a) Brindisi to Patras sea crossing.

(5b) Patras to Athens.

An example:
Departure: 0958 hrs, day ferry crossing, change of train at Paris to the Parthenon Express, one night on the train and arrive at Brindisi at 1850 hrs. Embark on the ferry-boat, departing at 2000 hrs, night on the ferry-boat and disembark at 1300 hrs the next day. Take the coach to Athens arriving at 1600 hrs.

The second class single fare costs from £124.90.

On all these services children benefit from reduced fares, depending on their age. Couchettes and sleepers are usually available at extra cost and Jetfoil sea crossings are subject to a surcharge.

The above are only a guide and up-to-date details must be checked with the relevant offices.

Details of fares and timetables are available from *British Rail Continental Enquiries*. Should enquiries fail at that address try the *European Rail Passenger Office* or *The Hellenic State Railways (OSE)*. The most cogent, helpful and informative firm through whom to book rail travel must be *Victoria Travel Centre*. I have always found them to be extremely accommodating.

It is well worth contacting *Thomas Cook Ltd*, who have a very useful range of literature and timetables available from their Publications Department.

From the Continent & Scandinavia to Athens

Pick up one of the above main lines by using the appropriate connections detailed in Illustration 1.

Departure terminals from Scandinavia include Helsinki (Finland), Oslo (Norway), Gothenburg, Malmo, Stockholm (Sweden), Fredrikshavn and Copenhagen (Denmark).

BY COACH

This means of travel is for the more hardy voyager and/or the young. If the description of the train journey has caused apprehension, the tales of passengers of the less luxurious coach companies will strike terror into the recipient. Common 'faults' include lack of 'wash and brush up' stops, smugglers, prolonged border custom investigations, last minute changes of route and breakdowns. All this is on top of the forced intimacy with a number of widely disparate, enforced companions, some wildly drunk, in cramped, uncomfortable surroundings.

For details of the scheduled *Euroways Supabus* apply c/o Victoria Coach Station or to the *National Express Company*. A single fare costs £62 and a return ticket £115 This through service takes 4 days plus, with no overnight layovers but short stops at Cologne, Frankfurt and Munich where there is a change of coach. Fares include ferry costs but exclude refreshments. Arrival and departure in Greece is at the Peloponissou Railway Station, Athens. The timetable is as follows:

Departure from London, Victoria Coach Station, Bay 20: Friday and Saturday at 2030 hrs arriving at 1100 hrs 4½ days later.

Return journey
Departure from Filellinon St, Syntagma Sq, Athens: Wednesday and Friday at 1300 hrs arriving London at 0800 hrs, 4 days later.

Express coach companies include *Consolas Travel*. This well-established company runs daily buses during the summer months, except Sunday, and single fares start at about £35 with a return ticket from £69. Other services are run by the various 'pirate' bus companies, the journey time is about the same and, again, prices, which may be slightly cheaper, do not include meals. On a number of islands, travel agents signs refer to the *Magic Bus*, or as a fellow traveller so aptly put it — *The Tragic Bus*, but the company that ran this renowned and infamous service perished some years ago. Imitators may well perpetuate the name.

In the United Kingdom it is advisable to obtain a copy of the weekly magazine *Time Out* wherein the various coach companies advertise. For return trips from Athens, check shop windows in Omonia Sq, the American Express office in Syntagma Sq, or the Students Union in Filellinon St, just off Syntagma Sq.

BY CAR (Illustration 2)

Usually only a worthwhile alternative method of travel if there are at least three adults and you are planning to stay for longer than three weeks, as the journey from England is about 1900 miles and will take approximately 50 hrs non-stop driving.

One of the shortest routes from the United Kingdom is via car-ferry to Ostend, (Belgium), on to Munich, Salzburg (Germany), Klagenfurt (Austria) and Ljubljana (Yugoslavia). There the Autoput E94 is used, on to Zagreb, Belgrade (Beograd) and Nis on the E5, where the E27 and E55 are taken via Skopje to the frontier town of Gevgelija/Evzonoi. Due to major rebuilding works, the Yugoslavian road between Zagreb and Nis can be subject to lengthy delays.

The main road, through Greece, to Athens via Pirgos, Larissa and Lamia, is good but the speed of lorries and their trailer units can be disquieting. Vehicles being overtaken are expected to move right over and tuck well into the hard shoulder. From Evzonoi to Athens via Thessaloniki is 340 miles (550 kms) and some of the major autoroute is a toll road.

Personally my own favourite choice of route involves crossing the Channel to Le Havre, cutting down through France, which holds few perils for the traveller, via Evreux, Chartres, Pithiviers, Montargis, Clamecy, Nevers, Lyon and Chambery to the Italian border at Modane. Here the faint-hearted can take the tunnel whilst the adventurous wind their way over the Col du Mont Cenis.

Once over the border into Italy, bypass Turin (Torino) and proceed to Piacenza, Brescia, Verona, Padua (Padova), Venice and cut up to Trieste.

I say bypass because the ordinary Italian roads are just 'neat aggravation' and the cities are impossible. Although motorways involve constant toll fees they are much quicker and less wearing on the nerves. Note that Italian petrol stations have a nasty habit of closing for the midday siesta between 1200 and 1500 hrs.

An alternative route is via Turin, Milan, Bergamo, Brescia, Verona and on to Trieste. This route leads around the southern edge of a few of the lakes in the area of Brescia. Excursions to Padua and Venice are obvious possibilities.

ROAD ROUTES

Two   European car routes & ferry-boat connections

From Trieste the most scenic (and winding) route is to travel the Adriatic coast road via Rijeka, Zadar and Split to Dubrovnik. The lovely medieval inner city of Dubrovnik is well worth a visit. At Petrovac the pain starts and the road swings up to Titograd around to Kosovska Mitrovika, Pristina, Skopje and down to the border at Gevgelija. The stretch from Skopje to the Greek frontier can be rather unnerving. Sign-posting in Yugoslavia is usually very bad; always obtain petrol when the opportunity crops up and lastly but not least city lights are often turned out at night, making driving extremely hazardous. To save the journey from Petrovac, it is possible at the height of season to take a ferry from Dubrovnik or take the pretty coastal road on to the port of Bar and catch a boat to Igoumenitsa or Patras on the Greek mainland.

On the return journey it is possible to vary the route by driving across Greece to Igoumenitsa, catching a ferry-boat to Italy and driving along the Adriatic seaboard, but the northern coast of Italy is not very attractive.

Detailed road reports are available from the Automobile Association but I would like to stress that in the Yugoslavian mountains, especially after heavy rain, landslips can (no will)

result in part of the road disappearing at the odd spot as well as the surface being littered with rocks. There you go!

General Vehicle & Personal Requirements

Documents required for travel in any European country include an *International Driving Licence*, and a *Carnet de Passages en Douanes* (both issued by the AA and valid for one year) as well as a *Green Insurance Card*. It is recommended to take the vehicle's registration documents as proof of ownership and the vehicle must have a nationality sticker of the approved pattern and design.

Particular countries' requirements include:

Italy

Import allowances are as for Greece but the restriction on the importation of Italian currency equals about £100.

A recent requirement for all cars entering Italy is that they must possess both right and left hand, external driving mirrors.

Switzerland

If intending to drive through Switzerland remember that the Swiss will require the vehicle and all the necessary documents to be absolutely correct. (They would). The authorities have a nasty habit of stopping vehicles some distance beyond the frontier posts.

Yugoslavia

A valid passport is the only personal document required for citizens of, for example, Denmark, West Germany, Finland, Great Britain and Northern Ireland, Republic of Southern Ireland, Holland and Sweden. Americans and Canadians must have a visa and all formalities should be checked with the relevant Yugoslavian Tourist Office.

It is compulsory to carry a warning triangle, a first-aid kit in the vehicle and a set of replacement vehicle light bulbs. If you plan to travel during the winter it is advisable to check the special regulations governing the use of studded tyres. The use of spotlights is prohibited.

Visiting motorists cannot obtain fuel without petrol coupons, which are available at the frontier and, supposedly, from travel agents 'Kompas' or 'Putnik'. Carefully calculate the amount of coupons required for the journey and pay for them in foreign currency at the frontier as the rate allowed is very advantageous compared to that if the coupons are paid for in Yugoslavian dinars. Petrol stations can be far apart, closed or out of petrol, so fill up when possible.

Photographers are only allowed to import five rolls of film; drinkers a bottle of wine and a quarter litre of spirits and smokers 200 cigarettes or 50 cigars. Each person may bring in unlimited foreign currency but only 1500 dinars.

Fines are issued on the spot and the officer collecting the fine should issue an official receipt.

To obtain assistance in the case of accident or breakdown dial 987 and the 'SPI' will come to your assistance.

Greece

It is compulsory to carry a first-aid kit as well as a fire extinguisher in a vehicle and failure to comply may result in a fine. It is also mandatory to carry a warning triangle and it is forbidden to carry petrol in cans. In Athens the police are empowered to confiscate and detain the numberplates of illegally parked vehicles.

The use of undipped headlights in towns is strictly prohibited.

Customs allow the importation of 200 cigarettes or 50 cigars, 1 litre of spirits or 2 litres of wine and only 3000 drs, but any amount of foreign currency. Visitors from the EEC may import 300 cigarettes or 75 cigars, 1½ litres of spirits or 4 litres of wine.

Speed Limits

See table below — all are standard legal limits which may be varied by signs.

	Built-up areas	Outside built-up areas	Motorways	Type of vehicle affected
Greece	31 mph (50 kph)	49 mph (80 kph)	62 mph (100 kph)	Private vehicles with or without trailers
Yugoslavia	37 mph (60 kph)	49 mph (80 kph) 62 mph* (100 kph)*	74 mph (120 kph)	Private vehicles without trailers

*Speed on dual carriageways.

BY FERRY-BOAT (Illustration 2)

Some of the descriptive matter under the heading **BY TRAIN** in this chapter refers to inter-country ferry-boat travel.

Due to the popularity of the ferry port of Brindisi travellers, at the height of the season, must be prepared for crowds, lengthy delays and the usual ferry-boat scrum (scrum not scum). Other irritants include the exasperating requirement to purchase an embarkation pass with the attendant formalities which include taking the pass to the police station on the second floor of the port office to have it punched! Oh, by the way, the distance between the railway station and the port is about 200 m and it is absolutely necessary to clock in at least 3 hrs before the ferries departure otherwise you may be 'scratched' from the fixture list, have to rebook and pay again. That is why the knowledgeable head for the other departure ports, more especially Otranto.

Great care must be taken when purchasing international ferry-boat tickets especially at Igoumenitsa. The competition is hot and tickets may well be sold below the published price. If so and you are amongst the 'lucky ones' do not count your drachmae until on board. The port officials check the tickets and if they find any that have been sold at a discount then they are confiscated and the purchaser made to buy replacements at the full price. Ouch!

See **Chapter 10 (Greek Mainland ports)** for particular details.

Do not forget that the availability of ferry-boat sailings must be continually checked as must airline and bus timetables. This is especially necessary during the months of October through to the beginning of May when the services are usually severely curtailed, so be warned.

Please refer to the individual mainland port and island chapters for full details of the inter-country ferry-boat timetables.

Useful names & addresses

The Automobile Association, Fanum House, Basingstoke, Hants RG21 2EA.   Tel. (0256) 20123

The Greek National Tourist Organization, 195-197 Regent St., London W1R 8DL.
Tel. 01-734 5997

The Italian State Tourist Office, 1 Princes St., London W1R 7AR.   Tel. 01-408 1245

The Yugoslav National Tourist Office, 143 Regent St., London W1R 8AE.   Tel. 01-734 5243

British Rail Continental Enquiries, Sealink (UK) Limited, PO Box 29, London SW1V 1JX.
Tel. 01-834 2345

European Rail Passenger Office, Paddington Station, London W2 1HA.   Tel. 01-723 7000

The Hellenic State Railways (OSE), 1-3 Karolou St., Athens, Greece.   Tel. 01-5222-491

Thomas Cook Ltd, Publications Dept., PO Box 36, Thorpewood, Peterborough, PE3 6SB
Tel. 01-0733-63200

Other useful names & addresses mentioned in the text include:

Time Out, Southampton St., London. WC2E 7HD

Owners Abroad Ltd, Valentine House, Ilford Hill, Ilford, Essex IC1 2DG   Tel. 01-514 8844

Olympic Airways, 164 Piccadilly, London W1 — Tel. 01-846 9080
Allsun Holidays, 164 Piccadilly, London W1 — Tel. 01-846 9080
Aegina Club Ltd, 25A Hills Rd., Cambridge CB2 1 NW. — Tel. 0223 63256
Ramblers Holidays, 13 Longcroft House, Fretherne Rd., Welwyn Garden City, Herts. AL8 6PQ.
Tel. 07073 31133
Greek Islands Club, 66 High St., Walton on Thames, Surrey KT12 1 BU — Tel. 0932 220477
Cricketer Holidays, 4 The White House, Beacon Rd., Crowborough, E. Sussex. TN6 1 AB
Tel. 08926 64242
Simply Simon Holidays Ltd, 1/45 Nevern Sq, London SW5 9PF — Tel. 01-373 1933
World Wide Student Travel, 38-39 Store St., London WC1 E 7BZ. — Tel. 01-580 7733
Victoria Travel Centre, 52 Grosvenor Gdns., London SW1. — Tel. 01-730 8111
Transalpino, 214 Shaftesbury Ave. London WC2H 8EB. — Tel. 01-836 0087/8
London Student Travel (Tel. 01-730 4473) and **Eurotrain** (Tel. 01-730 6525) both at
   52 Grosvenor Gdns., London SW1 N 0AG.
Euroways Supabus, c/o Victoria Coach Stn., London SW1. — Tel. 01-730 0202
   or c/o National Express Co.
   The Greek address is: 1 Karolou St., Athens. — Tel. 5240519/6
National Express Co, Westwood Garage, Margate Rd., Ramsgate CT12 6SL. — Tel. 0843 581333
Consolas Travel, 29-31 Euston Rd., London NW1. — Tel. 01-278 1931
   The Greek address is: 100 Eolou St., Athens. — Tel. 3219228

Amongst others, the agencies and offices listed above have, over the years, and in varying degrees, been helpful in the preparation of the guides and I would like to extend my sincere thanks to all those concerned. Some have proved more helpful than others!

Olympic Airways overseas office addresses are as follows:

America: 647 Fifth Ave., New York, NY 10022. — Tel. (0101-212)
(Reservations) 838 3600
(Ticket Office) 750 7933
Montreal: 200 McGill College Ave., Suite 1250 Montreal, Quebec. — Tel. 0101 514) 878 9691
Toronto: 80 Bloor St. West, Suite 406, Toronto. — Tel. (0101 416) 925 2272
Sydney: Suite 917, Australia Sq., Sydney, NSW 2000. — Tel. (01061 2) 241 1751
Johannesburg: Bank of Athens Buildings, 116 Marshall St, Johannesburg. — Tel. (0102711) 836 5683
Denmark: 4 Jembadegade DK 1608, Copenhagen. — Tel. (010451) 126 100
Sweden: 44 Birger Jarlsgatan, 11429 Stockholm. — Tel. (010468) 101203

Other useful overseas names & addresses include:
Let's Go Travel Services, Harvard Student Agencies, Thayer Hall B, Harvard University, Cambridge. MA02138 USA. — Tel. 617 495 9649
Canadian Universities Travel Service, 44 George St, Toronto ONTM5S 2E4, Canada.
Tel. 979 2406
Automobile Association and Touring Club of Greece (ELPA), 2 Messogion Street, Athens.
Tel. (01) 7791615
Italian Government Travel Office, 630 5th Ave, Suite 1565, New York, NY 10111.
Tel. (0101-212) 245 4825
Greek National Tourist Organisation, 645 5th Ave, New York, NY 10022.
(0101-212) 421 5777
   627 West 6th St, Los Angeles, CA 90017. — Tel. (0101-213) 626 6696
   168 North Michigan Ave, Chicago, IL 60601 — (0101-312) 782 1084
   Suite 67, 2 Place Ville Marie, Esso Plaza, Montreal, Quebec H3B 2C9
Yugoslav State Tourist Office, 630 5th Ave, New York, NY 10111 — (0101-212) 757 2801

Ferry Lines — US Offices
Adriatica, 437 Madison Ave, New York — Tel. (0101-212) 838 2113
Chandris, 666 5th Ave, New York — Tel. (0101-212) 586 8370
Hellenic Mediterranean Lines, 200 Park Ave, New York — Tel. (0101-212) 697 4220
Karageorgis, 1350 Avenue of the Americas, New York — Tel. (0101-212) 582 3007

AIR, RAIL, FERRY AND ROAD ROUTES

Three   Greek air, ferry, rail & road routes to the Ionian islands

3 Travel Between Athens & the Ionian

I see land. I see the end of my labour. *Diogenes*

The Greek islands are very thick on the water, numbering between 1000 and 3000, depending upon which authority you wish to believe, of which approximately 100 are inhabited. Historically, a specialised and efficient system of water-borne travel developed and in years gone by, the only way of setting foot on an island was to make for the relevant port and board a ferry-boat. The advent of international air flights direct to the larger islands, and the opening up of a number of airfields on the smaller islands (which must be regarded as a mixed blessing), has made it possible to fly to Athens and take a flight to the islands of Corfu, Cephalonia and Zakynthos, or Preveza (Aktion) for Lefkas.

Travellers must note all fares have risen quite substantially in recent years. For example, in 1985 there were two price uplifts, the last in June amounting to some 20%. Illustration 3 details the various travel connections between the mainland and Ionian islands.

BY AIR

It can prove difficult to purchase tickets on the spot, especially at the height of the tourist season, and it may be more convenient to book prior to departure, through the local Olympic office. Greeks utilise the services extensively, despite the extra cost of flying compared to other forms of travel which logically should discourage their use.

Travellers arriving in Athens other than by aircraft and wanting a domestic flight from the West airport can catch one of the Olympic coaches to the airport. These depart from the Olympic terminal and offices, 96-100 (Leoforos) Sygrou, between 0600 hrs and midnight and cost 45 drs compared to the 350/400 drs odd charged by a taxi. Relevant city buses are listed in Chapter 9 (Athens) in amongst the details of the bus timetable. An irate reader has taken me to task for not pointing out that approximately an hour must be allowed between catching the airline bus and the relevant plane check-in time.

Many travellers do not wish to stop over in Athens. If this is the case, and arriving other than on an Olympic flight, they can travel, directly after landing, to the domestic, West airport, using the connecting bus service.

The staff of Olympic, the Greek airline, are usually very helpful and their English good, although occasionally it is possible to fall foul of that sporadic Greek characteristic, intransigence. I remember arriving, heavily laden and tired, at the Olympic terminal offices about 1 am early one morning. On asking for advice about the location of any suitable hotel, I was politely directed, by the girl at the enquiries desk, to the Tourist police, which would have involved an uphill walk of at least a mile, weighed down by an assortment of bags. There was a hotel, in which we stayed, immediately around the corner from the terminal.

It is well worth considering utilising internal flights on one leg of a journey, if Athens is the point of arrival or departure. The extra cost of the flight, over and above the overland and ferry fares, must be balanced against the time element. For instance, Athens to Corfu by air takes some 50 mins whilst the ferry takes some 17 hours. One other advantage of domestic air travel is that the fares can be paid for by the use of American Express or Diners card, possibly saving precious drachmae, especially at the end of a holiday.

Athens to the Ionian islands
Scheduled Olympic domestic flights to:
Corfu (50 mins): A minimum of three flights daily. One-way fare 3470 drs.
Cephalonia (45 mins): A minimum of one flight daily. One-way fare 2390 drs.

Zakynthos (45 mins): A minimum of one flight daily. One-way fare 2390 drs.
Please refer to the individual island chapters for more details.

Ionian island airports
Corfu, Cephalonia and Zakynthos are at the smarter end of island airports bearing little resemblance to some of their 'country cousins' on the remoter islands.
Please refer to Athens (Chapter 9) and the relevant island chapters for full details of aircraft timetables.

BY BUS
There are daily scheduled bus services to the mainland ports (Chapter 10) that connect by ferry-boat to the various Ionian islands.
Please refer to Athens (Chapter 9), Mainland Ports (Chapter 10) and the relevant island chapters for full details of bus timetables.

BY FERRY-BOAT
In the following comments I am calling on my experience of travelling third and tourist class on any number of ferry-boats.

In general if sleeping arrangements are available they will be satisfactory if certain basic rules are followed. First claim a bunk by depositing luggage on the chosen berth, it will be quite safe as long as money and passports are removed. The position of a berth is important. Despite the labelling of 'Men' and 'Women' sleeping areas, a berth can usually be selected in either, but try to choose one adjacent to stern deck doors to ensure some ventilation. Due to the location of the third and tourist class accommodation it can get very hot and stuffy. Last tip is to lay a towel over plastic bunk covering, in order to alleviate what may well prove to be a sticky, uncomfortable night. The third class lavatories are often in an unsightly condition even prior to the craft's departure. To help enjoy reasonable surroundings and have the use of a shower, quietly trip into the next class and use their facilities (but don't tell everybody). Both the toilets and the showers suffer from the usual deficiencies listed under Greek bathrooms in Chapter 4, so be prepared.

Important points to take into account when inter-island ferry-boating include the following:

1. The ferries are owned by individual steamship companies and an employee of one Line will be unable or unwilling to give you information in respect of another company's timetable. Incidentally this individual ownership, can lead to a wide disparity in quality of service and general comfort.

2. The distances and voyage times are quite often lengthy and tiring. Additionally the duration of the passage sometimes, (no always), results in the timetable going to the wall with delays in scheduled departure times, on islands well into a ferry's voyage.

3. There are usually four basic fare classes: first, second, tourist and third/deck class. The published fares on scheduled ferries are government controlled and the third/deck class represents extremely good value. Ensure that you state the fare class you require. If you do not, you may well be sold a tourist instead of the cheaper deck class ticket. Note that there are a number of luxury ferries usually on a particular island-to-island journey, and tourist trip boats, on which charges are considerably higher. There are also hydrofoil 'Flying Dolphins', which result in journey times of under half those of the scheduled ferries but at approximately double the cost. Apart from the aforementioned four categories, there can be a variety of first- and second-class sleeping accommodation, including private and shared cabins.

4. Food and drink on the ferries used to be comparatively expensive, but price rises on the land have not been mirrored at sea. On the other hand the service is often discourteous and inefficient so it may be advantageous to pack provisions for a long voyage.

Wholesome and inexpensive ferry-boat picnic food includes: tomatoes, cucumber, bread, salami, ham, Sunfix orange juice and a bottle of wine (or two!). Take some bottled water. Greek chocolate (especially with nuts) is very good but does not keep well in the ambient daytime temperatures.

5. The state of the toilets and the lack of basic supplies makes it mandatory that one or two lavatory rolls are packed, easily to hand, as it were. The usual lack of washroom facilities commends the stowage of a pack of 'wipes'.

Quite frankly, on some occasions it will be necessary to stand on the rim of the toilet bowl as the only way of using the facility. Sorry!

6. Tickets should be purchased from a ticket agency prior to a voyage, as they can cost more when purchased on the boat. Ticket agency offices vary from 'the plush' to boxed-in back stairs, but check the scheduled prices and you should not go wrong. On the other hand be sure your list is up to date. In 1985 the prices went up twice by June and the last increase was 20%.

7. At the height of the season, the upper deck seats are extremely hot during the day and uncomfortably chilly at night. It is advisable to stake a claim to a seat fairly quickly, as the ferries are usually very crowded during the summer months.

8. Travellers should ensure they have a good, fat book and a pack of cards to while away the longer sea voyages. Despite the awesome beauty of the islands and the azure blue sea, there are often long, unbroken periods of Mediterranean passage to be endured, interrupted only by the occasional passing ship and the dramatic activity and ructions that take place during a port call.

9. Travellers sensitive to discordancy and who find disagreeable, a cacophany, a clamour of sound, may well find unacceptable the usual raucous mix experienced in the average 3rd class lounge. This is made up of two televisions, tuned to different programmes (the picture constantly flickering, suffering a snowstorm or horizontally high jumping in a series of flickering stills) accompanied by an overlaying wail of Greco-Turkish music piped over the ships tannoy system. Best to fly!

One delight is to keep a weather eye open and hope to observe some dolphins diving and leaping in the ship's wake. Their presence is often made discernible by the loud slapping noise they make when re-entering the water.

Ferry-boaters must take care when checking the connections, schedules and timetables as they can, no do, change during the year, especially outside the inclusive months of May to September, as well as from one year to another. So be warned!

Do not forget, when the information is at its most confusing, the Port police are totally reliable, but often a little short on English. Their offices are almost always on, or adjacent to, the quayside.

Please refer to the Mainland Ports (Chapter 10) and the relevant island chapters for full details of ferry-boat timetables.

BY TRAIN

The Peloponnese main line allows connection with Patras and Killini ports for ferry-boats to various Ionian islands.

Please refer to the individual Chapter 9 (Athens) and 10 (Mainland Ports) for full details of the train timetables.

CRUISE SHIPS

Fly/cruise packages on offer are usually rather up-market and in the main are based on seven days or multiples thereof. The cruise ships call in at selected islands for a part or full day, with excursions where applicable.

Other vacationers should note that the large influx of this genus of fun loving holiday-maker can have quite an impact on an island, and the cognoscenti normally vacate the particular port of call for that day.

GREEK ISLAND PLACE NAMES

This is probably the appropriate place to introduce the forever baffling problem which helps to bedevil the traveller — Greek place names. For instance, the island of Zakynthos is often designated Zante.

The reason for the apparently haphazard nomenclature lies in the long and complicated territorial ownership of Greece and its islands, more especially the islands. The base root may be Greek, Latin, Turkish or Venetian. Additionally the Greek language has three forms — Demotic (spoken), Katharevousa (literary) and Kathomiloumeni (compromise), of which the Demotic and Katharevousa have each been the offical linguistic style. Even as recently as 1967-74 the Colonels made Katharevousa once again the authorised form but Demotic is now the official language. Help!

Street names can be equally confusing and I have plumped for my personal choice and stated the alternatives, but where this is not possible, well, there you go! I mean how can Athens main square, Syntagma be spelt Syntagina, Sintagma or Syntagmatos?

Hotel and pension titles will also give rise to some frustration as can official guides using Greek script names, with two or three alternatives, including a similar meaning, Roman scripted appellation.

Street names are subject to some obscurity as the common noun Odhos (street) is often omitted, whilst Leoforos (avenue) and Plateia (square) are usually kept in the name. The prefix Saint of St. is variously written as Agios, Aghios, Ayios, Ag or Ai.

A *nome* approximates to a small English county, a number of which make up a province such as the *Peloponnese* or *Thessaly*.

At this stage, without apologies, I introduce my own definition to help identify an unspoilt, Greek town as follows: where the town's rubbish is collected by donkey, wooden panniers slung across its back, slowly wending its way up the hillside street, the driver, not in sight, probably languishing in a stray taverna.

Map nomenclature	Greek	Translation
Agios/Ag/Ayios/Aghios	Αγιου	Saint
Akra/Akrotiri	Ακρωτηρι	Cape/Headland
Ano	Ανω	Upper
Archeas/Oloyikos(horos)	Αρχαιοζ/Δογικοζ	Ancient (site)
Chora/Horo/Horio/Khorio	Χωριο	Village
Kato		Lower
Kolpos	Κολποδ	Gulf
Leoforos		Avenue
Limni	Διμνη	Lake/Marsh
Limin		Port harbour
Moni/Monastiri	Μοναστηρι	Monastery
Naos	Ναοζ	Temple
Nea/Neos	Νεο	New
Nissos		Island
Odhos/Odos	Δρομοξ	Street
Ormos		Bay
Oros		Mountain
Plateia	πλατεια	Square
Palios/Palaios	παλιοξ	Old
Potami	ποταμι	River
Spilia	Σπηλια	Cave
Vuno	Βουνο	Mountain

Useful Greek

English	Greek	Sounds like
Where is...	Που ειναι	Poo eene...
...the Olympic Airways office	τα γραφεια της Ολυμπιακης	...ta grafia tis Olimbiakis

...the railway station	ο σιδηροδρουικος σταθμος	...sidheerothropikos stathmos
...the bus station	ο σταθμος των λεωφορεων	...stathmos ton leoforion
...the boat	το πλοιο	...to plio
...the nearest underground station	ο πλησιεστερος σταθμος του ηλεκτρικου	...o pleessiestehros stathmos too eelektrigoo
...the ticket office	το εκδοτηριο των ειοιτηριων	...to eckdhoterio ton essidirion
...the nearest travel agency	το πλησιεστερος πρακτορειον ταξιδιων	...to pleessiestehros praktorion taxidion
I'd like to reserve...	θελω να κρατησω	Thelo na kratiso...
...seat/seats on the	θεοη/ θσειδ λια	...these/thessis ghia
...to	για	...yia
...plane	αεροπλανο	...aeroplano
...train	τραινο	...treno
...bus	λεωφορειο	...leoforio
...ferry-boat	πλοιο	...plio
When does it leave/arrive	Ποτε φευγει/φθανει	Poteh fehvghi/fihanee
Is there...	Υπαρχει	Eebarhee...
...from here to	απ εδωστο	...abethosodo
...go to	στον	...ston
Where do I get off	Που κατεβαινομε	Poo katevenomhe
I want to go to	θελω να παω οτονζ	Thelo na bao stoos...
I want to get off at	θελω να κατεβω στο	Thelo na katevo sto..
Will you tell me when to get off	Θα μον πτε πον να κατεβω	Thah moo peete poo nah kahtehvo
I want to go to...	θελω να παω οτονζ	Thelo na bao stoos
Stop here	Στοματα εδω	Stamata etho
How much is it	Ποσο ειναι	Posso eene
How much does it cost	Ποσο κανει η μεταρορα	Posso kano imedano
...to	στο	...sto
Do we call at	θα σταματησωμε οτην	Tha stamadisomee stin

Signs often seen affixed to posts & doors

Greek	English
ΑΘΞΙΣ	ARRIVAL
ΑΝΑΧΩΡΗΣΙΣ	DEPARTURE
ΣΤΑΣΙΣ	BUS STOP
ΕΙΣΟΔΟΣ	ENTRANCE
ΕΞΟΔΟΣ	EXIT
ΚΕΝΤΡΟ	CENTRE (as in town centre)
ΕΙΣΟΔΟΣ ΕΛΕΥΘΕΡΑ	FREE ADMISSION
ΑΜΑΓΟΡΕΥΕΤΑΙ ΗΕΙΣΟΔΟΣ	NO ENTRANCE
ΕΙΣΙΤΗΡΙΑ	TICKET
ΠΡΟΣ ΤΑΣ ΑΠΟΒΑΘΡΑΣ	TO THE PLATFORMS
ΤΗΛΕΦΩΝΟΝ	TELEPHONE
ΑΝΔΡΩΝ	GENTLEMEN
ΓΥΝΑΙΚΩΝ	LADIES
ΑΠΑΓΟΡΕΤΕΤΑΙ ΤΟ ΚΑΠΝΗΣΜΑ	NO SMOKING
ΤΑΜΕΙΟΝ	CASH DESK
ΤΟΥΑΛΕΤΕΣ	TOILETS
ΑΝΟΙΚΤΟΝ	OPEN
ΚΛΕΙΣΤΟΝ	CLOSED
ΩΘΗΣΑΤΕ	PUSH
ΣΥΡΑΤΕ	PULL

4 Island Accommodation

How oft doth man by care oppressed, find in an inn a place of rest   *Combe*

Package, villa and tour organised holiday-makers will have accommodation arranged prior to arrival in Greece. If travelling around, then the most important matter is undoubtedly the procurement of lodgings, especially the first overnight stay on a new island or at an untried location.

The choice of accommodation is bewildering, varying from private houses (usually very clean but with basic bathroom facilities) to luxury class hotels able to hold their own with the most modern European counterpart. The deciding factor must be the budget and a person's sensibilities. My comments in respect of standards reflect comparisons with Western Europe establishments. Those referring to prices are usually in comparison with other Greek options.The standard of accommodation on the Ionian naturally varies not only from island to island but from place to place. For instance, even amongst the long established tourist resorts of Corfu, accommodation can range from the indecently plush to extremely simple island *pooms**.

Travellers stepping off a ferry-boat, will usually be part of a swarming throng made up of Greeks, tourists and back-packers engulfed by a quayside mass of Greeks, tourists and back-packers struggling to get aboard the ferry-boat. Visitors may well be approached by men, women and youngsters offering rooms. It is a matter of taking potluck there and then, or searching around the town oneself. The later in the day, the more advisable it is to take an offer, unseen. It is mandatory to establish the price, if the rooms are with or without shower and how far away they are located. It is unnerving to be 'picked up' and then commence on an ever-lengthening trudge through the back streets of a strange place, especially as Greek ideas of distance are rather optimistic.

Any accommodation usually calls for passports to be relinquished. A passport is also required to change money and to hire a car or a scooter, so it is a good idea, if married or travelling with friends, to have separate documents. Then, if necessary, one passport can be left at the abode and another kept for other purposes, as required.

Official sources and many guide-books lay much emphasis on the role of the Tourist police in finding accommodation, but this must not be relied upon as the offices may well be closed on arrival. Moreover recent changes in the structure of the various police forces is resulting in the once separate and independent Tourist police being integrated into the offices of the Town police. I regret that this may well be a very retrograde step. Such a pity that the Greeks, the innovators of this excellent service should now abandon the scheme, more especially in the light of the ever increasing numbers of tourists.

It can prove fruitful to enquire at a convenient taverna, which, more often than not, will result in an introduction to a room or pension owner. Failing that, they will usually send out for someone.

A poom is a descriptive noun coined after sighting on Crete, some years ago, a crudely written sign that simply stated POOMS! The accommodation on offer was crude, low-ceilinged, raftered, earth-floored, windowless rooms simply equipped with a truckle bed and rickety oil-cloth covered washstand — very reminiscent of typical Cycladean cubicles of the 1950/60s period.

BEDROOMS
Greek bedrooms tend to be airy, whitewashed and sparsely furnished. The beds are often hard, as are the small pillows, and the unyielding mattresses may well be laid directly on to bed-boards and not springs.

It is advisable to inspect bedroom walls for blood-red splats of flattened, but once blood gorged, mosquitoes resulting from a previous occupant's night-time vigil. Well-designed rooms usually have a top-opening window screened off with gauze so that they can be left ajar without fear of incursions by winged creepy-crawlies. Where no gauze is in evidence, it is best to keep the windows tightly closed at night, however alien this may seem. Those not in possession of a proprietory repellent will have to reconcile themselves to a sleepless night, any tell-tale buzzing echoing in the ears indicating one has already been bitten. It is comparable to being attacked by Lilliputian Stuka night-fighters.

Hanging points are noticeable by their absence. Often there will be no wardrobe but if present there is every chance that there will be no hangers, not even the steel-wire type, and the doors may be missing. A rather idiosyncratic feature is that clothes hooks, when present, are often very inadequate, looking as if they have been designed, and are only suitable for, hanging coffee mugs by the handles.

Even more maligned and even more misunderstood than Greek food is

THE GREEK BATHROOM

I use the descriptive word bathroom, rather than refer simply to the toilets, because the total facility requires some elucidation. The following will not apply to luxury, A or B class hotels. Well, it should not!

The plumbing is quite often totally inadequate and instead of the separate wastes of the bath, shower and sink being plumbed into progressively larger soil pipes, thus achieving a 'venturi' effect, they are usually joined into a similar diameter tube to that of the individual pipes. This inevitably causes considerable back pressure with inescapable consequences. The toilet waste is almost always insufficient in size. Even normal, let alone excessive, use of toilet paper will result in dreadful things happening, not only to your bathroom, but probably to a number of bathrooms in the building, street and possibly the village. If this were not enough... the header tank usually does not deliver sufficient 'flush'. The Greeks have had, for many years, to be economic in the use of water and some islands ration it, turning off the supply for a number of hours per day, at the height of the summer.

Common faults are to find the lavatory without a seat; flooded to a depth of some inches; the bathroom light not working; no toilet roll; door locks not fitted; dirty WC pan and or any combination of the above. Furthermore, the wash basin may well be without a drain plug. Amongst other reasons, the lack of a plug is to stop flooding if a sink tap is accidently left turned on when the mains water is switched off, and not turned off when the water supply is resumed.

The most common type of en suite bathroom is an all purpose lavatory and shower room. Beware! The shower head, after years of research, is usually positioned in such a way as to not only shower the occupant but to drench the (amazingly) absorbent toilet roll, his or her clothes, towel and footwear. Incidentally the drain point is located to ensure that the bathroom is kept awash to a depth of between 1″ and 3″.

It is not unusual for there to be no hot water, even if a heating system is in evidence. Government energy conservation methods, the comparatively high cost of electricity and the use of moderately sized solar heating panels, all contribute to this state of affairs. Where solar panels are the means of heating the water, remember to beat the rush and shower as early as possible, for the water soon loses its heat. Why not share with a friend? If hot water is available but it is not heated by solar energy then it will be necessary to locate the relevant electric switch. This is usually a 4 way position ceramic knob hidden away behind a translucent panel door. On the other hand. . .

One stipulation on water-short islands that really offends the West European (and North American?) sense of delicacy, is the oft present, hardly legible sign, requesting guests to put their 'papers' in the waste-bin supplied and not down the pan! I must own up to not always obeying this dictum and have had to make a hurried departure from an island, let alone a pension or village, when the consequences of my profligate use of toilet paper have become apparent.

Room charges are often increased by 50 to 100 drs per day for the use of a shower, but this will be detailed on the Government-controlled price list that should be displayed in every room, and is usually suspended on the back of the door.

THE BEACH

Some back-packing youngsters utilise the shore for their night's accommodation. In fact all island ferry-boaters must be prepared to consider the beach as a stand-by during the months of July and August in the more crowded locations although I have only had to spend one or two nights on the beach in the seven or eight years of island ferry-boating excursions. The weather could not be more ideal, the officials do not seem too fussed and may well direct you to a suitable spot. Beware of mosquitoes and tar.

CAMPING

In direct contrast to *ad hoc* sleeping out on the beach, camping, except on approved sites, is strictly forbidden, but the law is not always rigorously applied. The restriction comes about from a wish to improve general hygiene, to prohibit and discourage abuse of private property and as a precaution against forest fires. Usually the NTOG own the sites but there are some authorised, privately run camping grounds, which are price controlled. There are quite a few camp sites on Corfu and several on Cephalonia and Zakynthos. A *Carnet-Camping International*, although not normally requested, affords campers world-wide, third-party liability cover and is available to United Kingdom residents from the AA and other similar organisations.

If moved on by any official for sleeping out on the beach or illegally camping, it is advisable not to argue and go quietly. The Greek police have fairly wide and autonomous powers and it is preferable not to upset them unnecessarily.

YOUTH HOSTELS (ΞΕΝΩΝΑΖ ΝΕΩΝ)

Establishments include the YMCA (**ΧΑΝ**), YWCA (**ΧΕΝ**) in Athens and the YHA in Athens and Corfu.

Greek youth hostels are rather down at heel and tend to be operated in a somewhat slovenly manner. None of the old get-up-and-go familiar to some other countries members — morning ablutions in ice-cold water and placing used razor blades in disused tobacco tins nailed to the wall.

It is preferable to have current YHA membership, taking the Association's card along. Approximate prices per night at the YMCA and YWCA are 450 drs and in a Youth Hostel, 250 drs.

ROOMS (ΔΩΜΑΤΙΑ)

The story goes that as soon as a tourist steps off the ferry, he (or she)is surrounded by women crying 'Rooms' (Dhomatio), and whoops, in minutes he is ensconced in some wonderful, Greek family's private home.

History may well have been like that, and in truth the ferries are still met at almost every island, the inhabitants offering not only rooms but pensions and the lower category hotels. Rooms are the cheapest accommodation, generally very clean and sometimes including the option of breakfast, which is ordinarily charged extra. Prices reflect an island's popularity and the season, but usually the mid-season cost will be between 700 and 1000 drs for a double room, depending upon the classification.

Apart from being approached leaving the ferry, the Tourist police would in the past advise of rooms to let but their role is being drastically reduced with their planned amalgamation with the Town police. Householders display the sign 'Ενοικαζονται δωματιοί, or simply 'Δωματια', when they have a room to rent. If the rooms are government approved and categorised, which they should be to be officially recognised, there will be a tariff, and they will be slightly more expensive than the free-lance householders. The Tourist police office will be signed 'ΤΟΥΡΙΣΤΙΚΗ ΑΣΤΥΝΟΜΙΑ', if at all (but their absorption into the other local police organisations will probably result in total emasculation).

A general point relates to a cautionary tale told to us by a delightful French couple. They were in the habit of replying to a room owners query as to how many nights they wished to stay by saying Tonight. One lady room owner interpreted this to mean two nights! Beware the inaccurate transcription.

PENSIONS (ΠΑΝΣΙΟΝ)
This type of lodging was a natural progression from **Rooms** and now represents the most easily found and reasonably priced accommodation on offer.

The older type of pension is rather reminiscent of those large Victorian English houses, split up into bed-sits. In the main though, they have been purpose built, usually during the Colonels' regime (1967-74) when government grants were freely available for the construction of tourist quarters. The owner often lives on one floor and acts as concierge. The rooms are functional and generally the guests on each level share a bathroom and shower and, a rather nice touch when provided, a communal refrigerator in which visitors can store their various provisions and drinks. Mid-season charges vary between 800 and 1200 drs for a double room.

Sometimes a breakfast of coffee, bread and jam, perhaps butter and a boiled egg, is available for about 150 drs and represents fair value compared with the cost of a cafe breakfast.

TAVERNAS (ΤΑΒΕΡΝΑ)
Tavernas are, first and foremost, eating places but some tavernas, especially those situated by, or near, beaches, have rooms available. The only drawback is that the more popular the taverna, the less likely guests are to get a full night's sleep, but of course the more involved they will be with the taverna's social life which will often continue on into the small hours.

HOTELS (ΞΕΝΟΔΟΧΕΙΟΝ)
Shades of difference and interpretation can be given to the nomenclature by variations of the bland, descriptive noun hotel. For instance ΞΝΟΔΟΧΕΙΟΝ ΥΠΝΟΥ indicates a hotel that does not serve meals and ΠΑΝΔΧΕΙΟΝ a low grade hotel.

Many back-packers will not consider hotels their first choice. The higher classification ones are more expensive than pensions and the lower grade hotels often cost the same, but may well be rather seedy and less desirable than the equivalent pension. Greek hotels are classified L (Luxury) A, B, C, D and E and the prices charged within these categories (except L) are controlled by the authorities.

It is unfortunately difficult to differentiate between hotels and their charges as each individual category is subject to fairly wide standards, and charges are subject to a multitude of possible percentage supplements and reductions as detailed below:

Shower extra (C, D and E hotels); number of days stayed less than three: plus 10 per cent; air conditioning extra (A and B hotels); out of season deduction (ask); high season extra: plus 20 per cent, ie the months of July, August and the first half of September; single occupancy: about 80 per cent of a double-room rate. The higher classification hotels may well insist on guests taking demi-pension terms, especially in high season. The following table must be treated as a guide only.

Class	Comments	Indicated mid-season double-bed price
L	All amenities and a very high standard and price. Probably at least one meal in addition to breakfast will have to be purchased. Very clean. Very hot water.	
A	High standard and price. Most rooms will have en suite shower or bath. Guests may well have to accept demi-pension terms. Clean. Hot water.	2500 drs
B	Good standard. Many rooms will have en suite shower or bath, clean, hot water.	2000 drs
C	Usually an older hotel. Faded elegance, shared bathroom, cleanish, possibly hot water.	1500 drs
D	Older hotel. Faded. Shared bathroom, which may well be 'interesting'. A shower, if available, will be an 'experience', and the water cold.	1000 drs
E	Old, faded and unclean. The whole stay will be an 'experience'. Only very cold water.	750 drs

The prices indicated includes government taxes, service and room occupancy until noon.

THE XENIAS
Originally Government owned to ensure the availability of high-standard accommodation at important tourist centres but now often managed by private enterprise. Only A, B and C rated categories and they are of a better standard than hotels in a similar class.

FLATS & HOUSES
During the summer months this type of accommodation, referred to by travel agents and package tour operators as villas, is best booked prior to arriving in Greece. Not only will pre-booking be easier but, surprisingly, will prove cheaper than flying out and snooping around.

The winter is a different matter, but probably not within the scope of most of our readers.

Further useful names & addresses
The Youth Hostel Association, 14 Southampton St., London WC2E 7HY. Tel. 01-836 8541

Useful Greek

English	Greek	Sounds like
I want...	θελω	Thelo...
...a single room	ενα μονο δωματιο	...enna mono dhomatio
...a double room	ενα διπλο δωματιο	...enna thiplo dhomatio
...with a shower	με ντουζ	...me doosh
We would like a room for...	Θα θελαμε ενα δωματιο για	Tha thelome ena dhomatio yia...
two/three days/a week/ until	δυο/τρειζ μερεζ/μια εβδομαδα/μεχρι	thio/trees meres/meea evthomatha/ mekhri
Can you advise of another...	ερετε κανενα αλλο	Xerete kanena alo...
house with rooms	σπεετι με δωματιο	speeti meh dhomatio
pension	πανσιον	panseeon
inn	πανδοχειο	panthokheeo
hotel	ζενοδοχειο	ksenodhokheeo
youth hostel	ξενοναζ νεων	xenonas neon
How much is the room for a night?	Ποσο κανει το δωματιο για τη νυχτα	Poso kanee dho dhomatio yia ti neektah
That is too expensive	Εωαι πολυ ακριβα	Eene polee akriva

35

Have you anything cheaper?	Δεν εχετε αλλο πιο φθηνο	Dhen ekhete ahlo pio theeno
Is there...	Υπαρχει	Eeparkhee
a shower	ενα ντουζ	doosh
a refrigerator	ευα ψυγειο	psiyeeo
Where is the shower?	Που ειναι το ντουζ	Poo eene dho doosh
I have to leave...	Πρεπει να φυγω	Prebee na feegha...
today	σημερα	simera
tomorrow	αυριο	avrio
very early	Πολυ νωριζ	polee noris
Thank you for a	Ευχαριστω για την	Efkareesto gia tin
nice time	συμπαθτκοζωρα	simpathitikosora

5 Travelling around an island

A man is happier for life from having once made an agreeable tour *Anon*

A few introductory remarks may well be apposite here in respect of holiday-makers' possessions and women in Greece. The matter will also be discussed elsewhere but it is not out of place to reiterate one or two points (Rosemary calls it 'carrying on').

Personal Possessions
Do not leave airline tickets, money, travellers cheques and or passports behind at your accommodation. A man can quite easily acquire a wrist-strap handbag in which to conveniently carry these items. The danger does not, even today, lie with the Greeks, but with fellow tourists, down-and-outs and professional thieves working a territory.

Women
There has been a movement towards the 'Spanish-costa' percentage ploy. Young Greek men, in the more popular tourist areas, have finally succumbed and will now sometimes try it on. It's up to you girls, there is no menace, only opportunities.

Now back to the main theme of the chapter but before expanding on the subject, a few words will not go amiss in respect of:-

Beaches
Surprisingly, quite a few beaches are polluted in varying degrees, mainly by washed up plastic and some tar.

Jellyfish and sea urchins can occasionally be a problem in a particular bay, jellyfish increasingly so. One of my Mediterranean correspondents advises me that cures for the sting include, ammonia, urine (ugh) and a paste of meat tenderiser (it takes all sorts I suppose).

The biggest headache (literally) to a tourist is the sun, or more accurately, the heat of the sun at the height of the summer season. The islands especially benefit from the relief of the prevailing wind, but, to give an example of the extreme temperatures sometimes experienced, in Athens a few years ago birds were actually falling out of the trees, and they were the feathered variety. Every year dozens of holidaymakers are carted off, suffering from acute sunburn. A little often, (sun that is), must be the watchword.

It is very pleasant to observe more and more middle-aged Greek ladies taking to the sea, usually in an all enveloping black costume and a straw hat. Some to preserve their modesty, appear to swim in their everyday clothes

Despite the utterly reasonable condemnation of modern day advances in technology by us geriatrics, one amazing leap for all travelling and beach bound mankind is the Walk-Master personal stereo-cassettes. No more the strident, tinny beat of the transistor (or more commonly the 'Ghetto-Blaster'), now simply jigging silence of ear-muffed, face transfused youth. Splendid!

It may well be that you are a devoted sun worshipper and spend every available minute on the beach or terrace; if so do not read on. On the other hand if your interests range beyond the conversion of the sun's very strong rays into painful, peeling flesh and you wish to travel around an island, the question of modus operandi must be given some thought.

First, purchase an island map and one of the colourful and extremely informative tourist guides available on the larger islands. An excellent map of Corfu and the Ionian, that can be acquired prior to departure from the United Kingdom, is produced by the very helpful

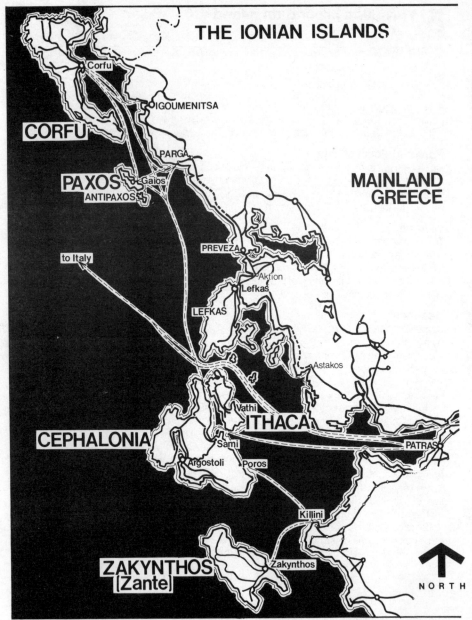

THE IONIAN ISLANDS

Corfu

IGOUMENITSA

CORFU

PARGA

PAXOS

Gaios

ANTIPAXOS

MAINLAND
GREECE

to Italy

PREVEZA

Aktion

Lefkas

LEFKAS

Astakos

Vathi

ITHACA

CEPHALONIA

Sami

PATRAS

Argostoli

Poros

Killini

NORTH

ZAKYNTHOS
[Zante]

Zakynthos

Four   The Ionian islands & mainland

firm, **Clyde Surveys Ltd., Reform Rd., Maidenhead, Berks SL6 8BU. Tel. (0628) 21371.**

Then consider the alternative methods of travel and appraise their value to your circumstances.

On Foot

Owing to the hilly terrain of the islands and the daytime heat encountered, you may well have enough walking to do without looking for trouble. A quick burst down to the local beach, taverna, shop or restaurant, and the resultant one hundred or so steps back up again, will often be quite enough to satiate any desire to go 'walkies'.

If you must, walking is often the only way to negotiate the more rugged donkey tracks and the minimum footwear required is a solid pair of sandals or 'trainers'.

Hitching

The comparative paucity of privately owned cars makes hitch-hiking an unsatisfactory mode of travel. On the other hand, if striking out to get to, or return from, a particular village on a dead end road, most Greek drivers will stop when thumbed down. It will probably be a lift in the back of a Japanese pick-up truck, possibly sharing the space with some chickens, a goat or sheep or all three!

Donkey

Although once a universal 'transportation module', now usually only available for hire on specific journey basis in particular locations. A personal prejudice is to consider donkey rides part of the unacceptable face of tourism added to which it is exorbitantly expensive.

Buses

Buses are the universal method of travel in Greece, so the services are widespread if, naturally enough, a little Greek in operation. Generally they run approximately on time and the fares are, on the whole, extremely reasonable.

The trick is to find the square from which the buses depart, and then locate the ticket office. Here the timetable and fares structure will be stuck up in the window or on a wall, and tickets are pre-purchased. On some bus routes the fares are collected by a conductor, although this is unusual. Be available well prior to the scheduled departure times as buses have a 'nasty habit' of departing early. Ensure any luggage is placed in the correct storage department, otherwise it may go missing.

Buses are often crowded, especially if the journey coincides with a ferry-boat arrival. They are, with the taxi, the islanders main form of transportation, so expect fairly bulky loads and, occasionally, livestock to share the seats, storage racks and central aisle. A bus rarely leaves a potential client, they just encourage everyone in. The fun comes if the bus is not only 'sardine packed', but fares are collected by the conductor. Somehow he makes his way through, round and over the passengers. The timetables are usually scheduled so that a bus or buses await a ferry-boats arrival, except perhaps very early or late craft.

Do not fail to observe the decorations, festooned around and enveloping the driver. Often these displays resemble a shrine, which, taking account of the way some of the drivers propel their bus, is perhaps not so out of place. Finally, do have the right change, coins are always in short supply.

A critic recently took me to task for not stressing that the summer bus schedules detailed are the subject of severe curtailment, if not total termination, during the winter months from October through to May. So, smacked hand Geoffrey and readers please note.

Taxis

Usually are very readily available, and can be remarkably modern and plush. On the other hand. . .

Ports and towns nearly always have a main square on which the taxis are ranked and very often they queue on the quayside to await a ferry-boat's arrival. Fares are governed by law and, at the main-rank, will be displayed giving examples of the cost to various destinations. The fares are reasonable by European standards, but it is essential to establish the cost prior to hiring a taxi.

It may come as a shock to have one's halting, pidgin Greek answered in 'pure' Australian or American. But this is not surprising when one considers that many island Greeks have spent their youth on merchant ships, or emigrated to the New World for 10 to 15 years. On their return home, with a relatively financially secure future, they have taken to taxi driving to supplement their income (and possibly to keep out of the little woman's way).

Bicycle, Moped, Scooter or Car Hire

Be very careful to establish what (if any) insurance cover is included in the rental fee, and that the quoted hire charge includes the various compulsory taxes. On the whole, bicycles are very hard work and poor value in relation to, say, the cost of hiring a Lambretta or Vespa scooter — an option endorsed when the mountainous nature of most islands, and the midday heat is taken into consideration. The ubiquitous Italian models are being replaced by semi-automatic Japanese motorcycles. Although they do away with the necessity to fight the gears and clutch they are not entirely suited to transporting two heavyweights. I have had the frightening experience, when climbing a steep mountainside track, of the bike jumping out of gear, depositing my passenger and I on the ground and the scooter whirling round like a crazed mechanical catherine-wheel.

It is amazing how easy it is to get a good tan while scootering. The moderate island wind draws the sun's heat, the air is laden with the smell of wild sage and oleanders and with the sun on your back. . . marvellous!

Very rarely is a deposit requested when hiring a bike or motorbike but your passport may be retained. If not the number will be required, as may the sight of a driving licence or an International driving permit which can be acquired from a tourist's relevant national driving organisation, and is valid for a period of one year.

Always shop around to check out various companies' hire rates; the nearer to a port, town or city centre you are, the more expensive they will be. A small walk towards the unfashionable quarters can be very rewarding.

Take a close look over the chosen mode of transport before settling up, as maintenance of any mechanical unit in Greece is poor to non-existent. Bicycles and scooters, a few years old, will be 'pretty clapped out'. More especially check the brakes — you will need them and do not allow the hirer to fob you off without making sure there is a spare wheel. Increasingly, the owners of two wheeled vehicles are hiring out dubious looking crash helmets. Flash young Greek motobike riders usually wear their space age outfits on the handlebars.

A useful tip when hiring a scooter is to take along a towel. It doubles up as useful additional padding for the pillion passenger's bottom on rocky roads and saves sitting on painfully hot plastic seating if a hirer has forgotten to raise the squab when parked up. Sunglasses are necessary to protect a riders eyes from air-borne insects. Out of the height-of-season and early evening it can become very chilly so a sweater or jumper is a good idea and females may well require a head scarf, whatever the time of day or night.

Fuel is served in litres and five litres of two-stroke costs about 250 - 300 drs. Fill up as soon as possible, fuel stations are in fairly short supply outside the main towns.

Typical daily hire rates are, for a bicycle 150 drs, a scooter/Lambretta 600 to 1000 drs, and a car between 2000 and 3000 drs. More and more often car hire companies require a daily deposit, which can be as much as 5000 drs per day. Out of season and period hire can benefit from negotiation. Increasingly the gap between the scooter and the car is being filled with more sophisticated machinery which include moon-tyred and powerfully engined Japanese motorbikes and beach-buggies.

Several words of warning will not go amiss. Taking into account the state of the roads do not hire a two-wheeled conveyance if not thoroughly used to handling one. There are a number of very nasty accidents every year, involving tourists and hired scooters. Additionally the combination of poor road surfaces and usually inadequate to non-existent lights should preclude any night time scootering. A hirer must ensure he (or she) is fully covered for medical insurance, including an unscheduled medi-care flight home, and check that a general policy does not exclude accidents incurred on hired transport. The glass fronted metal framed shrines mounted by the roadside are graphic reminders of a fatal accident at this or that spot. Incidentally, on a less macabre note, if the shrine is a memorial to a man, the picture and bottle usually present (more often than not of Sophia Loren and whisky) represent that person's favourite wishes. Back to finger-wagging. The importance of the correct holiday insurance cover cannot be over-stressed. The tribulations I have encountered in obtaining inclusive insurance combined with some readers disastrous experiences have resulted in the inclusion in the Guide of an all embracing scheme. This caveat should be coupled with the strictures in Chapter 1 drawing attention to the all-inclusive policy devised for readers of the *Candid Guides*, for details of which *See* page iii. Enough said!

Another area that causes unpleasant disputes is the increasing habit of the hire companies to charge comparatively expensively for any damage incurred. Your detailed reasons for the causes of an accident, the damage and why it should not cost you anything inevitably falls on deaf ears. Furthermore it is no use threatening to involve the police as they will not be at all interested in the squabble.

Roads

The main roads of Corfu are good, as are most of those on the other islands in the group; but metalled country lanes usually degenerate fairly alarmingly, becoming heavily rutted and cratered tracks. Much road building and reconstruction is under way. Beware as not all roads, indicated as being in existence on the official maps, are anything more than, at the best, donkey tracks and can be simply non-existent. Evidence of broken lines marking a road on the map must be interpreted as meaning there is no paved highway at all.

Useful Greek

English	Greek	Sounds like
Where can I hire a...	Που μπορω να νοικιασω ενα	Poo boro na neekeeaso enna...
...bicycle	ποδηλατο	...pothilato
...scooter	σκουτερ	...sckooter
...car	αυτοκινητο	...aftokinito
I'd like a...	Θα ηθελα ενα	Tha eethela enna...
I'd like it for...	Θα το ηθελα για	Tha dho eethela yia...
...a day	μια μερα	...mia mera
...days	μερεζ	...meres
...a week	μια εβδομαδα	...mia evthomadha
How much is it by the...	Ποσο κανει την	Poso kanee tin...
...day	μερα	...mera
...week	εβδομαδα	...evthomadha
Does that include...	Συμπεριλαμβανονται σαντο	Simberitamvanonte safto
...mileage	τα χιλιομετρα	...tah hiliometra
...full insurance	μικτη ασφαλεια	...meektee asfaleah

I want some	Θελω	Thelo
...petrol (gas)	βενζινη	...vehnzini
...oil	λαδι	...lathi
...water	νερο	...nero
Fill it up	Γεμιστε το	Yemiste to
...litres of petrol (gas)	λιτρα βενξινηζ	...litra vehnzinis
How far is it to...	Ποσο απεχει	Poso abechee...
Which is the road for...	Ποιοζ ειναι ο δρομοζ λια	Pios eene o thromos yia
Where are we now	Που ειμαστε τωρα	Poo emaste tora
What is the name of this place	Πωζ ονομαξεται αυτο το μεροζ	Pos onomazete afto dho meros
Where is...	Που ειναι	Poo eene...

Road Signs

STOP	ΑΛΤ
NO ENTRY	ΑΠΑΓΟΡΕΥΕΤΑΙ Η ΕΙΣΟΔΟΣ
NO THROUGH ROAD	ΑΔΙΕΞΟΔΟΣ
DETOUR	ΠΑΡΑΚΑΜΠΤΗΡΙΟΣ
REDUCE SPEED	ΕΛΑΤΤΩΣΑΤΕ ΤΑΧΥΤΗΤΑΝ
NO WAITING	ΑΠΑΓΟΡΕΥΕΤΑΙ Η ΑΝΑΜΟΝΗ
ROAD REPAIRS	ΕΠΓΑ ΕΠΙ ΤΗΣ ΟΔΟΥ
BEWARE (Caution)	ΚΙΝΔΥΝΟΣ
NO OVERTAKING	ΑΠΓΟΡΕΥΕΤΑΙ ΤΟ ΠΡΟΣΠΕΡΑΣΜΑ
NO PARKING	ΑΠΑΓΟΡΕΥΕΤΑΙ Η ΣΤΑΘΜΕΥΣΙΣ

6 Island Food & Drink

Let us eat and drink for tomorrow we die. *Corinthians*

It is a pity that many tourists, prior to visiting Greece, have 'experienced' the offerings masquerading as Greek food served up at sundry restaurants in Europe and America. Greek food does not seem to cross its borders very well and probably it is impossible to recreate Greek cooking away from the homeland. Perhaps this is because the food and wine owe much of their taste to, and are in sympathy with, the very air laden with the scent of the flowers and herbs, the very water, clear and chill, the very soil of the plains and scrub-clad mountains, the ethereal and uncapturable quality that is Greece. Incidentally many critics would say it was impossible to create Greek food, full stop, but be that as it may. . .

Salad does not normally send me into ectasy but, after a few days in Greece, the very thought of a peasant salad consisting of endive leaves, sliced tomatoes and cucumber, black olives, olive oil and vinegar dressing all topped off with feta cheese and sprinkled with oregano, parsley or fennel, sends me salivating to the nearest taverna.

Admittedly, unless you are lucky enough to chance across an outstanding taverna, the majority are surprisingly unadventurous and the choice of menu limited.

Mind you there are one or two restaurants serving exciting and unusual meals if the spelling mistakes are ignored. For instance I have observed over the years the following no doubt appetising dishes:- *omeled, spachetti botonnaise, shrings salad, bowels entrails, lump cutlets, limp liver, mushed pot, schrimps, crambs, kid chops, grilled meat bolls, spar rips, wine vives, fiant oven, sward fish, pork shops, staffed vine leaves, wild greens, string queens, wildi cherry, bater honi, gregg goti(!)* and *Creek salad* — sounds interesting.

A FEW HINTS & TIPS

Do not insist upon butter, the Greek variant is not very tasty to the European palate, is expensive and in the heat tends to dissolve into greasy pools.

Sample the retsina wine and after a bottle or two a day for a few days there is every chance you will enjoy it. Moreover, retsina is beneficial (well that's what I tell myself), acting as a splendid anti-agent to the comparative oiliness of some of the food.

Bread will be automatically served with a meal — and charged for — if you do not indicate otherwise. It is very useful for mopping up any excessive olive oil and requires no butter to make it more greasy. It has become a noticeable, and regrettable, feature in recent years that the charge for bread has increased to between 10 and 20 drs per head and I have seen it as high as 30 drs. Naughty!

Greek food tends to be served on the 'cool' side and even if the meal started out hot, and by some mischance is speedily served, it will arrive on a thoroughly chilled plate.

The selection of both food and drink usually served up is, almost always, limited and unenterprising, unless you elect to frequent the more international restaurants (but why go to Greece?). On the other hand the choice of establishments in which to eat and/or drink is unlimited, in fact the profusion is such that it can prove very confusing. If in doubt about which particular restaurant or taverna to patronise, use the well tried principle of picking one frequented by the locals; it will inevitably serve good quality food at reasonable prices.

It is generally a waste of time to ask a Greek for guidance in selecting a good taverna or restaurant for, as he would not wish to offend anyone, he will be reluctant to give specific advice in case you might be dissatisfied.

Especially in the more rural areas, do not be shy, ask to look over the kitchen to see what's cooking. If denied this traditional right, be on your guard as the food may well be pre-cooked, tasteless and plastic, particularly if the various meals available are displayed in a neon-lit showcase.

Do not order the whole meal all at once as you would at home, for if you do it will be served simultaneously and/or in the wrong sequence. Order course by course and take your time, everyone else does. You are not being ignored if the waiter does not approach the table for anything up to 20 minutes, he is just taking his time and is probably over-worked. At first the blood pressure does tend to rise inexorably as the waiter, seemingly, continues to studiously disregard your presence. It makes a visitor's stay in Greece very much more enjoyable if all preconceived ideas of service can be forgotten. Lay back and settle into the glorious and indolent timelessness of the locals' way of life. If in a hurry, pay when the order arrives for if under the impression that it took a disproportionate time to be served, just wait until it comes to settling up. It will probably take twice as long to get the bill (*logaristhimo*), as it did to receive the food.

Fish, contrary to expectations, is very expensive, even in comparison with European prices, so you can imagine the disparity with the cost of other Greek food. When ordering fish, it is normal to select the choice from '*the ice*', and, fish being priced by weight, it will be put on the scales prior to cooking.

Price lists are mandatory for most drinking and eating places, stating the establishment's category and the price of every item served. Two prices are shown, the first being net is not really relevant, the second, showing the price you will actually be charged, includes service and taxes.

Food is natural and very rarely are canned or any frozen items used, even if available. When frozen foods are included in the meal the fact must be indicated on the menu by addition of the initials *KAT*. The olive oil used for cooking is excellent, as are the herbs and lemons, but it can take time to become accustomed to the different flavour imparted to food.

Before leaving the subject of hints and tips, remember that olive oil can be pressed into service for removing unwanted beach-tar from clothes.

A most enjoyable road, quayside or ferry-boat breakfast is to buy a large yoghurt and a small pot of honey, mix the honey into the yoghurt and then relish the bitter-sweet delight. If locally produced, natural yoghurt (usually stored in small, cool tubs and spooned into a container) cannot be purchased, the brand named *Total* is an adequate substitute being made from cow or sheep milk. I prefer the sheep derived product and, when words fail, break into a charade of 'baa-ing'. It keeps the other shoppers amused if nothing else. The succulent water melon, a common and inexpensive fruit, provides a juicy lunch-time refreshment.

Apart from waving the table-cloth in the air, or for that matter the table, it is usually to call '*parakalo*' (please). It is also permissible to say '*gkarson*' or simply waiter.

THE DRINKS
Non-alcoholic beverages

Being a '*cafe*' (and '*taverna*') society, coffee is drunk at all times of the day and night. Greek coffee ('*kafe*') is in fact a left-over from the centuries long Turkish influence, being served without milk in small cups, always with a glass of deliciously cool water. Unless specified otherwise, it will come sickly sweet or *varigliko*. There are many variations but the three most usual are *sketto* (no sugar), *metrio* (medium) or *glyko* (sweet). Do not completely drain the cup, the bitter grains will choke you. Except in the most traditional establishments (*Kafeneions*), you can ask for *Nes-Kafe* or simply *Nes* which, as you would think, is an instant coffee but has a comparatively muddy taste. If you require milk with your coffee it is necessary to ask for *me ghala*. A most refreshing version is to have *Nes* chilled or *frappe*. French coffee (*ghaliko kafe*), served in a coffee pot with a separate jug of hot milk, espresso kafe and cappucino are found in the larger provincial cities, ports and international establishments. However, having made your detailed request, you may well receive any permutation of all the possibilities listed above, however carefully you think you have ordered.

Tea, (*tsai*), perhaps surprisingly, is quite freely available, made of course with the ubiquitous teabag, which is not so outrageous, since they have become so common-place. In more out of the way places, you may be served herbal tea.

Purchasing bottled mineral waters is not always necessary as, generally, island water is superb. Should you wish to have some stashed away in the fridge, brand names include *Loutrakri*, *Nigita*, and *Sarizo*. Sprite is fizzy and Lemnada/Lemonatha a stillish lemonade. Orangeade (*portokaladha*), cherry soft drink (*visinatha*) and fruit juices are all palatable and sold, as often as not, under brand names, as is the universal *Koka-Kola*.

A word of warning emanates from a reader who reported that, in the very hot summer months, some youngsters drink nothing but sweet, fizzy beverages. This can result in mouth ulcers caused by fermenting sugar, so drink some water every day.

Alcoholic beverages

Generally sold by weight. Beer comes in 330g tins or 500g bottles (have the 500g, it is a good measure) and wine in 340 to 430g (half bottle), 680 to 730g (1.1 pints) and 950g (1¾ pints) bottles.

Greek brewed or bottled beers represent very good value except when served in cans, which are the export version and a 'rip off'. This European habit should be resisted for no other reason than it means the cost is almost doubled. Now that *Fix Hellas* is rarely available, due to the founder's death, the only other, widely available, bottled beers are *Amstel* and *Henninger*. Draught lager, is insidiously, creeping in to various resorts and should be avoided, not only for purist reasons, but because it is comparatively expensive as are the imported stronger bottled lagers. No names, no pack drill but *Carlsberg* is one that springs to mind. A small bottle of beer is *mikri bira* and a large one, *meghali bira.*

Wine

Unresinated (*aretsinoto*) wine is European in style, palatable, and popular brands include red and white *Demestika* and *Cambas*. More refined palates will approve of the whites (aspro) and the reds (kokino) of AntiPaxos as well as the rosé and dry red wines of Cephalonia. Greek wine is not so much known for its quality but if quantity of brands can make up for this then Greece will not let you down.

Resinated wine is achieved, if you consider that to be the expression, by the barrels, in which the wine is to be fermented, being internally coated with pine-tree resin. The resultant liquid is referred to as retsina, most of which are white, with a kokkeneli or rosé version being available. Retsina is usually bottled, but in tavernas will quite often be served in a metal jug, or dispensed, for personal consumption, from large vats from side-street cellars, into any container you might like to use. The adjective 'open' is used to describe locally brewed retsina available on draught or more correctly from the barrel. Rumour has it that the younger retsinas are more easily palatable, but that is very much a matter of taste. A very good 'starter' kit is to drink a bottle or two of retsina twice a day for three or four days and if the pain goes. . .

Spirits & others

As elsewhere in the world, if you stick to the national drinks they represent good value.

Ouzo, much maligned and blamed for other excesses, is, in reality, of the aniseed family of drinks (which include Ricard and Pernod) and, taken with water, is a splendid 'medicine'. *Ouzo* is traditionally served with *mezethes* (or *mezes*), the Greek equivalent of Spanish *tapas*, consisting of a small plate of, for instance, a slice of cheese, tomato, cucumber and possibly smoked eel, octopus and an olive. When served they are charged for, costing some 20 to 30 drs, but the tradition of offering them is disappearing in many tourist locations. If you specifically do not wish to be served *mezes* then the request is made '*ouzo sketto*'. *Raki* is a stronger alternative to *Ouzo*, often 'created' in Crete.

Greek *Metaxa* brandy, available in three, five and seven star quality, is very palatable but with a certain amount of 'body', whilst *Otys* brandy is smoother. Greek aperitifs include *Vermouth, Mastika* and *Citro.*

DRINKING PLACES

Prior to launching into the various branches of this subject, I am at a loss to understand why so many cafe-bar and taverna owners select chairs that are designed to cause the maximum discomfort, even suffering. Often too small for any but a very small bottom, too low and made up of wicker-work or rafia that painfully impresses the pattern on the sitters bare (sun-burnt?) thighs.

Kafeneion (ΚΑΦΕΝΙΟΝ)

Greek cafe, serving only Turkish coffee. Very Greek, very masculine and I have never seen a woman in one. They are similar to a local working man's club, but with backgammon, worry beads and large open windows giving a dim view of the smoke-laden interior.

Ouzeries (ΟΥΞΕΡΙ)

As above, but the house speciality is (well, well) *Ouzo.*

Cafe-bar (ΚΑΦΕ-ΜΠΑΡ)

As above, but serving alcoholic beverages as well as coffee and women are to be seen.

Pavement cafes

French in style, with outside tables and chairs sprawling over the road as well as the pavement. Inside, the locals will be chatting to each other in that peculiar Greek fashion, giving the impression that a full-blooded fight is about to break out at any moment. In reality, they are just good friends, chatting to each other over the noise of a televised football match, or watching some plastic, sickly American soap opera or ghastly English 'comic' programme with Greek subtitles. Open from mid-morning, through the day to one or two o'clock the next morning. Snacks and sweet cakes are usually available.

Drinks can always be obtained at a taverna or restaurant, but you may be expected to eat, so read on.

You can drink at hotel cocktail bars but why leave home!

EATING PLACES

At the cheapest end of the market, and more especially found in Athens, are pavement-mounted stands serving doughnut-shaped bread which give an inexpensive nibble.

Pistachio nut & ice cream vendors

Respectively pushing their wheeled trolleys around the streets, selling a wide variety of nuts in paper bags for 10 drs or so and good-value ice cream in a variety of flavours and prices.

Galaktopoleio (ΓΑΛΑΚΤΟΠΩΕΙΟ)

A shop selling dairy products including milk (*gala*), butter, yoghurt (*yiaorti*), bread, honey, sometimes omelettes and fritters with honey (*loukoumades*). A traditional but more expensive alternative to a restaurant/bar in which to purchase breakfast.

Zacharoplasteion (ΖΑΧΑΡΟΠΛΑΣΤΕΙΟ)

A shop specialising in pastries, cakes (*glyko*), chocolates (which are comparatively expensive) and soft drinks as well as, sometimes, a small selection of alcoholic drinks.

Galaktozacharoplasteion

A combination of the two previously described establishments.

Snackbar (ΣΝΑΚ-ΜΠΑΡ, Souvlatzidika & Tyropitadika)

Snack bars, not so numerous in the less touristy areas, and often restricted to one or two in the main town. They represent marvellous value for a stand-up snack and the most popular offering is *souvlaki* — pita bread (or a roll) filled with grilled meat or kebab, (*doner kebab* — slices off a rotating vertical spit of an upturned cone of meat also called '*giro*'), a slice of tomato, chopped onion and a dressing. Be careful, as souvlaki is not to be muddled with *souvlakia* which, when served at a snack bar, consists of pieces of lamb, pork or veal meat grilled on a wooden skewer and is indistinguishable from *Shish-Kebab*, or (guess what) a *souvlakia* when served at a sit-down meal where the metal skewered meat pieces are interspersed with vegetables. Other goodies include *tiropites* — hot flaky pastry pies filled with cream cheese; *boogatsa* — a custard filled pastry, a wide variety of rolls and sandwiches (*sanduits*) with cheese, tomato, salami and other spiced meat fillings as well as toasted sandwiches (*tost*).

Pavement cafes

Serve snacks and sweets.

Pizzerias

Seem to be on the increase and are restaurants specialising in the imported Italian dish which prompts one to ask why not go to Italy. To be fair they usually represent very good value and a large serving will often feed two.

Tavernas (ΤΑΒΕΡΝΑ), Restaurants (ΕΣΤΙΑΤΟΡΙΟΝ), Rotisserie (ΨΥΣΤΕΡΙΑ) & Rural Centres (ΕΞΟΧΙΚΟΝ ΚΕΝΤΡΟΝ)

Four variations on a theme. The traditional Greek taverna is a family concern, frequently only open in the evening. More often than not, the major part of the eating area is outside under a vine-covered patio, down the pavement and/or on a roof garden.

Restaurants tend to be more sophisticated, possibly open all day and night, but the definition between the two is rather blurred. The price lists may include a chancy English translation, the waiter might be smarter and the table cloth and napkins could well be linen, in place of the taverna's paper table covering and serviettes.

As tavernas often have a spit-roasting device tacked on, there is often little, discernible difference between a rotisserie and a taverna. A grilled meat restaurant may also be styled ΨΗΣΤΑΡΙΑ.

The rural centre is a mix of cafe-bar and taverna in, you've guessed it, a rural or seaside setting.

Fish tavernas (ΨΑΡΟΤΑΒΕΡΝΑ)

Tavernas specialising in fish dishes.

Hotels (ΞΕΝΟΔΟΧΕΙΟΝ)

ΞΕΝΟΔΟΧΕΙΟΝ ΥΠΝΟΥ is a hotel that does not serve food, ΠΑΝΔΟΧΕΙΟΝ a lower category hotel and Xenia, a Government-owned hotel.

The Xenia will be well run, the food and drink international, the menu will be in French and the prices will reflect all these 'attributes'.

An extremely unpleasant manifestation to old fogey's like me is illustrated by one or two menus spotted in the more 'international' locations, namely Greek bills of fare set out Chinese restaurant style. You know, set 'Meal A' for two, 'Meal B' for three and 'C' for four and more. . .!

THE FOOD

Some of the following represents a selection of the wide variety of food available.

Sample menu

Ψωμι (Psomi)	Bread
ΠΡΩΙΝΟ	BREAKFAST

Αυγα τηγανιτο με μπεικον και τοματα	Fried egg, bacon and tomato
Τοστ βουτυρο μαρμελαδα	Buttered toast and marmalade
Το προγευμα (to pro-ye-vma)	English (or American on some islands) breakfast

ΑΥΓΑ — EGGS
- Μελατα — soft boiled
- Σφικτα — hard boiled
- Τηγανιτα — fried
- Ποσσε — poached

ΤΟΣΤ ΣΑΝΤΟΥΙΤΣ — TOASTED SANDWICHES
- Τοστ μετυρι — toasted cheese
- Τοστ (με)Ζαμπον καιτυρι — toasted ham and cheese
- Μπουρκερ — burger
- Χα Μπουρκερ — hamburger
- Τσισμπουρκερ — cheeseburger
- Σαντουιτσ λουκανικο — hot dog

ΟΡΕΚΤΙΚΑ — APPETIZERS/HORS D'OEUVRES
- Αντξουγιεξ — anchovies
- Ελιεζ — olives
- Σαρδελλεζ — sardines
- Σκορδαλιο — garlic dip
- Τζατζικι — tzatziki (diced cucumber & garlic in yoghurt)
- Ταραμοσαλατα — taramasalata (a fish roe pafe)

ΣΟΥΠΕΣ — SOUPS
- Σουπα φασολια — bean
- Αυγολεμονο — egg and lemon
- Ψαροσουπα — fish
- Κοτοσνπα — chicken
- Ντοματοσουπα — tomato
- Σουπα λαχανικων — vegetable

ΟΜΕΛΕΤΕΣ — OMELETTES
- Ομελετα μπεικου — bacon
- Ομελετα μπεικον τυρι τοματα — bacon, cheese and tomato
- Ομελετα τυρι — cheese
- Ομελετα ζαμπον — ham
- Ομελετα συκωτα κια πουλιων — chicken liver

ΣΑΛΑΤΕΣ — SALADS
- Ντοματα Σαλατα — tomato
- Αγγουρι Σαλατα — cucumber
- Αγγουστοματα Σαλατα — tomato and cucumber
- Χωριατικη — Greek peasant village salad

ΛΑΧΑΝΙΚΑ (ΛΑΔΕΡΑ)* — VEGETABLES
- Πατατεζ — potatoes
- Πατατεζ Τηγανιτεζ — chips (french fries)
- φρεοκα φασολακια — green beans
- Σπαραγκια — asparagus
- Κολοκυθακια — courgettes
- Σπανακι — spinach

*indicates cooked in oil.

Note various methods of cooking include:-
Baked — στο θουρνο; boiled — βραστα; creamed — με ασπρη σαλτσα; fried — τηγανιτα; grilled — στη σχαραρα; roasted — Ψητα; spit roasted — σουβλαζ.

ΚΥΜΑΔΕΣ — MINCED MEATS
- Μουσακαζ — moussaka
- Ντοματεζ Γεμιοτεζ — stuffed tomatoes (with rice or minced meat)
- Κεφτεδεζ — meat balls
- Ντολμαδακια — stuffed vine leaves (with rice or minced meat)

Πσπουτσακια	stuffed vegetable marrow (rice or meat)
Κανελονια	canelloni
Μακαρονια με κυμα	spaghetti bolognese (more correctly with mince)
Παστιτσιο	macaroni. mince and sauce
Σουβλακι	shish-kebab

PIZI — RICE
Πιλαφι	pilaff
Πιλαφι (με) γιαουρτι	with yoghurt
Πιλαφι συκωτακια	with liver
Σπανακοριζο	with spinach
Πιλαφι κυμα	with minced meat

ΠΟΥΛΕΡΙΚΑ — POULTRY
Κοτοπουλο	chicken. roasted
Ποδι κοταζ	leg of chicken
Στηθοζ κοταζ	chicken breast
Κοτοπουλο βραστο	boiled chicken
Ψητο κοτοπουλο στη συμβλα	spit-roasted chicken

ΚΡΕΑΣ — MEAT
Νεφρα	kidneys
Αρνι†	lamb†
Αρνιστεζ Μπριζολεζ	lamb chops
Παιδακια	lamb cutlets
Συκωτι	liver
Χοιρινο†	pork†
Χοιρινεζ Μπριζολεζ	pork chops
Λουκανικα	sausages
Μπιφτεκι	steak (beef)
Μοσχαρισιο	veal
Μοσχαρισιο Μπριζολεζ	veal chops
Μοσχαρι	grilled veal
Ψητο Μοσχαρακι	roast veal

† often with the prefix/suffix to indicated if roasted or grilled

ΨΑΡΙΑ — FISH
Σκουμπρι	mackerel
Σμναγριδα	red snapper
Μαριδεζ	whitebait
Οκταποδι	octopus
Καλαμαρια	squid
Μπαρμπουνι	red mullet
Κεφαλοζ	mullet
Λυθρινι	grey mullet

ΤΥΡΙΑ — CHEESE
φετα	feta (goat's-milk based)
Γραβιερα	gruyere-type cheese
Κασερι	cheddar-type (sheep's-milk based)

ΦΡΟΥΤΑ — FRUITS
Καρπουζι	water melon
Πεπονι	melon
Μηλα	apple
Πορτοκαλι	oranges
Σταφυλια	grapes
Κομποστα φρουτων	fruit compote

ΠΑΓΩΤΑ — ICE-CREAM
Σπεσιαλ	special

Παγωτο βανιλλια	vanilla
Παγωτο σοκολατα	chocolate
Παγωτο λεμονι	lemon
Υρανιτα	water ice
ΓΛΥΚΙΣΜΑΤΑ	DESSERTS
Κεικ	cake
ρουτοσαλατα	fruit salad
Κρεμα	milk pudding
Κρεμ καραμελ	cream caramel
Μπακλαβαζ	crisp pastry with nuts and syrup or honey
Καταιφι	fine shredded pastry with nuts and syrup or honey
Γαλακτομπουρεκο	fine crispy pastry with custard and syrup
Γιαουρτι	yoghurt
Μελι	honey
ΑΝΑΨΥΚΤΙΚΑ	COLD DRINKS/SOFT DRINKS
Πορτοκαλι	orange
Πορτοκαλαδα	orangeade
Λεμοναδα	lemonade made with lemon juice
Γκαζοζα (Gazozo)	fizzy lemonade
Μεταλλικο νερο	mineral water
Κοκα κολα	Coca-cola
Πεψι κολα	Pepsi-cola
Σεβεν-απ	Seven Up
Σοδα	soda
Τοηικ	tonic
Νερο (Nero)	water
ΚΑφΕΔΕΣ	COFFEES
Ελληνικοζ (Καφεζ)	Greek coffee (sometimes called Turkish coffee ie Toupkikos Καφε)
σκετο (skehto)	no sugar
μετριο (metrio)	medium sweet
γλυκο (ghliko)	sweet (very)

(Unless stipulated it will turn up 'ghliko'. Do not drink before it has settled.

Νεζ καφε	Nescafé
Νεζ (με γαλα) (Nes me ghala)	Nescafé with milk
Εζπρεσσο	espresso
Καπουτσινο	cappucino
φραπε	chilled coffee is known as 'frappé'
Τσαι	tea
Σοκολατα γαλα	chocolate milk
ΜΠΥΡΕΣ	BEERS
ΦΙΞ(ΕΛΛΑΣ) Μπυρα	Fix (Hellas) beer
φιαλν	bottle
κουτι	can
ΑΜΣΤΕΛ (Αμστελ)	Amstel
ΧΕΝΝΙΝΓΕΡ (Χεννινγκερ)	Henninger (300 g usually a can 500 g usually a bottle)
ΠΟΤΑ	DRINKS
Ουζο	Ouzo
Κονιακ	Cognac
Μπραντυ	Brandy
Μεταξα	Metaxa
3 ΑΣΤ	3 star
5 ΑΣΤ	5 star
Ουισκυ	Whisky

Τζιν	Gin
Βοτκα	Vodka
Καμπαρι	Campari
Βερμουι	Vermouth
Μαρτινι	Martini

ΚΡΑΣΙΑ	WINES
Κοκκινο	red
Ασπρο	white
Ροζε Κοκκινελι	rosé
Ξερο	dry
Υλυκο	sweet
Ρετσινα	resinated wine
e.g. θεοκρποξ	Theokritos
Αρετσινωτο	unresinated wine
e.g. Δεμεοτιχα	Demestica
	340 g is a ½ bottle
	680 g is a bottle
	950 g is a large bottle

Useful Greek

English	Greek	Sounds like
Have you a table for...	Εχετε ενα τραπεζι για	Echede enna trapezee ghia...
I'd like...	Θελω	Thelo...
We would like...	Θελουμε	Thelome...
a beer	μια μπυρα	meah beerah
a glass	ενα πορρι	ena poteeree
a carafe	μια καραφα	meea karafa
a small bottle	ενα μικρη μπουκαλι	ena mikri bookalee
a large bottle	ενα μεγαλη	ena meghali bookalee
bread	ψωμι	psomee
tea with milk	τσαι με γαλα	tsai me ghala
with lemon	τσαι με λεμονι	me lemoni
Turkish coffee (Greek)	Τουρκικο καφε	Toupkiko kafe
sweet	γλυκος	ghleekos
medium	μετριος	medreeo
bitter (no sugar)	πικρο	pikto
Black coffee	**Nescafe** χωρις γαλα	Nescafé horis ghala
Coffee with milk	**Nescafe** με γαλα	Nescafé me ghala
a glass of water	ενα ποτηρι νερο	enna poteeree nero
a napkin	ενα πετσετα	enna petseta
an ashtray	ενα σταχτοδοχειο	enna stachdothocheeo
toothpick	μια οδοντογλυθιδα	mea odontoglifadha
the olive oil	η ελεολαδο	ee eleolatho
Where is the toilet?	Που ειναι η τουαλεττα	Poo eene i(ee) tooaleta?
What is this?	Τι ειναι αυτο	Ti ine afto
This is...	Αυτο ειναι	Afto eene
cold	κρυο	kreeo
bad	χαλασμενο	chalasmeno
stale	μπαγιατικο	bayhiatiko
undercooked	αψητο	apseeto
overcooked	παραβρασμενο	paravrasmeno
The bill please	Το λογαριασμο παρακαλω	To loghariasmo parakalo
How much is that?	Ποσο κανει αυτο	Poso kane afto?
That was an excellent meal	Περιφημο γευμα	Pereefimo yefma
We shall come again	Θα ζαναρθουμε	Tha xanarthoume

7 Shopping & Public Services

Let your purse be your master. *Proverb*

Purchasing items in Greece is still quite an art form or subject for a degree course. The difficulties have been compounded by the rest of the western world becoming nations of supermarket shoppers, whilst the Greeks have stayed traditionally and firmly with their individual shops, selling a fixed number of items and sometimes only one type of a product.

Shopping for a corkscrew, for instance, might well involve calling at two or three seemingly look-alike ironmongers, but, no, they each specialise in certain lines of goods and do not stock any items outside those prescribed, almost as if by holy writ.

Bakers usually have to be diligently searched for and when found are frequently located tucked away in or behind other shops. A pointer is that there is often a pile of blackened, twisted olive wood stacked up to one side of the entrance.

Cake shops (zacharoplasteion) may sell bottled mineral water (ask for a cold bottle).

The question of good and bad buys must be highly personal but the items listed below are highlighted on the basis of value for money and quality.

Clothing and accessories that are attractive and represent good value include embroidered peasant dresses, leather sandals, woven bags and furs. Day-to-day items that are inexpensive take in Greek cigarettes, drinks including ouzo, *Metaxa* brandy and selected island wines. Suitable gifts for family and friends include ceramic plates, sponges, Turkish delight, and worry beads (*komboloe*). Disproportionately expensive items include camera film, toiletries, books and playing cards.

Do not forget to compare prices and preferably shop in the streets and markets, not in airport and hotel concessionary shops which are often more expensive.

Try not to run short of change; everybody else does, including bus conductors, taxi drivers and shops.

Opening Hours
Strict or old fashioned summer shop hours are:
Monday, Wednesday and Saturday: 0830-1400 hrs.
Tuesday, Thursday and Friday: 0830-1330 hrs & 1730-2030 hrs.

Generally shops in tourist areas, during the summer, are open Monday to Saturday from 0800-1300 hours, when they close until 1700 hours after which they open again until at least 2030 hours, if not 2200 hours. Sundays and Saints days are more indeterminate, but there will usually be a general shop open somewhere. In very popular tourist resorts and busy port shops are often open seven days a week.

Drink
Available either in the markets from delicatessen meat/dairy counters or from 'off-licence'-type shops.

Smokers
Imported French, English and American cigarettes are inexpensive, compared with European prices, at between 80 and 100 drs for a packet of 20. Greek cigarettes, which have a distinctive and different taste, are excellent. Try *Karellia*, which cost about 50 drs for a packet of 20 and note that the price is printed around the edge of the packet. Even Greek cigars are almost unheard of on the islands, while in Athens, they cost 5 -10 drs and Dutch cigars work out at about, say, 20 drs each, so if a cigar-smoker, take along your holiday requirements.

Newspapers & Magazines
The *Athens Daily News* and *Athens Daily Post* are both published in English. Overseas

newspapers are available up to 24 hours behind the day of publication, but note that all printed matter is comparatively expensive.

Photography (Fotografion -ΦΩΤΟΓΡΑΦΕΙΟΝ)
Travellers should bring their film with them if possible, being imported it is comparatively expensive. To counter the very bright sunlight, when using colour film, blue filters should be fitted to the lens.

Tourist Guides & Maps
Shop around before purchasing, as the difference in price of the guides can be as much as 150 drs, ie. from 150-300 drs.

Some major ports and towns have one authentic, well stocked bookshop, more often than not a little off the town centre. The proprietor may well speak adequate English and will courteously answer most enquiries.

SHOPS
BAKERS & BREAD SHOPS
(ΑΡΤΟΠΟΙΕΙΟΝ ΑΡΤΟΠΩΛΕΙΟΝ or ΠΡΑΤΗΡΙΟΝ ΑΡΤΟΥ)
For some obscure reason bakers are nearly always difficult to locate, being hidden away, and bread shops are few and far between. Bakers may also sell cheese and meat pies. They are almost always closed on Sundays and all holidays despite their ovens often being used by the local community to cook the Sunday meal.

The method of purchasing bread can prove disconcerting, especially when sold by weight. Sometimes the purchaser selects the loaf and then pays but the most bewildering system is where it is necessary to pay first then collect the goods. Difficult if the shoppers level of Greek is limited to grunts, 'thank you' and 'please'!

Greek bread also has another parameter of measure, that is a graduation in hours — 1 hour, 4 hours and so on. After the period is up it is usually completely inedible, having transmogrified into a rock-like substance.

BUTCHER (ΚΡΕΟΠΩΛΕΙΟΝ)
Similar to those at home but the cuts are quite different (surely the Common Market can legislate against this deviation!).

MARKETS
The smaller ports and towns may have a market street and the larger municipalities often possess a market building, thronged with locals, where all the basic necessities can be procured inexpensively, with fruit and vegetable stalls interspaced by butchers and dairy delicatessen shops. During their opening hours, the proprietors are brought coffee and a glass of water by waiters carrying the cups and glasses, not on open trays, but in round aluminium salvers with a deep lip, held under a large ring handle, connected to the tray by three flat arms.

SUPERMARKETS (ΥΠΕΡΑΓΟΡΑ/ΣΟΥΠΕΡΜΑΡΚΕΤ)
Very much on the increase and based on small-town, self-service stores but not to worry, they inherit all those delightful native Greek qualities including quiet chaos.

SPECIALITY SHOPS
Found in some big towns and Athens. While pavement browsing, you will espy little basement shops, down a flight of steps, specialising, for instance, in dried fruit, beans, nuts and grains.

STREET KIOSKS (Periptero/ΠΕΡΙΠΤΕΡΟ)
These unique, pagoda-like huts stay open remarkably long hours, often from early morning to after midnight and sell a wide range of goods including newspapers, magazines (surprisingly sometimes pornographic literature), postcards, tourist maps,

postage stamps, sweets, chocolates, cigarettes, matches and cigars but not on the islands. *See* earlier comments. Additionally they form the outlet for the pay-phone system and, at the cost of 5 drs, a local call may be made. It is rather incongruous, to observe a Greek making a possibly important business call, in amongst a rack of papers and magazines, with a foreground of jostling pedestrians and a constant stream of noisy traffic in the background.

Alternate Ways of Shopping
Then there are the other ways of shopping: from hand-carts, their street-vendor owners selling respectively nuts, ice creams, milk and yoghurt; the back of a donkey with vegetable-laden panniers or from two wheeled trailers drawn by fearsome sounding, agricultural rotovator power units, both with an enormous set of scales, swinging like a hangman's scaffold, from the back end, be it donkey or truck powered.

Frequently used shops include:

ΒΙΒΛΙΟΠΩΛΕΙΟΝ — Bookshop; ΙΧΘΥΟΠΩΛΕΙΟΝ — Fishmonger; ΟΠΩΡΟΠΩΛΕΙΟΝ — Greengrocer; ΠΑΝΤΟΠΩΛΕΙΟΝ — Grocer; ΚΑΠΝΟΠΩΛΕΙΟΝ — Tobacconist. You will note that the above have a similar ending and it is worth noting that all shop titles that terminate in 'ΤΙΩΛΕΙΟΝ/πωλειο' are selling something, if that's a help.

SERVICES
THE BANKS (ΤΡΑΠΕΖΑ)
The minimum opening hours are 0800 to 1330 hrs, Monday to Thursday and 0800 to 1300 hrs on Friday. Some banks, in the most tourist ravaged spots, open on Saturday and a few on Sunday but smaller towns, villages or for that matter islands will not have a bank but occasionally a local money changer acting as agent for this or that national bank. Do not forget that a passport is usually required to change traveller's cheques. In the larger cities, personal cheques may be changed at a selected bank when backed by a Eurocheque or similar bank guarantee card. A small commission charge of between 50 and 100 drs is made whatever the size of the transaction. The service is generally discourteous and one employee will, reluctantly, speak English.

Make sure you select the correct bank to carry out a particular transaction (such as changing a personal cheque) Each bank displays a window sticker giving an indication of the tourist services carried out. There is nothing worse, after queuing for half an hour or so, than to be rudely told to go away. I once chose the wrong bank to change a personal cheque, only to receive a loud blast of abuse about some long-departed foreigner's bouncing cheque. Most embarrassing.

The larger hotels change traveller's cheques, but naturally enough at a disadvantageous rate compared with the banks.

Another interesting source of taking currency abroad for United Kingdom residents is to use National Giro Post Office cheques which can be cashed at any Post Office in Greece. This is a very useful wheeze especially on busy tourist islands where the foreign currency desk will be subject to long queues. Detailed arrangements have to be made with the International branch of Giro.

The basis of Greek currency is the drachma. This is nominally divided into 100 lepta and occasionally price lists show a price of, say, 62.60 drs. As prices are rounded up (or down), in practice, you will not encounter the lepta.

At the time of writing, the British pound sterling was worth approximately 215 drs and the US $ 150 drs (February 1986).

Notes are in denominations of 50, 100, 500, and 1000 drs and coins in denominations of 1 and 2 drs (bronze), 5, 10 and 20 and 50 drs (nickel). Do not run out of change, it is always in demand. Repetitious I know, but well worth remembering.

MUSEUMS
The following is a mean average of the information to hand but each museum is likely to

have its own particular pecularities. In the summer season (1st April - 31st October) they open daily 0845-1500/1900 hrs, Sundays and holidays 0930-1430/1530 hrs and are closed Mondays or Tuesdays. They are closed 1st January, 25th March, Good Friday, Easter holiday and 25th December. Admission costs range from free to 100/150 drs, whilst Sundays and holidays may well be free.

THE POST OFFICE (ΤΑΧΥΑΔΡΟΜΕΙΟΝ/ΕΛΤΑ)

Stamps can be bought from kiosks and shops selling postcards as well as from Post Offices. Post boxes are scattered around, are usually painted yellow, are rather small in size and often difficult to find, being fixed, high up, on side-street walls.

Most major town Post Offices are modern and the service received, only slightly less rude than that handed out by bank staff.

When confronted by two letter-box openings, the inland service is marked Εχοτεβικοy and the overseas Εξοτερικοy. Letters can be sent for *poste-restante* collection, but a passport will be required. Post Offices are usually only open Monday to Friday between 0730-2030 hrs for stamps and registered mail, 0730-2000 hrs for poste-restante and 0730-1430 hrs for parcels.

Parcels have to be collected.

ΓΡΑΜΜΑΤΟΣΗΜΑ — stamps; ΔΕΜΑΤΑ — parcels.

TELEPHONE OFFICE (OTE)

A separate organisation from the Post Office and to accomplish an overseas or long-distance call it is necessary to go to the OTE office. Here there are separate booths from which to make calls but busy offices will usually experience queues. The counter clerk will indicate which compartment is to be used and in a bank alongside him are mounted the instruments to meter the cost, payment being made after completion of the call. Ensure that the relevant meter is zeroed prior to making a connection. Opening days and hours vary enormously. Smaller offices may only open weekdays for say 7 hours between 0830-1530 hrs whilst the larger city offices may open 24 hours a day, seven days a week.

Overseas dialling codes		Inland services	
Australia	0061	Directory enquiries	131
Canada and USA	001	Provincial enquiries	132
New Zealand	0064	General information	134
South Africa	0027	Time	141
United Kingdom and Ireland	0044	Medical care	166
Other overseas countries	161	City Police	100
		Gendarmerie	109
		Fire	199
		Tourist police	171
		Roadside assistance	104
		Telegrams/cables	165

To dial England, drop the '0' from four figure codes, thus making a call to Portsmouth, for which the code is 0705, dial 0044 705 and then the number. Do not give up, keep dialling but slowly, and split the numbers up i.e. 00 44 705 ......

The internal service is both very good and reasonably priced. Local telephone calls cost 5 drs and can be made from some bars and the pavement kiosks (Periptero). The presence of a telephone will often be indicated by the sign ΕΔΩ ΤΗΛΕΛΝΕΙΤΕ, a blue background indicating a local phone, and an orange one an inter-city phone. Another sign εδω τηλεφωνειτε, (the lower case equivalent), indicates 'telephone from here'. The method of operation is to insert the coin and dial. If you cannot make the connection place the receiver back on the cradle and the coin will be returned.

Telegrams may be sent from either the Post Office or the OTE.

Useful Greek

English	Greek	Sounds like
Where is...	Που ειναι	Poo enne...
Where is the nearest...	Που ειναι η πλησιεστερη	Poo eene dho bleesiesteri...
baker	ο φουρναρηζ/ψωμαζ/ Αρτοποιειον	foonaris/psomas/ artopieon
bank	η τραπεζα	i(ee) trabeza
bookshop	το βιβλιοπωλειο	to vivleeobolieo
butchers shop	το χασαπιχο	o hasapiko
chemist shop	το φαρμακειο	to farmakio
dairy shop	το γαλακτοπωλειο	galaklopolieon
doctor	ο γιατροζ	o yiahtros
grocer	το μπακαληζ	to bakalis
hospital	το νοσοχομειο	to nosokomio
laundry	το πλυνηριο	to plintireo
liquor store	το ποτοπωλειο	to potopolea
photographic shop	το φωτογραφειο	to fotoghrafeeo
post office	το ταχυδρομειο	to tahkethromeo
shoe repairer	το τσαγκαραδιχο	to tsangkaradiko
tailor	ο ραπτηζ	o raptis
Have you any...	Εχετε	Ekheteh...
Do you sell...	Πουλατε	Boulate...
How much is this...	Ποσο κανει αυτο	Posso kanee afto...
I want...	Θελω	Thelo...
half kilo/a kilo	ενα μισο κιλο/ενα κιλο	miso kilo/ena kilo
aspirin	η ασπιρινη	aspirini
apple(s)	το μηλο/μηλα	meelo/meela
banana(s)	η μπανανα/μπανανεζ	banana/bananes
bread	το ψωμι	psomee
butter	το βουτυρο	vutiro
cheese	το τυρι	tiree
cigarettes (filter tip)	το τσιγαρο (με φιλτρο)	to tsigharo (me filtro)
coffee	καφε	cafe
cotton wool	το βαμβαχι	to vambaki
crackers	τα χραχερζ	krackers
crisps	τσιπζ	tsseeps
cucumbers	το αγγουρι	anguree
disinfectant	το απολυμαντιχο	to apolimantiko
guide book	ο τουριστικοζ οδηγοζ	o touristikos odhigos
ham	το ξαμπον	zambon
ice cream	το παγωτο	paghoto
lemons	το λεμανια	lemonia
lettuce	το μαρουλι	to marooli
map	το χαρτηζ	o khartis
a box of matches	ενα χομτι σπιρτα	ena kuti spirta
milk	το γαλα	to ghalo
pate	πατε	pate
(ball point) pen	το μπιχ	to bikx
pencil	το μολυβι	to molivi
pepper	το πιπερι	to piperi
(safety) pin	μια παραμανα	mea paramana
potatoes	οι πατατεζ	patates
salad	ηφσαλατα	i salatah
salami	το σαλαμι	salahmi
sausages	το λουχανικα	lukahniko
soap	το σαπουνι	to sapooni
spaghetti	σπαγεττο	spayehto
string	ο σπαγγοζ	o spangos

sugar	η ζαχαρη	i zakhahree
tea	το τσαι	to tsai
tomatoes	η ντομφτες	domahdes
toothbrush	η οδοντοβουρτοα	odhondovourtsa
toothpaste	η οδοντοχρεμα	odhondokrema
writing paper	το χαρτι γραψιματος	to kharti grap-simatos

8 Greece: History, Mythology, Religion, Present-Day Greece, Greeks & their Holidays

All ancient histories, as one of our fine wits said, are but fables that have been accepted. Voltaire

Excavations have shown the presence of Palaeolithic man up to 100,000 years ago. Greece's history and mythology are, like the Greek language, formidable to say the least, with legend, myth, folk tales, fables and religious lore often inextricably mixed up. Archaeologists are now finding that some mythology is in fact based on historical fact. For instance the great Minoan civilisation centred on Crete, which may well have been the fabled Atlantis of pre-history, was mysteriously and suddenly destroyed. Recent, informed speculation leads to the conclusion that about 1700 BC a vast volcanic eruption, presumed to be centred on the island of Santorini (Thira) in the Cyclades, destroyed this flourishing and far reaching culture.

From then on Greeks fought Greeks, Phoenicians and Persians. Under Alexander the Great they conquered Egypt and vast tracts of Asia Minor. Then they in turn were conquered by the Romans. After the splitting of the Roman Empire into Western and Eastern Empires, the Greeks, with Constantinople as their capital, were ruled by the Eastern offshoot, only to fall into the hands of the Franks about AD 1200, then the Turks, with the Venetians, Genoese and finally the Turks ruling the islands.

In 1821 the War of Independence commenced, which eventually led to the setting up of a Parliamentary Republic in 1928. Incidentally, Thessaly, Crete and the Dodecanese islands remained under Turkish rule. By the time the Dodecanese had thrown out the Turks, the Italians had taken over. If you are now confused, give up, because it gets even more difficult to follow.

The Greek monarchy, which had come into being in 1833, and was related to the German Royal family, opted in 1913 to side with the Axis powers. The chief politician Eleftherios Venizelos, disagreed, was dismissed and set up a rival government, and the King, under Allied pressure, retired to Switzerland. After the war, the Turks and Greeks agreed, after some fairly bloody fighting to exchange a total of one and a half million people.

In 1936 a General Metaxas became dictator. He achieved immortal fame by booting out Mussolini's representative, when in 1940 Mussolini demanded permission for Italy's troops to traverse Greece, and received the famous *Ochi* (No). (This day has become a national festival known as *Ochi Day*, celebrated on 28th October). When the Italians demurred and marched on Greece, the Greeks reinforced their point by routing them, the Italians only being saved from total humiliation by the intervention of the Germans, who then occupied Greece for the duration of the Second World War. As German ascendancy declined, the Greek freedom fighters split into royalist and communist blocks and proceeded to knock as much stuffing out of each other as they had out of the Germans. After the end of hostilities, all the Italian-held Greek islands were reunited with mainland Greece.

Until the British intervention, followed by large injections of American money and weapons, it looked as if Greece would go behind the *Iron Curtain*. A second civil war broke out between 1947 and 1949 and this internal strife was reputed to have cost more Greek lives than were lost during the whole of the Second World War.

In 1951, Greece and Turkey became full members of NATO, but the issue of the ex-British colony of Cyprus was about to rear its ugly head, with the resultant, renewed estrangement between Greece and Turkey.

The various political manoeuvrings, the involvement of the Greek monarchy in domestic affairs and the worsening situation in Cyprus, led to the *coup d'état* by the *Colonels' Junta* in 1967, soon after which King Constantine II and his entourage fled to Italy. The Colonel's extremely repressive dictatorship was, seemingly, actively supported by the Americans and condoned by Britain. Popular country-wide feeling and, in particular, student uprisings between 1973-1974, initially put down in Athens by brutal tank attacks, led to the eventual collapse of the regime in 1974.

In the death-throes of their rule, the Colonels, using the Cyprus dream to distract the ordinary people's feeling of injustice, meddled and attempted to overthrow the vexatious priest, President Makarios. The net result was that the Turks invaded Cyprus and made an enforced divison of that unhappy, troubled island.

In 1974, Greece returned to republican democracy and in 1981 joined the EEC.

RELIGION

The Orthodox Church prevails everywhere but there are small pockets of Roman Catholicism and very minor enclaves of Turks on the Dodecanese and mainland western Thrace. The schism within the Holy Roman Empire, in 1054, caused the Catholic Church to be centred on Rome and the Orthodox Church on Constantinople.

The Turkish overlords encouraged the continuation of the indigenous church, probably to keep their bondsmen quiet, but it had the invaluable side effect of keeping alive Greek customs and traditions during the centuries of occupation.

The bewildering profusion of small churches, scattered 'indiscriminately' all over the islands, is not proof of the church's wealth, although the Greek people are not entirely convinced of that fact. It is evidence of the piety of the families or individuals who paid to have them erected, in the name of their selected patron saint, as thanksgiving for God's protection. The style of religious architecture changes between the island groups.

Many churches only have one service a year, on the name day of the particular patron saint, and this ceremony is named *Viorti* or *Panayieri*. It is well worth attending one of these self-indulgent, extravaganzas to observe and take part in Greek village, celebratory religious life and music. All-comers are welcome to the carnival festivities which include eating and dancing in, or adjacent to, the particular churchyard.

The words Byzantine and Byzantium crop up frequently with especial reference to churches and appertain to the period between the fourth and fourteenth centuries AD. During this epoch Greece was, at least nominally, under the control of Constantinople (Istanbul), which was built by the Emperor Constantine on the site of the old city of Byzantium.

Religious paintings executed on small wooden panels during this period are called *ikons*. Very, very few original ikons remain available for purchase, so beware if offered an apparent 'bargain'.

When visiting a church, you will observe pieces of shining, thin metal, placed haphazardly around or pinned to wooden carvings. These *tamata* or *exvotos* represent limbs or portions of the human body and are purchased by worshippers to be placed in the church as an offering, in the hope of an illness being cured and/or limbs healed.

GREEKS

In making assessment of the Greek people and their character, it must be remembered that, perhaps even more so than the Spaniards or the Portuguese, Greece has only recently emerged into the twentieth century. Unlike other newly discovered holiday countries, they have not, in the main, degraded or debased their principles or character, in the face of the on-rush of tourist wealth. For a people to have had so little as recently as the 1960s and to face so much demand for European necessities, would have strained a less hardy and well-balanced people.

Their recent emergence into the western world is well evidenced by the still partriarchal nature of Greek society supported, for instance, by the oft-seen spectacle of men lazing in the tavernas whilst their womenfolk work in the fields (and why not?)

Even the smallest village, on the remotest island, will usually have an English-speaking islander who has lived abroad, earning a living through seafaring, as a hotel waiter, or as a taxi driver. Thus, while making their escape from the comparative poverty at home, for a period of good earnings in the more lucrative world, a working knowledge of English, American (sic) or Australian (sic) will have been gained. Greek *strine*, or as usually contracted *grine*, simply has to be heard to be believed.

The greatest hurdle to understanding is undoubtedly the language barrier, especially if it is taken into account that the Greeks appear to have some difficulty with their own language in its various forms. Certainly, they seem, on occasions, not to understand each other and the subject matter has to be repeated a number of times. Perhaps that is the reason for all the shouting!

There can be no doubt that the traditional Greek welcome to the *xenos* or *singrafeus*, now increasingly becoming known as *touristas* has, naturally, become rather lukewarm in the more 'besieged' areas.

It is often difficult to reconcile the shrugged shoulders of a seemingly disinterested airline official or bus driver, with being stopped in the street by a gold-toothed, smiling Greek proffering some fruit. But remember the bus driver may realise the difficulty of overcoming the language barrier, it is very hot, he has been working long hours earning his living and you are on holiday.

Sometimes a drink appears mysteriously at your taverna table, the donor being indicated by a nod of the waiter's head but a word of warning here. Simply smile and accept the gift graciously. Any attempt to return the kindness by 'putting one in the stable' for your new found friend will only result in a 'who buys last' competition which you will lose. I know, I am speaking from battle-weary experience. A Greek may well be very welcoming and will occasionally invite you to his table, but do not expect more, they are reserved and have probably had previous experience of ungrateful, rude, overseas visitors.

To look over churches or monasteries visitors must ensure they are adequately covered, including legs and arms and should note that many religious establishments strictly apply the rules. It seems a pity for a tourist to have made a special excusion sometimes involving arduous walking, only to be turned away at the gate. Men must wear a shirt and trousers, not shorts, and women a modest blouse, a skirt and take a head scarf (as a back-stop).

Women tourists can travel quite freely in Greece without fear, except from other tourists. On the other hand females should not wear provocative attire or fail to wear sufficient clothing when coming into close social contact with Greek men, who might well be inflamed into action, or Greek women, whom it will offend. Certainly this was the case until very recently but the constant stream of 'available' young tourist ladies on the more popular islands, has resulted in the local lads taking a 'view', and a chance. It almost reminds one of the *Costa Brava* in the early 1960s. The disparate moral qualities of the native and tourist females is resulting in a conundrum for young Greek women. To compete for their men's affections they have had to loosen their principles with an unheard of and steadily increasing number of speedily arranged marriages, if you know what I mean.

Do not miss the Volta (Βολτα), the traditional family evening walkabout in city, town or village square. Dressed for the event, an important part of the ritual is for the family to show off their marriageable daughters. Good fun and great watching, but the Greeks are rather protective of their family and all things Greek... you may comment favourably, but keep criticism to yourself.

It is interesting to speculate on the influence of the early Greek immigrants on American culture, especially when you consider the American habit of serving water with every meal, the ubiquitous hamburger, (which is surely a poorly reproduced and inferior *souvlaki*), and some of the official uniforms, more particularly the flat peaked hats of American postmen and policemen.

THE GREEK NATIONAL HOLIDAYS

Listed below are the national holidays and on these days many areas and islands hold festivals, but with a particular slant and emphasis.

1st January	New Year's Day/The Feast of Saint Basil
6th January	Epiphany/Blessing of the Waters — a cross is immersed in the sea, lake or river, during a religious ceremony
The period 27th Jan to 17 February	The Greek Carnival Season
25th March	The Greek National Anniversary/Independence Day
April — Movable days	Good Friday/Procession of the 'Epitaph'; Holy Week Saturday/Ceremony of the Resurrection; Easter Sunday/open air feasts
1st May	May/Labour Day/Feast of the Flowers
1st to 10th July	Greek Navy Week
15th August	Assumption Day/Festival of the Virgin Mary, especially on the Cycladian island of Tinos (beware travelling at this time anywhere in the area)
28th October	National Holiday/'Ochi' Day
24th December	Christmas Eve/carols evening
25th December	Christmas Day
26th December	St Stephen's Day
31st December	New Year's Eve/carols, festivals

In addition to these national days, each island has festivals and holidays particular to them which are listed individually under each island description. Moreover, many of the various island churches have only one service a year.

A word of warning to ferry-boat travellers will not go amiss here — DO NOT travel to an island immediately prior to one of these festivals NOR off the island immediately after the event. It will be almost impossible to do other than stand if one has not been trampled to death in the various stampedes off and on the boats.

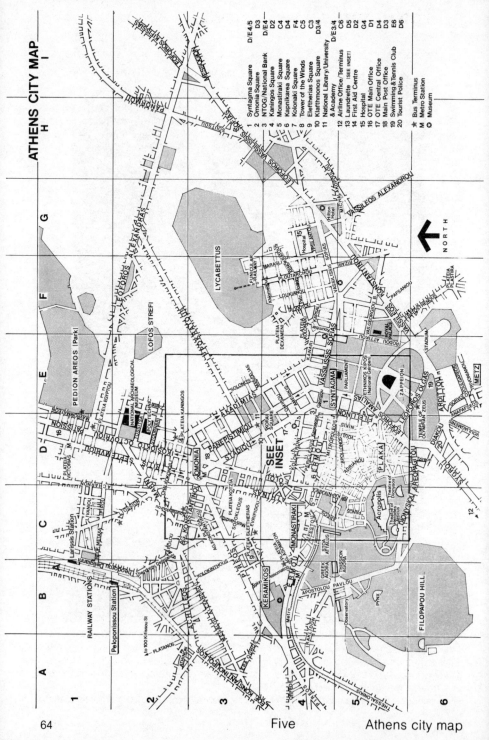

9 ATHENS CITY (ATHINA, AΘHNAI)

There is no end to it in this city; wherever you set your foot, you encounter some memory of the past. *Marcus Cicero.*

Tel. prefix 01

The capital of Greece and major city of Attica. Previously the springboard for travel to most of the Greek islands, but less so since a number of direct flights have become available. Experienced island travellers flying into Athens airport, often try to arrange their flight for an early morning arrival and head straight for either the West airport, Piraeus port, the railway station or bus terminal, so as to be able to get under way immediately.

ARRIVAL BY AIR

International flights other than Olympic Airways land at the

East airport

Public transport facilities include:

Bus No. 18:   East airport to Leoforos Amalias. Every 20 mins from 0600-2400 hrs. Fare 60 drs.

Bus No. 121:   East airport to Leoforos Olgas. 0650-2250 hrs. Fare 60 drs.

Bus No. 19:   East airport to Plateia Karaiskaki/Akti Tselepi, Piraeus port. Every hour from 0800-2000 hrs. Fare 60 drs.

Bus No. 101:   East airport via Leoforos Possidonos (coast road) to Klisovis/Theotoki St, Piraeus port. Every 20 mins from 0500-2245 hrs.

Domestic and all Olympic flights land at the

West airport

Public transport facilities include:

Bus No. 133:   West airport to Leoforos Square, Leoforos Amalias, Filellinon & Othonos Streets (Syntagma Sq). Every ½ hour from 0530-0030 hrs.

Bus No. 122:   West airport to Leoforos Olgas. Every 20 mins.

Buses No. 107: West airport via Leoforos Possidonos (coast road) to Klisovis St, Piraeus port.
& 109

In addition there are Olympic buses connecting West and East airports.

GENERAL (Illustrations 5 & 6)

Even if you are a European city dweller, Athens will come as a sociological and cultural shock to the system. In the summer it is a hot, dusty, dry, crowded, traffic-bound, exhaust polluted bedlam, but always friendly, cosmopolitan and ever on the move.

On arrival in Athens, and staying over, it is best to select the two main squares of Syntagma (*Tmr* 1.D/E4/5) and Omonia (*Tmr* 2.D3) as centres for the initial sally, and radiate out to the other squares or plateias.

There is no substitute for a city map which is issued free, yes free, from the Tourist Board desk in the National Bank of Greece on Syntagma Sq (*Tmr* 3.D/E4). *See* **NTOG — THE A to Z OF USEFUL INFORMATION (A to Z).**

Syntagma Square (Constitution or Parliament Square) (*Tmr* 1.D/E4/5)
The airport and many other buses stop off here. It is the city centre with the most elite hotels, airline offices, international companies including the American Express headquarters, smart cafes and the Parliament building all circumscribing the central, sunken square. In the bottom right hand corner of the plateia, bounded by Odhos Othonos and Leoforos Amalias, there are some very clean, attendant minded toilets. There is a charge for the use of the squatties.

To orientate, the Parliament building and Monument to the Unknown Warrior lie to the east of the square. To the north-east, in the middle distance, is one of the twin hills of Athens, Mt Lycabettus (Lykavittos). The other hill is the Acropolis, to the south-west, and not now visible from Syntagma Sq. due to high-rise buildings. On the west side of the square are the offices of American Express and a battery of pavement cafes, with Ermou St leading due west to Monastiraki Sq. To the north are the two parallel, main avenues of Stadiou (a one-way street down to Syntagma) and Venizelou or Panepistimiou (a one-way street out of Syntagma) that both run due north-west to:

Omonia Square (Concorde or Harmony Square) (*Tmr* 2.D3)
The Piccadilly Circus or Times Square of Athens but rather tatty really, with a constant stream of traffic bludgeoning its way round the large central island, which is crowned with an impressive fountain. Should you try to escape the human bustle on the pavements by stepping off into the kerbside, beware that you are not mown down by a bus, taxi or private car.

Constant activity night and day, with seemingly every nationality cheek by jowl, lends the square a cosmopolitan character all of its own. On every side there are hotels, varying from the downright seedy to the better-class tawdry, housed in rather undistinguished, 'neo city-municipal' style, nineteenth century buildings, almost unique to Athens.

Various underground train entrance/exits emerge around the square, similar to air raid shelters, spewing out and sucking in the metro travellers. The underground concourse has a Post office, telephones, a bank and, by the Dorou St entrance, a block of squatty toilets for which the attendant charges 5 drs for 2 sheets of paper.

Shops, cafes and booths fill the gaps between the hotels and the eight streets that converge on the square.

To the north-east side of Omonia, on the corner of Dorou St, is a taxi rank and beyond, on the right, a now rather squalid, covered arcade brimful of reasonably priced snack bars. Through this covered passage way, and turning to the left up 28 Ikosiokto Oktovriou (28th October St)/Patission St, and then right down Veranzerou St, leads to

Kaningos Square (*Tmr* 4.D2)
Serves as a bus terminal for some routes.

To the south of Omonia Sq is Athinas St, the commercial thoroughfare of Athens. Here every conceivable item imaginable including ironmongery, tools, crockery and clothing can be purchased, and parallel to which, for half its length, runs Odhos Sokratous, the city street market during the day and the red-light area by night.

Athinas St drops due south to:

Monastiraki Square (*Tmr* 5.C4)
This marks the northernmost edge of the area known as the Plaka (*Tmr* D5) bounded by Ermou St to the north, Filellinon St to the east, and to the south by the slopes of the Acropolis.

Many of the alleys in this area follow the course of the old Turkish streets, most of the houses are mid-nineteenth century and represent the 'Old Quarter'.

Climbing the twisting maze of streets and steps of the lower NE slopes of the Acropolis requires the stamina of a mountain goat. The almost primitive, island-village nature of some of the houses is very noticeable. This is due, it is said, to a Greek law passed after Independence to alleviate a housing shortage, and allowed anyone who could raise the roof of a dwelling between sunrise and sunset to finish and own the house. Some islanders from the Cyclades island of Anafi (Anaphe) were reputed to have been the first to benefit from this new law and others followed to specialise in restoration and rebuilding, thus bringing about a colony of expatriate islanders within the Plaka district.

From the south-west corner of Monastiraki Sq, Ifestou St and its associated byways house the **Flea Market**, which climaxes on Sunday into stall upon stall of junk, souvenirs, junk, hardware, junk, boots, junk, records, junk, clothes, junk, footwear, junk, pottery and junk. Where Ifestou becomes Astigos St, and curves round to join up with Ermou St, there are a couple of extensive second-hand bookshops with reasonably priced (for Greece that is), if battered, paperbacks for sale. From the south-east corner of Monastiraki, Pandrossou St, one of the only enduring reminders of the Turkish Bazaar, contains a better class of antique dealer, sandal and shoe makers, and pottery stores.

Due south of Monstiraki Sq is Odhos Areos, unfortunately the first 100 m or so of which is now host to a raggle-taggle band of European and Japanese drop-outs selling junk ie trinkets (not dope) from the pavement kerb. They seem to have driven out the original stallholders and shop keepers in this stretch. Climbing Odhos Areos skirts the Roman Agora, from which the various streets leading upwards, on ever upwards, contain a plethora of stalls and shops, specialising in leather goods, clothes and souvenirs. The further you climb, the cheaper the goods become. This interestingly enough does not apply to the tavernas and restaurants in the area, which seemingly become more expensive as one ascends.

The 'chatty' area known as the Plaka is 'littered' with eating places, a few good, some bad, some tourist rip-offs. The liveliest street in the Plaka is Odhos Kidathineon which is jam-packed with cafes, tavernas and restaurants and at night is bestrewn with music-playing layabouts, sorry students. The class, tone and price of the establishments improve as you progress north-eastwards. I have to admit to gently knocking the Plaka over the years but it must be acknowledged that the area offers the cheapest accommodation and eating places in Athens and generally appears to have been cleaned up in recent times.

From Monastiraki Sq, eastwards along Ermou St, the street is initially full of clothes and shoe shops. One third of the way to Syntagma Sq and Odhos Ermou opens out into a small square in which there is the lovely church of Kapnikarea (*Tmr* 6.D4). Continuing eastwards, the shops become smarter with a preponderance of fashion stores. Parallel to Ermou St is Odhos Ploutonos Nteka, which becomes Odhos Mitropoleos. Facing east, on the right, is the City's Greek Orthodox Cathedral, Great Mitropolis. The church was built about 1850 from the materials of 70 old churches, to the design of four different architects resulting, not unnaturally, in a building of a rather 'strange' appearance. Alongside and to the south is the diminutive medieval church, Little Mitropolis or Agios Eleftherios, dating back to at least the twelfth century but which has materials, reliefs and building blocks probably originating from the sixth century AD. A little further on is the intriguing and incongruous site of a small Byzantine church, built over and around by a modern office block, the columns of which tower above and beside the little church.

Leaving Syntagma Sq by the north-east corner, along Vassilissis Sofias, and turning left at Odhos Irodou Attikou, runs into:

Kolonaki Square (*Tmr* 7.F4)
The most fashionable square in the most fashionable area of Athens, around which most of the foreign embassies are located. The British Council is located on the square, as are some relatively expensive cafes, restaurants and boutiques.

To the north of Kolonaki, across the pretty orange tree planted Dexameni Sq, is the southern-most edge of Mt Lycabettus (*Tmr* F/G3) and access to the summit can be made, on foot, by a number of steep paths. The main, stepped footpath is on up Loukianou St beyond Odhos Kleomenous. A little to the east, at the top of Ploutarchou St, which breaks into a sharply rising flight of steps, is the cable car funicular railway. This runs in a 700ft long tunnel, emerging near to the nineteenth-century chapel, which caps the fir-tree-covered mountain, alongside a modern and luxuriously expensive restaurant. There are also some excellent toilets. The railway service opens at 0845 hrs, shuts down at 0015 hrs and the trip costs 35 drs one-way and 65 drs for a return ticket. A more relaxed climb, passing the open air theatre, can be made from the north end of Lycabettus.

The top most part of the mountain where the funicular emerges is surprisingly small if not doll-like. The spectacular panorama that spreads out to the horizon, the stupendous views from far above the roar of the Athens traffic, is best seen in the early morning or late afternoon.

Leaving Plateia Kolonaki from the south corner and turning right at Vassilissis Sofias, brings one to the north corner of:

The National Garden (Ethnikos Kipos) (*Tmr* E5)
Here peacocks, water fowl and songbirds blend with a profusion of shrubbery, subtropical trees, ornamental ponds, various busts and cafe tables through and around which thread neat gravel paths.

To the south of the gardens are the Zappeion Exhibition Halls. To the north-west, the Greek Parliament buildings, the old Royal Palace and the Tomb or Monument to the Unknown Warrior, guarded by the traditionally costumed **Evzones**, the Greek equivalent of the British palace guards (for more details of which *See* **Places of Interest (A to Z)**). South-east of the National Gardens is the Olympic Stadium erected in 1896 on the site of the original stadium, built in 330 BC, and situated in a valley of the Arditos Hills. South-west across Leoforos Olgas are the Olympic swimming pool, the Tennis and Athletic Club. To the west of these sporting facilities is the isolated gateway known as the Arch of Hadrian overlooking the busy traffic junction of Leoforos Olgas and Leoforos Amalias. Through the archway, the remains of the Temple of Olympian Zeus are outlined, 15 only of the original 104 Corinthian columns remaining.

Leaving Hadrian's Arch, westwards along Odhos Dionysiou Areopagitou brings one to the south side of:

The Acropolis (Akropoli) (*Tmr* C5)
A 10-acre rock rising 750 ft above the surrounding city and surmounted by the Parthenon Temple, built in approximately 450 BC, the Propylaia Gateway, the Temple to Athena Nike and the triple Temple of Erechtheion. Additionally, there has been added the modern Acropolis museum, discreetly tucked away almost out of sight.

At the bottom of the southern slope are the Theatres of Dionysos, originally said to seat up to 30,000 but more probably 17,000, and the smaller, second century AD, Odeion of Herodes Atticus, which has been restored and is used for plays and concerts during the summer festival.

The west slope leads to the Hill of Areopagos (Areios Pagos) where, in times of yore, a council of noble men dispensed supreme judgements. Across Apostolou Pavlou St lie the other tree-covered hills of Filopapou (Philopappos/Mouseion), or Hill of Muses, from whence the views are far-reaching and outstanding; Pnyx (Pnyka), where The Assembly once met and a son et lumière is now held, and the Asteroskopeion (Observatory), or the Hill of Nymphs, whereon stands, surprise, surprise, an observatory.

Descending from the Asteroskopeion towards and across Apostolou Pavlou St is:

The (Greek) Agora (*Tmr* B/C4)
The gathering place from whence the Athenians would have approached the Acropolis. This market-place cum civic centre is now little more than rubble, but the glory that once was is recreated by a model.

Nearby the Temple of Hephaistos or Thission (Theseion) sits on a small hill overlooking the Agora and to one side is the recently reconstructed market-place, Stoa Attalus. The cost of this project was met from private donations raised by American citizens.

A short distance to the east of the Greek Agora is the site of:

The Roman Forum (or Agora) (*Tmr* C5)
Close by is the Tower of the Winds (*Tmr* 8.C5), which remarkable octagonal tower, probably built in the first century BC, acted as a combination waterclock, sundial and

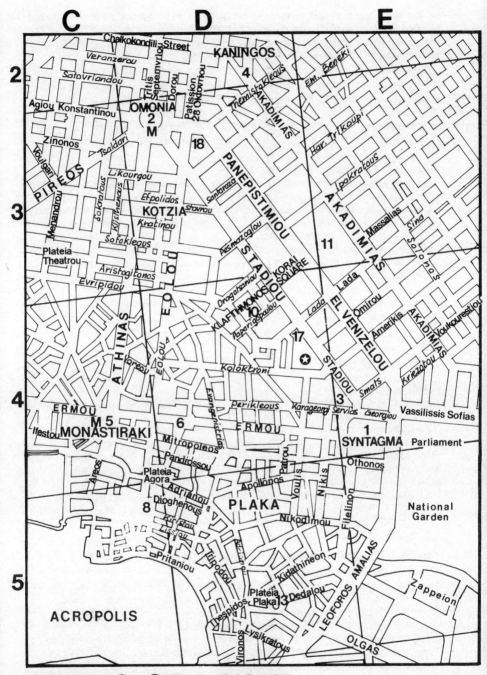

ATHENS CITY INSET

weathervane. Early descriptions say the building was topped off with a bronze weathervane represented by the mythological Triton complete with a pronged trident. The carved eight gods of wind can be seen, as can traces of the corresponding sundials, but no interior mechanism remains and the building is now used as a store for various stone antiquities.

A short distance to the north-west is an area known as The Keramikos (*Tmr* B4), a cemetery or graveyard, containing the Street of the Tombs, a funeral avenue laid out about 400 BC.

In a north-easterly direction from Keramikos along Pireos St, via Eleftherias Sq bus terminal (*Tmr* 9.C3), turning right down Evripidou St, across Athinas and Eolou Streets, leads to:

Klafthmonos Square (Klathmonos) (*Tmr* 10.D3/4).
Supposedly the most attractive Byzantine church in Athens, Aghii Theodori is positioned in the west corner of the square.

Looking north-east across Stadiou St, up Korai St (the site of another bus terminal), and across Panepistimiou Ave, reveals an imposing range of neo-classical buildings (*Tmr* 11.D/E3/4), fronted by laid-out gardens. These comprise the University flanked by, to the left (facing), the National Library, and to the right, the Academy. Behind and running parallel to Stadiou and Panepistimou, is Akadimias St, on which is another major bus terminal. Just off Akadimias St, in Massalias St, is the Hellenic-American Union, many of whose facilities are open to the general public. These include an English and music library, as well as a cafeteria. In the summer a schedule of concerts and plays is staged in English.

North-west of Klafthmonos Sq, to the left of Eolou St, is:

Kotzia Square (*Tmr* D3)
A very large plateia in which, on Sunday at least, there is a profusion of flower sellers' stalls.

Fokionos Negri
Actually a street, if not more an avenue rather than a square. Rather distant, almost in the suburbs to the north, and usually just off the street plans of Athens. To reach it from Omonia Sq proceed up 28 (Ikosiokto) Oktovriou, which runs into Patission St, on past the National Archaeological Museum and Green Park (Pedion Areos), on the right, to where Agiou Meletiou St runs across Patission St. Fokionos Negri starts as a fairly small side-street to the right, but widens out into a tree-lined, short, squat avenue with a wide, spacious centre pedestrian way once gravelled and being extensively resurfaced in 1985. Supposedly the **Dolce Vita** or **Via Veneto** of Athens but not out of the ordinary if quiet wealth is normal. Extremely expensive cafes edge the square half way up on the right and it certainly becomes extremely lively after nightfall.

A number 5, 11, 12 or 13 trolley-bus, going north, will take you there.

THE ACCOMMODATION & EATING OUT
The Accommodation
On the islands, pensions and (even) 'E' class hotels can be recommended, but in Athens I only include some 'B', 'C' and some better 'D' class hotels. There are a few reasonable Class 'E' hotels and good pensions but. . . .

On Adrianou St (*Tmr* D5) (Plaka district) there are a few very cheap dormitories and students' hostels, where a certain amount of roof-top sleeping is also allowed, costing upwards of 350 drs per night. Unless well off the main roads, a set of ear-muffs or plugs is almost obligatory to ensure a good night's sleep.

On a cautionary note, since the end of 1981 the Greek authorities have been closing a number of the more 'undesirable', unlicensed hotels, so your favourite over-night stop may no longer be in business.

Most of the Athenian hotel charges are priced at the 1985/86 rates which averaged out in 1985 as follows.

Class	Single	Double	
A	4000/4900 drs	5000/6200 drs	en suite bathroom
B	2500/3000 drs	3200/4000 drs	& breakfast included
C	1500/1900 drs	2400/3000 drs	sharing bathroom and
D	600/700 drs	900/1100 drs	room rate only

SYNTAGMA AREA (Tmr 1.D/E4/5)

Hotel Cleo (Cleopatra) (*Tmr* D4) (Class D) 3 Patrou St.   Tel. 322-9053
Directions: Leaving Syntagma Sq, walk down Mitropoleos St, towards Monastiraki Sq and take the fourth turning left.

Well recommended if threadbare. Ground floor dormitory, free baggage store. Double rooms from 1150 drs.
N.B. The owners also have a guest house nearby in 18 Apollonos St.

Pension John's Place (*Tmr* D4) (Class C) 5 Patrou St.   Tel. 322-9719
Directions: As for Hotel Cleo above.

Not surprisingly the affable old Papa is named John. Well kept, with singles from 650 drs and doubles from 800 drs rising to 900 drs and 1100 drs respectively, naturally sharing bathroom facilities.

George's Pension (*Tmr* D4) (Class B) 46 Nikis St.   Tel. 322-9569
Directions: As for Hotel Cleo, but take the first left-hand turning.

Recommended by four American Texas college girls, met on the train to Patras a few years ago and whose first stopover in Greece was this guest house. Shared bathroom and hot water in the evening, if you are quick. Doubles from 800 drs.

Hotel Kimon (*Tmr* D5) (Class D) 27 Apollonos   Tel. 323-5223
Directions: Mid-way on Apollonos St, one block down from Mitropoleos St.

Old but renovated. Single rooms sharing 560 drs increasing to 650 drs whilst double rooms start at 740 drs rising to 925 drs sharing a bathroom and 925 drs to 1110 drs en suite.

YMCA (XAN) (*Tmr* E4) 28 Omirou St.   Tel. 362-6970
Directions: North-east corner of Syntagma Sq up Panepistimiou St, third turning right and across Akadimias Avenue, on the right.

Institutional and not inexpensive accommodation costing some 550 drs for a single, and 900 drs for a double per night.

YWCA (XEN) (*Tmr* E4) 11 Amerikis St.   Tel. 362-4291
Directions: All as above but second turning off Panepistimiou St and on the left.

Self-service restaurant, hairdressing salon, library and laundry facilities.

OMONIA AREA (Tmr 2.D3)

Any hotel or pension rooms facing Omonia square must be regarded as very noisy

Hotel Omonia (*Tmr* D3) (Class C) 4 Omonia Sq   Tel. 523-7210
Directions: Just stand in Omonia Sq and swivel on your heels, north side of the square.

The reception is on the first floor, as is a cafe-bar and terrace, overlooking the square and its action. Modern and 'worn' international look to the place. You may well have to take demi-pension terms. A double room en suite costs from 1300 drs, breakfast 150 drs and a meal from 600 drs.

Hotel Banghion (*Tmr* D3) (Class C) 18b Omonia Sq.   Tel. 324-2259
Directions: As for Hotel Omonia but south side of the square.

Elegant and ageing. From 1200 drs for a double room sharing a bathroom, increasing to 1450 drs, with breakfast available at 180 drs.

Hotel Carlton (*Tmr* D3) (Class C) 7 Omonia Sq.   Tel. 522-3201
Directions: As for Hotel Omonia.

Very Greek and old fashioned. Single rooms 900 drs and double rooms between 1st April - 31st December 1100 drs, both sharing a bathroom. Breakfast costs 200 drs.

Hotel Europa (*Tmr* D2) (Class C) 7 Veranzerou St.   Tel. 522-3081
Directions: North of Omonia Sq, the second main street up, lying east/west. This is very often listed as Chateaubriandou (Satovriandou) St but the local authorities either have, or have not, been notified of the change. The street is now a pedestrian precinct.

'Greek Provincial', the remarkably ancient lift of this hotel creaks its way up and down to the various floors. The rooms are adequate, even have a wardrobe and the floors are covered with brown linoleum. To use the shower the concierge must be asked for the relevant key in mime, if your Greek is sketchy, as the staff's knowledge of English is very limited. When produced, the key might well be adjudged large enough to open the doors of the **Bastille**. Weighed down by this instrument, the moment of truth is about to dawn, for when the door is opened, sheer disbelief may well be your first reaction, especially if it is your first stop off in Athens, as it was my own years ago. A cavernous and be-cobwebbed room reveals plumbing that beggars description. Enough to say the shower was most welcome, even if the lack of a point to anchor the shower head, whilst trying to soap oneself down, required interesting bodily contortions.

The single room rate is 600 drs while a double rises from 760 drs to 1000 drs.

Hotel Alma (*Tmr* 2.D2/3) (Class C) 5 Dorou   Tel. 524-0858
Directions: Dorou St runs north from the north-east corner of Omonia Sq.

Modern, the rooms with a verandah are on the seventh and eighth floors. From 1000 drs for a double room with breakfast costing 200 drs.

Hotel Parnon (*Tmr* D2) (Class C) 20 Tritis Septemvriou/21 Chalkokondili Tel. 523-5196
Directions: North of Omonia Sq on the junction of Tritis Septemvriou and Chalkokondili St.

Modern and noisy at 1300 drs for a double room with bath (April to October) and breakfast from 200 drs.

Hotel Eva (*Tmr* C2) (Class D) 31 Victoros Ougo   Tel. 522-3079
Directions: West of Omonia, parallel to and two blocks back from Ag Konstantinou.

Well recommended with single rooms from 760 drs and double rooms 1150 drs en suite. Breakfast 150 drs.

Hotel Marina (*Tmr* C3) (Class C) 13 Voulgari   Tel. 522-4769
Directions: South-west from Omonia along Odhos Pireos, 4th turning to the right.

Single rooms from 705 drs, double rooms 1010 drs sharing the bathroom and 970 drs and 1230 drs respectively en suite. Breakfast costs 150 drs.

Hotel Vienna (*Tmr* C3) (Class C) 20 Pireos   Tel. 524-9143
Directions: South-west off Omonia Sq.

New, clean and noisy, at about 1600 drs for a double in the early summer and breakfast 190 drs.

Hotel Athinea (*Tmr* C2) (Class C) 9 Vilara   Tel. 523-3884
Directions: Westwards on Ag Konstantinou and situated on one side of the small square of Agiou Konstantinou.

Old but beautifully positioned although cabaret night life can intrude. A restaurant and cake shop are close by as is a taxi rank. A single room starts at 1200 drs and a double 1600 drs en suite. Breakfast 200 drs.

Hotel Pythagorion (*Tmr* C2/3) (Class C) 28 Ag Konstantinou   Tel. 524-2811
Directions: West of Omonia Sq.
A single room from 1200 drs and a double room, both with bath from 1650 drs, breakfast is 140 drs and lunch/dinner from 450 drs.

Hotel Florida (*Tmr* C3) (Class C) 25 Menandrou   Tel. 522-3214
Directions: Third turning left, south-west along Pireos St.
Single rooms from 490/650 drs and doubles from 940 drs both without a bathroom, and en suite, 750 drs and 1150 drs respectively. Breakfast 150 drs.

Hotel Alcestis (Alkistis) (*Tmr* C3) (Class C) 18 Plateia Theatrou   Tel. 321-9811
Directions: Off Pireos St, either south down Sokratous or Menandrou St, and across Sofokleous St.
Despite its chromium-plated appearance, all glass and marble with a prairie-sized lobby awash with Americans, it is a Class C hotel in a commercial square. Popular, with double rooms from 1333 drs, breakfast 175 drs and lunch/dinner from 600 drs.

MONASTIRAKI AREA (*Tmr* 5.C4)
Hotel Tembi/Tempi (*Tmr* D4) (Class D) 29 Eolou (Aioulu/Aeolou)   Tel. 321-3175
Directions: A main street north of Ermou St, opposite the church of Ag Irini.
Pleasant rooms with singles sharing the bathroom starting at 500 drs and rising to 570 drs for the period 1st June - 30th September. Double rooms sharing cost from 750 drs and ensuite 880 drs advancing to 950 drs and 1100 drs respectively. Laundry facilities available.

Hotel Ideal (*Tmr* D4) (Class D) 39 Eolou/2 Voreou   Tel. 321-3195
Directions: On the left of Eolou walking up from Odhos Ermou and on the corner with Voreou St.
A perfect example of a weather-worn, 19th century Athens neo classical building complete with old fashioned metal and glass canopy entrance and matchbox sized wrought iron balconies. The accommodation lives up to all that the exterior promises. A telephone, TV room, bar and luggage is stored. The bathroom facililties are shared, with the basic single room rate 500 drs and double room 750 drs rising, for the period 16th June - 20th September, to 600 drs and 900 drs respectively.

Hotel Hermion (*Tmr* C/D4) (Class D) 66c Ermou St   Tel. 321-2753
Directions: East of Monastiraki adjacent to Kapnikarea Church and Sq.
Old but clean with the reception up the stairs. All rooms share bathrooms with the single rate starting off at 600 drs and the double rooms from 880 drs.

Hotel Attalos (*Tmr* C3/4) (Class C) 29 Athinas   Tel. 321-2801
Directions: North from Monastiraki Sq.
Recommended to us by a splendidly eccentric lady English artist who should know — she has been visiting Greece for some 20 years.
Between 16th March - 30th June singles 800 drs and doubles 1200 drs rising for the period 1st July - 30th September to 900 drs and 1500 drs. Breakfast costs 180 drs.

Hotel Cecil (*Tmr* C4) (Class D) 39 Athinas   Tel. 321-7079
Directions: North from Monastiraki Sq and two buildings up from the Kalamida St turning on the left-hand side. This is the other side of the road from a very small chapel, incongruously stuck on the pavement.
Clean looking with a single room costing 695 drs and a double 1048 drs. The bathrooms are shared.

PLAKA/METZ STADIUM AREAS (*Tmr* D5 & D/E6)
The Plaka is rich in accommodation, as it is in most things. .

Hotel Phaedra (*Tmr* D5) (Class D) 4 Adrianou/16 Herephontos   Tel. 323-8461
Directions: Situated close by a multi-junction of various streets including Lysikratous,

Galanou, Adrianou and Herephontos, opposite the Byzantine church of Ag Aikaterini and its small, attractive gardens.

Pretty area by day, noisy by night. Family hotel with a ground-floor bar. Double rooms 1300 drs. Breakfast costs 130 drs.

Students' Inn (*Tmr* D5) 16 Kidathineon St. Tel. 324-4808
Hostelish but recommended as good value with hot showers en tap (sorry) and an English-speaking owner. Roof top available as is a snack bar and the use of a washing machine. Clean with the basic double rooms complete with a rickety oil-cloth covered table and a mug costing 1000 drs.

Hotel Solonion (*Tmr* D5) (Class E) 11 Sp Tsagari/Dedalou Tel. 322-0008
Directions: To the right of Kidathineon St, facing Syntagma Sq, between Dedalou St and Leoforos Amalias. Odhos Tsagari is a continuation of Asteriou St.

A pleasant, smiling Asian lady runs the old, faded but refurbished building. The accommodation is 'student provincial', the rooms being high ceilinged and the rather dodgy floor boards covered in brown linoleum. Hot water all day and on a fine day. . . you can espy the Acropolis. . . well a bit of it.

No singles, a double room sharing the bathroom costs 925 drs and en suite 1100 drs, 1st May - 31st October.

Close by the Hotel Solonion are the

Hotel Kekpoy (Cecrops) (*Tmr* D5) (Class D) 13 Tsagari Tel. 322-3080
Directions: On the same side as the *Solonion* but a building or two towards Leoforos Amalias.

Similar to the *Solonion* with almost identical rates.

Hotel Phoebus (Fivos) (*Tmr* D5) (Class C) Asteriou/12 Peta Tel. 322-0142
Directions: Back towards Kidathineon, on the corner of the Asteriou and Peta Streets.

Rather more up market that the 3 previously listed hotels. A double room en suite costs 1260 drs with the month of June - September rising to 1500 drs. Breakfast 160 drs.

A few side streets towards the Acropolis is the

Hotel Ava (*Tmr* D5) Lysikratous St
Directions: As above.

I have no personal experience but the establishment has been mentioned as a possibility.

New Clare's House (*Tmr* E6) (Class C Pension) 24 Sorvolou St Tel. 922-2288
Directions: Rather uniquely, the owners have had a large compliments slip printed with a pen and ink drawing on the face, and on the reverse side, directions in Greek entitled: **Show this to the taxi driver.**

This includes details of the location, south of the Stadium on Sorvolou St between Charvouri and Voulgareos Streets on the right, half-way down the reverse slope with the description **'white house with the green windows'**. From Syntagma take Leoforos Amalias, the main avenue south, and keep to the main avenues hugging the Temple of Olympian Zeus and along Odhos Diakou. Where Diakou makes a junction with Vouliagmenis and Ardittou Avenues, Odhos Anapavseos leads off in a south-east direction and Sorvolou St crescents off to the left. Trolley buses 2, 4, 11 & 12 will drop one off by the Stadium. It is quite a steep climb up Sorvolou St, which breaks into steps, to the pretty and highly recommended area of Metz (highly regarded by Athenians that is). Plus points are that the narrow nature of the lanes, which suddenly become steps, keeps the traffic down to a minimum and the height of the hill raises it above the general level of smog and pollution.

The pleasant flat fronted pension is on the right and has a marble floor entrance hall. Inside, off to the left is a large reception/lounge/bar/breakfast room and the right, the lift.

The self assured, English speaking, owner presides from a large desk in the reception area and is warily helpful. The lady staff receptionists do not exactly go wild in an orgy of energy sapping activity, tending to indulge in a saturnalia of TV watching. Guests in the meantime can help themselves to bottles of beer (75 drs) and Coke from the bar and pay when convenient to them and the receptionist.

The nice double rooms share a red and black appointed bathroom with one other double room. Despite the self assured aura of excellence there are a collection of the usual faults — cracked loo seats, no hot water* (due to a plumbing fault we were airily advised), no locking mechanism on the lavatory door and the toilet had to be flushed by pulling a string. A double room and breakfast sets a guest back 1900 drs which at first and for that matter second impression appears on the expensive side. That is until it is realised that the 4th floor has a Common Room with balcony and a kitchen complete with cooker and a fridge. Added to this the 5th floor contains a laundry room with an iron and 2 roof-top clothes lines which facilities of course make a great deal of difference to the cost of a room.

The management create an atmosphere that will suit the young, very well behaved student and the older traveller but not exuberant rowdies as hands are smacked if guests lay around eating a snack on the front steps, hang washing out of the windows or make a noise especially between the hours of 1330 and 1700 hrs and after 2330 hrs. You know lights out boys and no smoking in the dorms...

Originally recommended by Alexis on the island of Kos but for 1986 is included in one or two of the smaller tour companies brochures for the Athens overnight stop.

THISSION AREA (Thesion) (*Tmr* B/C4/5)
First south-bound metro stop after Monastiraki and a much quieter area.

Hotel Phedias (*Tmr* B4) (Class C) 39 Apostoulou Pavlou   Tel. 345-9511
Directions: South of the metro station. Modern and friendly with double rooms from 1500 drs and breakfast 160 drs per head.

OLYMPIC OFFICE AREA (*Tmr* C6)
Hotel Karayannis (*Tmr* C6) (Class C) 94 Leoforos Sygrou   Tel. 921-5903
Directions: On the corner of Odhos Byzantiou and Leoforos Sygrou, opposite the side exit of the Olympic terminal office.

'Interesting', tatty and noisy, but very necessary, if travellers arrive really late at the terminal. Rooms facing the main road should be avoided. The Athenian traffic, which roars non-stop for a full 24 hours, appears to make the journey along Leoforos Sygrou, via the hotel's balconies, even three or four storeys up. Picturesque view of the Acropolis from the breakfast and bar roof-top terrace, even if it is through a maze of television aerials. Single rooms sharing the bathroom 1200 drs and a double room 1626 drs, with a double room en suite 1698 drs. Breakfast for one costs 190 drs.

Best to splash out for the en suite rooms as the Karayannis shared facilities are of the 'thought provoking' type with a number of the unique features detailed under the general description of bathrooms in the introductory chapters.

Whilst in this area it would be inappropriate not to mention the:

Cafe/Restaurant Behind the Olympic office.
Excellent service and snack bar food, reasonably priced. Closed on Sundays.

Youth Hostels (i.e. the official ones)
I am never quite sure why overnighters use the Athens YHAs. Other accommodation is usually less expensive, cleaner and do away with the need to share dormitories. If you

---

*I must point out that Peter (an Aegean yachtsman who almost always spends some of the winter at **Clares**) insists that I include his disclaimer. He has never found the water anything but hot.

must, about 300 drs per person per night, including sheets.

(a) 57 Kypselis St and Agiou Meletiou 1   Tel. 822-5860
Area: Fokionos Negri, north Athens
Directions: Along 28 (Ikosiokto) Oktovriou/Patission Street from Omonia Sq beyond
Pedion Areos Park to Ag Meletiou St. Turn right and follow until the junction with Kypselis
St. Trolley-buses, No 3, 5, 11, 12 & 13.

(b) 1 Drossi St and Leoforos Alexandras 87 (*Tmr* G2)   Tel. 646-3669
Area: North-east Athens.
Directions: East of Pedion Aeros Park along Leoforos Alexandras almost until the junction
with Ippokratous St. Odhos Drossi is on the left. Trolley-bus No 7 from Panepistiou or No 8
from Kanigos Sq or Akadimias St.

(c) 3 Hamilton St and 97 Patission St (*Tmr* D1)   Tel. 822-6425
Area: North Athens.
Directions: North from Omonia Sq along 28 (Ikosiokto) Oktovriou St as far as the top end
of Pedion Areos Park. Hamilton St is on the left. Trolley-buses 2, 3, 4, 5, 11, 12 & 13.

If intending to stay at one of the Youth Hostels, it is favourite to go to the central
office.

YHA Head Office (*Tmr* D3/4) 4 Dragatsaniou   Tel. 323-4107
Directions: The north side of Plateia Klafthmonos on the left hand side of Stadiou St.
   Open Monday - Friday, 0900 - 1400 hrs and 1830 - 2030 hrs (but not Tuesday evening)
and Saturday between 0900 - 1400 hrs. They advise of vacancies in the various youth
hostels and issue international youth hostel cards.

LARISSIS STATION AREA (*Tmr* B/C1)
See **Trains, A to Z.**

CAMPING
Sample daily site charges per person vary between 170 - 210 drs and the hire of a tent
between 150 - 185 drs.
   Sites include the following:-

Distance from Athens	Site Name	Amenities
8 km	**Athens Camping,** 198 Athinon Ave. On the road to Dafni (due west of Athens). Tel. 581-4113	Open all year, 25 km from the sea. Bar, shop and showers
10 km	**Dafni Camping,** Dafni. On the Athens to Corinth National Road. Tel. 581-1562	Open all year. 5 km from the sea. Bar, shop, showers, disco and kitchen facilities

For the above: Bus 853 Athens - Elefsina departs Koumoundourou Sq/Deligeorgi St (*Tmr* C2/3) every
20 mins between 0510 - 2215 hrs.

14.5 km	**Patritsia,** Kato Kifissia, N. Athens. Tel. 801-1900	Open June - October. Bar, shop, showers, laundry and kitchen facilities
15 km	**Neo Evropaiko,** Nea Kifissia, N. Athens. Tel. 808-3482	Open April - October. 18 km from the sea. Bar, shop, showers, kitchen facilities and swimming pool
16 km	**Nea Kifissia,** Nea Kifissia, N. Athens. Tel. 801-0202	Open all year. 20 km from the sea. Bar, shop, showers, swimming pool and laundry
18 km	**Dionyssiotis,** Nea Kifissia, N. Athens. Tel. 807-1494	Open all year
25 km	**Papa-Camping,** Zorgianni Ag Stefanos. Tel. 814-1446	Open June - September. 25 km from the sea. Laundry, bar and kitchen facilities

For the above (sited on or beside the Athens National Road, north to Lamia): Lamia bus from 260 Liossion St (*Tmr* C1/2), every hour from 0615 to 1915 and at 2030 hrs.

35 km	**Marathon Camping,** Kaminia, Marathon NE of Athens. Tel. 0294-55577	On a sandy beach. Open all year. Showers, bar, laundry, restaurant, shop, swimming pool (1½ km) and kitchen facilities
35 km	**Nea Makri,** 156 Marathonos Ave, Nea Makri. NE of Athens just south of Marathon. Tel. 0294-92719	Open April - October. 220 m from the sea. Sandy beach, laundry, bar and shop

For the above: The bus from Odhos Mavromateon, Plateia Egyptou (*Tmr* D1), every ½ hour from 0530 to 2200 hrs.

26 km	**Cococamp,** Rafina. East of Athens. Tel. 0294-23413	Open all year. On the beach, rocky coast. Laundry, bar, showers, kitchen facilities, shop and restaurant
29 km	**Kokkino Limanaki Camping,** Kokkino Limanaki, Rafina. Tel. 0294-26602	On the beach. Open April - October.
29 km	**Rafina Camping,** Rafina. East of Athens. Tel. 0294-23118	Open all year, 4 km from the sandy beach. Showers, bar, laundry, restaurant and shop

For the above: The Rafina bus from Mavromateon St, Plateia Egyptou (*Tmr* D1). Twenty-nine departures from 0550 to 2200 hrs.

20 km	**Voula Camping,** 2 Alkyonidon St, Voula. Just below Glyfada and the airport. Tel. 895-2712	Open all year. On the sandy beach. Showers, laundry, bar, shop and kitchen facilities
27 km	**Varkiza Beach Camping,** Varkiza. Coastal road Athens-Vouliagmenis-Sounion. Tel. 897-3613	Open all year. By a sandy beach. Bar, shop, laundry and kitchen facilities
60 km	**Sounion Camping,** Sounion. Tel. 0292-39358	Open all year. By a sandy beach. Bar, shop, laundry, kitchen facilities and a swimming pool
76 km	**Vakhos Camping,** Assimaki near Sounion. On the Sounion to Lavrion Road. Tel. 0292-39263	Open June - September. On the beach

For the above: Buses from Mavromateon St, Plateia Egyptou (*Tmr* D1) every hour from 0630 to 1730 hrs. Note to get to Vakhos Camping catch the Sounion bus via Markopoulon and Lavrion.

The Eating Out

Where to dine out is a very personal choice and in a city the size of Athens there are so many restaurants and tavernas to choose from that only a few recommendations are made.

In general, steer clear of Luxury and Class A hotel dining rooms, restaurants offering international cuisine and tavernas with Greek music and/or dancing. They may be very good but will be expensive.

In Athens and the larger, more cosmopolitan, provincial cities, it is usual taverna practice to round up prices, which can prove a little disconcerting until you get used to the idea.

In despair it is noted that some restaurants and tavernas climbing the slopes of the Acropolis up Odhos Markou Avrilou, south of Eolou St, are allowing 'Chinese menu' style collective categories (A, B, C etc) to creep in to their Greek menu listings.

PLAKA AREA (*Tmr* D5)

A glut of eating houses ranging from the very good and expensive, the very expensive and bad, to some inexpensive and very good.

Taverna Thespis 18 Thespidos St   Tel. 323-8242
Directions: Up a lane across the way from Kidathineon St, across the bottom or south east end of Adrianou St.
Recommended with friendly service and reasonably priced. The house retsina is served in metal jugs. A two-hour slap-up meal of souvlaki, Greek salad, fried zucchini, bread and two carafes of retsina totals some 1000 drs plus for two.

Plaka Village 28 Kidathineon
Directions: In the block edged by the streets of Adrianou and Kidathineon.
An excellent souvlaki-bar but (as is now prevalent in the Omonia Sq souvlaki arcade) to sit down costs an extra 16 drs per head. Price lists do not make this plain and the annoying habit can cause, at the least, irritation. A large bottle of beer costs 80 drs.

Gerani Ouzerie 14 Tripodou
Directions: Up the slope from the Thespidos/Kydathineon junction one to the left of Adrianou (facing Monastiraki Sq) and on the left. Distinguishing the establishment is not difficult as the 1st floor balcony is embellished with a large, stuffed bird and two large antique record player horns mounted on the wrought iron balustrade. The taverna, standing on its own evokes a provincial atmosphere and it is necessary to arrive early as it is well patronised by the locals.

Eden Taverna Flessa St
Directions: Off Adrianou St, almost opposite Odhos Nikodimou and on the left. Mentioned because their menu includes many offerings that excellently cater (sorry) for vegetarian requirements.

Platanos Taverna 4 Dioghenous
Directions: Parallel to, but one down and to the top, Monastiraki end, of Adrianou St.
Conventional taverna serving inexpensive lunch and dinner. Closed Sundays.

Michiko Restaurant 27 Kidathineon
Directions: On the right beyond the junction with Asteriou St (in a north east direction towards Syntagma Sq) opposite a small square and church.
Japanese, if you must, and extremely expensive.

Xynou/Xynos 4 Arghelou Geronda (Angelou Geronta)
Directions: Left off Kidathineon St (facing Syntagma Sq).
One of the oldest and most reasonably priced tavernas in the Plaka, highly rated and well patronised by Athenians. Evenings only and closed on Sundays. A friend advises me that it is now almost obligatory to book in advance.

Plateia Agora, a lovely, elongated, chic Plaka Sq formed at the junction of the bottom of Eolou, the top of Adrianou and Kapnikareas Streets, spawns a number of cafe-bar restaurants. The include the *Possidion* and *Apollon*, the canopied chairs and tables of which edge the street all the way round the neat, paved plateia. There is a clean public lavatory at the top (Monastiraki) end. The *Apollon* has a particularly wide range of choice and one can sit at the comfortable tables for an hour or so over a coffee (84 drs), have a fried egg breakfast (220 drs) or a full blown meal. Hope your luck is in and the organ grinder wanders through.

STADIUM (PANGRATI) AREA (*Tmr* E/F6)
Karavitis Taverna (ΚΑΡΑΒΙΤΗΣ) 4 Pafsaniou (Paysanioy)
Directions: Beyond the Stadium (*Tmr* E/F6) going east (away from the Acropolis) along Vasileos Konstantinou, and Pafsaniou is 3rd turning to the right. The taverna is on the left.
A small, leafy tree shaded gravel square fronts the taverna which is so popular that there is an extension across the street through a pair of 'field gates'. Our friend Paul will probably berate me (more if he was not less of a gentleman) for listing this gem. Unknown to visitors

but extremely popular with Athenians more especially those who, when college students, frequented this jewel in the Athens taverna crown as young men. A meal for 4 of a selection of dishes including lamb, beef in clay, giant haricot beans, garlic flavoured meat balls, greens, ztatziki, 2 plates of feta cheese, aubergines, courgettes, bread and 3 jugs of retsina from the barrel for some 1700 drs. Beat that, but some knowledge of Greek will help.

Also in this area is the

To Fanari (*Tmr* F6) Plastira Sq
Directions: South-east of the National Gardens, leaving the Stadium to the right, turn down Eratosthenous St from Vasileos Konstantinou to Plateia Plastira.

Very Greek and off the Plaka, Syntagma and Omonia Square 'tourist beat' and therefore comparatively inexpensive.

SYNTAGMA AREA (*Tmr* 1.D/E4/5)
Corfu Restaurant (*Tmr* E4) 6 Kriezotou St
Directions: North of Syntagma Sq and first turning right off Panepistimiou (Venizelou) St.

Extensive Greek and European dishes in a modern, friendly restaurant.

Delphi Restaurant (*Tmr* D4) 15 Nikis St
Directions: From the south-west corner of Syntagma Sq, east along Mitropoleos and the first turning left.

Modern, reasonably priced food and friendly. Extensive menu.

Sintrivani Restaurant (*Tmr* D/E5) 5 Filellinon St.
Directions: South-west corner of Syntagma Sq and due south.

Garden restaurant serving a traditional menu at reasonable prices.

Vassillis Restaurant (*Tmr* E4) 14A Voukourestiou
Directions: North of Syntagma Sq and the second turning off Panepistimiou St to the right along Odhos Smats and across Akadimias St.

Variety, in traditional surroundings.

Ideal Restaurant (*Tmr* D/E4) 46 Panepistimiou St
Directions: Proceed up Panepistimiou from the north-east corner of Syntagma Sq and the restaurant is on the right.

Good food at moderate prices.

YWCA 11 Amerikis St
Directions: North-west up either Stadiou or Panepistimiou St and second or third road to the right, depending which street is used.

Cafeteria — the food is inexpensive.

There are many cafes in or around Syntagma. Recommended but expensive are:

Brazilian Coffee Cafes
Two close by Syntagma Sq, one at the bottom of Stadiou St on the square and the other in Voukourestiou St, both serving coffee, tea, toast, butter and jam, breakfast, ice creams and pastries.

Zonar's 9 Panepistimiou (Venizelou)

OMONIA AREA (*Tmr* 2.D3)
Ellinikon (*Tmr* D2) On the corner of Dorou and Satovriandou Streets.
Directions: North of Omonia Sq along Dorou St and almost immediately on your left.

Good value, if a little showy.

Taverna Kostoyannus (*Tmr* E2) 37 Zaimi St
Directions: Leave Omonia northwards on 28 (Ikosiokto) Oktovriou, turn right at Odhos Stournara to the near side of the Polytechnic School, and Zaimi St is the second road

CANDID GUIDE TO IONIAN

along. The taverna is to the left approximately behind the National Archaeological Museum.

Satisfactory food and prices. Well recommended but, as in the case of many other Athenian tavernas, it is not open for lunch or on Sundays.

Snack Bars
Probably the most compact, reasonably priced 'offerings' in grubby surroundings lie in the arcade between Dorou St and 28 (Ikosiokto) Oktovriou, off Omonia Sq, wherein are situated cafes and stalls selling almost every variety of fast Greek convenience food. A 'standard' souvlaki costs 35 drs and a 'spezial' or de-luxe 50/55 drs BUT do not sit down unless you wish to be charged an extra 15 - 20 drs per head. A beer costs 55/65 drs.

Note the standard version is a preheated slab of meat and the 'spezial' the traditional giro meat-sliced offering.

Cafes
Everywhere of course, but on Omonia Sq, alongside Dorou St and adjacent to the Hotel Carlton, is a magnificent specimen of the traditional Kafeneion. Greek men sip coffee and tumble their worry beads, as they must have done since the turn of the century.

Flocas *(Tmr D/E3/4)* 4 Korai St
Directions: Half way down Panepistimiou St opposite the University.

Fair value, fast service for a range of dishes.

Odhos Sokratous south of Omonia Sq (parallel and west of Athinas St) is during the day almost one great market, mainly meat. In amongst the stalls and counters are 3 inexpensive tavernas of some note.

LYCABETTUS (LYKAVITOS) AREA *(Tmr F4)*
Je Reviens Restaurant *(Tmr F/G4/5)* 49 Xenokratous St
Directions: North-east from Kolonaki Sq, up Patriachou Ioakim St to the junction with and left at Marasli St until it crosses Xenokratous St.

French food, creditable but "middlingly" expensive. Open midday and evenings.

L'Abreuvoir 51 Xenokratous St
Directions: As for *Je Reviens* as are the comments, but more expensive.

Al Convento Restaurant *(Tmr G4)* 4 Anapiron
Directions: North-east from Kolonaki Sq along Patriarchou Ioakim to Marasli St. Turn left and then right along Odhos Souidias and Anapiron St is nearly at the end.

Stage Coach Restaurant 14 Voukourestiou
Directions: From the north-west corner of Plateia Kolonaki, take Odhos Skoufa, which crosses Voukourestiou St.

Wild West in decor, air-conditioned, the food is American in style and content, and is not cheap with steaks as a house speciality. Why not go to the good old US of A? Lunch and evening meals, open 1200 to 1600 and 1900 to 0100 hrs.

THE A TO Z OF USEFUL INFORMATION
AIRLINE OFFICES & TERMINUS *(Tmr 12.C6)*
Referred to in the introductory paragraphs as well as under *Accommodation*, the busy offices are to the left (facing Syntagma Sq), of the frantic Leoforos Sygrou. As with other Olympic facilities the office doubles as a terminus for airport buses arriving from and departing to East and West Airports.

Aircraft Timetables
See **Chapter 3** for the islands described in this guide that are serviced from Athens and the individual islands for details of the actual timetables.

BANKS (Trapeza — ΤΡΑΠΕΖΑ)

Normal opening times, 0900 to 1300 hrs, Monday-Friday. Do not forget to take your passport and note, that if a bank strike is under way (apparently becoming a natural part of the tourist season high-jinks) the National Bank in Syntagma Sq stays open and in business. However, it becomes more than usually crowded in these circumstances. Banks opening after normal hours include the:

National Bank of Greece (*Tmr* 3.D/E4) 2 Karageorgi Georgiou, Syntagma Sq
Open 0800 - 1300 and 1400 - 2100 hrs, Monday-Friday, 0800 - 2000 hrs Saturday and Sunday.

Ionian and Popular Bank (*Tmr* D/E4/5) 1 Mitropoleos St
Open 0800 - 1300 and 1400 - 1730 hrs, Monday-Saturday and 0900 - 1200 hrs, Sunday.

Commercial Bank of Greece (*Tmr* E4) 11 Panepistimiou (Venizelou)
Open 0800 - 1300 and 1400 - 1530 hrs, Monday-Saturday and 0900 - 1200 hrs, Sunday.

BEACHES

Athens is not on a river or by the sea, so to enjoy a beach it is necessary to leave the main city and travel to those suburbs by the sea. Very often these beaches are operated under the aegis of the NTOG, or private enterprise in association with a hotel. The NTOG beaches usually have beach huts, cabins, tennis courts, a playground and catering facilities. Entrance charges vary from 25-100 drs.

There are beaches and/or swimming pools at

Paleon Faliron/Faliro	A seaside resort	Bus No. 126: Departs from Odhos Othonos, south side of Syntagma Sq (*Tmr* E5).
Alimos	NTOG beach	Bus No. 133: Departs from Odhos Othonos, south side of Syntagma Sq (*Tmr* E5).
Glyfada (Glifada)	A seaside resort	Bus No. 129: Departs from Leoforos Olgas, south side of the Zappeion Gdns (*Tmr* E5).
Voula	Class A NTOG beach	Bus No. 122: Departs from Leoforos Olgas, south side of the Zappeion Gdns (*Tmr* E5).
Voula	Class B NTOG beach	Bus No. 122.
Vouliagmeni	A luxury seaside resort and yacht marina. NTOG beach	Bus No. 118: Departs from Leoforos Olgas, south side of the Zappeion Gdns (*Tmr* E5).
Varkiza	A seaside resort and yacht marina. NTOG beach	Bus No. 115: Departs from Leoforos Olgas, south side of the Zappeion Gdns (*Tmr* E5).

There are other beaches all the way down to Cape Sounion (Sounio) via the coast road. Buses from 14 Mavromateon St (*Tmr* D/E1) (west of Pedion Areos Park, north of Omonia Sq). The Athens/Cape Sounion bus departs every hour from 0630 hrs and leaves Sounion for Athens every hour from 0800 - 1900 hrs, the one way fare costing about 250 drs and the journey takes 1½ hrs.

BOOKSELLERS

Apart from the aforementioned Plaka **Flea Market** secondhand bookshops, there are three or four on Odhos Nikis (west of Syntagma Sq) and Odhos Amerikis (north-west of Syntagma Sq) as well as one on Lysikratous St (*Tmr* D5) opposite the small church. There is also a book trade stall on the Kidathineon St edge of the Plateia Plaka.

Of all the above it is perhaps invidious to select one but . . . .

The Compendium Bookshop (& Computors) 28 Nikis St   Tel. 3226931
Well recommended for a wide range of English language publications. The **Transalpino Travel** office is in the basement.

BREAD SHOPS
In the more popular shopping areas.

BUSES & TROLLEY BUSES
These run variously between 0500 and 0030 (half an hour past midnight) and are usually crowded, but excellent value, fares costing between 10 and 20 drs Travel between 0500 and 0800 hrs is free.

BUSES
The buses are blue (and green) and bus stops are marked Statis (ΣΤΑΣΙΣ).
   Some one-man-operated buses are utilised and a few buses have an honesty box for fares.

TROLLEY-BUSES
Yellow coloured vehicles and bus stops. Usually entered via the door at the rear marked Eisodos (ΣΙΣΟΔΟΣ), with the exit at the front, marked Exodus (ΕΞΟΔΟΣ).

Do have the correct money to hand as the driver and/or conductor may not have any change.

Major City Terminals & turn-round points† (see footnote)
Kaningos Sq: (*Tmr* 4.D2) North-east of Omonia Sq
Korai Sq: (*Tmr* D3/4) Opposite the University between Stadiou and Panepistimiou Streets and Omonia and Syntagma Squares
Liossion St: (*Tmr* C1) North-west of Omonia Sq
Eleftherias Sq: (*Tmr* C3) North-west of Monastiraki Sq
Leoforos Olgas: (*Tmr* E5/6) South of the National Gardens
Mavromateon St†: (*Tmr* D/E1) West of Pedion Areos Park, north of Omonia Sq
Egyptou Place (Aigyptou/Egiptou): (*Tmr* D1) Just below the south-west corner of Pedion Areos Park, alongside 28 (Ikosiokto) Oktovriou
Agion Asomaton Place: (*Tmr* B4) West of Monastiraki Sq
Koumoundourou St: (*Tmr* C2/3) West of Omonia Sq, third turning right off Ag Konstantinou

† The tree shaded north-south street is lined with bus departure points. The Rafina bus leaves from about a third of the way up the street and the Lavrion bus from the square at the south end, on the junction with Leoforos Alexandras.

Trolley-buses timetables
Some major city routes include:
No. 1:   Plateia Attiki (metro station) (*Tmr* C1), Stathmos Larissis (railway station) (*Tmr* B/C1) Karaiskaki Place, Ag Konstantinou, Omonia Sq, Syntagma Sq, Kallithea suburb (SW Athens). Every 10 mins from 0505-2350 hrs.
No. 2:   Pangrati (*Tmr* F6), Leoforos Amalias (Central), Syntagma Sq, Omonia Sq, (28 Ikosiokto Oktovriou) Patission St, Kipseli (N Athens). From 0630-0020 hrs.
No. 10:   N Smirni (S Athens), Leoforos Sygrou, Leoforos Amalias, Syntagma Sq, Panepistimiou St, Korai St (*Tmr* D3/4) (opposite the University). From 0500-2345 hrs.
No. 12:   Leoforos Olgas (*Tmr* D/E5/6), Leoforos Amalias, Syntagma Sq, Omonia Sq, 28 Ikosiokto Oktovriou (Patission) St (N Athens). From 0630-2235 hrs.

Other routes covered by trolley-buses include:
No. 3:   Patissia to Erythrea (N to NNE Athens suburbs). From 0625-2230 hrs.
No. 4:   Odhos Kypselis (*Tmr* E1) (North of Pedion Areos park), Omonia Sq, Syntagma Sq, Leoforos Olgas to Ag Artemious (SSE Athens suburbs). From 0630-0020 hrs.
No. 5:   Patissia (N Athens suburb), Omonia Sq, Syntagma Sq, Filellinon St, Koukaki (S Athens suburb). From 0630-0015 hrs.
No. 6:   Ippokratous St (*Tmr* E3), Odhos Panepistimiou, Omonia Sq to N Filadelfia (N Athens suburbs). Every 10 mins from 0500 - 2320 hrs
No. 7:   Odhos Panepistimiou (*Tmr* D/E3/4), 28 Ikosiokto Oktovriou (Patission) St, to Leoforous Alexandras (N of Lycabettus). From 0630-0015 hrs.

No. 8:   Plateia Kaningos (*Tmr* D2), Odhos Akadimias, Vassilissis Sofias, Leoforos Alexandras, 28 Ikosiokto Oktovriou, (Patission) St. From 0630-0020 hrs.

No. 9:   Kypseli St (*Tmr* E1), 28 Ikosiokto Oktovriou (Patission) St, Stadiou St, Syntagma Sq, Petralona (W Athens suburb — far side of Filopapou). Every 10 mins from 0455 - 2345 hrs

No. 10:   Korai St (*Tmr* D3/4), Stadiou St, Syntagma Sq, Filellinon St, Leoforos Sygrou, Nea Smirni (S Athens suburb). Every 10 mins from 0500 - 2345 hrs

No. 11:   Koliatsou (NNE Athens suburb), 28 Ikosiokto Oktovriou (Patission) St, Stadiou St, Syntagma Sq, Filellinon St, Plastira Sq, Eftichidou St, N Pangrati (ESE Athens suburb). Every 5 mins from 0500 - 0010 hrs.

No. 13:   28 Ikosiokto Oktovriou (Patission) St, Akadimias St, Vassilissis Sofias, Plateia Papadiamantopoulou, Leoforos Kifissias, Neo Psychiko (NE Athens suburb). Every 10 mins from 0500-2400 hrs.

Bus timetables

Bus numbers are subject to a certain amount of confusion, but here goes! Some of the routes are as follows:

No. 022:   Kaningos Sq (*Tmr* D2), Akadimias, Kanari, Patriarchou Ioakim, Marasli, Genadiou St (SE Lycabettus). Every 10 mins from 0520 - 2330 hrs

No. 024:   Leoforos Amalias (*Tmr* D/E 5), Syntagma Sq, Panepistimiou St, Omonia Sq, Tritis Septemvriou, Stournari, Acharnon, Sourmeli, Liossion St. *NB This is the bus that delivers passengers to 260 Liossion St (Tmr C2), one of the main bus terminals.*

No. 040:   Filellinon St (Syntagma Sq), Leoforos Amalias, Leoforos Sygrou to Vassileos Konstantinou, Piraeus port. Every 10 mins, 24 hours a day. Green Bus.

No. 045:   Kaningos Sq (*Tmr* D2), Akadimias St, Vassilissis Sofias, Leoforos Kifissias to Kefalari and Politia (NE Athens suburb). Every 15 mins from 0600 - 0100 hrs

No. 049:   Athinas St (*Tmr* C/D3), (S of Omonia Sq), Sofokleous St, Pireos St, Sotiros St, Filonos St, to Plateia Themistokleous, Piraeus port. Every 10 mins, 24 hours a day. Green Bus.

No. 051:   Off Ag Konstantinou (*Tmr* C2/3), W of Omonia Sq, corner of Menandrou/Vitara Streets, Kolonou St, Platonos St (W Athens suburb). *NB This is the bus that connects to the 100 Kifissou St (Tmr A2), a main bus terminal.*

No. 115:   Leoforos Olgas (*Tmr* E5/6), Leoforos Sygrou, Leoforos Possidonos (coast road) to Varkiza. Every 20 mins, 24 hours a day

No. 118:   Leoforos Olgas (*Tmr* E5/6), Leoforos Sygrou, Leoforos Possidonos (coast road) to Vouliagmeni. Every 20 mins from 1245 - 2015 hrs

No. 122:   Leoforos Olgas, Leoforos Sygrou, Leoforos Possidonos (coast road) to Voula. Every 20 mins from 0530 - 2400 hrs

No. 132:   Othonos St (Syntagma Sq) (*Tmr* E5), Filellinon St, Leoforos Amalias, Leoforos Sygrou to Edem (SSE Athens suburb). Every 20 mins from 0530 - 1900 hrs

No. 224:   Polygono (N Athens suburb), 28 Ikosiokto Oktovriou (Patission) St, Kaningos Sq, Vassilissis Sofias, Democratias St, (Kessariani, E Athens suburb). Every 20 mins from 0500 - 2400 hrs

No. 230:   Ambelokipi (E Athens suburb), Leoforos Alexandras, Ippokratous St, Akadimias St, Syntagma Sq, Leoforos Amalias, Dionysiou Areopagitou St, Apostolou Pavlou, Thission. Every 10 mins from 0500 - 2320 hrs

No. 510:   Kaningos Sq (*Tmr* D2), Akadimias St, Ippokratous St, Leoforos Alexandras, Leoforos Kifissias to Dionyssos (NE Athens suburb). Every 20 mins from 0530 - 2250 hrs

No. 527:   Kaningos Sq (*Tmr* D2), Akadimias St, Leoforos Alexandras, Leoforos Kifissias to Amaroussion (NE Athens suburb). Every 15 mins from 0615 - 2215 hrs.

† The Athens-Attica bus services detailed above cover the city and its environs. The rest of Greece is served by:
1) KTEL: A pool of bus operators working through one company from two terminals: 260 Liossion St* and 100 Kifissou St**.
2) OSE (the State Railway Company) from an aggressive bus terminal alongside the main railway station of Stathmos Peloponissou. Apart from the domestic services, there is a terminal for other European capitals including Paris, Istanbul and Munich.

*Liossion St (*Tmr* D2) is to the east of Stathmos Peloponissou Railway Station. The terminus serves Halkida, Edipsos, Kimi, Delphi, Amfissa, Kamena Vourla, Larissa, Thiva, Trikala (Meteora) Livadia, Lamia. *See* the bus route No. 024 to get to the terminus.
**Kifissou St is to the west of Omonia Sq, beyond the 'steam railway' lines, across Leoforos

Konstantinoupolos and up Odhos Platonos. The terminus serves Patras, Pirgos (Olympia), Nafplio (Mikines), Andritsena (Vasses), Kalamata, Sparti (Mistras), Githio (Diros), Tripolis, Messolongi, Igoumenitsa, Preveza, Ioanina, Corfu, Zakynthos, Cephalonia, Lefkas, Kozani, Kastoria, Florina, Grevena, Veria, Naoussa, Edessa, Seres, Kilkis, Kavala, Drama, Komotini, Korinthos, Kranidi, Xilokastro. *See* the bus route No. 051 to get to the terminus.

For any bus services connecting to the islands detailed in this guide, refer to the relevant Mainland Ports and Island chapters.

CAMPING
See **Accommodation.**

CAR HIRE
As any other capital city, numerous offices, the majority of which are lined up in the smarter areas and squares, such as Syntagma Sq and Leoforos Amalias. Typical is

Pappas, 44 Leoforos Amalias   Tel. 3220087

CAR REPAIR
Help and advice can be obtained by contacting:-

The Automobile and Touring Club of Greece (ELPA) at 2 Messogion St (*Tmr* 13)
Tel. 779-1615

For immediate, emergency attention dial 104.

There are dozens of back-street car repairers, breakers and spare-part shops parallel to Leoforos Sygrou, in the area between the Olympic office and the Temple of Olympian Zeus.

CHEMIST
See **Medical Care.**

CINEMAS
There are a large number of out-door cinemas. Do not worry about a language barrier, the majority of the films have English dialogue with Greek subtitles.

Aigli in the Zappeion is a must and is situated at the south end of the National Garden. Other cinemas are bunched together in Stadiou, Panepistimiou and 28 Ikosiokto Oktovriou (Patission) Streets.

CLUBS, BARS & DISCOS
Why leave home? But if you must, there are enough to satiate the most voracious desires.

COMMERCIAL SHOPPING AREAS
A very large street market ranges up Odhos Athinas (*Tmr* C3/4), Sokratous St and the associated side streets from Ermou St almost all the way up to Omonia Sq during the daylight hours. After dark the shutters are drawn down, the stalls canvassed over and the ladies of the night appear.

Plateia Kotzia (*Tmr* D3) spawns a flower market on Sundays whilst the Parliament Building side of Vassilissis Sofias (*Tmr* E4) is lined with smart flower stalls that open daily.

Monastiraki Sq (*Tmr* 5.C4) and the various streets that radiate off are abuzz, specialising in widely differing aspects of commercial and tourist trade. Odhos Areos contains a plethora of leather goods shops; the near end of Ifestou is edged by stall upon stall of junk and tourist 'omit-abilia' (the forgettable memorabilia); Pandrossou lane contains a better class of shop and stall selling sandals, pottery and smarter 'memorabilia' while the square itself has a number of hawkers and their handcarts.

The smart department stores are conveniently situated in or around Syntagma Sq, and the main streets that radiate off the square including Ermou, Stadiou and Panepistimiou.

DENTISTS & DOCTORS
See **Medical Care.**

EMBASSIES

Australia: 15 Messogion Av.	Tel. 775-7650
Canada: 4 Ioannou Gennadiou St.	Tel. 723-9511
Great Britain: 1 Ploutarchou and Ypsilantou Sts.	Tel. 723-6211
Ireland: 7 Vassileos Konstantinou.	Tel. 723-2711
New Zealand: 15-17 An. Tsoha St.	Tel. 641-0311
South Africa: 124 Kifissias/Iatridou.	Tel. 692-2125
USA: 91 Vassilissis Sofias.	Tel. 721-2951
Denmark: 15 Philikis Etairias Sq.	Tel. 724-9315
Finland: 1 Eratosthenous and Vas Konstantinou Streets.	Tel. 751-5064
Norway: 7 Vassileos Konstantinou St.	Tel. 724-6173
Sweden: 7 Vassileos Konstantinou St.	Tel. 722-4504
Belgium: 3 Sekeri St.	Tel. 361-7886
France: 7 Vassilissis Sofias.	Tel. 361-1663
German Federal Republic: 3 Karaoli/Dimitriou Sts.	Tel. 36941
Netherlands: 5-7 Vassilissis Konstantinou	Tel. 723-9701

HAIRDRESSERS
No problems with sufficient in the main shopping areas.

HOSPITALS
See **Medical Care.**

LAUNDRETTES (*Tmr* 13.D5)
There may be others but... this '**Self Service, The only Coin-Op in Athens**' is signposted from Kidathineon St (proceeding towards Syntagma Sq). At the far end of Plateia Plaka turn right down Angelou Geronda across Dedalou and the laundrette is on the right hand side. A machine load costs 200 drs, 9 mins of dryer 20 drs and powder 50 drs. In respect of the detergent, why not pop out to Kidathineon St and purchase a small packet of **Tide** for 38 drs. Open in the summer daily 0800-2100 hrs. Note that my lavatorial obsession would not be satisfied without mentioning that there is a public WC sited on Plateia Plaka.

LOST PROPERTY
The main office is situated at 14 Messogion St (*Tmr* 12/3) Tel. 770-5771. But contact the relevant lost property office if you mislay anything, first asking the Tourist police for the correct address. Each form of transport has its own lost property office, as do the city authorities.

It is true to say that you are far more likely to 'lose' personal belongings to other tourists, than to Greeks.

LUGGAGE STORE
A number of offices where one would expect them on Filellinon and Nikis Streets off Syntagma Sq. Charges from 50 drs per case per day.

MEDICAL CARE
Chemists/Pharmacies (Farmakio — ΦΑΡΜΑΚΕΙΟ)
Identified by a green or red cross on a white background. Normal opening hours and a rota operates to give a 'duty' chemist cover.

Dentists & Doctors
Ask at the First Aid Centre for the address of the School of Dentistry where free treatment is available. Both Dentists and Doctors advertise widely and there is no shortage of practitioners.

First Aid Centre (KAT)
21 Tritis Septemvriou St (*Tmr* 14.D2), beyond the Chalkokondili turning, parallel to 28 Ikosiokto Oktovriou, and on the left.   Tel. 150
Hospital (*Tmr* 15.G4)
Do not go direct to a hospital (first to GO!). No seriously folks, initially attend the First Aid Centre. If necessary they will direct a seriously ill patient to the correct destination.
Medical Emergency: Tel. 166

METRO/ELEKTRIKOS (HΣAM)
The Athens underground or subway system, which operates underground in the heart of the city and over-ground for the rest of the journey. It is a simple one track layout from Kifissia (north-east Athens suburb) to Piraeus (south-west Athens port), and represents marvellous value with two rate fares of 20 and 40 drs. You must have the requisite coin to obtain a ticket from the machine prior to gaining access to the platforms.

Everyone is most helpful and will, if the ticket machine 'frightens' you, show how it should be operated. Beware, select the ticket value first, then put the coin in the slot(I think) and keep your ticket to hand in to the ticket collector at the journey's end. The service operates between 0505 and 0015 hrs and travel before 0800 hrs is free. Keep an eye out for the old-fashioned wooden carriages.

Station Stops
There are 20 which include Kifissia (NE suburb), Stathmos Atiki (for the main railway stations), Plateia Victorias (N Athens), Omonia Sq, Monastiraki Sq (Plaka), Pl Thission (for the Acropolis) and (Piraeus) Port. From the outside, the Piraeus terminus is rather difficult to locate, the entrance being in the left-hand corner of what appears to be an oldish waterfront building.

MUSIC & DANCING
See **Clubs, Bars & Discos.**

NTOG (EOT)
The headquarters of the National Tourist Organisation (NTOG or in Greek, EOT—Ellinikos Organismos Tourismou— **EMHNIKOΣ ΟΡΓΑΝΙΣΜΟΣ ΤΟΥΡΙΣΜΟΥ**) is on the 5th floor at 2 Amerikis St, near Syntagma Sq, but this office does not normally handle the usual tourist enquiries.

The Information desk, from whence maps and some advice, information folders, bus and boat schedules and hotel facts may be obtained, is situated just inside, on the left, of the foyer of the

National Bank of Greece (*Tmr* 3.D/E4) 2 Karageorgi Servias, Syntagma Sq
                                                                          Tel. 322-2545.
Do not hope to obtain anything other than the usual pamphlets, it would be unrealistic to expect personal attention from staff besieged by wave upon wave of tourists of every hue, race and colour. Open Monday - Saturday, 0800 - 2000 hrs.

A note of caution concerns the agencies inability to admit to their being any E class hotels.

There is also an office conveniently situated at the East Airport.

OPENING HOURS
(Summer months)
These are only a guide-line and apply to Athens (as well as the larger cities).

Note that in country and village areas, it is more likely that shops will be open Monday-Saturday for over 12 hours a day, and on Sundays, holidays and Saints days, for a few hours either side of midday. The afternoon siesta will usually be taken between 1300/1400 hrs and 1500/1700 hrs.

Trade Stores & Chemists
Monday, Wednesday and Saturday 0800-1430 hrs. Tuesday, Thursday and Friday 0800-1300 hrs and 1700-2030 hrs.

Food Stores
Monday, Wednesday and Saturday 0800-1500 hrs. Tuesday, Thursday and Friday 0800-1400 hrs and 1730-2030 hrs.

Art & Gift Shops
Weekdays 0800-2100 hrs. Sundays (Monastiraki area) 0930-1445 hrs.

Restaurants, Pastry Shops, Cafes & Dairy Shops
Seven days a week.

Museums
See the individual museums.

Public Services (including Banks)
See the relevant subheading.

OTE
There are OTE offices at 85, 28 Ikosiokto Oktovriou/Patission St (*Tmr* 16.D1) (open 24 hrs a day), 15 Stadiou St (*Tmr* 17.D4) (open Monday to Friday 0700-2400 hrs, Saturday and Sunday 0800-2400 hrs), 53 Solonos (*Tmr* E3/4) and 7 Kratinou (Plateia Kotzai) (*Tmr* D3) open between 0800 and 2200 hrs. There is also an office on Athinas St (*Tmr* C3).

PHARMACIES
See **Medical Care.**

PLACES OF INTEREST
Parliament Building (*Tmr* E4/5) Syntagma Sq
The Greek equivalent of the British changing of the Guard at Buckingham Palace. The special guards are spectacularly outfitted with tasselled red caps, white shirts (blouses do I hear?), coloured waistcoats, a skirt, white tights, knee-garters and boots topped off with pom-poms. The ceremony is officially at 1100 hrs on Sunday morning but seems to kick off at about 1045 hrs. Incidentally there is a band thrown in for good measure.

Museums:
Seasons are split as follows: Winter: 1st November - 31st March; Summer: 1st April - 31st October.
Museums are closed on: 1st January, 25th March, Good Friday, Easter Day and Christmas Day.
Sunday hours are kept on Epiphany, Ash Monday, Easter Saturday, Easter Monday, 1st May, Whit Sunday, Assumption Day, 28th October and Boxing Day. They are only open in the mornings on Christmas Eve, New Year's Eve, 2nd January, Good Thursday and Easter Tuesday.
Museums are closed Tuesday (unless otherwise indicated), admission is in the main free on Sundays and students with cards will achieve a reduction in fees.

Acropolis (*Tmr* C5)
The museum exhibits finds made on the site. Of especial interest are the sixth century BC statues of Korai women.
Entrance charges are included in the entrance fee to the Acropolis site, 250 drs per head. Summer: 0730 - 1930 hrs; Sunday and holidays 0800 - 1800 hrs.
The museum is open 0730 - 1930 hrs; Tuesdays 1100 - 1700 hrs; Sundays and holidays, 0800 - 1800 hrs.

Benaki (*Tmr* E/F4)
On the corner of Vassilissis Sofias and Koubari (Koumbari) St, close by the Plateia Kolonaki. A very interesting variety of exhibits made up from private collections.

Particularly diverting is a collection of national costumes.
Summer: daily 0830 - 1400 hrs. Entrance 100 drs.

Byzantine (*Tmr* F4/5) 22 Vassilissis Sofias
As you would think from the name — Byzantine art.
Summer: daily 0800 - 1900 hrs; Sunday and holidays, 0800 - 1800 hrs. Closed Mondays. Entrance 150 drs.

Goulandris, 13 Levidou St, Kifissia, N Athens
Natural history.
Summer: daily 0900 - 1300 and 1700 - 2000 hrs. Closed Fridays. Entrance 70 drs.

Kanelloupoulos (*Tmr* C5) On the corner of Theorias and Panos Sts, (Plaka)
A smaller version of the Benaki Museum at the Monastiraki end of Adrianou St.
Summer: daily 0845 - 1500; Sunday and holidays 0930 - 1430 hrs. Entrance 100 drs which is charged Sundays and holidays.

Keramikos (*Tmr* B4), 148 Ermou St
Finds from Keramikos cemetery.
Summer: daily 0845 - 1500 hrs; Sunday and holidays, 0930 - 1430 hrs. The museum is closed Thursdays. Entrance to the site and museum 100 drs.

National Gallery & Alexandros Soutzos (*Tmr* F/G4/5), 46 Vassileos Konstantinou/Sofias
Mainly 19th and 20th century Greek paintings.
Summer: 0900 - 1500 hrs; Sunday and holidays 1000 - 1400 hrs. Closed Mondays. Admission free.

National Historical & Ethnological (*Tmr* D4), Kolokotroni Square, off Stadiou St.
Greek history and the War of Independence.
Summer: 0900 - 1400 hrs; Sunday and holidays 0900 - 1300 hrs. Closed Mondays. Entrance 100 drs, Thursday free.

National Archaeological (*Tmr* D/E2), 1 Tositsa St, off 28 Ikosiokto Oktovriou/Patission St
The largest and possibly the most important Greek museum, covering a wide variety of exhibits. A must if you are a museum buff.
Summer: 0800 - 1900 hrs; Sunday and holidays 0800 - 1800 hrs. Closed Mondays. Entrance 200 drs, includes entrance to the Santorini and Numismatic exhibitions (*See* below).

Numismatic In the same building as the National Archaeological
Displaying, as you would imagine, a collection of Greek coins, spanning the ages.
Summer: 0830 - 1330 hrs; Sunday and holidays 0900 - 1400 hrs.
Also housed in the same building are:
The Epigraphical Collection: Summer: 0830 - 1330 hrs; Sunday and holidays 0900 - 1400 hrs.
Santorini Exhibits: Summer: 0800 - 1900 hrs; Sunday and holidays 0800 - 1800 hrs. Closed Monday.
and
The Casts and Copies Exhibition: Summer: 0800 - 1900 hrs; Sunday and holidays 0800 - 1800 hrs.

Popular Art (*Tmr* D5), 17 Kidathineon St, The Plaka
Folk art, folklore and popular art.
Summer: 0845 - 1500 hrs; Sundays and holidays 0930 - 1430 hrs. Closed Mondays. Entrance free.

War (*Tmr* F4/5) 2 Rizari St, off Leoforos Vassilissis Sofias
Warfare exhibits covering a wide variety of subjects.

Summer: daily 0900 - 1400 hrs. Closed Mondays. Entrance free.

Theatres & Performances

For full, up to date details enquire at the **NTOG** office (*Tmr* 3.D/E4). They should be able to hand out a pamphlet giving a precise timetable for the year. As a guide the following are performed year in, year out:

Son et Lumière

From the Pnyx hill-side, a *Son et Lumière* features the Acropolis. The English performance starts at 2100 hrs every evening, except when the moon is full, and takes 45 minutes. There are French versions at 2200 hrs daily except Tuesdays and Fridays when a German commentary is enacted. Tickets are available for 180 drs (students 70 drs) at the entrance of the church, Ag Dimitros Lombardiaris, on the way to the show. Catch a No. 230 bus along Dionysiou Areopagitou St, getting off one stop beyond the Odeion (Theatre) of Herodes Atticus and follow the sign-posted path on the left-hand side.

Athens Festival

Takes place in the restored and beautiful Odeion of Herodes Atticus, built in approximately AD 160 as a Roman theatre, seating about 5000 people and situated at the foot of the south-west corner of the Acropolis.

The festival lasts from early June to the middle of September, and consists of a series of plays, ballet, concerts and opera. The performances usually commence at 2100 hrs and tickets, which are on sale up to 10 days before the event, are obtainable from the Theatre or from the **Athens Festival booking office**, 4 Stadiou St, Tel. 322-1459.

Dora Stratou Theatre

A short stroll away on Mouseion or Hill of Muses. On the summit stands the Monument of the Filopapou (Philopappos) and nearby the Dora Stratou Theatre, where an internationally renowned troupe of folk dancers, dressed in traditional costumes, perform a series of Greek dances and songs. Performances here are timed to coincide with the ending of the Son et Lumière, on the Pynx. The show, produced between early May and the end of September, costs between 300 and 430 drs per head, starts at about 2215 hrs, lasts approximately one hour, and is worth a visit.

Lycabettus Theatre

On the north-east side of Lycabettus Hill (Lykavitos, Likavittos, Lykabettos, etc, etc). Concerts and theatrical performances take place in the hill-side open-air theatre between the middle of June and the first week of September from 2100 hrs. Tickets can be purchased from the theatre box office one hour before the event or from the **Athens Festival booking office** referred to above.

The Hellenic-American Union puts on a series of concerts and plays (*See* **Klafthmonos Sq** in the introductory paragraphs).

POLICE
See **Tourist Police.**

POST OFFICES (Tachidromio — TAXIΔPOMEION)

Weekday opening hours, as a guide, are 0800 to 1300 hrs.

The Central Post Office is at 100 Eolou St (*Tmr* 18.D3) close by Omonia Sq and is open Monday - Friday, 0730 - 2030 hrs and Saturday, 0730 - 1500 hrs.

Branch offices are situated on the corner of Othonos and Nikis Streets (Syntagma Sq); at the Omonia Sq underground in the Metro concourse and Dionysiou Areopagitou St on the corner of Tzireon St (*Tmr* D6).

The telephone and telegraph system is run by a separate state organisation. *See* **OTE.**

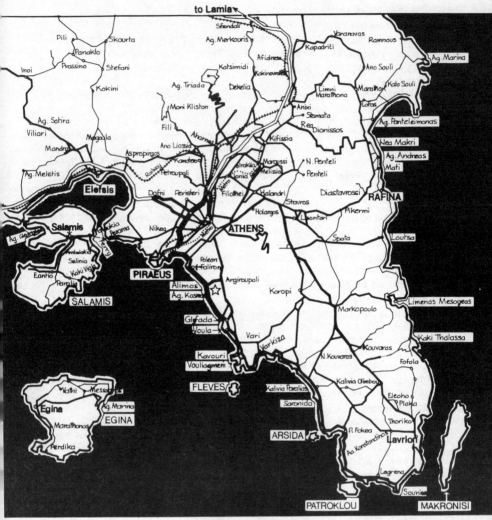

THE ENVIRONS OF ATHENS

Motorway
Road
Railway
Metro
☆ Airport

NORTH

Seven   Athens environs, suburbs, bus & metro routes

PHOTOGRAPHY (Fotografion – ΦΩΤΟΙΓΡΑΦΕΙΟΝ)
If you require photographs for various membership cards, there is an instant photo-booth in the underground concourse beneath Omonia Sq (*Tmr* 2.D3).

SHOPPING HOURS
See **Opening Hours.**

SPORTS FACILITIES
Golf
There is an 18 hole course, the **Glifada Golf Club** close by the East(ern) Airport. Changing rooms, restaurant and refreshment bar.

Swimming
There is a Swimming (and Tennis) Club on Leoforos Olgas (*Tmr* 19.E6), opposite the Zappeion Public Gardens.

The *Hilton Hotel* (*Tmr* G4) has a swimming pool but, if you are not staying there, it will cost the price of a (expensive) meal.
See **Beaches.**

Tennis
There are courts at all the NTOG beaches as well as at the Ag Kosmas athletics centre, close by the West airport.

TAXIS (ΤΑΞΙ)
Used extensively, although a little expensive, but the drivers are, now, generally without scruples. Fares are metered and are costed at about 20 drs per kilometre, but are subject to various surcharges including 10 drs for each piece of baggage, 5-10 drs for hours between midnight and 0600, 100 drs per hour of waiting time and 5 drs for picking up at, or delivering to, public transport facilities.

When standing at a taxi rank they must take your fare, but are not obliged to do so when cruising. The sign **EΛEYΘEPON** indicates they are free for hire.

TELEPHONE
See **OTE.**

TOURIST OFFICE/AGENCIES
See **NTOG** & **Travel Agents.**

TOURIST POLICE (*Tmr* 20.D6)
I understand despite the reorganisation of the service that the Athens headquarters is to remain in operation. They are situated at 7 Sygrou (Leoforos Sygrou/Syngrou/Singrou Av). Open daily 0800 - 2100 hrs, Tel. 923-9224.
Tourist information in English is available from the Tourist police on the telephone, Tel. 171
There are also offices at **Larissis Railway Station**, open 0700 - 2300 hrs, Tel. 821-3574 and the **East Airport**, open 0600 - 2400 hrs, Tel. 981-4093.

TOILETS
Apart from the various bus terminii and the railway stations there is a super public toilet on the south-east corner of Syntagma Sq as there is a pretty grim squatty in the Omonia Sq metro concourse.

The Plaka is well endowed with one at Plateia Plaka, (on Odhos Kidathineon) and another on the Plateia Agora at the other end of Odhos Adrianou. Visitors to Mt Lycabettus will not be caught short and the toilets are spotless.

TRAINS
They arrive at (or depart from) either (a) Larissis Station (Stathmos No. 1) or (b) Peloponissou Station (Stathmos No. 2).

(a) Larissis Station (Stathmos No 1) (*Tmr* B/C1)   Tel. 821-3882

The main, more modern station of the two. Connections to the Western European services and the northern provinces of Central Greece, Thessaly, Macedonia and Thrace.

The National Bank of Greece has a branch in the station building open daily between 0800 - 2000 hrs. Through to the front of the station there is a pavement cafe-bar (a coffee 56 drs) and an elongated square, well more a widening of the road. With the station behind one there is to the right, across the concourse, on the corner, the:-

Hotel Lefkos Pirgos (Class E), 27 Neof. Metaxa/Stathos Larissis   Tel. 821-3765
Directions: As above.

  Seedy looking with double rooms sharing a bathroom starting at 725 drs, rising to 930 drs.

Hotel Nana (Class C), 29 Neof. Metaxa   Tel. 884-2211
Directions: Alongside the *Hotel Lefkos Pirgos*.

  Smarter, well it is C class, with the charges reflecting this eminence. A double room en suite starts off at 1575 drs but for the period between 16th March - 31st October this becomes 1945 drs.

Directly opposite the main station entrance is the

Hotel Oscar (Class B), 25 Samou/Filadelfias   Tel. 883-4215
Directions: As above.

  I hardly dare detail the room rates which for a double kick off at 2515 drs rising to 2960 drs, en suite naturally.

Even early and late in the summer a number of the hardier stretch out on the pavements (and at the *Hotel Oscar's* rates I'm not surprised). Arrivals, even whilst on the train, are bombarded with offers of accommodation, so much so that the touts are a nuisance.

Buses: Trolley-bus No 1 pulls up to the right of the station as do the Nos 2 and 4. The fare to Syntagma Sq is 20 drs.

Advance Booking Office (*Tmr* D/E4)
81 Panepistimiou (Venizelou), opposite the University buildings.

(b) Peloponissou Station (Stathmos No 2) (*Tmr* B1/2)   Tel. 513-1601

The station for trains to the Peloponnese, the ferry connections for some of the Ionian islands and international ferries to Italy from Patras.

Advance Booking Office (*Tmr* C/D2/3)
18 Ag Konstantinou (Ay Konstandinou), west from Omonia Sq.

Tickets: (Peloponissou Station)

The concept behind the acquisition of a ticket is similar to that of a lottery. On buying a ticket, a compartment seat is also allocated, and in theory this is a splendid scheme, but in practice the idea breaks down in a welter of bad-tempered arguments over whom is occupying whose seat. Manners and quaint old-fashioned habits of giving up one's seat to older people and ladies are best avoided. I write this from the bitter experience of offering my seat to elderly Greek ladies only for their husbands to immediately fill the vacant position. Not what one had in mind! Find your seat and stick to it like glue and if you have made a mistake feign madness, admit to being a foreigner, but do not budge.

  The mechanics of buying a ticket takes place in organised bedlam. The ticket-office 'traps' open half an hour prior to the train's departure. Scenes reminiscent of a cup-final crowd develop, with prospective travellers pitching about within the barriers of the ticket hatch, and all this in the space of about 10 metres by 10 metres. To add to the difficulty, at Peloponissou Station, there are two hatch 'slots' and it is anybody's guess which one to select. It really is best to try and steal a march on this 'extra-curricula' activity, diving for a hatch whenever one opens up.

When booking a return journey train ticket to Europe and travelling via Italy ensure the ticket is from Patras, not Athens. (Yes Patras). Then purchase a separate Athens to Patras train ticket which will ensure a traveller gets a seat. A voyager boarding the train with an open ticket will almost surely have to stand for almost the whole of the 4 hour journey. Most Athens-Patras journeys seems to attract an 'Express' train surcharge of some 40 drs which is charged by the train ticket collector.

Incidentally, the general architecture of the Peloponissou building is delightful, especially the ceiling of the main booking-office hall, which is located centrally, under the main clock face. To the left, on entering the building, there is a glass-fronted information box with all the train times listed on the window. The staff manning this desk are extremely helpful and speak sufficient English to pose no problems in communication (the very opposite of the lack-lustre disinterest shown at the NTOG desk in the National Bank of Greece, on Syntagma Sq).

Trains General
Toilets
The station toilets usually, well always, lack toilet paper.

Sustenance (on the trains)
An attendant brings inexpensive drinks and snacks around from time to time and, at major stations on the route, hot snacks are available from platform trolleys.

Railway Head Office (*Tmr* C2)
Hellenic Railways Organisation (OSE) 1-3 Karolou St.   Tel. 522-2491
The far, west end of Ag Konstantinou from Omonia Sq.

Provisions
Shopping in the area of the railway stations is a bit of a task. A bread and a very good pie shop are located in an area to the east of the railway. From Larissis station wander off along Filadelfias into Livaniou or down Liossion St. From Peloponissou station walk down the station approach road southwards, over the railway bridge and up Mezonos or Favierou Streets.

Access to the stations
Bus/Trolley-bus
From the Airport, take the Olympic bus to the down-town terminal at 96-100 Leoforos Sygrou (which for 45 drs is extremely good value). Then catch a bus (Nos. 133, 040, 132, 155, 903 and 161 amongst others) from across the street to Syntagma Sq and a No. 1 trolley-bus to the station via Omonia Sq. It is also possible to walk west from Leoforos Sygrou to the parallel street of Odhos Dimitrakopoulou and catch a No. 1 trolley-bus all the way to the stations.

From Piraeus Port catch the No. 40 (green) bus on Leoforos Vassileos Konstantinou (parallel to the quay) to Syntagma Sq, or the No. 049 from Plateia Themistokleous to Athinas St, close by Omonia Sq.

Metro
The metro station for both railway stations is **ATIKI** from whence ('undergrounding' from the South) dismount and turn right down into the underpass to come out the far or west side of the station on Odhos Liossion. Turn left and walk to the large irregular Plateia Attikis (with the *Hotel Lydia* on the right) and proceed down Domokou St, the road that exits half right on the far side of the square and which spills into Plateia Deligiani edged by Stathmos Larissis. A more long-winded alternative is to take the metro to Omonia Sq, walk west along Ag Konstantinou to Karaiskaki Sq and then up Odhos Deligianni or catch a No. 1 trolley-bus.

Taxi

A taxi is a reasonable indulgence if in a hurry although it must be noted that in the crowded traffic conditions of Athens it can often be quicker to walk than catch a cab.

Station to Station

To get from one to the other, say Larissis to Peloponissou it is necessary to turn right out of the station and, after about 5 mins walk, turn right again over the bridge spanning the railway lines that angles back and round to the right onto the forecourt or plateia in front of Peloponissou. Almost, but not quite, adjacent as some guides put it, if 200 m on a very hot day, laden down with cases seems contiguous.

TRAIN TIMETABLES — Peloponissou Station

It is easy to read the timetable and come to the conclusion that a large number of trains are leaving the station at the same time. On seeing the single-line track, a newcomer cannot be blamed for feeling apprehensive that it will prove difficult to select the correct carriages.

The mystification arises from the fact that the trains are detailed separately from Athens to Corinthos, Mikines, Argos, Tripolis, Pirgos and etc, etc. There is no mention that the railway line is a circular layout, with single trains circumscribing the route and that each place name is simply a stop on the journey.

Making changes for branch lines can be 'exciting'! Stations are labelled in demotic script and there is no understandable announcement from the guard, thus it is easy to fail to make an exit on cue!

Athens : (Stathmos Peloponissou)	Depart	0641, 0830, 1022, 1310, 1542, 2147 hrs
Patras Port :	Arrive	1058, 1215, 1459, 1700, 1959, 0203 hrs

Fares: Athens to Patras 390 drs.

TRAVEL AGENTS

Tourist offices for tickets for almost anything to almost anywhere include:

ABC 59 Stadiou St. Tel. 321-1381
CHAT 4 Stadiou St. Tel. 322-2886
Key Tours 2 Ermou St. Tel. 323-3756
Viking* 3 Filellinon St. Tel. 322-9383
*Probably the agency most highly regarded by students for prices and variety.

International Student & Youth Travel Service (SYTS) 11 Nikis St. Tel. 323-3767 For FIYTO membership. Second floor, open Monday - Friday 0830 - 1900 hrs and Saturday from 0900 to 1400 hrs.

Filellinon and the parallel street of Odhos Nikis to the west of Syntagma Sq are jam packed with tourist agencies and student organisations including one or two express coach and train fare companies.

YOUTH HOSTEL ASSOCIATION
See **Accommodation.**

10 Greek Mainland Ports

Fortune and Hope farewell! I've found the port: you've done with me; go now with sport.

From a Greek epigram

This guide concerns itself with Corfu and the Ionian islands so this chapter is only a resumé of the relevant mainland ports (*See* Illustration 4) from which a traveller can effect a connection with the various islands.

IGOUMENITSA: Epirus Region, NW Greece
Tel. prefix 0665
Not recommended for any more than whatever stop-over is necessary to make the requisite island ferry-boat connections.

A 'frontier' port with almost the whole of Ag Apostolou, the sign-ridden quay road, occupied by 'fast' ferry-boat ticket agencies, which, with the other shops, stay open quite late at night.

The port is really two streets, Ag Apostolou which runs out at the north end of the town, alongside the football stadium, and Odhos Kyprou which parallels the Esplanade in the main body of the town.

Some attempt has been made to beautify the waterfront and there is a pleasant, lineal public garden edging the main road.

THE ACCOMMODATION & EATING OUT
The Accommodation
A number of reasonably priced C & D class hotels and pensions.

Kalami Beach Camping is located at Plataria 4 km south of Igoumenitsa — Tel. 71211/71245. Open March - October.

The Eating Out
Yes! Fast foods and cafe bars all advertising their presence with neon signs.

THE A TO Z OF USEFUL INFORMATION
BANKS
The Commercial Bank
In Ag Apostolou St, the Esplanade road, beyond the main ferry-boat quay. Usual hours but there will be an exchange office open every day and most of the night.

BREAD SHOPS
Close to the bus terminal.

BUSES
The terminal is to the right off Ag Apostolou by the **Commercial Bank**, and left at the small park.

Bus timetable
From Athens to Igoumenitsa (475 km via Rion-Antirion) 100 Kifissou St. Tel. 5125954.
Daily   0630, 1200, 1915 hrs.
Return journey
Daily   0800, 1100, 1815 hrs.
One-way fare: 1510 drs, duration 8½ hrs.

For those travelling south to the island of Lefkas there is now a bus service to Preveza whence connections can be made to Lefkas. For fuller details *See* **Preveza** but briefly departures are as follows:

From Igoumenitsa to Preveza
Daily   1145, 1500 hrs.
Duration 2 hrs.

Igoumenitsa to Parga (50 km)
Daily   0600, 1115, 1315 hrs.
Sunday/holidays 0630, 1700 hrs.
Duration 1 hr.

COMMERCIAL SHOPPING AREA

There are sufficient shops opposite the bus terminal including a dairy and grocer.

FERRY-BOATS

A whopping great quay advertising the internationalism of the set-up (instead of the normal informal Greek chaos) with ticket offices, officials and covered-ways.

A thought provoking sight to motorists is the jumble of damaged cars heaped together to one side at the end of the main quay.

Not only domestic connections but international ferries to the Italian ports of Brindisi, Bari, Otranto and Ancona as well as Bar, Dubrovnik, Rijeka and Split in Yugoslavia.

Ferry-boat timetable: International
Igoumenitsa - Ancona (Italy)

Depart			Arrive			Vessel	
Every	Monday	2030 hrs	Tuesday	2100 hrs	C/F Ionian Victory	Tel. 4129815
Every	Tuesday	0800 hrs	Wednesday	0700 hrs	C/F El Greco	Tel. 7512356
Every	Tuesday	2400 hrs	Thursday	1000 hrs	C/F Princess M	Tel. 4110777
Every	Wednesday	2030 hrs	Thursday	2000 hrs	C/F Ionian Star	Tel. 4129815
Every	Friday	0730 hrs	Saturday	0830 hrs	C/F Ionian Victor	Tel. 4129815
Every	Friday	1000 hrs	Saturday	0830 hrs	C/F El Greco	Tel. 7512356
Every	Saturday	2100 hrs	Sunday	2100 hrs	C/F Princess M	Tel. 4110777
Every	Sunday	0730 hrs	Monday	0800 hrs	C/F Ionian Star	Tel. 412 9815

Return

Every	Monday	2200 hrs	Tuesday	2230 hrs	C/F Ionian Star	
Every	Tuesday	2330 hrs	Wednesday	2330 hrs	C/F Ionian Victory	
Every	Wednesday	1300 hrs	Thursday	1200 hrs	C/F El Greco	
Every	Thursday	2000 hrs	Friday	2200 hrs	C/F Princess M	
Every	Thursday	2300 hrs	Friday	2330 hrs	C/F Ionian Star	
Every	Saturday	2000 hrs	Sunday	2100 hrs	C/F Ionian Victory	
Every	Saturday	2100 hrs	Sunday	2100 hrs	C/F El Greco	
Every	Sunday	2400 hrs	Tuesday	0600 hrs	C/F Princess M	

Igoumenitsa - Bari (Italy)

Depart		Arrive		Vessel	
July:					
Even days	0630 hrs	even days	1630 hrs	C/F Patra Express	Tel. 4181001
Even days	2330 hrs	odd days	1130 hrs	C/F Bari Express	Tel 4181001
August:					
Odd days	0630 hrs	odd days	1630 hrs	C/F Patra Express	Tel. 4181001
Odd days	2330 hrs	even days	1130 hrs	C/F Bari Express	Tel. 4181001
September 2nd - 22nd:					
Even days	0630 hrs	even days	1630 hrs	C/F Patra Express	Tel. 4181001
Return					
July:					
Odd days	1900 hrs	even days	0700 hrs	C/F Bari Express	Tel. 4181001
Even days	2000 hrs	odd days	0900 hrs	C/F Patra Express	Tel. 4181001
August:					
Odd days	2000 hrs	even days	0900 hrs	C/F Patra Express	Tel. 4181001
Even days	1900 hrs	odd days	0700 hrs	C/F Bari Express	Tel. 4181001

September 2nd - 22nd:

Even days	2000 hrs	odd days	0900 hrs	C/F Patra Express	Tel. 4181001

Igoumenitsa - Brindisi (Italy)

Depart		Arrive		Vessel	
Daily	0700 hrs	daily	1600 hrs	C/F Corfu Island or C/F Corfu Sea	Tel. 4125249
Daily	0700 hrs	daily	1700 hrs	C/F Egnatia C/F Appia or C/F Esp. Grecia	Tel. 4174341

August 15th - 30th:

Daily	0730 hrs	daily	1630 hrs	C/F Egli	Tel. 8221285

August:

Even days	0630 hrs	even days	1600 hrs	C/F Eolos	Tel. 8221285

August 1st - 13th:

Odd days	0700 hrs	odd days	1600 hrs	C/F Elli	Tel. 8221285

June - October

Odd days	0630 hrs	odd days	1600 hrs	C/F Eolos	Tel. 8221285

Up to 31st July:

Even days	0630 hrs	even days	1530 hrs	C/F Ionian Glory	Tel. 4129815

June - July & September - October:

Even days	0700 hrs	even days	1600 hrs	C/F Elli	Tel. 8221285

July:

Odd days	0730 hrs	odd days	1700 hrs	C/F Summer Star	Tel. 7232016

August:

Odd days	0630 hrs	odd days	1530 hrs	C/F Ionian Glory	Tel. 4129815

August:

Even days	0730 hrs	even days	1700 hrs	C/F Summer Star	Tel. 7232016

Return

Daily	2215 hrs	daily	0730 hrs	C/F Corfu Island or C/F Corfu Sea	Tel. 4125249
Daily	2230 hrs	daily	0900 hrs	C/F Egnatia, C/F Appia or C/F Esp. Grecia	Tel. 4174341

August 1st - 13th:

Odd days	2100 hrs	even days	0800 hrs	C/F Elli	Tel. 8221285

August 15th - 30th:

Daily	2000 hrs	daily	0630 hrs	C/F Elli	Tel. 8221285

August:

Even days	2100 hrs	odd days	0830 hrs	C/F Eolos	Tel. 8221285

June - July & September - October:

Odd days	2100 hrs	even days	0830 hrs	C/F Eolos	Tel. 8221285
Even days	2100 hrs	odd days	0800 hrs	C/F Elli	Tel. 8221285

June 22nd - July 30th & September 2nd - 14th:

Even days	2200 hrs	odd days	0745 hrs	C/F Ionian Glory	Tel. 4129815

July:

Odd days	2215 hrs	even days	1000 hrs	C/F Summer Star	Tel. 7232016

August:

Odd days	2200 hrs	even days	0745 hrs	C/F Ionian Glory	Tel. 4129815
Even days	2215 hrs	odd days	1000 hrs	C/F Summer Star	Tel. 7323016

Igoumenitsa - Otranto (Italy)

Depart		Arrive			Vessel
Daily except Monday & Sunday	1000 hrs	daily		1900 hrs	C/F Roana

Every Sunday	2100 hrs	every Monday	0630 hrs	C/F Roana	

September 15th - 30th:

Every Tuesday	2100 hrs	every Wednesday	0630 hrs	C/F Roana
Every Thursday	2100 hrs	every Friday	0630 hrs	C/F Roana

Return

Daily except Saturday, Sunday	2230 hrs	daily Monday Sunday	0800 hrs	C/F Roana
Every Saturday	2300 hrs	every Sunday	1000 hrs	C/F Roana

September 15th - 30th:

Every Monday	2300 hrs	every Tuesday	1000 hrs	C/F Roana
Every Wednesday	2300 hrs	every Thursday	1000 hrs	C/F Roana

Igoumenitsa - Bar (Yugoslavia)   Tel 4520244

Depart		**Arrive**		**Vessel**
Every Wednesday	1400 hrs	every Thursday	0430 hrs	C/F Liburnija

September 3rd - October 8th

Every Tuesday	1400 hrs	every Wednesday	0420 hrs	C/F Liburnija

Return

Every Tuesday	2130 hrs	every Wednesday	1300 hrs	C/F Liburnija

September 1st - October 6th

Every Monday	2130 hrs	every Tuesday	1300 hrs	C/F Liburnija

Igoumenitsa - Dubrovnik (Yugoslavia)   Tel. 4520244

Depart		**Arrive**		**Vessel**
Every Wednesday	1400 hrs	every Thursday	0900 hrs	C/F Liburnija
Every Friday	1500 hrs	every Saturday	0800 hrs	C/F Liburnija

July 9th - August 27th:

Every Tuesday	0730 hrs	every Tuesday	2330 hrs	C/F Liburnija

September 3rd - October 8th:

Every Tuesday	1400 hrs	every Wednesday	0900 hrs	C/F Liburnija

Return

Every Monday	1330 hrs	every Tuesday	0600 hrs	C/F Liburnija
Every Tuesday	1700 hrs	every Wednesday	1300 hrs	C/F Liburnija

July 3rd - September 4th:

Every Thursday	2000 hrs	every Friday	1400 hrs	C/F Liburnija

September 1st - October 6th:

Every Monday	1700 hrs	every Tuesday	1300 hrs	C/F Liburnija

Igoumenitsa - Rijeka (Yugoslavia)   Tel. 4520244

Depart		**Arrive**		**Vessel**
Every Tuesday	0730 hrs	every Wednesday	1930 hrs	C/F Liburnija
Every Wednesday	1400 hrs	every Friday	0730 hrs	C/F Liburnija
Every Friday	1500 hrs	every Sunday	0730 hrs	C/F Liburnija

September 3rd - October 8th:

Every Tuesday	1400 hrs	every Thursday	0730 hrs	C/F Liburnija

Return

Every Monday	1800 hrs	every Wednesday	1300 hrs	C/F Liburnija
Every Wednesday	2230 hrs	every Friday	1400 hrs	C/F Liburnija

July 7th - August 25th:

Every Sunday	1800 hrs	every Tuesday	1600 hrs	C/F Liburnija

September 1st - October 6th:

Every Sunday	1800 hrs	every Tuesday	1300 hrs	C/F Liburnija

Igoumenitsa - Split (Yugoslavia)

Tel. 4520244

Depart		Arrive		Vessel
Every Tuesday	0730 hrs	every Wednesday	0745 hrs	C/F Liburnija
Every Wednesday	1400 hrs	every Thursday	1755 hrs	C/F Liburnija
Every Friday	1500 hrs	every Saturday	1755 hrs	C/F Liburnija

September 3rd - October 8th:

Every Tuesday	1400 hrs	every Wednesday	1755 hrs	C/F Liburnija

Return

Every Thursday	1000 hrs	every Friday	1400 hrs	C/F Liburnija

September 1st - October 6th:

Every Monday	0800 hrs	every Tuesday	1300 hrs	C/F Liburnija

Ferry-boat timetable: domestic
Igoumenitsa to Corfu

Daily   0530, 0700, 0900, 1000, 1100, 1200, 1300, 1400, 1500, 1600, 1700, 1800, 1900, 2030, 2200 hrs.

Return

Daily   0600, 0700, 0800, 0900, 1000, 1100, 1200, 1300, 1400, 1500, 1600, 1730, 1900, 2000, 2130 hrs.

One-way fare 275 drs, duration 1 hr 55 mins.

FERRY-BOAT TICKET OFFICES
Oh my goodness yes, any number of them, but be careful. The officials check the tickets carefully and any found sold beneath the statutory listed prices will be confiscated and the unfortunate purchaser made to go and buy correctly priced replacements. Oh dear!

OTE
On the right of Odhos Evangelistrias which is the major street connecting Ag Apostolou and the parallel street of Odhos Kyprou.

POLICE
Tourist
Over the Town police office.

Town
Sited across main road from the waterfront.

POST OFFICE
On the right of Odhos Evangelistrias, next door to the OTE.

TELEPHONE NUMBERS & ADDRESSES
Hospital 15 Filiates St.   Tel. 22205
Tourist Police Ag Apostolou.   Tel. 22302

TRAVEL AGENTS
See **Ferry-boat Ticket Offices.**

PARGA: Epirus Region, NW Greece
Tel. prefix 0684

This small, very picturesque town and port is hunched and spread around the waterfront, crowded in by steep, heavily wooded hillsides. The main town of whitewashed houses winds up one of these hills in a maze of narrow streets and unexpected steps in the fashion of a careless, Cornish fishing village.

The beautiful cove on which the port lies is hemmed in by tall, gnarled, rocky islets. Around the headland, which is topped off by a Norman fort, is a larger bay with sandy shores set at the foot of a backdrop of tiered Olive and Orange trees.

The town has had a convoluted history in which the Venetians, Turks, Russians, French British and Turks all had a hand (in that order), controlling the area until it was reunited with Greece in 1913.

The beauty of the overall scene, a landscape painters dream has ensured that the locale is popular with both Greeks and tourists and therefore crowded and comparatively expensive.

The approach road crosses soft but massive mountains and drops quite steeply to the outskirts of Parga where a left-hand fork leads to a beach and *Parga Camping*.

Road vehicles progress from hereon is now barred by a battery of 'no-entry' signs alongside a small crescent shaped beach, ringed by very large rocks that appear to have been dropped into the sea by a celestial body. The roadway curves and drops sharp right towards the centre of the town, along the waterfront road of Anexartissias St in the middle of which is the small, concrete ferry-boat finger pier.

THE ACCOMMODATION & EATING OUT
The Accommodation
There are a number of rooms and pensions including those of *Mitsoulis, Petros* and *Vassilas* all with doubles at about 800 drs. The two travel agents on the waterfront Esplanade will also suggest alternatives.

Hotels include the C class *Alcyon, Avra*; the D class *Calypso, Paradissos* and *Tourist* as well as the expensive E class *Acropole*.

Parga Camping is down the last left-hand turning of the approach road before Odhos Anexartissias, the Esplanade road. A recommended site close by the sea and open May to the end of October. Tel. 31586. There are 3 other camp sites within 3 km.

The Eating Out
Generally expensive and mainly massed on and around the waterfront. At the left-hand uphill end of the Esplanade (*Fsw*) are two adjacent restaurants with fair offerings. They have raised, shaded patios, across the road above the sea's edge, the benches and tables of which have to be reached by small flights of steps.

THE A TO Z OF USEFUL INFORMATION
BREAD SHOP
The bakery is beyond the *Hotel Paradissos*, in the town.

BUSES
The turn-round is at the widened part of the approach road, where the traffic is barred from further progress.

Bus timetable
From Athens to Parga (500 km) 100 Kifissou Sts.		Tel. 5129252
Daily	0700, 1330, 2000 hrs.	
Return journey		
Daily	0700, 1000, 1815 hrs.	
One-way fare 1450 drs.		

There is a bus service between Igoumenitsa and Preveza (*See* either).

COMMERCIAL SHOPPING AREA
There is a supermarket beyond the *Hotel Paradissos* as well as the normal jumble of shops and stalls scattered about the village.

DISCOS
Two 1960s discos and the more traditional *Funny Bar,* wherein Greek music and dancing.

FERRY-BOATS
For a ferry to thread its way through the rocky surrounds of the small irregular bay appears to be a difficult task, which it may well be.

They moor up at the small quay in the centre of the waterfront. The only domestic connection is on the local ferry-boat plying between Corfu Town and Paxos that stops off at Parga on a 'now and then' basis — now they do, now they don't.

FERRY-BOAT TICKET OFFICES
See **Travel Agents.**

OTE
En route to the village from the bus and vehicle turnround.

PLACES OF INTEREST
Obviously the castle that dominates the town and surrounding coastline must be included in the list if only for the view. Climb the steps from the upper village. Entrance costs 50 drs.

The travel agents offer a fascinating excursion into Greece's mythological past with a boat trip up the river Acheron, that was known as the Styx. This is followed by a walk to the Necromanteion of Ephyra, oracle for the dead, and the Sanctuary of Persephone and Hades. One occasionally day dreams of a particularly disliked relative making the one way trip. . . .

POST OFFICE
In a cluster with the Police station, close by the vehicle park and turnround on the outskirts of the Town.

POLICE
As above.

TRAVEL AGENTS
Two on the Esplanade, one of which is

West Travel, 10 Anexartissias St.   Tel. 31223
and the other

Parga Tours.

PREVEZA: Epirus region NW Greece
Tel. prefix 0682
A bustling, cosmopolitan commercial harbour town situated on the tip of a peninsula at the entrance to the Bay of Amvrakikos. Preveza, whilst not unattractive, has little to commend it to the island traveller but, due to vagaries of the local bus services, an overnight stop may be necessary.

Founded in 290 BC by King Pyrrhu, the town and its surroundings are steeped in history. It is the site of the Roman city of Nicopoli and the remains of an aqueduct, baths, amphitheatre, basilica and several Roman roads are dotted around the area. In common with other towns in the region there was a convoluted series of overlords and up until 1912 it was on the border between Greece and the Ottoman Turkey. The remains of an old Venetian Fort can still be seen.

The town extends northwards from the long east-west quayside road. The ferry from Aktion (across the narrow neck of the bay) ties up at the western end of the Esplanade (*Tmr* 1.B1) while to the east there is the busy commercial port area. There are a number of restaurants and cafes across the road from the quay, together with banks and the Post Office. The main shopping area is located in the street which runs one block back and parallel to the quayside road whilst the police station and bus terminal are located at the north-eastern end of the town.

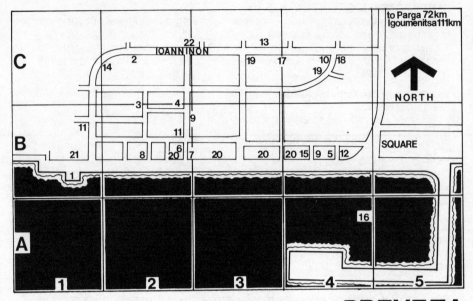

PREVEZA

KEY

1	Aktion Ferry	B1
2	Hotel Preveza City	C2
3	Hotel Minos	B/C2
4	Hotel Dioni	B/C2
5	Hotel Aktaeon	B4
6	Hotel Metropolis	B2
7	Petrol Station	B2/3
8	Petrol Station	B2
9	Banks	B2/3&B4
10	Bus Terminus	C4
11	Bread Shop	B1&B2
12	Cinema	B4
13	Police Station	C3
14	O.T.E.	C1/2
15	Post Office	B4
16	Commercial Port	A4/5
17	Supermarket	C3/4
18	Fish Shop	C4
19	Pharmacy	C4
20	Cafés/Tavernas	B2,3&4
21	Preveza Travel	B1
22	School	C2/3

Eight   Preveza port plan

THE ACCOMMODATION & EATING OUT
The Accommodation
There are few, if any rooms to rent in the town and the majority of the hotels tend to be on the pricey side, catering almost solely for business and commercial travellers.

Hotel Preveza City (*Tmr* 2.C2) (Class C) 81-83 Ioanninon   Tel. 27370
Directions: At the western end of the northern perimeter road, approached by following the street running north from the quayside road, almost opposite the point where the Aktion ferry ties up.
   Smart, comfortable and modern. A double room en suite costs from 1400 drs per night.

Hotel Minos (*Tmr* 3.B/C2) (Class C) 11, 21st Octovriou   Tel. 28424
Directions: From the Aktion ferry walk east and take the street running north beside the Shell petrol station (*Tmr* 8.B2). The hotel lies about 200 yards up on the left-hand side. Modern and comfortable with double rooms from 1400 drs per night en suite.

Hotel Dioni (*Tmr* 4.B/C2) (Class C) 4, I Kalou   Tel. 22269
Directions: On the left-hand side of the street running east opposite the *Hotel Minos.*
   Clean and comfortable with doubles from 1400 per night en suite.

Hotel Aktaeon (*Tmr* 5.B4) (Class C) 1 Kolovou   Tel. 22258
Directions: In the last street off the eastern end of the quayside road prior to the town square.
   Noisy and rather neglected. Doubles sharing from 1050 drs.

Hotel Metropolis (*Tmr* 6.B2) (Class C) 1 Parthenagogiou   Tel. 22235
Directions: On the street beside the Mobil filling station (*Tmr* 7.B2/3) behind and adjoining the cafe on the corner.
   Probably the best value C class hotel in Preveza. Spotlessly clean, simple and friendly. A double room sharing the bathroom from 1050 drs.

There are a number of D and E class hotels.

The Eating Out
There is an abundance of restaurants, tavernas, cafes and bars (as well as a discotheque) on the quayside road which bustles with activity in the evening. It's simply a question of shopping around but they are all fairly pricey.

THE A TO Z OF USEFUL INFORMATION
AIRLINE OFFICE & TERMINUS
There is a local airport on the Aktion side of the bay, but labelled Preveza.

Aircraft timetables
Preveza to Athens
Monday, Wednesday, Friday, Saturday, Sunday   1520 hrs.
From 23rd June additionally
Tuesday, Saturday, Sunday   1645 hrs.

Athens to Preveza
Monday, Wednesday, Friday, Saturday, Sunday   1340 hrs.
From 23rd June additionally
Tuesday, Saturday, Sunday   1520 hrs.
One-way fare 2390 drs, duration 1 hr 20 mins.

BANKS (*Tmr* 9.B2/3 & B4)
There are two, one in the street beside the Mobil station almost opposite the *Hotel Dioni* and another at the eastern end of the quayside road at the end of the cafe strip.

BEACHES
None in the town itself but there are several sandy beaches to the east of the town, further round the bay.

BUSES
There are daily services to Athens, Igoumenitsa and the surrounding towns from the main bus terminus at the eastern end of the northern perimeter road (*Tmr* 10.C4).

Bus timetables
From Athens, 100 Kifissou Sts.   Tel. 5129252
Daily   0700, 1330, 2000 hrs.
Return journey
Daily   0915, 1300, 1830 hrs.
One-way fare 1310 drs, duration 7 hrs.

Preveza to Arta:
Daily   0730, 1000, 1230, 1430, 1630 hrs.

Preveza to Ioannina:
Daily   0600, 0715, 0900, 1030, 1300, 1445, 1530, 1730, 1830 hrs.

Preveza to Igoumenitsa:
Daily   1100, 1515 hrs.

Preveza to Parga:
Daily   0630, 1045, 1415, 2000 hrs.

BOOKSELLERS
None.

BREAD SHOPS (*Tmr* 11.B1 & B2)
One on the corner of the street behind the *Hotel Metropolis*. Another on the left-hand side of the street running up from the quayside road, opposite the point where the Aktion ferry ties up.

CINEMA (*Tmr* 12.B4)
Beyond the *Hotel Aktaeon* at the eastern end of the quayside road.

COMMERCIAL SHOPPING AREA
In the roads and interconnecting streets running behind the quayside road. There is a supermarket (*Tmr* 17.C3/4) on the perimeter road diagonally across from the police station and a fish shop (*Tmr* 18.C4) further along the same road, on the right-hand side, just beyond the bus terminus.

FERRY-BOAT QUAY (*Tmr* 1.B1)
At the western end of the quayside road. The ferry to Aktion operates at 30 minute intervals from 0600 to 2200 hrs and hourly between 2300 - 0600 hrs, takes 10 mins and costs some 25 drs. The return journey (Aktion to Preveza) operates to the same periodicity but 10 minutes past the hour.
   A service is rumoured to operate direct to Lefkas from Preveza during the height-of-summer months.

FERRY-BOAT TICKET OFFICES
From the kiosk on the quayside close by where the ferries tie up or, if closed, on the ferry itself.

MEDICAL CARE
A pharmacy (*Tmr* 19.C4).

NTOG
None but for inquiries *See* **Police.**

OTE (*Tmr* 14.C1/2)
On the right, at the top of the street running up from the western end of the quayside road, opposite the ferry-boat quay.

POLICE (*Tmr* 13.C3)
On the left, halfway along the northern perimeter road of Odhos Ioanninon.

POST OFFICE (*Tmr* 15.B4)
At the eastern end of the quayside road beyond the cafe-bar/taverna gauntlet.

PORT — COMMERCIAL (*Tmr* 16.A4/5)
At the far right of the harbour (*Sbo*).

TAXIS
Telephone Nos. 28030, 22887, 28470.

TRAVEL/TOURIST OFFICES (*Tmr* 21.B1)
Preveza Travel
Opposite the Aktion ferry-boat quay, provides information on air schedules to and from Athens and boat excursions.

The Lefkas connection (via Preveza & Igoumenitsa)

During the height-of-summer months there is a splendid caique/trip-boat service operating out of Vassiliki, Lefkas connecting with the islands of Ithaca and Cephalonia but as has been mentioned, Lefkas is the least accessible of the Ionian islands, from the point of view of conventional ferry-boat, inter-island travel. The journey between Lefkas and the northern islands of Paxos and Corfu is no less arduous, despite their relative proximity, than the trek from the southern islands. In view of the lack of any direct ferry-boat connections between Lefkas and either of the two aforementioned islands, it is necessary to return to the mainland and make a fairly extensive bus journey to the mainland port of Igoumenitsa.

At the peak of the summer season there are very strong rumours of a ferry link between Lefkas and the busy mainland port of Preveza. However for most of the year it is necessary to take the ferry from Preveza across the harbour entrance to Aktion and then bus to Lefkas Town. The Lefkas bus to Aktion leaves from the main bus station and the thirty minute journey passes through a rather unattractive marshy coastal plain past the small military/civilian airport which serves Lefkas. The Aktion-Preveza ferry deposits travellers at the left-hand end of the town quay (facing the port) and it is quite a hike from here to the town bus station from whence the Igoumenitsa bus departs.

There are only two buses a day to Igoumenitsa and the early morning bus from Lefkas to Aktion connects with the 1515 hrs bus. Travellers wishing to catch the 1100 hrs bus to Igoumenitsa, and so arrive at a reasonable hour, are advised to take a taxi from Lefkas to the Aktion side of the ferry-boat connection. Those who miss the last bus, will have to reconcile themselves to a night in Preveza which, like Igoumenitsa, has little to commend it to the transient voyager.

The bus between Preveza and Igoumenitsa takes about 2 hours and passes through some truly beautiful and, at times, dramatic countryside. From Preveza, the bus travels east following the line of the bay before swinging north and climbing up over the densely wooded coastal mountains. It then drops down to the shores of the Ionian Sea, which it follows for several miles to Loutsa before cutting inland again across a fertile plain to Kanalaki, the first sizeable community since leaving Preveza. The route then continues up a long valley, on which sheep graze, there are fields of corn, olives and cotton whilst roses and lime trees grow in profusion in cottage gardens. Beyond the village of Gliki, the road crosses a rickety Bailey bridge over the oft swollen Acheron river. The narrow valley is edged with rugged, steep scree slopes, cloud-capped mountains to the right and, to the left, gentle, rolling hills resembling a colony of slumbering hippos.

At the end of the valley, the route joins the road from Parga after which it switchbacks over the lower slopes of the mountains, passing through the village of Paramithia, before descending steeply through a pass to a wide plain. Here it connects with the main Ioannina to Igoumenitsa highway from whence it follows the line of the wide Thiamis river before gently climbing again, over red sandstone to yet another fertile valley and finally over a further range of hills before dropping gently down to the sea and the port of Igoumenitsa.

The bus station is in the centre of the town and the quayside is reached by continuing down the sloping street. The ferries to Corfu and Paxos tie-up at the near, southern end of the quay.

ASTAKOS: Epirus region, NW Greece
Tel. prefix 0646
Worth a mention as in 1984 a new, regular, all-year-round ferry service was inaugurated between Astakos and the islands of Cephalonia and Ithaca.

Hotels include the D class *Akti Beach* and the *Byron.*

BUSES
Buses journey to Agrinion from whence connections can be caught to Athens, the island of Lefkas and other mainland ports including Preveza.

Bus timetable
Athens to Agrinion, 100 Kifissou St.   Tel. 5129293
Daily   0600 and every hour, on the hour, to 1800, 2000, 2200 hrs.
Return journey
Daily   0600, 0700, 0830, 0900, 1000, 1100, 1200, 1300, 1400, 1600, 1700,
                               1800, 1900, 2200 hrs.
One-way fare 1,000 drs, duration 5 hrs.

Ferry-boat timetable
Astakos - Vathi (Ithaca)
Daily   1400 hrs.
Return
Daily   1100 hrs.
One-way fare 363 drs, duration 1¾ hrs.

Astakos - Ag Evfimia (Cephalonia)
Daily   1400, 2030 hrs.
Return
Daily   0900, 1800 hrs.
One-way fare 490 drs, duration 3½ hrs.

Hotels include the D class *Akti Beach* and the *Byron.*

PATRAS (Patra, Patre, Patrai): Peloponnese
Tel. prefix 061
RELIGIOUS HOLIDAYS & FESTIVALS
Include: the Patras Carnival which lasts for some three weeks in February and early March. Officially starts 10 days before Lent. Great goings on and good fun. On the 30th November there is a feast to celebrate St. Andrew, the city's patron saint.

GENERAL
Bearing in mind that Patras is the third largest city in Greece, as well as being a commercial centre, seaport and railway terminal it is not surprising that the place has an industrial, cosmopolitan bustling, noisy ambiance. The majority of immediate needs are spread along Odhos Othonos Amalias, across the way from, and parallel to the quay wall

alongside which the main town railway line ranges. To add to the confusion a shunting train shares the Esplanade road with the confused traffic of cars and humans. Keep an eye and ear open.

The modern city was rebuilt in the grid layout in the 1820s, after the Turks had razed it to the ground in 1821. It is quite possible that any stop-off will only be to change ferries or disembark from bus or train to embark on a ferry.

The key to the town is the Esplanade quayside road Othonos Amalias, which sweeps from the north end of Patras' waterfront, where it is named Iroon Politechnou, past the North Harbour, (*Tmr* 1.A2), the NTOG offices (*Tmr* 2.A2), the Athens bus terminal (*Tmr* 3.A/B3) and at the end of which is the Railway Station (*Tmr* 4.A4). The railway station is almost adjacent to Plateia Trion Symmahon which palm-tree'd square, edged by cafes, restaurants and newsagents, is the hub of Patras.

The Tourist police (*Tmr* 6.A/B4) are just across the road from the railway station. One block back in Odhos Agios Andreou is the Port police office (*Tmr* 5.B4) as is another bus terminal for Pelopponnese buses. Beyond the Square of Trion Symmahon, in a south-east direction, Odhos Agios Nikolaou runs straight and true to a flight of steps to one side of the Acropolis of Patras.

After dark, Plateia Trion Symmahon comes alive and families stroll through the square whilst others sit under the trees drinking coffee or ouzo served from one of the many little cafe's on the periphery. A pleasant after dinner walk is to perambulate along the jetty (*Tmr* A4) opposite the square watching the old men fishing — no rod, just a line resting through their fingers using bread as bait. There is a cafe/snack bar at the end of the quay which serves excellent pizzas for about 350 drs.

South along the Leoforos Othonos Amalias stretches past the private yacht moorings to the South Harbour.

THE ACCOMMODATION & EATING OUT
The Accommodation
There are a profusion of rooms, pensions and hotels on Agios Nikolaou and the parallel Ermou St. Being an epicentre for travellers, accommodation tends to be more expensive with 'C' class hotels costing, on average, 1500 drs for a double room and 'D' class 1000 drs.

Hotel Adonis (*Tmr* 7.B3) (Class C) Zaimi/9 Kapsali Sts.   Tel. 225260
Directions: Behind the Athens bus terminal by the English church of Agios Andreas in the area where, across the Esplanade road, the quayside wall of the North Harbour turns sharply.

Clean and modern with a double room costing from 1340 drs en suite.

Hotel Splendid (*Tmr* 8.A/B 3/4) (Class D) 28 Agios Andreou   Tel. 276521
Directions: Almost opposite the railway station. Splendid it may have been once but alas not now. . . . However it is clean and acceptable for an overnight stop.

Hotel Acropole (*Tmr* 9.A/B3/4) (Class C) 39 Othonos Amalias   Tel. 279809
Directions: Virtually next door to the Hotel Splendid and rather more modern and (naturally) expensive. Has triple rooms for 2400 drs a night.

Hotel Delphi (Class D) 63 Agios Andreou   Tel. 273050
Directions: Bordering the Plateia Trion Symmahon (*Tmr* A/B4). Depending on your viewpoint, unclean and noisy, or dirty and downright clamorous.

No single rooms as such but a double let as single costs from 480 drs a night and doubles, both sharing a bathroom, from 690 drs.

Hotel Mediterranee (*Tmr* 10.B4) (Class C) 18 Ag Nikolaou/Riga Fereou Sts Tel. 279602
Directions: From Plateia Trion Symmahon straight on up Agios Nikolaou St and on the right, in the corner of the second block up.

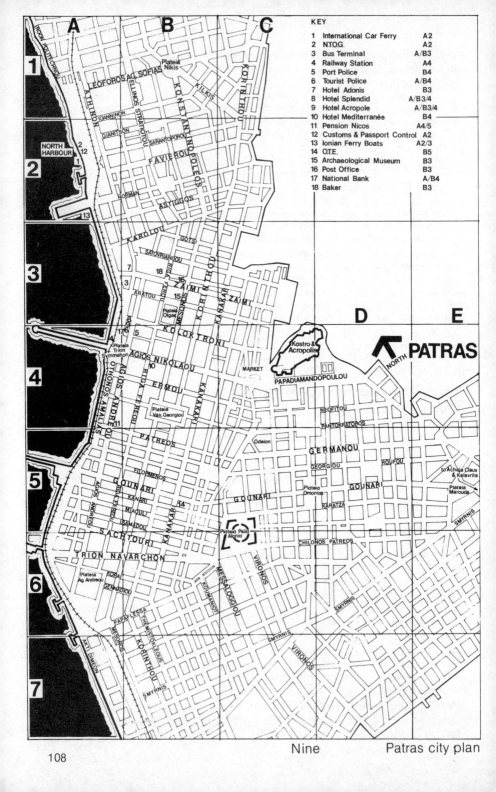

Nine   Patras city plan

Well appointed and comfortable with doubles en suite costing 1540 drs per night.

Nicos Pension (*Tmr* 11.A4/5) 3 Patreos/121 Ag Andreou .... Tel. 276183
Directions: South or right (*Sbo*) from Plateia Trion Symmahon along Ag Andreous St and on the corner of the third turning left.

Accommodating (sorry) and helpful. Single, double and rooms for 3, hot showers, breakfast, snacks and a bar. A room for two starts off at about 800/900 drs.

Youth Hostel 68 Iroon Politechnou St   Tel. 427278
Directions: Turn left on leaving any ferry and proceed along the quayside northwards some 800 or 900 metres. The old but restored Victorian style house was once used by the Germans during the Second World War as an HQ.

Inexpensive but cramped, cheap meals and laundry facilities.

CAMPING
Agia-Patras Camping   Tel. 424131
An NTOG site five kilometres north from Patras situated at Agia Patron on the coast road towards Rio close to a bus stop. Pleasantly located by the sandy seashore with lawns, trees, car parking, showers, laundry, a bar, restaurant and shop.

The Eating Out
Tavernas and restaurants are grouped along and around Othonos Amalias, Agios Nikolaou and Plateia Trion Symmahon (what isn't?) But the average cost of a meal is expensive. For instance bread, tzatziki, moussaka, a Greek salad, retsina and coffee for one costs about 650 drs.

Another good hunting ground for tavernas is in the area of the upper-town market, two-thirds of the way along Odhos Agios Nikolaou, on the way to the Acropolis.

THE A TO Z OF USEFUL INFORMATION
BANKS (*Tmr* 17.A/B4)
The National Bank of Greece
Changes Eurocheques and is conveniently situated on the edge of Plateia Trion Symmahon. There are other major banks in the area.

BEACHES
None in town, it being necessary to go five kilometres north along the coast to Agia Patron (where there is also an NTOG seaside campsite).

BREAD SHOPS
A baker on the left of Odhos Zaimi (*Tmr* 18.B3).

BUSES
Apart from the main routes to Athens, Ioannina, Volos and Thessaloniki; down the west coast of The Peloponnese for Killini, Pirgos, Pilos and Kalamata, there are local services to Rio. The major terminal (*Tmr* 3.A/B3) is situated across the road from the waterfront where the quay takes a left turn. There is an information office in the terminal which opens at 0700 hrs, and the staff speak basic English. The service to Killini is direct and connects with the ferry to the islands of Zakynthos and Cephalonia.

Bus timetables
Athens to Patras: 100 Kifissou St.   Tel. 5124914
Daily   0630, 0730, 0815, 0900, 0945, 1030, 1130, 1230, 1330, 1415, 1500,
                             1545, 1630, 1715, 1800, 1900, 2000, 2115 hrs.
Return journey
Daily   0630 every hour to 2130 hrs.
One-way fare 680 drs, duration 3½ hrs.
Note: most of the ferries which dock at Patras make connections with buses to Athens, a four-hour journey crossing the Corinth Canal.

Patras to Killini Port
Daily   0915*, 1445 hrs.
One-way fare 220 drs, duration 1½ hrs.
Return journey
Daily   0900, 1100, 1500 hrs.
*Connects with 1200 hrs ferry to Zakynthos.

BOOKSELLERS
Papachristou at 16 Agios Nikolaou and **Calitas** on Ermou St.

COMMERCIAL SHOPPING AREA
Sited in the upper town, halfway along Odhos Agios Nikolaou. There are a number of small shops on Odhos Gounari (*Tmr* B/C5).

CUSTOMS (*Tmr* 12.A2)
Customs and passports in the one single storey block, at the north end of the harbour where the international ferries berth.

FERRY-BOATS
From the North and South harbours, with the International (*Tmr* 1.A2) and Ionian (*Tmr* 13.A2/3) ferry-boat terminals at the North Harbour end of the waterfront.

Ferry-boat timetables: International
International:
Patras - Ancona (Italy)

Depart		Arrive		Vessel	
Every Monday	1200 hrs	Tuesday	2100 hrs	C/F Ionian Victory	Tel. 4129815
Every Monday	2100 hrs	Wednesday	0800 hrs	C/F Medit. Sea	Tel. 4173001
Every Monday	2330 hrs	Wednesday	0700 hrs	C/F El Greco	Tel. 7512356
Every Tuesday	2100 hrs	Thursday	0800 hrs	C/F Medit. Star	Tel. 4173001
Every Tuesday	2400 hrs	Wednesday	0800 hrs	C/F Princess M	Tel. 4110777
Every Wednesday	1200 hrs	Thursday	2000 hrs	C/F Ionian Star	Tel. 4129815
Every Wednesday	2100 hrs	Friday	0800 hrs	C/F Medit. Sky	Tel. 4173001
Every Thursday	2200 hrs	Saturday	0830 hrs	C/F Ionian Victory	
Every Thursday	2330 hrs	Saturday	0830 hrs	C/F El Greco	
Every Friday	0200 hrs	Saturday	1000 hrs	C/F Medit. Sea	
Every Saturday	0200 hrs	Sunday	1000 hrs	C/F Medit. Star	
Every Saturday	1200 hrs	Sunday	2100 hrs	C/F Princess M	
Every Saturday	2200 hrs	Monday	0800 hrs	C/F Ionian Star	
Every Sunday	1300 hrs	Monday	2000 hrs	C/F Medit. Sky	

Return

Every Monday	2200 hrs	Wednesday	0800 hrs	C/F Ionian Star
Every Monday	2400 hrs	Wednesday	0800 hrs	C/F Medit. Sky
Every Tuesday	2330 hrs	Thursday	0900 hrs	C/F Ionian Victory
Every Wednesday	1300 hrs	Thursday	2000 hrs	C/F El Greco
Every Wednesday	1300 hrs	Thursday	2200 hrs	C/F Medit. Sea
Every Thursday	1300 hrs	Friday	2200 hrs	C/F Medit. Star
Every Thursday	2000 hrs	Saturday	0700 hrs	C/F Princess M
Every Thursday	2300 hrs	Saturday	0800 hrs	C/F Ionian Star
Every Friday	2100 hrs	Sunday	0800 hrs	C/F Medit. Sky
Every Saturday	2000 hrs	Monday	0700 hrs	C/F Ionian Victory
Every Saturday	2100 hrs	Monday	0700 hrs	C/F El Greco
Every Saturday	2100 hrs	Monday	0800 hrs	C/F Medit. Sea

Patras - Bari (Italy)

Depart		Arrive		Vessel	
July:					
Odd days	2100 hrs	even days	1630 hrs	C/F Patra Express	Tel. 4181001
Even days	1700 hrs	odd days	1130 hrs	C/F Bari Express	"

August:

Odd days	1700 hrs	even days	1130 hrs	C/F Bari Express	"
Even days	2100 hrs	odd days	1630 hrs	C/F Patra Express	"

September:

Odd days	2100 hrs	even days	1630 hrs	C/F Patra Express	"

Return

July:

Odd days	1900 hrs	even days	1400 hrs	C/F Bari Express	"
Even days	2000 hrs	odd days	1700 hrs	C/F Patra Express	"

August:

Odd days	2000 hrs	even days	1700 hrs	C/F Patra Express	"
Even days	1900 hrs	odd days	1400 hrs	C/F Bari Express	"

September:

Even days	2000 hrs	odd days	1700 hrs	C/F Patra Express	"

Patras - Brindisi (Italy)

Depart		Arrive		Vessel	
Daily	1700 hrs	daily	0830 hrs	C/F Appia or C/F Castalia	Tel. 4174341
Daily	2200 hrs	daily	1530 hrs	C/F Atlas III, IV	Tel. 4181095
Daily	2200 hrs	daily	1700 hrs	C/F Egnatia, C/F Appia or C/F Esp. Grecia	Tel. 4174341
Daily	2215 hrs	daily	1600 hrs	C/F Corfu Island or C/F Corfu Sea	Tel. 4125249

June 17th - July 31st & September

Odd days	2030 hrs	even days	0930 hrs	C/F Flavia	Tel. 4520135

August:

Odd days	2130 hrs	even days	1600 hrs	C/F Eolos	Tel. 822185

June 21st - July 31st & September 1st - 13th:

Odd days	2130 hrs	even days	1530 hrs	C/F Ionian Glory	Tel. 4129815

June - October

Even days	2130 hrs	odd days	1600 hrs	C/F Eolos	Tel. 8221285

July:

Even days	2200 hrs	odd days	1700 hrs	C/F Summer Star	Tel. 7232016

August:

Even days	2030 hrs	odd days	0930 hrs	C/F Flavia	Tel. 4520135
Even days	2130 hrs	odd days	1530 hrs	C/F Ionian Glory	Tel. 4129815
Odd days	2200 hrs	even days	1700 hrs	C/F Summer Star	Tel. 7232016

Return:

Daily	2000 hrs	daily	1300 hrs	C/F Appia or C/F Castalia	Tel. 4174341
Daily	2130 hrs	daily	1530 hrs	C/F Atlas III, IV	Tel. 4181095
Daily	2215 hrs	daily	1600 hrs	C/F Corfu Island or C/F Corfu Sea	Tel. 4125249
Daily	2230 hrs	daily	1800 hrs	C/F Egnatia, C/F Appia, or C/F Esp. Grecia	Tel. 4174341

June 18th - July 30th & September 2nd - 22nd:

Even days	2000 hrs	odd days	1100 hrs	C/F Flavia	Tel. 4520135

August:

Even days	2100 hrs	odd days	1700 hrs	C/F Eolos	Tel. 8221285

June - October:

Odd days	2100 hrs	even days	1700 hrs	C/F Eolos	Tel.. 8221285

June 22nd - July 30th & September 2nd - 14th:
Even days   2200 hrs odd days   1630 hrs C/F Ionian Glory   Tel. 4129815

July:
Odd days   2215 hrs even days   1700 hrs C/F Summer Star   Tel. 7232016

August:
Odd days   2000 hrs even days   1100 hrs C/F Flavia   Tel. 4520135
Odd days   2200 hrs even days   1630 hrs C/F Ionian Glory   Tel. 4129815
Even days   2215 hrs odd days   1700 hrs C/F Summer Star   Tel. 7232016

Ferry-boat timetable: Domestic

Depart	Departure time	Ferry-boat	Ports/Islands of Call
Daily	1330 hrs	C/F Argostoli and/or C/F Kefallinia	Sami (Cephalonia), Vathi (Ithaca)
Thursday*	2330 hrs	C/F Ionian Glory	Sami (Cephalonia), Vathi (Ithaca), Gaios† (Paxos), Corfu

* This connection increases to every even day at the height of the summer.
† Well it should stop-off at Paxos but check.
One-way fares, Patras to Sami   850 drs : duration, 3½ hrs
                          Vathi   850 drs :   5 hrs
                          Gaios   1450 drs :   9 hrs
                          Corfu   1450 drs :   10¼ hrs

Remember ferry-boat timetables are subject to a number of variables which include the season, the availability of boats and changes in planned schedules from year to year. It is necessary to check, double check and check again.

FERRY-BOAT TICKET OFFICES
Lie in profusion along the Esplanade, across the road from the quay, mostly in the area between the Railway Station and the North Harbour.

NTOG (*Tmr* 2.A2)
In the new complex at the North Harbour, as are the Customs and Passport controls.

OTE (*Tmr* 14.B5)
On the corner of Odhos Gounari and Kanakari.

PLACES OF INTEREST
The Acropolis (*Tmr* C4)
At the top of Ag Nikolaou St are the huge flight of access steps. A fort was built in the early Middle Ages on the site of the ancient Acropolis and has been the subject of much alteration over the years.

The Odeion (*Tmr* C5)
To the south-west of the Acropolis, or immediate left (*Fsw*), is the theatre, re-discovered in the 1800s. Subject of heavy 'restoration' due to the acquisitive nature of local builders who used much of the original stonework for their own jobs!.

Archaeological Museum (*Tmr* 15.B3) Aratou St, Plateia Olgas
Three blocks back from the quayside. Not outstanding.

The Church of Agios Andreas (*Tmr* A6)
Overlooking Plateia Andreou at the far south-west end, down around the corner of the quay front. A modern but colourful church in honour of St Andrew, martyred on a crucifix in the form of an X, and repository of his gold and silver encased head.

Achaia Clauss
Admittedly a few kilometres from Patras but the site of the well-known winery that 'grapes'

some well known bottles. Good for a wine-tasting sojourn.

POST OFFICE (*Tmr* 16.B3)
On Odhos Zaimi near the corner with Mesonos St.

POLICE
Tourist (*Tmr* 6.A/B4).
On the town side of the quay road in the area of the Railway Station, to the north side of Trion Symmahon Square.

Port (*Tmr* 5.B4)
Same area, one block back.

TELEPHONE NUMBERS & ADDRESSES

NTOG	Tel. 420304/5
Hospital	Tel. 222812
Tourist Police	Tel. 220902/3

TRAINS
Railway Station (*Tmr* 4.A4)
Bounded by the quayside and Odhos Othonos Amalias, diagonally opposite Plateia Trion Symmahon. There is an information office inside the booking hall (open daily 0800 - 1300 hrs) where the young lady speaks reasonable English.

Train timetables
Patras to Kavasila Junction (for Killini port*)
Daily   1100, 1220, 1508, 1700, 2000, 0205 hrs.
One-way fare 180 drs, duration about 1 ½ hrs.

Patras to Athens:
Daily   0815, 1059, 1349, 1700, 1858, 0205 hrs.
Duration: 3 hrs 20 mins - 3 hrs 40 mins.

*See Killini (next port description) for connection details between Kavasila and the Port.

YOUTH HOSTEL
See **Accommodation.**

KILLINI (Kilini, Kyllini): Peloponnese
Tel. prefix 0623
A rather scruffy, fly-blown if not god-forsaken port but the only ferry-boat connection to the island of Zakynthos as well as a link with the better served Cephalonia.

ARRIVAL BY BUS
Buses pull up in Killini on the ferry-boat quay and the ferry ticket office is the little kiosk on the left-hand side (*Fsw*).

Another method of attaining Killini port is:-

ARRIVAL BY TRAIN
Really a story on its own, for the journey to Killini involves an interesting ride on the Athens to Pirgos train (*See* Athens for further details). This entails a change for Killini at Kavasila which incidentally is not detailed on most of the official small-scale maps. It is vital to realise that the train has arrived at the railway junction of Kavasila for it is easy to miss and proceed on round the Peloponnese. The railway halt (the word 'terminus' would give a false impression of grandeur), and the associated railway works are reminiscent of scenes of the South American railways so beautifully portrayed in the film **Butch Cassidy and The Sundance Kid** — dusty, desolate, deserted and dilapidated. You now should have the picture.

113

The branch line train lurks in the siding usually with the odd chicken hopping in and out of the drivers cab. The driver, clients and friends may well be found playing cards or backgammon on rickety tables and stools scattered about on the actual railway line. Travellers can be forgiven for not realising that the seemingly immobile piece of machinery is the passport and carriage to the shores of Killini, but there you go. . . .

The Station Master is a short but important man topped off with a red-banded, peaked hat. Unfortunately, he speaks no English and loses interest as well as concentration after a verbal exchange of any length. He also appears to be the ticket collector, station clerk and general factotum.

The train hurtles down the single line track, stopping at the occasional halt, finally finishing up at the deserted end-of-the-line station of Killini. It would appear the train occasionally proceeds on to the actual port quay, but on what basis I cannot advise.

On descending from the train, take off diagonally to the right across the sandy station environs, left up a hedgerowed lane then right spilling out on to the sprawling, rather disjointed layout that is the port and town. On the right is the huge quay with the town straggling away to the left.

The ferries moor up stern-on to the outside or sea face of the wall whilst the harbour formed by the upside down 'L' shaped quay is the home port for a fair number of medium sized, high prowed and sterned fishing boats.

On the approach road to the quay area there are a couple of hotels on the left, but even the C class one requires some 1700 drs for a double room. Take my advice and board the ferry as soon as you can.

An NTOG campsite is shown at and named after Killini but it is situated about 5 km away at Vartholomia so may well be of no practical use for an overnight stay.

Ferry-boat timetables
Killini to Poros (Cephalonia)
Daily	1230, 1730, 2130 hrs.
Return	
Daily	0900, 1500, 1900 hrs.

One-way fare 445 drs, duration 1½ hrs.

Killini to Zakynthos
Daily	0800, 1000, 1200, 1400, 1600, 1800, 2000, 2200 hrs.
Return	
Daily	0600, 0800, 1000, 1200, 1400, 1600, 1800, 2000 hrs.

One-way fare 345 drs, duration 1¼ hrs.

PART THREE
11 Introduction to the Ionian Islands

Compared with other Greek island groups not only are the Ionian islands widely spread out but they are off the western coast of the Greek mainland, set out in the sparkling blue Ionian Pelagos. Inter-island travel is not always easy, it being more difficult to get from say Zakynthos to Cephalonia than from Italy or Athens to Corfu.

The islands grouped together and described in this second edition include Corfu, Paxos, AntiPaxos, Lefkas, Cephalonia, Ithaca and Zakynthos.

It is usual to find Kithira included in guide books of this grouping, but I have omitted the island as it has never been considered one of the Ionian other than as an administrative manoeuvre during a period of colonial administration. Perhaps more importantly, Kithira cannot be reached directly from any of the other Ionian islands. It is arguable that Lefkas is, strictly speaking, not an island. The ancient cutting separating Lefkas from the mainland is a man-made channel, excavated in the fifth century BC and deepened in the nineteenth century AD.

Scheduled ferry-boat transport between the islands and the mainland is reasonably easy, with the exceptions of Zakynthos (from which island it is necessary to return to the mainland in order to reach the other islands) and Lefkas (which must be reached from the mainland, no inter-island ferry-boats making the connection).

Air travel can be used to reach Corfu, Cephalonia and Zakynthos. There is also an airport at Preveza, (well really Aktion on the mainland) from which Lefkas can be attained. Additionally various bus services and the Peloponnese train circuit make connections using the ferry-boat links. However, the frequency of all the services depends on the time of year. Outside the months of June, July, August and September schedules may only operate two or three times a week and some are suspended altogether. Hydrofoils (Flying Dolphins) may still connect the mainland port of Patras to Cephalonia and Zakynthos during the summer months.

Owing to their location on the western side of the mainland, the Ionian islands do not constantly reflect Turkish historical intrusion. The usual medieval Byzantine influence is blended with that of Venice as well as, due to the expansionist nature of the European Colonial powers, France and the United Kingdom. The Cantades, a Venetian based folk music, is one of the pointers to the different route to the twentieth century taken by the Ionian islands (as compared to the Aegean islands) and is a very welcome change to the ubiquitous bouzouki.

As a result of the earthquakes that have devastated the islands over the ages much of historical note has been damaged or destroyed beyond practical use, serving only as a basis for archaeological enquiry. Corfu, Paxos and Lefkas have suffered less, but Cephalonia, Ithaca and Zakynthos lie adjacent to a geographical fault or faults and have experienced a number of sizeable earthquakes in the last four or five hundred years. The last, most serious tremors in 1953 destroyed up to 70 per cent of the last three island's buildings. This explains the lack of old houses and conversely the rather twentieth century, prefabricated look of recent building replacements, which have been constructed with an eye to withstanding future seismic disturbances rather than aesthetic considerations. A pity, but practical.

Naturally, a sizeable chunk of the Ionians prosperity is now related to tourism, but there is a very strong agricultural prop to their economy, based on vines, olives, currants, almonds, vegetables, dairy herds, sheep and goats whilst commercially, shipping has and does play an important part in the various budgets.

The most likely member of the wild life family to bother a tourist is the mosquito, although the islands do sport the occasional jackal, and snakes are comparatively common but are not renowned for any poisonous powers. Care should be taken if marching about in wild countryside, not only for snakes which seem much more interested in evading one's approach than in any aggressive intent, but also in respect of the very seldom seen scorpion. Bird life takes in golden orioles, hoopoes, kingfishers and birds of prey including buzzards, kestrels, the golden eagle and osprey. Turtles come ashore on certain southern Zakynthos beaches to lay their eggs at the appropriate season.

The islands are exceptionally green compared to their Aegean counterparts and Pine, Olive and Cypress trees are abundant. Underfoot vegetation, including bracken, is thick and lush, even at the height of the hottest summer months. One of the reasons for the luxurious nature of the flora is the comparatively heavy rainfall experienced in the winter months. Even in the summer season it is not unusual to experience short, heavy and sometimes prolonged rainstorms which are occasionally accompanied by the most spectacular lightning and deafening thunder. But it is 'warm' rain.

Naturally, due to the connections with Homer's Odyssey, the islands have received more than their fair share of mythological and archaeological attention. During the period between 1800 and the early 1900s, it must have been difficult to avoid tripping over wild-eyed chaps, wielding trowels and shovels and every so often shouting 'Eureka' (or the archaeological equivalent). Despite all this scholarly activity certain Homeric questions and various island claims to this, or that have not been finally clarified or unequivocally substantiated. If anything, this has saved possibly embarrassing inter-island strife breaking out, and they can each claim that which suits them, with various amounts of 'tongue in cheek'.

The Corinthians were in occupation of the islands during the eighth century BC, but by the sixth century BC, Corfu decided to go it alone and won the subsequent sea-battle with the Corinthians. During the fifth to third centuries BC, Athens and the Peloponnese (in the Spartan camp) had a long, drawn out scrap, with Athens gaining the support of the Ionian islanders.

The Romans were invited to take over the administration of Corfu about 230 BC and slowly, during the next hundred years, took over the rest of the Ionian. All was fine until the Romans decided to have their own internecine squabbles, into which the various islands were drawn on one side or the other, with unfortunate consequences for those who backed the loser. Fortunately the last years of the decline of the Roman Empire were comparatively peaceful for the islands.

From AD 300 to 1100, the Ionian were part of the Byzantine domain, suffering bouts of pillaging from various piratical groups. About 1100 the Normans were expanding their Western European Kingdom. To help keep the Normans at bay the Greeks sought an alliance with the City State of Venice in exchange for freedom of trade and various concessions. As a result of "misunderstandings" between the Allies, the Normans slipped in and occupied Corfu, Cephalonia, Ithaca and Zakynthos.

By AD 1200 the Byzantine Empire had collapsed, due to the usual amount of double dealing, and between AD 1200 and 1500 the Venetians, although nominally in control of the Ionian, left the various feudal families to run them as their own personal fiefdoms. The increasing threat of the advancing Turks decided the Venetians to formalise their control and administer the islands directly but they still suffered severe savaging at the hands of the raiders, over the next 300 years.

In 1797 Napoleon Bonaparte, after overcoming the Venetians elsewhere in the European theatres of war, decided once and for all to take the Ionian islands under his wing. As soon as he achieved this feat, a coalition of Russia and Turkey overthrew the French leaving the Russians in control. It is interesting to note that the Czars were running a school of insurgency as long ago as the 1770s which dissident Cephalonians, Corfiots and Zantiots attended. Is nothing new?

In the meantime (1803) Britain and France declared war (on each other) and Napoleon repossessed the Ionian islands as part of his global strategy. This brought the British into this part of the world and by 1807 the British had taken Cephalonia, Ithaca and Zakynthos followed by Lefkas in 1811. Corfu was extremely strongly garrisoned by the French and, to save unnecessary bloodshed, the British haphazardly blockaded the island for the next six years. At a meeting of The Great Powers, (Great Britain, Austria, Prussia and Russia) following the final defeat of the French in Europe, the administration of the Ionian islands was formally granted to Britain, who ruled until 1864.

Lasting monuments to British rule, (or misrule, according to your viewpoint) must include encouraging the island farmers to implement comparatively revolutionary advances in agriculture. These were coupled with the necessary and complementary land drainage, extensive road building, some administrative buildings of note, British cemeteries and, on Corfu, cricket and ginger beer.

After various misadventures, Lord Palmerston handed over the Ionian islands to the Greeks in 1864. As is often the case, the locals had been vociferous in their wish to rid themselves of the 'appalling and oppressive' British, but once they departed the islands suffered heavy emigration due to the rapid decline of the agricultural underpin to the economy. Incidentally the British, had sneakily taken over Cyprus, thus storing up big problems for the future.

The Second World War brought in its train further dramatic upheavals, and the Germans gave the Italians administrative control in 1941. They seized it back in 1943, after some fairly bloodthirsty events, when the Italians sided with the Greek freedom fighters. Fortunately the islanders were little involved in the Greek Civil War uprisings which erupted at the end of the Second World War, but did not escape scot-free for, in 1953, a horrendous earthquake laid waste Cephalonia, Ithaca and Zakynthos.

The most recent pages of Ionian history involve the upsurge of tourism that really took off in the 1960s, was given a fillip during the 'Colonels' regime and is now, seemingly, proceeding headlong if not almost totally out of control.

The dominant religion is Greek Orthodox but there is a thriving Catholic enclave on Corfu, a few of Jewish faith on several of the islands (remnants of prevously large ghettos), and one or two Anglicans.

There are very few Byzantine churches standing, due to the centuries of earthquakes, but the later Ionian version is better represented. The separately constructed bell towers, or more correctly walls, pierced by bell arches and topped off with small, overhanging, tiled roofs, are named Campaniles. Inside the churches, the altar area is separated from the worshippers by a 'screen' of timber or stonework, usually honeycombed by a number of doors, varying from the very simple to the most ornately carved and fretworked constructions. The Icons, revered and displayed in the churches, are simple paintings from the Byzantine age, normally executed on small wooden 'canvasses', and often mounted on the screens.

In the following island chapters, a format has been devised and developed over the years to make the layout as easy to use as is possible, without losing the informative nature of the text. Each island is treated in a similar manner, giving the traveller easy identification of the immediate requirements. Below are detailed notes in respect of the few symbols occasionally used, and following that an alphabetical list of the islands included in my treatment of the Ionian.

SYMBOLS

Where inserted a star system of rating indicates my judgement of an island, its accommodation and restaurant standards by the incorporation of one to five stars.
1 star signifies bad, 2 basic, 3 good, 4 very good, and 5 excellent.

I must admit the inclusion of ratings are carried out on idiosyncratic, whimsical grounds and are based purely on personal observation. For instance where an island or establishment receives a detailed critique I may consider that sufficient unto the day.... The absence of a star symbol or any mention at all has no detrimental significance, and might, for instance, indicate that I did not personally visit the establishment.

The text is faced by the relevant island, port and town maps with descriptions and text tied into the various island routes. The key *Tmr* is used as a map reference to aid easy location on port and town maps. Other keys used include *Sbo* or Sea behind one, *Fsw* or Facing seawards, *F-bqbo* or Ferry-boat quay behind one and OTT or Over The Top.

A new standard or rating has been 'encouraged on me' by Richard Evetts, who helped out with this edition of the guide. This is the 'GROCs' Rating for measuring the excellence or otherwise of beaches based on a 'sand or pebble scale' of 1 to 10 (blame him not me if you do not agree!). GROCs Rating 1 indicates a simply awful, dirty beach, probably rocky and polluted. GROCs Rating 10 would be a superb situation with lovely sand, sparkling seawater and ideal swimming conditions.

Ionian islands described include:

Island Name(s)	Capital	Port(s)	Ferry Connections (M = mainland)
AntiPaxos (Antipaxoi, Antipaxi Andipas)		Agrapiolas (Agrapidia)	Trip boats from Paxos
Cephalonia (Kefallinia, Kefalonia Kephallenia, Cefalonia)	Argostoli	Sami Poros Argostoli Fiscardon Lixouri*	Corfu, Ithaca, Paxos, Killini (M), Patras (M), Brindisi (Italy)
*which only connects with Argostoli			
Corfu (Kerkira, Kerkyra, Corfou)	Corfu	As capital	Patras (M), Igoumenitsa (M), Paxos, Ithaca, Cephalonia, Ancona (Italy), Bar (Yugoslavia), Bari (Italy) Brindisi (Italy), Dubrovnik (Yugoslavia), Otranto (Italy), Rijeka (Yugoslavia), Split (Yugoslavia), Zadar (Yugoslavia)
Ithaca (Ithaki)	Vathi (Ithaki)	As capital	Cephalonia, Corfu, Paxos, Astakos (M), Patras (M)
Lefkas (Lefkada, Levkas)	Lefkas	As capital, Nidri Vassiliki	Trip boats from Ithaca, Preveza (M)
Paxos (Paxoi, Paxi)	Gaios (Paxi)	As capital	Corfu, Cephalonia, Ithaca, Patras (M)
Zakynthos (Zante, Zakinthos)	Zakynthos	As capital	Killini (M)

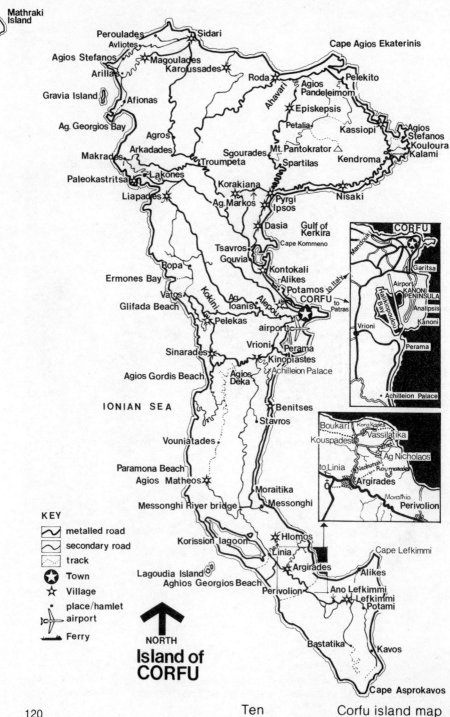

Island of CORFU

NORTH

KEY

~~~ metalled road
~~~ secondary road
⋯⋯ track
✪ Town
☆ Village
• place/hamlet
✈ airport
⚓ Ferry

12 Corfu (Kerkira, Kerkyra, Corfou) Ionian Islands

***

FIRST IMPRESSIONS
Smells; dust; clamour of clashing brass band and pop music; swifts and swallows; gracious crumbling buildings; green countryside, olive-tree and fern covered.

SPECIALITIES
Mandolato nougat; the liquer *Coum Cout*; *Koummkuat* candy; pastitsada (spiced braised veal and macaroni) and sofrito (spiced, fried and then baked meats); author Lawrence Durrell.

RELIGIOUS HOLIDAYS & FESTIVALS
include: 21st May— Ionian islands union with Greece; 14th August at Mandouki (suburb of Corfu Town) — Assumption of the Holy Virgin; Palm Sunday, the following Saturday, the 11th August and the first Sunday in November — Church services and Corfu Town processions accompanied by the remains of St Spirodon.

VITAL STATISTICS
Tel. prefix 0661. The island is 50 km long, has a maximum width of 27½ km, with an overall population of about 93,000, of which Corfu Town contains up to 29,000.

GENERAL
Corfu island comes as a pleasant surprise, for after the years of exposure to tourism, it would not be unreasonable to expect that the island, its people and their culture, should have wilted under the strain. Not so! Naturally, coastline development has intruded on areas of natural loveliness previously visited only by the more adventurous visitors and there is possibly more coach-trip exploitation of certain beauty spots. Probably the most annoying evidence of the tourist invasion is the ability of waiters to politely hear out a visitors halting efforts at Greek, only to respond in excellent English, American or German!

Much in evidence is the island peasant's dependence on the donkey as a beast of burden and it is still a common sight to observe women, dressed in traditional costume, sitting side-saddle on well-laden, clip-clopping donkeys. The people are very friendly and more than ordinarily hospitable.

Corfu is an amazing admixture of all possible permutations of typical Greek countryside, from mountains, verdant valleys, precipitous cliffs, sandy shores, picturesque inland and coastal fishing villages, as well as highly developed tourist areas, some squalor and urban sprawl. The only surprising omission is the paucity of archaeological remains. Well, well!

Due to a quirk of history, the British administered the Ionian islands as a Protectorate, from as early as 1809, only relinquishing control in 1864. This period of administration resulted in some lasting pecularities on Corfu, including the *Malta feel* of much of Corfu Town; the cricket pitch (albeit of sandstone) on the Esplanade; the British cemetery, as well as the availability of ginger beer. The island is also remarkable for the presence of a thriving Roman Catholic population.

CORFU: capital, main port & airport
Corfu Town varies from the vaguely squalid to the very beautiful, with an interesting blend of Venetian, French and British architecture. The Old Town or Quarter is a maze of narrow

streets, lanes and alleyways piercing the tall, eighteenth century buildings; washing strung haphazardly between cast-iron balustrades high above the street and caged birds trilling in the deep shadows of the shabby, careworn facades of the houses. The Old Town is built on a headland hill with, all round, lovely seascapes. Streets quite often come to an end at a flight of steps which, in turn, spill out on to unexpected squares, edged by abandoned, ruined churches and houses, the whole overlayed with a cacophony of disparate music and shrieking, diving, swooping swifts and swallows.

Corfu has quite surprisingly a large number of brass bands and the often discordant noise of their practising actually manages to even drown out the relentless beat of pavement pop music, the hubbub of the crowds and the chatter of side street printing presses.

Corfu can be reached by scheduled domestic and international ferries as well as by bus and air from various European countries and Athens.

ARRIVAL BY AIR
The airport is, unusually, very close to the Town, being built across Halikiopoulou Bay or lagoon, formed by the peninsula of land south of Corfu Town (the Paleopolis peninsula, usually referred to as Kanoni). There is no city bus from the airport, only various hotel buses and an Olympic airline coach, so travellers requiring transport and arriving on a charter flight will have to take a taxi. Unfortunately the fare is about 250 - 300 drs which is exorbitant by usual standards. The most inexpensive advice to the impecunious is to walk into Town which will take little more than 40 minutes and is quite a pleasant stroll.

If planning to stay in Corfu Town without pre-arranged accommodation, it is possibly best to proceed direct to the NTOG office on Samara Sq (*Tmr* 20.D4), between the streets of N Mantzarou and St Dessila.

ARRIVAL BY BUS
London and the other major European capitals spawn a number of private bus and coach operators, of a varying degree of professionalism, who journey to Corfu island, transhipping from Italy or Igoumenitsa on the Greek mainland. They usually run between mid June and September on an intermittent basis and the London to Corfu one-way fare is about £69. There is a scheduled service from Athens to Corfu, via Rio-Antirio and Igoumenitsa completing the trip on the ferry. (*See* **Buses, A to Z**).

ARRIVAL BY FERRY
The ports are due north in the area of the New Fort. The inter-island and mainland ferries dock at the east end between the New Fort and the Old Fort (*Tmr* D1) whilst the international ferries call at the west-end of the harbour in the Mandouki area beyond the New Fort on Xenofontos Stratigou St (*Tmr* A1).

To the left of the domestic quayside (*Tmr* D1), Donzelot Parade rises quickly from sea level, follows the cliff edge around the headland and merges into Arseniou Parade, which contains a multitude of tourist offices renting out rooms, scooters, boat trips and goodness knows what else.

If arriving at, or planning to make an early departure from the international ferry terminal which also serves Patras – gateway to the southern Ionian islands of Cephalonia, Ithaca and Zakynthos — then it is preferable to seek accommodation in the Mandouki.

There are two very good little hotels, the *Aegli* (D class) and *Europa* (C class). Both are in the back streets behind the ferry terminal and less than 5 minutes walk from the departure building — a useful factor when one realises that many departures are prior to 0600 hrs!

There is a launderette in the *Hotel Europa* and a multitude of cheap scooter hire and simple souvlaki establishments in the area all of which helps to make it a good quarter in which to make a base.

THE ACCOMMODATION & EATING OUT
The Accommodation
There is a very wide choice of accommodation including many rooms to let in private houses. The NTOG office (*Tmr* 20.D4) has extensive lists detailing them (as well as many other subjects including bus timetables), but all this information usually has to be extracted slowly, very slowly.

Immediately across from the inter-island/mainland quay is a very large grass square named after King George II, behind which rises the Old Quarter, wherein lie many houses with **Rooms**. In crossing the square, head towards the *Hotel Constantinoupolis* (*Tmr* 1.D1/2) and *Acropolis* (*Tmr* 2.D1/2) (both D class), which, if one is not 'picked up' before reaching them, will offer more than adequate accommodation.

Hotel Acropolis (*Tmr* 2.D1/2) (Class D) 3c Zavitsianou   Tel. 39569
Directions: In the street parallel to and immediately opposite the ferry-boat quayside, from which it is separated by George II Square.

Clean, seedy, late Victorian Greek hotel (two classes better than its counterpart, traditionally featured in those 1950, black and white films). Well situated with a single room for about 650 drs and a double room, both sharing a bathroom, from about 850 drs.

Hotel Constantinoupolis (*Tmr* 1.D1/2) (Class D) 11c Zavitsianou   Tel. 39826
As for the *Acropolis* from which it is separated by a lane.

Hotel New York (Nea Yorki) (*Tmr* 3.D1) (Class D) Donzelot Parade or 21 Ypapantis
Tel. 39922
Directions: Instead of crossing George II Sq turn towards Donzelot Parade to the left of the quay (*Sbo*), which doubles back on the harbour rising up to follow the cliff round the bluff of the Old Quarter headland. On the right hand side as one manoeuvres on to Donzelot.

A single and double room costs respectively some 700 and 900 drs sharing the bathroom.

Hotel Metropolis (*Tmr* 4.D1) (Class D) 24 Leoforos Konstantinou   Tel. 31156
Directions: In a small side street/square/cul-de-sac, in the far corner formed by Zavitsianou and Donzelot Streets.

Hotel Spilia (*Tmr* 5.D2) (Class E) 2 Solomou St   Tel. 34097
Directions: On the right-hand side walking up from the Central Bus Station (*Tmr* 21.C2). Typical of an E class hotel but quite adequate for an overnight stop.

A double room with shared bathroom costs 850 drs per night.

Hotel Criti (*Tmr* 6.D2) (Class E) 23 Nikiforou Theotoki   Tel. 38691
Directions: They should sound easy, nevertheless actuality blunts the clarity of my descriptive powers, but here we go. Plateia George II is split north/south by an avenue which joins Zavitsianou St the other side of which is a side street. This jinks right and then left and is the start of Nikiforou Theotoki St, which runs south for two blocks and then turns up, off left, in a south-east direction at the square of the Roman Catholic church of Agios Franciscos. The shops on the right are colonnaded and the street widens out immediately beyond the point where the colonnades cease. On the left is a small colonnaded shopping arcade, above which is the Hotel Criti. Phew!

As you would expect for an E class hotel with a 'provincial' double sharing the 'rustic' bathroom for 800 drs.

Following Odhos Nikiforou Theotoki on, it makes a junction with Kapodistriou St. To the left is the

Hotel Suisse (*Tmr* 7.E2) (Class C) 13 Kapodistriou   Tel. 39815
Directions: As above.

Nineteenth century house in a splendid location on The Liston, a gracefully arcaded

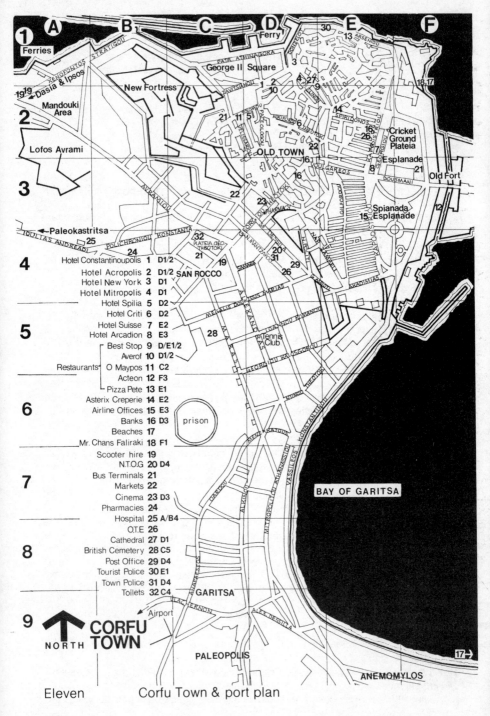

1 Ferries

A Ferries

XENOFONTOS STRATIGOU

19 19 ← Dasia & Ipsos

2 Mandouki Area

Lofos Avrami

B

New Fortress

3

AVRAMIOU

← Paleokastritsa

IOULIAS ANDREADI

POLICHRONIOU KONSTANTA

25

24

PAT. ATHINAGORA

George II Square

C

D Ferry

30

13 ARSENIOU

E

F

ZAVITSIANOU

3

4 27

1 2

10

2

9

21   11 5

NIKIFOROU THEOTOKI

6

22

SPIRIDONOS

14

16

26

57

OLD TOWN

16

OU GAREOS

8

GILFORDOU

16

23   N. THEOTOKI

DOUSMANI

Cricket
Ground
Plateia

Esplanade

21

Old Fort

12

22

PLATEIA GEO.
THEOTOK

32

N. KANTAROU

Spianada
Esplanade

15

DONKISSIS MARIAS

4

Hotel Constantinoupolis **1** D1/2

21   19

SAN ROCCO

20

31

29

26

AKADIMIAS

Hotel Acropolis **2** D1/2
Hotel New York **3** D1
Hotel Mitropolis **4** D1

5

Hotel Spilia **5** D2
Hotel Criti **6** D2
Hotel Suisse **7** E2
Hotel Arcadion **8** E3

28

IOANNOU KASOGIORGI

Tennis
Club

Best Stop **9** D/E1/2
Averof **10** D1/2

Restaurants

O Maypos **11** C2
Acteon **12** F3
Pizza Pete **13** E1

GEORGIOU THEOTOKI

NIRIDI

6

Asterix Creperie **14** E2
Airline Offices **15** E3
Banks **16** D3
Beaches **17**
Mr. Chans Faliraki **18** F1

prison

MEN KRATOIN

7

Scooter hire **19**
N.T.O.G **20** D4
Bus Terminals **21**
Markets **22**
Cinema **23** D3
Pharmacies **24**

VASSILEOS K. CONSTANTINOU

BAY OF GARITSA

8

Hospital **25** A/B4
O.T.E **26**
Cathedral **27** D1
British Cemetery **28** C5
Post Office **29** D4
Tourist Police **30** E1
Town Police **31** D4
Toilets **32** C4

GARITSA

9

Airport

NORTH **CORFU
TOWN**

VLAG LERNON

ALEX DESSILA

PALEOPOLIS

17 →

ANEMOMYLOS

Eleven   Corfu Town & port plan

124

French-style building, with large suspended lamps, illuminating the Esplanade at night.

To the right is

Hotel Arcadion (*Tmr* 8.E3) (Class C) 44 Kapodistriou   Tel. 37671
Directions: As above.

Again a splendid location looking out over the park of the Esplanade.
A double room en suite, reflecting the position, costs from 1650 drs.

Back round the headland to the Mandouki area, left of the *Tmr* grid A2 off the edge of the town map and there are the

Hotel Aegli (Class C)
Directions: In the street running up behind the international ferry terminal, and well signposted.

Usually full by mid-day so arrive early. Clean and simple with a single room sharing the bathroom costing 800 drs and a double room, 1000 drs.

Hotel Europa (Class D) Neos Limin   Tel. 39304
Directions: Defies description being located in the maze of streets behind the international ferry terminal. Just ask.

Clean, simple and friendly with a single room sharing a bathroom costing 700 drs. A double room costs 1000 drs sharing and en suite 1400 drs.

The hotel is the proud possessor of a laundromat costing 500 drs for wash and a dry.

At the far end of the Bay of Garitsa which it overlooks, on the Esplanade road of EM Theotoki, is the

Hotel Marina (Class B) E M Theotoki   Tel. 32783
Directions: As above.

Comfortable but rather expensive with a double room en suite costing 2100 drs.

The list of rooms to rent in private houses, obtainable from the NTOG, is so very extensive that I will not list the half dozen I have stayed in. The majority are in the Old Town or Quarter, which is a veritable rabbit-warren of streets and buildings with lodgings. Double room rates range from 700 drs to 900 drs per night depending upon the facilities.

YHA & CAMPING
There are none in or adjacent to Corfu Town but the two Youth Hostels and various campsites on the island are listed under the island text description of:

Kontokali	YHA & Camping	7 kms NW of Corfu Town on the east coast
Agios Ioanis	YHA	9 kms W of Corfu Town. Inland.
Kato Kommeno, Tsavros	Camping	11 kms NW of Corfu Town on the east coast
Dasia	Camping	12 kms NW of Corfu Town on the east coast
Ipsos	Camping	14½ kms NW of Corfu Town on the east coast
Pyrgi	Camping	16 kms N of Corfu town on the east coast
Vatos	Camping	13 kms W of Corfu Town, 2 kms inland of the west coast
Messonghi	Camping	19 kms S of Corfu Town on the east coast
Paleokastritsa	Camping	11 kms NW of Corfu Town on the west coast

The Eating Out
Best Stop (*Tmr* 9.D/E1/2) Filelinon St, Old Quarter
Directions: Situated at the far (port) end of Filelinon St in the little square just above the Cathedral. A choice of stools inside or tables in the square, with daily life throbbing all around and, alongside, a printing press chattering away.

Excellent breakfast of two fried eggs, bacon and tomatoes 120 drs. Toast, butter and marmalade (well, Corfu jam) 70 drs, coffee 40 drs. There are occasions, if away for a month or so, when it's a delight to sink one's teeth into bacon and eggs. Greek salad, omelette and Amstel beer for two cost some 500 drs.

Restaurant Averof (*Tmr* 10.D1/2)

Directions: On the corner of Odhos Alipiou and Prossalendou, conveniently reached by slipping down the alleyway between the *Hotels Acropolis* and *Constantinoupolis* from Odhos Zavitsianou alongside Plateia George II.

A truly Greek restaurant operating with the obligatory arm-waving and shouting, and packed with Greeks. No shortage of waiters here and the service is excellent. The whole performance is reigned over by a seated Mama and Papa overlooking and supervising proceedings from behind the raised cash register. Sitting outside, under the passageway awning, one can watched the friendly competition between the *Averof* and the restaurant opposite, for passing custom. Both employ a waiter to 'influence' the passing 'punters'. Ensure you inspect the offerings in the kitchen, it is good form. Greek salad, moussaka, bread, a bottle of retsina and coffee for two, 900 drs. Taramosalata, green beans, chef's speciality of veal (veal bedded on sliced aubergine, wrapped in sliced potato and topped off with creamed potato), a bottle of retsina and coffee for two cost 650 drs. On one occasion my companion was of the opinion that the veal might be goat's meat but, whatever, it was very good.

O Maypos (*Tmr* 11.C2) 20 Solomou St

Directions: Just off the New Fortress terminal and Market Sq (*Tmr* C2), on the right coming from the square. The family and their formica-topped restaurant tables lack any charm, but the meals are certainly reasonably priced, with meat balls, beans, retsina and bread for two at 600 drs.

Self-Service Restaurant (*Tmr* C/D2) Solomou St

Directions: On the left-hand side of Solomou St, about 50 metres up from the New Fortress Bus station. Inexpensive but plentiful, well cooked food — ideal if you find your budget getting a bit low near the end of a holiday. Macaroni pie, tomato and onion salad, bread and beer for one costs just 195 drs.

Makis Grill Bar (*Tmr* D2) 38 St Basilios St

Directions: From Kapodistriou walk along Odhos Nikiforou Theotoki. This little establishment is to be found tucked away in the alleyway on the left prior to the start of the colonnades on that side, just beyond the Hotel Criti (*Tmr* 6.D2). This is one of the 'best buys'. John Makis and his wife, Koula, assisted by their two daughters, Mary and Marinella, run one of the foremost souvlaki and grill establishments in Corfu Town. Unlike a lot of the smarter restaurants where most of the food is prepared using modern equipment, all John's dishes are cooked over charcoal in the traditional manner. In addition the prices are extremely reasonable — grilled chicken, Greek salad, bread and a bottle of retsina for one, costing 245 drs.

It was whilst Richard was 'troughing' here that he observed the Tourist police in action. Two neatly dressed gentlemen entered the establishment, selected three uncooked souvlakis from the tray, weighed each in turn and then demanded that one of them be cooked. Once prepared the kebab was reweighed and sampled. The police inspectors not only pronounced themselves satisfied with John's offerings, but also gave him permission to increase his prices! Incidentally, by the same token, had they not been happy with the food they could have closed the place down, there and then. I wonder how many United Kingdom restaurants could stand such a 'spot check' scrutiny!

In the Old Quarter, if you have enough courage, there are a number of cellar restaurants serving up very cheap, simple meals, which will help keep daily costs to a minimum.

In the smarter, west part of town, where the road borders the far end of the Esplanade, overlooking the canal separating the Old Fort or Citadel from the mainland, is located:

The Restaurant Acteon (*Tmr* 12.F3)
Directions: As above.

Outside tables, splendidly sited, the restaurant is rather 'chi-chi' with the prices reflecting this 'attribute' without the food doing likewise.

Another magnificent location is exploited by two or three restaurants along the Arseniou cliff-top road, which looks over Potamos Bay with Vidos island in the near distance. The tables are on the cliff edge under awnings and the kitchens are across the road inside the establishment's building. Let's hope none of the staff are knocked down by passing traffic, it could make the meal very drawn out!

Pizza Pete (*Tmr* 13.E1)
Directions: As above.

One of the restaurants referred to above that springs to mind, another is the *Aegli.*

Mr Chans Faliraki (*Tmr* 18.F1)
Directions: Close by Arseniou. (*See* **Beaches, A to Z**)

A charming diversion is to take refreshment at one of the Kafeneions, or cafes, situated in The Liston and watch the ramblas or volta of the Corfiots and tourists, endlessly wandering up and down the parade of Georgiou A (*Tmr* E2/3). There are tables and chairs five or six deep on the far side of the road, on the edge of the Esplanade. Coffee and cakes are expensive, but nobody seems to mind you sitting at a table for hours over one cup and there is no hustling by the waiters.

Incidentally, the roads that encircle the Esplanade and the pathways that run through the park, are thronged with ambling couples and families on most summer evenings.

Asterix Creperie (*Tmr* 14.E2)
Directions: Half-way up the steps running off the far end of Ag Spiridonos St from Odhos Kapodistriou. Nice for a change, especially an early or late evening snack. Excellent selection of savoury and sweet pancakes from about 150 drs.

THE A TO Z OF USEFUL INFORMATION
AIRLINE OFFICES & TERMINUS (*Tmr* 15.E3)
The Olympic premises are towards the south end of Kapadistriou St.

Note that nearby, across the road on the edge of the Esplanade, is a public toilet, a rare Ionian facility.

Aircraft timetables
Corfu to Athens
A minimum of 3 flights daily 0715, 1940, 2310 hrs.
From 23rd June additionally 2140 hrs.

Athens to Corfu:
A minimum of 3 flights daily 0545, 1810, 2140 hrs.
From the 23rd June additionally 2010 hrs.
One-way fare 3470 drs, duration 50 mins.

BANKS
There are four or five major banks. Probably the two most convenient are the:
National Bank of Greece, to one side, and the **Commercial Bank**, on the other of Eug Voulgareos, where it divides around a building in the middle of the road. (*Tmr* 16.D3).

Another useful bank (*Tmr* 16.E2) is situated on Kapodistriou St, close by the corner with Spiridonos St, next door to the OTE offices (*Tmr* 26.E2).

The usual weekday opening hours.

BEACHES

Corfu Town is not well endowed with beaches.

Beach 1: One spot rarely found by short-stay tourists is situated just below the small headland, overlooked by the north side of the Old Fort and its little yacht harbour (*Tmr* 17.F1). Where Arseniou Parade joins Kapodistriou St there is a sharply downwards inclined, short, metalled path, leading to a blockhouse of some description. At the bottom, turning left through the arch gives access to a small open area. To the left is a ruined church or chapel, left into a building end-ways on to the sea, which was possibly a fish-packing factory or similar. The landward end of this building has been converted into an extremely smart and fairly expensive Chinese restaurant
Mr Chans Faliraki (*Tmr* 18.F1).
Complete with Chinese waiters (Birmingham yes, Corfu no!). Tomato and onion salad 150 drs, chicken and green peppers 400 drs.

To the right, through a turnstile, admission costing 20 drs is gained to a rather shabby, tree-sheltered lido. There is no beach but access to a buoyed-off area of sea is by way of a set of steps, The seabed is hard sand, and fairly clean. There are changing rooms, open-air showers, toilets and sunbathing beds, in an area bounded by a crumbling, low-columned parapet and a very small cafe sells drinks and a limited range of food. The central part of the area is free with its own passage to the sea.

Beach 2: Plage Mon Repos is another beach at the southern promenade end of Vassileos Konstantinou. The beach is opposite Mon Repos, a 'once royal' villa with park-like gardens, built in 1824 as the summer residence of the British High Commissioners. It became the property of the Greek Royal Family and (perhaps of particular interest to British tourists) the Duke of Edinburgh was born here.

Beach 3: The third and probably the most pleasant beach within walking distance of the town is below the *Hilton Hotel* at the far end of the Kanoni Peninsula. This is reached by walking south around the bay of Garitsa and then out along the headland. The road comes to a dead-end with the grounds of the Hilton sloping up to the left, a large tourist hotel to the right, and a cafe-bar perched on the terrace overlooking Corfu's famous twin islets. Take the steps beside the cafe down the cliff-side and then the path over the rocks behind the little beach shop/cafe. The beach is man-made but is quite pleasant and the water clean. There is a kiosk bar on the beach, selling a selection of hot snacks and ice-cream at quite reasonable prices, reasonable that is bearing in mind that it is run by the *Hilton Hotel*. Boats can be hired and if tiring of 'neat sunbathing' then why not climb back up the cliffs, have a drink on the cafe terrace and watch the aircraft taking off and landing at the airport below. When all this activity proves too tiring it is possible to catch a bus back from the top of the cliff. They run about every 30 minutes for a fare to the town centre of about 20 drs.

BICYCLE, SCOOTER & CAR HIRE

Numerous establishments hiring all three modes of transport are grouped around the New and Old Port, Alexandras, Arseniou and Kapodistriou Streets and the Plateia Georgiou Theotoki (San Rocca Sq).

The best scooter buy's (*Tmr* 19) are to be found amongst those establishments located on and around the junction of Xenofontos Stratigou with Avramiou St near the New Port (*Tmr* A1/2). Prospective hirers should shop around and ensure that they are seen to be doing just that by the various proprietors. It is possible to get as much as 300 drs knocked off the original price requested for a scooter. That is after the owner has observed a visit to his competitors.

Prices range from:- Bicycle 150 drs, moped 300 drs and a scooter 600 drs. Five litres of 2 stroke mix costs about 250 drs.

Incidentally, it comes as quite a shock to find that on Corfu tourists have imported light-fingeredness to the point that the aforesaid conveyances are supplied with cable locks.

Although stressed in the introductory chapters it must be reiterated that car hire is becoming tiresomely expensive if not a total 'rip off'. Daily deposits, to be paid up-front, average about 5000 drs and the hire costs some 2500 - 3000 drs per day. Woe betide the hirer who incurs any damage, even to the wheel trims! You have been warned.

BOOKSELLERS

Being a large and cosmopolitan town, there are a number of booksellers with an international flavour. There is even a book published on the island about and written by long-standing English expatriates, as there is also a free issue English language newspaper, **The Corfu News**. This is supposedly published fortnightly, is available from the NTOG office (*Tmr* 20.D4), is full of extremely useful information including travel details, entertainment, museums, general articles of interest, lists of dentists, doctors and chemists, as well as names and addresses of the various sports clubs. It is well worth winkling out a copy.

BREAD SHOPS
See **Commercial Shopping Area.**

BUSES
Three bus terminals accommodate the island's buses.

Bus timetables
Corfu Town to Athens, 100, Kifissou St.   Tel. 5129443
Daily   0700, 0900, 2000 hrs.
Return journey
Daily   0700, 1930, 2030 hrs.
One-way fare 1530 drs (plus ferry-boat fare).

1. The Cricket Ground/Esplanade (*Tmr* 21.F3)
The nearest to a Town bus serving the suburbs of Kanoni and Mandouki.
Bus No. 2
Daily including
Sundays/holidays   0645 to 2200 hrs, every ½ hour
Return journey:
Daily including
Sundays/holidays   0700 to 2230 hrs, every ½ hour
NB. *See* Horse Drawn Carriages, A to Z for an alternative method of town travel.

2. The Plateia Geo Theotoki (San Rocco Sq) (*Tmr* 21.C4)
From Corfu Town to Potamos, Evropouli (for Folklore village), north-west of Corfu Town:
Bus No. 4
Daily   0545, 0645, 0720, 0845, 0930, 1030, 1130, 1230, 1300, 1350,
                               1425, 1545, 1630, 1730, 1830, 1930, 2030, 2215 hrs
Sundays/holidays   0800, 1000, 1300, 1700, 1830, 2000, 2200 hrs
Return journey
Daily   0540, 0610, 0750, 0900, 0945, 1045, 1145, 1245, 1320, 1400,
                               1445, 1600, 1650, 1745, 1845, 1945, 2045, 2125, 2235 hrs
Sundays/holidays   0820, 1015, 1320, 1720, 1845, 2020, 2215 hrs
From Corfu Town to Vrioni, Milia, Kouramades (Nr Sinarades), south-west of Corfu Town:
Bus No: 5
Daily   0530, 0600, 0700, 0715, 0830, 0900, 1100, 1200, 1300, 1355,
                               1415, 1515, 1615, 1800, 1900, 2115, 2215 hrs
Sundays/holidays   0700, 1100, 1300, 1515, 1600, 1800, 1900, 2100, 2200 hrs
Return journey
Daily   0545, 0625, 0725, 0825, 0845, 0925, 1130, 1225, 1325, 1405,
                               1445, 1555, 1645, 1825, 1925, 2125, 2235 hrs
Sundays/holidays   0725, 1125, 1325, 1540, 1625, 1825, 1925, 2125, 2215 hrs

From Corfu Town to Benitses, south of Corfu Town: Bus No. 6

Daily	0700, and then every hour on the hour till 2130 hrs
Sundays/holidays	0800, 1000, 1200, 1400, 1530, 1730, 1930, 2100 hrs
Return journey	
Daily	0715, 0830, and then every hour on the half hour till 2200 hrs
Sundays/holidays	0830, 1030, 1230, 1430, 1600, 1800, 2000, 2130 hrs

From Corfu Town to Kontokali, Dasia, north-west of Corfu Town: Bus No. 7

Daily	0700, and then every hour on the hour till 2200 hrs
Sundays/holidays	0800, 0900, 1100, 1300, 1500, 1600, 1800, 2000, 2130 hrs
Return journey	
Daily	0730, and then every hour on the half hour till 2230 hrs
Sundays/holidays	0830, 0930, 1130, 1330, 1530, 1630, 1830, 2030, 2200 hrs

From Corfu Town to Agios Ioanis, west of Corfu Town: Bus No. 8

Daily	0530, 0615, 0700, 0745, 0800, 0845, 1000, 1200, 1300, 1345, 1430, 1515, 1600, 1800, 2015, 2200 hrs
Sundays/holidays	0700, 1000, 1200, 1515, 1700, 1900, 2010, 2200 hrs
Return journey	
Daily	0545, 0635, 0720, 0800, 0820, 0855, 1020, 1220, 1320, 1530, 1620, 1820, 2030, 2215 hrs
Sundays/holidays	0745, 1020, 1220, 1530, 1720, 1935, 2015, 2220 hrs

From Corfu Town to Achilleion (for Achilleion Palace), south of Corfu Town: Bus No. 10

Daily	0700, 0900, 1100, 1415, 1700, 2100 hrs
Sundays/holidays	0800, 1000, 1400, 1700, 1900, 2100 hrs
Return journey	
Daily	0720, 0920, 1140, 1435, 1740, 1920, 2120 hrs
Sundays/holidays	0820, 1040, 1420, 1740, 1920, 2120 hrs

From Corfu Town to Pelekas (for the Kaisers Throne), west, south-west of Corfu Town: Bus No. 11

Daily	0645, 1030, 1200, 1415, 1700, 1930 hrs
Sundays/holidays	0900, 1900 hrs
Return journey	
Daily	0715, 1100, 1445, 1730, 2000 hrs
Sundays/holidays	0930, 1930 hrs

3. The New Fortress/Citadel Square (Spillia) (*Tmr* 21.C2)

(Note, no numbers — well, it helps the confusion!)

From Corfu Town to Kavos (Beach), southern end of the island:

Daily	0630, 0900, 0930, 1030, 1130, 1230, 1330, 1445, 1530, 1700, 1930 hrs
Sundays/holidays	0930, 1930 hrs
Return journey	
Daily	0600, 0615, 0800, 1115, 1315, 1330, 1715 hrs
Sundays/holidays	0700, 1600 hrs

From Corfu Town to Agios Matheos, south, south-west of Corfu Town:

Daily	0515, 0700, 1200, 1430, 1630 hrs
Sundays/holidays	0930 hrs
Return journey	
Daily	0600, 0745, 1330, 1415, 1530, 1730 hrs
Sundays/holidays	1600 hrs

From Corfu Town to Messonghi, south of Corfu Town:

Daily	0830, 0900, 1030, 1230, 1430, 1800, 1930 hrs
Return journey	
Daily	0915, 1115, 1345 hrs

From Corfu Town to Sidari, Avliotes, north-west of Corfu Town:

Daily	0530, 0900, 1100, 1300, 1530, 1930 hrs
Sundays/holidays	0930 hrs

Return journey
Daily   1100, 1430, 1715 hrs
Sundays/holidays   1600 hrs

From Corfu Town to Roda, Karoussades, north, north-west of Corfu Town:
Daily   0530, 0900, 1330, 1600 hrs
Sundays/holidays   0930 hrs
Return journey
Daily   1100, 1730 hrs
Sundays/holidays   1600 hrs

From Corfu Town to Afionas, Arillas, west, north-west of Corfu Town:
Daily   0530, 1330 hrs
Return journey
Daily   0700, 1500 hrs

From Corfu Town to Kassiopi, north-east of Corfu Town:
Daily   0530, 0645, 0900, 1000, 1100, 1200, 1430, 1615 hrs
Sundays/holidays   0930 hrs
Return journey
Daily   0645, 0800, 1030, 1400, 1600, 1715 hrs
Sundays/holidays   1600 hrs

From Corfu Town to Petalia, Lauki, north inland of Corfu Town:
Tues/Thurs/Saturday   0530, 1430 hrs
Return journey
Tues/Thurs/Saturday   0700, 1500 hrs

From Corfu Town to Vatos, west of Corfu Town:
Daily   0700, 0900, 1000, 1100, 1200, 1300, 1430, 1530, 1600, 1730,
                             1900, 2000 hrs
Sundays/holidays   0900, 1100, 1630 hrs
Return journey
Daily   0730, 1130, 1445, 2030 hrs
Sundays/holidays   0930, 1130, 1700 hrs

From Corfu Town to Glifada Beach, west of Corfu Town:
Daily   0900, 1100, 1200, 1300, 1430, 1530, 1600, 1730, 1900, 2000 hrs
Return journey
Daily   0945, 1145, 1615, 2045 hrs

From Corfu Town to Ipsos, Pyrgi, north, north-west of Corfu Town:
Daily   0715, 0900, 1000, 1100, 1200, 1300, 1400, 1700, 1800, 1930,
                             2100 hrs
Sundays/holidays   0900, 1100, 1300, 1600, 1700, 1900 hrs
Return journey
Daily   0745, 0930, 1130, 1230, 1445, 1730 hrs
Sundays/holidays   0930, 1130, 1330, 1630, 1730, 1930 hrs

From Corfu Town to Paleokastritsa, west, north-west of Corfu Town:
Daily   0830, 0900, 1000, 1100, 1200, 1300, 1400, 1700, 1800, 1930,
                             2100 hrs
Sundays/holidays   1000, 1600 hrs
Return journey
Daily   0945, 1045, 1145, 1315, 1500, 1745 hrs
Sundays/holidays   1045, 1645 hrs

From Corfu Town to Agios Gordis Beach, west, south-west of Corfu Town:
Daily   1230, 2000 hrs
Return journey
Daily   1315, 2045 hrs

Oft reiterated, I know, but please note that timetables alter from year to year. Despite this they are listed in order to give a good grounding of the type and frequency of service to be expected.

CHEMIST
See **Medical Care.**

COMMERCIAL SHOPPING AREA
Corfu Town can be confusing till certain major streets are absorbed into the geographical part of the memory. From the Plateia Geo Theotoki (*Tmr* C4) (also known as San Rocco), along Georgiou Theotoki, which has a number of large department type stores, the second turning on the left is Ag Sofias. This leads up into the elongated fire station square, whereon is located the Cabbage market, a very large, open, fish and vegetable market (*Tmr* 22.C3).

Georgiou Theotoki runs into Eug Voulgareos and, taking the left-hand fork, past the National Bank of Greece (*Tmr* 16.D3), bears into a small square with colonnaded shops on the left. The buildings tower skywards, overshadowing the tiny side streets. I say tiny but every so often a vehicle will improbably squeeze its way out of a narrow alleyway. In this area (*Tmr* 22.D/E2) both the streets of Ag Bazileioy and M Theotoki are cluttered with vegetable, fruit and fish shops as well as the occasional and most welcome snack and pie counter.

At the bottom of M Theotoki St, across Nikif Theotoki, is Odhos Filarmonikis in which are located two bread shops as well as a couple of very good yoghurt and dairy shops. At the end of the constantly climbing Filarmonikis St, a flight of steps leads up to the narrow Filelinon St, which runs off to the left and the entrance to which is surrounded by greengrocers. In this narrow claustrophobic lane is a smaller, cleaner 'Plaka look-alike' (of Athens fame).

The other commercial area of shops, stalls and even a hardware shop is the area of the New Fortress Sq and Solomou St (*Tmr* C/D2).

CINEMAS
There are four or more, including **The Pallas** (*Tmr* 23.D3) in Georgiou Theotoki St, which usually shows English, American, German or French films with Greek subtitles:

DENTISTS & DOCTORS
See **Medical Care.**

DISCOS
One publication advises that 'Discos abound'! I'm sure they do.

FERRY BOATS
Old Port (*Tmr* D1)
Island and local ferry-boats dock here, including those to and from Igoumenitsa (M) and Paxos. Note that Patras (M) ferries via Cephalonia and Ithaca berth at the New Port, (*Tmr* A1).

Much of the unfathomable, inscrutibility attributable to the Greek ferry-boat system is nowhere better illustrated than in the Ionian islands so please bear in mind all the strictures listed in Chapter Three.

I must admit a certain level of defeat in the detail of the Ionian island ferries, for the information given is often found to be incorrect, the ferry has been withdrawn, new services introduced and different offices for different lines give different information, which is all very confusing when planning inter-island visits.

The Patras to Corfu link via Cephalonia and Ithaca is a particularly difficult route to follow but there is definitely a weekly connection.

Ferry-boat timetable
Corfu to Patras

Day	Departure time	Ferry-boat	Ports/Islands of Call
Thursday	2330 hrs		Vathi (Ithaca), Sami (Cephalonia), Patras (M)

Note: this service also returns from Patras up the chain on Thursday nights departing at 2330 hrs.
One-way fares and duration are as follows:

Corfu - Paxos	350 drs, 1¼ hrs
Corfu - Ithaca	850 drs, 5¼ hrs
Corfu - Cephalonia	850 drs, 6¾ hrs
Corfu - Patras	1450 drs, 10¼ hrs

The **Ionian Lines** also operate a ferry that runs between Corfu, Paxos, Ithaca, Cephalonia and Patras.

Corfu to Patras

Day	Departure time	Ferry-boat	Ports/Islands of Call
Tuesday	0700 hrs		Paxos, Fiscardon & Sami (Cephalonia), Patras (M)

Note: this service departs from Patras on Monday night at 2100 hrs.

The same company run a daily service between Patras, Sami (Cephalonia) and Ithaca (for fuller details *See* the relevant island chapter) so connections can be made to facilitate inter-island travel.

Corfu to Paxos

Day	Departure time	Ferry-boat	Ports/Islands of Call
Mon/Tue	1430 hrs	FB Paxi	Paxos
Thurs/Fri			
Wed/Sat	1400 hrs		

One-way fare 347 drs, duration 3 hrs.
Note: this service returns from Paxos daily, except Sundays, at 0730 hrs. But I am sure there is a Sunday ferry!

Corfu to Igoumenitsa (M):

Daily	0600, and then hourly on the hour till 1600, 1730, 1900, 2000, 2130 hrs
Return	
Daily	0530, 0700, 0900, 1000 and then hourly on the hour till 1900, 2030 and 2200 hrs

One-way fare 275 drs, duration 1 hr 55 mins.

New Harbour, Xenofontos Stratigou (*Tmr* A1)

The international ferries dock here, that is the Greek-Italian and Yugoslavian liners. Some of these craft make inter-island calls on the connections between Patras to Ancona/Bari and Brindisi; Igoumenitsa to Bar; Igoumenitsa to Bari; Igoumenitsa to Dubrovnik; Igoumenitsa to Otranto and Igoumenitsa to Rijeka (or vice versa). But note in planning journeys that travellers may not be able to disembark at will, as some shipping lines do not allow stopover or a break in the journey despite the fact that they make a port call whilst others will only allow this if the ticket is marked thus at the time of purchase.

Typical of the international ferries that make domestic calls are the ferry-boats, **Ionian Star** and **Ionian Glory**, of Strintzis Lines, *en route* from Patras to Brindisi which take in Sami (Cephalonia), Igoumenitsa (M) and Corfu.

FERRY-BOAT TICKET OFFICES

A number of ferry-boat ticket agencies are located in the wall created by Donzelot Parade as it sweeps up the hillside, (rather similar to walled-in railway arches) at the left-hand side of the Old Port (*Sbo*). Do not forget that each office usually only deals with one particular ferry company, will not advise you in respect of their competitors' sailings AND remember to ask more than once!

As a last resort, tickets for the international ferries can be purchased at the time of travel from the kiosks inside the terminal building in the New Port BUT there is invariably a crush of people and it is rather less bruising to get tickets in advance, if at all possible.

HAIRDRESSERS

Sufficient unto the day thereof. . .

HORSE DRAWN CARRIAGES (Monipo)
These extremely colourful horse-drawn, brightly painted, Victorian carriages are 'ranked' on the Esplanade and the Old Port. The horses and carriages are decked out with an assortment of brasses and ornaments and the horses are quite often 'straw be-hatted' with holes cut for the ears. Charges are by the hour and these must be checked prior to hiring this interesting way of touring the town. Rates, which are controlled, are about 1000 drs per hour.

HOSPITAL
See **Medical Care.**

LAUNDRY
The *Hotel Europa* (*Tmr* A1 & left) has a laundrette with wash and dry. *See* **The Accommodation** for details and directions.

MEDICAL CARE
Chemists & Pharmacies (*Tmr* 24)
One on Odhos Ioulias Andreadi (*Tmr* 24.A4), another in the same area but close to Plateia Geo Theotoki (*Tmr* 24.C4) as well as one on Odhos Georgiou Theotoki. A 24 hr rota system is in operation.

Casualty Clinic
In the square behind the Commercial Bank (*Tmr* 16.D3) reached down the lane to the right, on the nearside of the bank approaching from the direction of Plateia Geo Theotoki.

Dentists & Doctors
A number in the town, the addresses of which can be obtained from the *Corfu News* and or the NTOG offices (*Tmr* 20.D4).

Hospital (*Tmr* 25.A/B4)
From Plateia Geo Theotoki along Odhos Polichroniou Konstanta which runs into Ioulias Andreadi and on the right. A 24 hr casualty service in addition to which English is spoken.

NTOG (*Tmr* 20.D4)
A shining example to all countries and certainly one of the best of the NTOG establishments throughout Greece (a plaudit shared with the Chania (Crete) and the Rhodes Town offices).

This is not to say that to dig out information does not require quite a lot of perseverance, but it is there in profusion. The building is situated in an elongated square facing the Municipal Theatre with access from either N Mantzarou or St Dessilla St, off Odhos Georgiou Theotoki.

OPENING HOURS
Banks
Daily 0800 - 1400 hrs (Fridays close 1330 hrs) but not Saturday, Sunday or holidays.

Summer, general
Monday, Wednesday, Saturday 0830 - 1400 hrs
Tuesday, Thursday, Friday 0830 - 1330 as well as 1730 - 2000 hrs

Kiosks, tourists and dairy shops
On average open 0830 - 2000 hrs including Sundays.

OTE
See **Post Office**

PETROL
In Corfu Town petrol is obtainable on the south side of Plateia Geo Theotoki (*Tmr* C4), at

the top of Alexandras St (*Tmr* C4) and on Xenofontos Stratigou (*Tmr* A1) in the area of the New Port.

Out of town supplies are patchy. Fairly frequently available north of Corfu Town as far as Dasia. There are stations at Pelekito, Karoussades, Ag Nikolaos (near Pelekas) and Moraitika. Additionally there are a number of petrol stations sited on the Corfu to Sinarades road.

PHARMACIES
See **Medical Care.**

PLACES OF INTEREST
Although the continual military character of the town over the centuries has resulted in very few early remains being left, there are architecturally interesting buildings and forts. Possibly the most eye-catching area, probably established as a clear field of fire, is

The Esplanade (*Tmr* E/F2/3)
This is split up into the sandy Plateia, whereon are arranged the rather unexpected cricket matches, and the grassy Spianada, on which are sited the wrought iron bandstand, where some of the town's many bands play, and an Ionic Rotunda.

To the east of the Esplanade is the

Old Fort or Citadel (*Tmr* F2/3)
Built of great blocks of stone, where a Son et Lumiere of Corfu's history is staged on summer evenings.

On the western side of the Esplanade are the:

Liston Buildings (*Tmr* E2/3)
French inspired, designed and constructed with large colonnades and arcades. Fashionable cafes and Kafeneions are located in the ground floor and great lamps are suspended from above the arches.

To the north of the Esplanade is the:

Palace of St Michael and St George (*Tmr* F1/2)
An impressive, if solid pile, complete with triumphal arches, a flank of which is pierced by the road off the Esplanade. Built by the British as an administrative building, after Independence, the Greek Royal family took it over and used it as a Royal residence until 1913, when it fell into disrepair. It has been restored and the town museum and public library are now located within the Palace. The oriental collection of an erstwhile Greek ambassador makes a rather incongruous, if interesting, exhibition.

Cathedrals & Churches
The Greek Orthodox Cathedral (*Tmr* 27.D1)
Approached by a flight of steps at the end of Konstantinou St, off the left-hand corner (*Sbo*) of Plateia King George II. At most times of the day there are constant comings and goings and the Cathedral is the repository for the headless remains of St Theodora. Look out for the small, colour-painted signs over the doors of a now coffin makers' workshop but which was most likely a taverna, to the right of the Cathedral (sea still behind one). They probably represent soldiers and regimental colours, dating from the British occupation.

The Church of Spirodon (*Tmr* E2)
On Ag Spiridonos St, between the Esplanade and Filelinon alley, deserves a mention as it houses the remains of the much revered St Spirodon which are paraded around the town four times a year. He is credited with having saved the Corfiots from death and destruction on a number of occasions. Not surprisingly Spiro is an extremely popular christian name for Corfiot males.

The Catholic Church of St Francis (*Tmr* D2)
At the west-end of Nikif Theotoko St, as is the Catholic infant school.

135

The New Fort (*Tmr* B/C1/2)
Built about 1580 to improve the capital's fortifications and the subject of late improvements by the British immediately prior to their rather swift departure. It is still in use by the Greek Navy and is not open to the public.

The Archaeological Museum
Sited to the south side of the *Corfu Palace Hotel*, on Vassileos Kontantinou. It contains several unique exhibits as well as a varied and interesting range of items on show and is well worth a visit.

The British Cemetery (*Tmr* 28.C5)
Contains many interesting headstones of soldiers who served during the British Protectorate, as well as those of British soldiers and sailors who fell during the two world wars. The well-kept gardens are reached by turning down Odhos Dimoulitsa off the top west corner of Plateia Geo Theotoki. Two hundred yards or so along, on the left is Kolokotroni St down which, on the left again, is the entrance to the cemetery.

POLICE
Tourist (*Tmr* 30.E1)
In Arseniou St, the cliff top road along the northern-most part of the Old Quarter.

Town (*Tmr* 31.D4)
In the same block as the NTOG offices.

Port
Well, really customs and passport office, by the yacht harbour supply station (*Tmr* A1), in the New Harbour on Xenofontos Stratigou.

POST OFFICE (& the OTE) (*Tmr* 29.D4)
The Post Office, and an OTE office (*Tmr* 26.D4) are in the same block as the NTOG offices. There is another OTE office (*Tmr* 26.E2) on Odhos Kapodistriou near the junction with Spiridonos St.

SPORTS FACILITIES
Corfu island is very well endowed, almost awash, with sporting facilities for the energetic visitor. I consider lifting a glass briskly is usually quite enough activity. . . .

Cricket
Temporary membership for a game from either the Gymnastics Syllogos (Tel. 23027) or The Byron Club (Tel. 39504).

Gambling
(Is this a sport?) *See* **Achilleion Palace**. Tel. 30360.

Golf
See **Corfu Golf Club**, Vatos. Tel. 94320.

Horse Riding
See **Gouvia.**

Scuba Diving
See **The Baracuda Club**, Paleokastritsa. Tel. 41211.

Squash
See the *Korkyra Beach Hotel,* Gouvia. Tel. 30770.

Tennis
The Corfu Tennis Club (*Tmr* D5), Ioannou Romanou St has four courts, bar and changing rooms. There is also the Corfu Town Club, 4 Vraila St. Tel. 37021.

Ten Pin Bowling
See the *Hilton Hotel,* Tel. 36540.

TAXIS
Various ranks including those on the central road through Plateia George II (*Tmr* C/D1/2), Plateia Geo Theotoki (San Rocco) (*Tmr* C4) and the Esplanade (*Tmr* E/F2/3).

TELEPHONE NUMBERS & ADDRESSES
Tourist Police (Corfu Town): 31 Arseniou St	Tel. 100
Tourist Police (Country): Plateia Geo Theotoki (San Rocco)	Tel. 109
Hospital: Ioulias Andreadi St (off Plateia Geo Theotoki)	Tel. 30562
NTOG: Odhos Samara	Tel. 39730
Harbour Master: The Old Port	Tel. 32655
British Vice-Consulate (*Tmr* E4): 2 Nap Zambeli St	Tel. 30055
(1000 - 1200 hrs — lucky fellow!)	

TOILETS (*Tmr* 32)
Public WCs are comparatively rare on the Ionian islands, thus worthy of note. This list includes those amenities at the Old Port, Plateia Geo Theotoki Sq and the Esplanade (opposite the Olympic office (*Tmr* 15.E3)).

It is necessary and accepted, to use restaurant and hotel facilities in towns and villages. In the countryside take to a bush!

TRAVEL AGENTS
Apart from the ferry-boat ticket offices referred to, there are a number of agencies strung out along Arseniou and Kapodistriou Sts.

ROUTE ONE
To Karoussades via Kassiopi (41 km)
North of Corfu Town (well, north-east due to the curve of the bay), the sea-road hugs the coast and can be followed all the way round around the outline of the island to the seaside village of Roda.

The Gulf of Kerkira is a lovely bay, but the road out past Alikes as far as Kontokali has experienced rather cheap, ramshackle and tatty semi-industrial building as well as 'rapid-rise' hotel development. The traffic is comparatively heavy as far as Tsavros, a major road junction beyond Gouvia. I feel very sorry for those package holidaymakers on this stretch where their hotel is the opposite side of the highway to the water's edge. Not only is there traffic noise to contend with, but the job of crossing the road is quite enlivening (or not if you see what I mean). In addition the sea-shore is muddy and reedy.

The first settlement is

KONTOKALI (Kondakali) (7 km from Corfu Town)
A Greek village, which has been subject to speculative building with dusty, unmade, pot-holed roads, villas, apartments, 'traditional' Greek tavernas, pubs, charcoal grills, restaurants, cafe-bars, scooters for rent "In Cheap" (sic), 'ye olde gifte shoppe', all cheek by jowl and overlayed with a pervading smell of drains, frying chips and shish kebabs as well as sun blistered bodies. Not a lot to do with a Greek village really!

The vast Gouvia yacht marina dominates the Kontokali seafront. Incidentally, there is an NTOG office here to cater for those visitors to the island who arrive on board boats.

Hotels include: the D class *Panorama* and *Pyrros*. There are plenty of rooms available as well as a rather basic Youth Hostel and a camping site
Kontakali Beach International,   Tel. 91202.
On the beach and open from April to October.

Just to the north at Gouvia there are squash courts at the *Korkyra Beach Hotel* and an equestrian establishment.

TSAVROS (10 km from Corfu Town)

Here the road forks right following the coast (and left for Paleokastritsa, Sidari and Magoulades). There is a camping site

Dionyssos Camping, Kato Kommeno, Tsavros.

Open April to October.

Keeping along the coast road leads to

DASIA (12 km from Corfu Town)

The village is to the right, off the main road at the crossroads and is Greek 'primitive'. The original Olive groves are now sprinkled with discreet hotels, pink-painted cafe-bars, discos, space invader machines, beach gear, gift and Greek 'original' art shops as well as tour buses and an all pervading, swampy, frying oil smell.

The sandy earth approach road widens out through the Olive trees and decants on to a thin ribbon of shingly beach (GROC Rating 7/10) layered with peeling, burning Western European tourists, the occasional English voice breaking through the continuous hubbub. A neat concrete wall edges the beach and finger piers occasionally protrude into the muddy blue sea. There are caique trips, water-skiing and para-skiing. It is smarter than Kontokali.

Dotted about is the occasional, extremely expensive, select hotel, tree and beach surrounded, and recognisable by the canopy, under which air conditioned pullman coaches and taxis disgorge their well groomed occupants.

Lesser hotels include the *Dassia* (C class) and *Scheria* (D class) as well as private rooms.

IPSOS & PYRGI (14.5 and 16 km from Corfu Town)

These were originally small hamlets tucked away at either end of a pleasant, long sweeping bay, with a narrow, shingly foreshore (GROC Rating 7/10) which has now been developed into a 'fishing village resort'. The coastal road edges the beach and the few original valley farmhouses have been swamped in the ribbon development that has occurred over the last 10 years.

The rather pathetic little mole once utilised by local fishermans caiques has now been taken over by, and overflows with tatty fibreglass speedboats.

Hotels embrace the C class *Platanos, Mega, Ionian Sea, The Port* and D class *Costas* and *Ionia*.

Camp sites include

Corfu Camping Tel. 93244, *Ypsos Camping*, Ipsos and *Pyrghi Village Camping*, Pyrgi.

The above are open between April and October.

After Pyrgi there are two turnings off to the left. The first leads to the village of

AGIOS MARKOS (& on to Korakiana)

At Agios Markos is a chapel dating from 1075 and a church with wall paintings and icons dating from 1576.

The second turning leads to

SPARTILAS

Continuing on through this village the road proceeds to Sgourades, Episkepsis, Agios Pandeleimom and back on to the main, coast road at Ahavari, thus circumnavigating Mt Pantokrator. At Sgourades, if a right-hand turning is taken on the unsurfaced road and then another right, between the villages of Strinilas and Petalia, access can be made to the summit of Mt Pantokrator. This is topped off by a much modified monastery and a radio mast. As can be imagined, the view is phenomenal and on 'a very clear day' you are supposed to be able to see a smidgen of the coastline of Italy. Nonetheless the views do include the islands north of Corfu, the

Albanian coast and the Lake of Butrinto, the Greek mainland beyond the Albanian headland, the island of Paxos and of course much of the island of Corfu all of which are dramatically laid out beneath any intrepid climber.

Back on the coast road, it is 'Villa' country but the buildings are fairly well scattered and usually discreetly out of sight, the only indication of their presence being the smart signboards, neat gates, and surfaced driveways. In fact the road from Pyrgi to Nisaki becomes more pleasantly Greek in character, passing through hill-hugging Olive groves. These quickly drop away, on the sea side, to a rocky coastline edged by blue sea and, on the inland side, rise quite sharply towards craggy mountainous peaks.

The road and coastline continues to skirt Mt Pantokrator, which dominates this part of the island.

NISAKI (22 km from Corfu Town)
There are two free-entry, shingle beaches (GROC Rating 7/10), as long as you can face the long walk down and, conversely, the even more arduous climb back up.

There are another two, similar, rather commercialised beaches on the road to

KENDROMA (26 km from Corfu Town)
Although it is a prodigiously long way down, one or two small hotels allow access to their private beach. Incidentally, all the free-entry beaches must be reached on foot. There are rooms to let.

The road winds up to Kendroma and slightly down to Gimari (Guimari), where there are more rooms to let and 'free access' to the beach.

The road from Pyrgi to Gimara traces a lovely, if somewhat downwardly distant shoreline. If the thought of the long walk either way is too much for a traveller (and for whom would it not be?) then there is no need to fret, for a few kilometres beyong Gimari, a turning off leads down to either Kalami or Kouloura.

KALAMI (30 km from Corfu Town)
A very, very pleasant small caique fishing village wherein a dozen old houses (some rather grand), a couple of reasonably priced restaurant bars and a taverna (let into the side of a larger dwelling house) are situated on the edge of a shingly beach (GROC Rating 7/10). They are delightfully set out on a curving bay which is framed by hillsides, dotted with Cypress trees to landward and the coastline of Albania shutting out the seaward background. Some development is taking place however, so be warned.

KOULOURA (30 km from Corfu Town)
On the northern side of the headland that separates it from Kalami. An enchanting spot with the small, slanted bay running along the edge of the hillside and a mole forming a small, attractive harbour for local fishing vessels. There is a taverna, a church connected to some extensively refurbished terraced houses and a dozen or so craft moored bow on to the bay cliff side. The little beach is of shingle (GROC Rating 8/10). A beautiful spot to while away a few hours.

The hills above the road from the Kalami/Kouloura junction, as far as the Agios Stefanos turn-off are much gentler, while the coastline is very beautiful.

At Agnitsini village a track leads down to a shingle beach (GROC Rating 8/10) in a beautiful setting with some facilities but largely undeveloped.

After less than 1/2 km an unmade and fairly circuitous road branches off to the right and drops down to

AGIOS STEFANOS
The deep bay is lovely, even if the shore is rather seaweedy and the small amount of

beach stony (GROC Rating 6/10). A number of boats are moored up, there is a small mole jutting into the water, two tavernas (where is there not?) and a few new houses! Albania is at its closest and almost seems to blank off the sea end of the bay.

The road cuts inland across the headland to

KASSIOPI (36 km from Corfu Town)
This seaside village has been 'treated' to become a typical 'Greek fishing village resort' with trip boats, coaches and most of the modern day refinements necessary to cope with holidaymakers. The stony beach (GROC Rating 6/10) is around Cape Kassiopi, to the left beyond the ruins of the old castle. *Rooms* are available in a number of private houses.

From Ipsos all the way round to Roda there are villas and apartments let into the coastline; on the road from Kassiopi to Pelekito the hillsides are rather monotonous and from Pelekito to Ahavari the shoreline is low lying and sand-duney. In fact from Cape Agios Ekaterinis right around and past Roda the seashore is very sandy, although somewhat narrow. (GROC Rating 8/10).

At Ahavari they have built beach chalets — say no more.

RODA (37 km from Corfu Town, via the inland village of Troumpeta)
Flat, low-lying surrounding countryside, with a narrow, sandy, shelving beach (GROC Rating 8/10) and reasonably priced restaurants and bars. *John and Jackies* is an example of the moderate charges for refreshments available here. Nescafe with milk 40 drs, ouzo 30 drs and a beer at 45 drs. Oh! there is para-skiing as well.

Hotels include the C class *Village Roda Inn, Aphroditi, Silver Beach* and the E class *Ninos. Rooms* are also available.

From Roda, in a westerly direction, the road links inland to

KAROUSSADES (41 km from Corfu Town)
This pleasant Greek inland town overlooks a fertile plain. Here the surfaced road runs out and is replaced by a deeply potholed track which provided a traveller perseveres, will at length lead to the Sidari road. But beware, signposting is either non-existent or, when present confusing.

From the turning off to the left to Karoussades it is possible to turn right down a track to

ASTRAKEN (43 km from Corfu Town)
The beach (GROC Rating 7/10) is muddy, rather scruffy and busy.

ROUTE TWO
To Afionas via Troumpeta (49 km)
The journey inland from Corfu Town directly to Karoussades in a north-westerly direction passes through lovely countryside and remains totally unspoilt after the left turn at the Tsavros junction. Towards Troumpeta village the road climbs steeply over the spine of the hill range, which runs from the bottom corner of Mt Pantokrator to Paleokatritsa. There are magnificent views of the east coast with Corfu Town in the distance.

One or two of the villages and their settings on this route are very reminiscent of the French Dordogne. Close to the summit of the hill range, the road forks right to Roda and left for Sidari.

The drive from this junction via Arkadades to Sidari is very pleasant, but I am not sure that it is worth making the effort.

SIDARI (37 km from Corfu Town)
Reminiscent of a straggling Canvey Island, with a surprisingly substantial, almost commercial quay alongside which are moored up a few fishing boats. The main 'beach' is

in truth a muddy foreshore and holidaymakers have to walk west out of the village and around the headland to a beach (GROC Rating 7/10) where there is a collection of straw thatched restaurants.

Rooms to let, apartments, villas and hotels. Hotels include the C class *Mimosa*, *Three Brothers* and the D class *Sidari*.

From Sidari the road leads to the beautifully squalid Greek village of

PEROULADES (40 km from Corfu Town)
A sign 'To the Sea' leads to a landslipped promontory about 65 m above the sea. The 'C' class approach road is super value, with the odd snake slithering across the Olive tree bowered lane. On Sundays the Greek women sit out on the front doorsteps in their Corfiot 'get up'.

AGIOS STEFANOS (44 km from Corfu Town)
Corfu in common with some other Greek islands has a "naughty little habit" of using similar names for places miles apart. Agios Stefanos (west coast) as distinct from Agios Stefanos (north-east coast) exemplifies this confusing custom.

Agios Stefanos (west coast) has a lovely sandy bay (GROC Rating 8/10) with seabreakers rolling in across the gently shelving beach, but the surrounding coastal plain, fishing.boat mole and church are being overtaken by the slow but steady encroachment of newly constructed tavernas, restaurants, a mini-market, villas and apartments. All well spread out at the moment but one fears for the future.

Even the kelpy seaweed, on the left-hand side of the bay, adjacent to the fishing quay, is cleared off the beaches by a digger and lorries. Some way off-shore is the island of Mathraki with a smaller island in the foreground.

Hotels include the C class *Nafsika* and *Agios Stefanos*.

Around the cape is the village of

ARILLAS (46 km from Corfu Town)
Comments are much as for Agios Stefanos. There are no fishing boats but the breakers are larger with a splendid pebble and sandy beach (GROC Rating 8/10) and, close inshore, the craggy, uninhabited island of Gravia.

Hotels include the C class *Marina* and *Arila Beach*.

From Arillas it is worth making one's way to the sprawling, agricultural headland village of

AFIONAS (49 km from Corfu Town)
High up on the cliff-top from whence there are stunning views to the south-east with the massive headland of Cape Falakron forming a splendid backdrop and way down below the impressive bay of

AGIOS GEORGIOU
The long sandy beach is pebbly (GROC Rating 8/10) but quite pleasant even close up.

ROUTE THREE
To Liapades via Paleokastritsa (32 km)
The road from the Troumpeta village junction (*See* ROUTE TWO) to Makrades, is similar to a hot, Welsh mountain road (if such a thing is possible). The views over the hillsides to the northern coast and to the south-west, over the bay of Kerkira, are nothing short of spectacular. This is the real Corfu, the little villages and hamlets untouched by the great tourist explosion which has intruded along the coastal region, their gentle way of life only disturbed by the klaxons of the tour-buses as they transport their air conditioned occupants from one 'beauty-spot' to the next.

From Makrades village turn inland to Lakones in order to reach

PALEOKASTRITSA (25 kms from Corfu Town)

The most dramatic area from which to view this tourist magnet is on this route. At a spot a kilometre or so before the village of Lakones, at about 330 m above sea level, to the right, are a few remains of the cliff-top Castle of Angelokastro, from which signals used to be received in Corfu Town.

The view is dramatic but of course the hotels, villas and general development associated with tourism have detracted from the beauty of the scene. The Monastery of Paleokastritsa appears to hang out over the sea's edge, being built on a promontory 100 m up. Of the five or six bays overlooked by the religious house, some form a clover-leaf like shape.

Paleokastritsa is, alas, a typical example of how uncontrolled packaged tourism can 'transform' a once, truly idyllic spot. *Olympic Holidays* appear to have a monopoly on most of the properties on the outskirts while the shoreline is completely dominated by large hotels. Even the once relative solitude of the little sandy coves across the bay have been destroyed due to the flotilla of water taxis which ply constantly back and forth with their cargoes of tourists ever hopeful that they will find a few, free square metres of sand on which to blazon their multi-hued, multi-shaped bodies.

On the other hand it is perhaps noteworthy that Edward Lear, whilst living on the island, commented that he would have to flee the scene of Paleokastritsa due to the impending arrival of picnic parties, and that was sometime in the 1860s. Well, well!

Prices in all establishments tend to be, no are, expensive. C class hotels include the *Apollon, Hermes* and *Odysseus*; the D class *Zephyros*, and E class *Meltemi*. There are a lot of *Rooms* to let.

Paleokastritsa Camping   Tel. 41204
Open April to October.

From Paleokastritsa the road makes its way to

LIAPADES (32 km from Corfu Town)

Here there are reasonably priced *Rooms* to rent in the village and a rather pebbly, weed-strewn beach (GROC Rating 7/10) approached by a steep, narrow road.

The main road then bears down to the Plain of Ropa.

ROUTE FOUR
To Ag Gordis via Ermones Beach (14 km)

The road westwards from Corfu Town proceeds via Alepou, where there are a number of *Rooms* to let, and leads to

AGIOS IOANIS (9 km from Corfu Town)

The unmade turning to the right leads to a Youth Hostel, housed in a faded, converted mansion. There are also *Rooms* to let in the village.

At Kefalovrisso a left-hand turning goes to Kokini close by the junction with the major Pelekas/Ermones road. Turn right here and the other Pelekas road is joined at

VATOS

There are *Rooms* to let in the village.

Vatos Camping   Tel. 94393
The site possesses good facilities which include hot showers, a bar, restaurant, shops as well as car and bike rental.

Beyond Vatos the road passes over an irrigation ditch bridge, after which the Corfu Golf Club turning is to the right and the road swings left to

ERMONES BEACH (15½ km from Corfu Town)

The right-hand hillside (*Fsw*) has, superimposed upon its steep sides, a cliff cable-car, leading to the landscaped *Ermones Beach Hotel* chalets, set on the mountain side.

Thatched straw beach shelters are planted out on a fairly pleasant, if slightly weedy beach (GROC Rating 7/10). A beach bar restaurant, at the far or left-hand side of the small bay, can be reached by tripping over a rather primitive wooden plank, fording the fast-running stream flowing into the sea. The beach bar can also be arrived at by road from Vatos village, turning left back on the main road prior to the irrigation ditch bridge.

On the Ermones/Vatos to Pelekas road, a turning to the right, close to Pelekas, meanders down to

GLIFADA BEACH
Set in a lovely, Olive-groved bay (GROC Rating 8/10), but with a large *Olympic Hotel* complex at the far left or south end. By sticking to the north end, one has only to cope with relatively more modest hotels and beach restaurants. *Rooms* are available.

Between Ermones and Glifada Beach, and reached from Vatos on foot, is a rather isolated monastery overlooking Mirtiotissa beach, in a setting of Olive groves.

South from Glifada Beach is the hillside village of

PELEKAS (13 km from Corfu Town)
Its fame is due to a hilltop viewing platform, which, in daylight hours and good weather, gives a marvellous view over the surrounding countryside and at night makes a splendid spot from which to observe the setting evening sun. Linked with the First World War's German King, the view is known as the Kaiser's Throne.

Many *Rooms* to let and a path down to a commercialised but sandy beach (GROC Rating 8/10).

After Pelekas, the road advances to

KALAFATIONES (18 km from Corfu Town)
In the village a side turning drops down to another commercialised but sandy beach (GROC Rating 8/10).

From Sinarades a splendid, second-class, one-way, mountain road drops over, around and down through a narrow defile to

AGIOS GORDIS BEACH (21 km from Corfu Town)
The vines spread right down to the strip of bamboos separating them from the sandy beach (GROC Rating 8/10) which opens out in a long narrow coastal strip. Plitiri Point rears up in the background to the right (*Fsw*), where the beach degenerates into rocks, and to the left a towering islet marks the end of the bay.

Apart from the magnificence of the scenery Ag Gordis has little to recommended it being rather reminiscent of the more popular, south Cornish harbour village beauty spots — you know, absolutely nowhere to park and double yellow lines down both sides of the street. In fact almost unbelievably the natives have taken to renting out their gardens to motorists for 50 drs and at the end of the road, where it mingles with the beach, there are a couple of small Greek versions of the British, post war, bombsite car parks.

There is, naturally, the mandatory massive hotel blotting out part of the natural beauty of the bay but admittedly this complex is a breathtaking, cliff-hanging, honey-comb, concrete fabrication.

The central one of the three spaced out beach bars is counter, not waiter, service. Not a habit to be encouraged.

On the approach road hotels include the C class *Chrysses Folies*, D class *Diethnes* (ex International) and there are a number of *Rooms* to let.

ROUTE FIVE
To Kanoni Peninsula via Kavos (47 km)
South-west from Corfu Town the road through Kinopiastes and Ag Deka winds down the centre of the island to the Messonghi River bridge (about 20 km from Corfu Town). Prior to

crossing over the bridge a turning left makes its way back to the main coastal road from Messonghi to Corfu Town, but more of that later.

Just over the bridge a turning to the right leads to the village of Agios Matheos (25 km from Corfu Town) skirting the mountain of the same name and passing, on the left, the 13th century Gardiki Castle. Beyond the castle the first unsurfaced road off to the right leads, via Vouniatades back to the Agios Gordis area and the unmetalled turning to the left winds down to

PARAMONA BEACH on Makroulo Bay (27 km from Corfu Town)
The sandy beach (GROC Rating 8/10) is not too busy and there are some amenities.

Returning to the Messonghi River bridge, the road continues down the centre of the island all the way to Kavos, with spur roads off to the left and right which give access to various coastal villages.

At the village of Linia, very nearly opposite the left-hand turning to Hlomos, is a track down to the southern part of

KORISSION LAGOON (28 km from Corfu Town)
The lagoon is still used to net fish and the surroundings are very reminiscent of Norfolk but then time and time again Corfu reminds one of other places in the world. The track peters out amongst sand dunes beyond which, in my opinion, lies the most marvellous and yet undiscovered beach on the whole island — just miles and miles of golden sand. (GROC Rating 9/10, almost 10/10). Apart from a small mobile snack bar perched in the dunes to one side and which sells cold drinks and toasted sandwiches, there are absolutely no amenities on the beach at all. A marvellous spot to escape from it all.

The next turning right off the main road, before the village of Argirades, leads down to the beach of

AGIOS GEORGIOS (31 km from Corfu Town)
This is, in effect, a continuation of the deserted beach described above (GROC Rating 8/10), but the sandy foreshore is considerably narrower and the area is being developed at a rapid rate, with the resultant unsatisfactory jumble of bar/restaurants and villas for let. However, not a bad spot, as yet, especially further south.

There are a few *Room* to let.

At Argirades, the left turning drops down to an Olive-groved plain, with a rather confusing road system. A few kilometres after the village of Neohoraki, a left-hand turning leads to

KOUSPADES (31 km from Corfu Town)
From this village a turning to the left leads to the small cove of Boukari, (GROC Rating 6/10) complete with the C class *Hotel Boukari* and a taverna.

Right in Kouspades sallys forth to the villages of Vassilatika and Korakades. At the latter the road is mainly rock and the villagers are not so inured to tourists that they will not come out on to the roadside and wave. It is possible, by persevering along the track to wind down, through a heavily wooded plantation, and come out at the far end of

PETRETI (32 km from Corfu Town)
Lies in a lightly wooded, flat plain. There is a surprisingly large quay with craft moored up and a number of caiques chocked up here and there on the shore. The waterfront is rather seaweedy and scruffy (GROC Rating 6/10) and were it not for the heat and the spread-out taverna, with a large marquee covered hardstanding, the scene could well be the Cornish Helford river at middle tide.

If, back at Neohoraki, the right-hand turning is taken, the narrow road leads through well spread out, aged Olive groves with scattered settlements and herds of sheep and goats tended by one of the family. A further fork results in a left-handed turning and the road to Petreti, whilst the right-hand turning leads to the hamlets of Agios Nikolaos and

Roumanades.

Back at Argirades, the main road goes on to Perivolion, where a left turn advances down a steep and accelerating descent to a coastal bay, whereon two beach restaurant bar owners scrap it out in a rather undignified manner to secure visitors patronage. The trees grow right down to the seafront and there is a small quay to which are moored up local caiques and fishing boats.

The road system and signposting on the route to Ano Lefkimmi and Lefkimmi is, to understate the matter, rather confusing. This section has been under repair for the last 3 years and appears to be heading for another 3 years of repair, or disrepair depending on your point of view, making for some rather exciting moments especially on a scooter! In Ano Lefkimmi there is a turning left to the coastal hamlet of

ALIKES (43 km from Corfu Town)
The beach (GROC Rating 7/10) is sandy, busy but not bereft of space. Another turn-off at Ano Lefkimmi sallys forth to the inland villages of Bastatika, Neohori, Kritika, Paleohori, Dragotina and Spartero.

POTAMI (Potamos) (41 km from Corfu Town)
The village possesses a fine Bailey bridge crossing a cutting resembling a canal, but which is in fact a river. The scene is most surprising, for there are caiques and small boats lineally moored up on both sides of the river, a sight that puts one in mind of Holland or a very hot Midlands canal scene, not Corfu!

Incidentally, in 1985, the local residents blockaded the bridge for a few days, cutting off road communications to Kavos. This 'theft of the highway' was in protest at height-of-summer water shortages which were blamed on the tourists. Naturally, as an ill wind doesn't blow everybody ill, the local boat owners made a financial killing ferrying in and out-going Kavos area package holiday-makers to and from Corfu Town and the airport.

A couple of hotels and numerous *Rooms* to let.

From Potami, the road passes through a plain, heavily wooded with Olive trees and groves to

KAVOS (47 km from Corfu Town)
The original settlement has been subject to villa type, ribbon development, with dusty streets and a very fly-blown feel. The awful beach (GROC Rating 5/10) is to be avoided at all costs being reminiscent of Southend on a hot, August Bank Holiday. The expensive, rather grotty beach-bars are constantly packed with pink 'tranny' carrying youngsters — the majority of whom are decidedly the worse for an excess of alcohol by mid-afternoon. Admittedly by proceeding northwards along the 5 km sweeping beach the ambience becomes progressively more acceptable (GROC Rating 7/10).

Accommodation includes the C class *Hotel Kavos* and many *Rooms* to let.

A great pity that it is on this note that the description of the southern tip of Corfu must end. Perhaps it might be as well to walk on to the cliffs overlooking the bay alongside Cape Asprokavos, passing the site of a ruined monastery and the surrounding buildings. This area and the approach are very beautiful, with old Olive trees and the now familiar and almost exotic growth of bracken covering much of the ground.

Back at the Messonghi River bridge once again, the main road to Messonghi leads on to the major coastal road and the most intense development on Corfu, stretching all the way from Messonghi up to Perama, across the bay from the Peninsula of Kanoni.

MESSONGHI & MIRANGI BAY (23 km from Corfu Town)
Both are becoming thoroughly despoiled although on this stretch of the coast lovely groves of Olive trees still grow down to the narrow, crowded beach (GROC Rating 7/10).

Hotels include the C class *Rossis, Roulis* and *Melisa Beach* and there are a number of rooms to let as well as a camping site, *The Sea Horse Camping.*

MORAITIKA (20 km from Corfu Town)
Heavily developed though still attractive with the C class *Hotels Sea Bird* and *Margarita.*

From here to Benitses, the development increases, in a 1960s low rise, Spanish style, 'Costa-built-up', culminating in the depredation of

BENITSES (12½ km from Corfu Town)
Well, yes! Benitses is still billed by many holiday brochures as a genuine Corfiot fishing village. I must admit, as long ago as 1983, to seeing a caique towing its attendant fishing boats with their large sardine lanterns slung over the stern, so I suppose, with some poetic licence, it can still be referred to as a fishing village, maybe! It possesses a narrow, seaweed festooned beach which is usually very packed (GROC Rating 6/10).

Hotels include C class *Corfu Maris,* the D class *Benitsa,* the E class *Eros* and *Riviera* and there are **Rooms** to let.

From here it is only a kilometre to the

ACHILLEION PALACE (10 km from Corfu Town)
Built for Empress Elizabeth of Austria in 1891, subsequently owned by the German Kaiser, the Greek Government and then finally leased to private interests, who now use part of the building as a casino. This is only open to non-Greeks, so take your passport to prove nationality, The architecture is often airily criticised, but one pile of 'neo' this or that looks much like another (does it not?) but I must admit it does resemble a large wedding cake.

From the Achilleion Palace, the road proceeds up the coast to

PERAMA (7 km from Corfu Town)
From here can be viewed the much photographed twin islets of Kanoni. On one of them, reached by a causeway, is built Vlacherna Monastery from which it takes its name. The other, Pondi Konnisi, which is part wooded, has a chapel. In the background are the Halikiopoulou lagoon, the south end of the Kanoni Peninsula and the airport strip.

A causeway enables one to walk or scooter across the mouth of the lagoon and a trip boat plies hither and thither.

Hotels include the C class *Continental, Aegli, Pontikonisi* and E class *Perama.* **Rooms** to let.

The road swings left to Vrioni, where it joins up with the main Kinopiastes to Corfu Town road.

KANONI
This was a pretty, tree-covered peninsula south of Corfu Town, but the builders of the high-rise hotels, and apartments as well as the villa developers have sorted that all out! The road system is a flattened, circuitous one-way route. *See* **Beaches, A to Z** for further description of Kanoni's appeals.

The *Hilton Hotel* 'sports' a four-lane, ten-pin bowling alley, which might interest some home-sick tourists. I am not sure I would wish to stay in a hotel, overlooking the swamp created by the position of the airport runway in the lagoon and deafened by the intermittent thunder of aircraft taking off and landing, but it must be enjoyable, mustn't it? However, as has been commented upon, the little man-made beach below the Hilton Hotel is quite pleasant for swimming.

One other thought-provoking view as one boards any departing plane are the designated areas, on the peninsula side of the runway, covering several football-pitch-sized enclosures, each piled high with discarded, lost, unclaimed and mouldering luggage.

Perhaps the Corfiot character is best summed up by a notice once pinned to some Olive trees on the edge of one of the island villages which was reprinted in a national English newspaper some years ago. In essence this politely requested tour buses to turn around and leave the village and its inhabitants to their own devices so as not to spoil the intrinsic character of their life. Nice that!

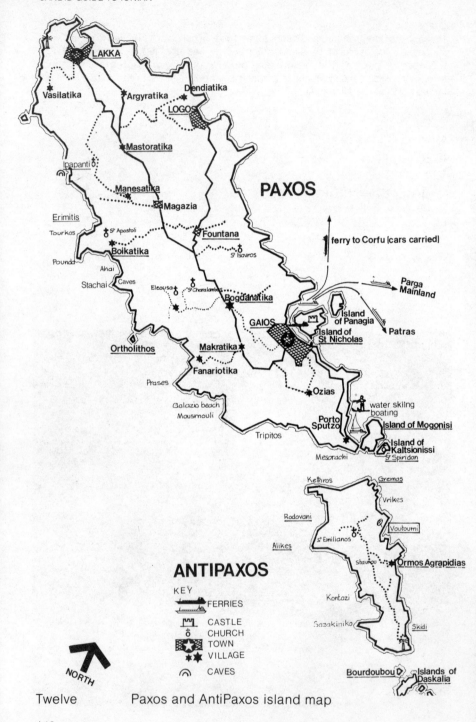

LAKKA

Vasilatika

Argyratika

Dendiatika

LOGOS

Mastoratika

Ipapanti

Manesatika

Magazia

Erimitis

Tourkos St Apostoli

Boikatika

Pounda

Ahai

Stachai Caves

Eleousa St Charalambos

Fountana

St Isavros

PAXOS

ferry to Corfu [cars carried]

Parga
Mainland

Bogdanatika

GAIOS

Island
of Panagia

Island of
St Nicholas

Patras

Ortholithos

Makratika

Fanariotika

Prases

Galazio beach
Mousmouli

Tripitos

Ozias

water skiing
boating

Porto
Sputzo

Island of Mogonisi

Island of
Kaltsionissi

Mesorachi

St Spiridon

Kelkiros

Gremos

Vrikes

Rodovani

St Emilianos

Voutoumi

Alikes

Stavrou

Ormos Agrapidias

ANTIPAXOS

Kontozi

KEY

FERRIES

Sazakiniko

Skidi

CASTLE

CHURCH

TOWN

VILLAGE

Bourdoubou

Islands of
Daskalia

CAVES

NORTH

Twelve   Paxos and AntiPaxos island map

13 PAXOS (Paxoi, Paxi) and ANTIPAXOS
Ionian Islands

****

FIRST IMPRESSIONS
Boulder strewn hillsides and dry river beds; Olive groves; narrow, olive-blackened roads; old ruined buildings; the smell of olive dross.

SPECIALITIES
Olives, olive oil and the wine of Antipaxos.

RELIGIOUS HOLIDAYS & FESTIVALS
include: Assumption (Dormition) Day, 15th August.

VITAL STATISTICS
Tel. prefix 0662. The island is 9½ km long and 4 km wide. Paxos has about 2250 inhabitants of which some 500 live in Gaios port.

GENERAL
Paxos, like Ios in the Cyclades, is a reasonably priced island and probably for the same reasons. The major factor may well be the preponderance of British tourists, who are rather less free-spending than other Europeans, or just more careful, depending upon your viewpoint. Although averagely inexpensive a few items are noticeably more costly probably because nearly all supplies, including groceries, have to be 'imported'.

Paxos is very different from any of the other Ionian islands, with an 'enchanted forest' feel when driving on the minor roads. These wind up and down through boulder strewn, rambling, cool, shady, Olive groves, and the olive-blackened lanes are often set above the surrounding land, which seems to have been sculpted away. Many of the Olive groves are extremely old and the individual trees are gnarled, twisted and of immense size.

In common with the other Ionian islands, Paxos is extremely verdant, due to the comparatively high winter rainfall experienced. This fact is evidenced by the deep, summer-dry, rocky river-beds, which interweave with the roads and are criss-crossed by stone built bridges, an unusual sight on a Greek island.

The island's agriculture is almost entirely based on the olive. Prior to harvest time, the rolled up nets are almost everywhere in evidence. When the olives are 'in season' the nets are opened out and laid on the ground beneath the spreading branches. A curious sight are the large bells strapped to and hanging down from convenient branches. These are to sound a warning in case of fire, of which the islanders are truly very apprehensive, well all right, terrified. For this reason random camping is strictly forbidden, a stricture which must be obeyed.

It takes a little time to realise that the houses, often comparatively massively constructed of dressed stone, are, unusually, not painted white. Apparently derelict buildings and old olive presses are littered about amongst the forests of Olive trees and impart an ethereal overlay to the cool, fairy-tale, almost medieval atmosphere.

A number of factors combine to make Paxos a difficult island on which to find accommodation, and a backpacker's nightmare at the height of the season. For instance, the two Gaios hotels usually listed are block-booked by a sailing school and a tour operator. To make matters more difficult for unplanned short-term stopovers, the three main towns (port/villages really) have become family, holiday-villa territory. The various specialist tour companies have staked out nearly all the houses and flats, with every nook and cranny exploited to create more accommodation of this type.

Unlike Corfu, the government officials speak very little, if any English, so visitors cannot expect to have their most searching inquiries met with anything more than a shrug of the shoulders.

(Porto) GAIOS (Paxi): capital & main port

Gaios town and harbour is positioned in a small bay into which the large island of St Nicholas fits, leaving a wide channel running all the way round the quay. The New Port is at the far north side of the harbour and is separated from the main port and waterfront by a curving, dusty, unsurfaced road, resulting in a rather tiring trudge, especially if disembarking late at night.

Gaios, which has a rather piratical air about it, spreads along the quayside, radiating out from the attractive town square in the narrow, sea-level valley. In fact the town is extremely beguiling and many a traveller planning a short visit might well stay on and on and on. . . .

Vessels of all types including trip boats, small tramp-like ferries, large luxury motor cruisers, yachts, caiques and small sailing dinghies are anchored gunwhale to gunwhale, bow or stern on to the quayside which they fill from end to end. On the way round from the New Port, the sailing school dinghies are the first craft to be encountered. These are followed by the larger vessels, with the bigger pleasure boat caiques centred alongside the main square part of the quay, then private yachts and finally the smaller fishing boats and caiques towards the south-east end of the quay road.

This is definitely a 'Greek town' as defined towards the end of Chapter Three. The rubbish is collected daily by a bell ringing character, a look-alike for Zorba's father, who bestrides a Greek cross between a dumper truck and a motorised palett cart.

ARRIVAL BY FERRY

The larger inter-island ferries dock at the New Port or quay, at the end of the unmade cul-de-sac to the north of Gaios. After landing it is only possible to turn left for the 200 to 300 m walk to the heart of the port. The smaller, local ferry docks conveniently on the northern edge of the town. Following the harbour wall round to the left leads, after only two or three blocks (or another 150 m) to the main square.

The local **FB Kamelia** is an interesting ferry in that it is a representative example of the average island ferry-boat prior to the mid-1970s. A tiddler compared to the modern-day giants, the small flush stern deck may hold, for instance, two or three cars wedged in and a truck stacked high with household contents (which seem mainly to consist of old bedsteads). Additionally, there might well be two or three goats tethered to the taffrail and a few crates holding chickens. The small main deck cabin is on the same level as the deck and houses the purser, a snack bar, bolted down tables, padded bench seats and squatty loos. The ferry makes the occasional mainland stop at Parga on a basis that I do not comprehend.

THE ACCOMMODATION & EATING OUT

The lop-sidedness of the tourist development, concentrating as it does on villa-lets, has distorted the normal island mix of accommodation. Due to the self-catering nature and the number of the villas, compared to other islands, there are not so many tavernas, more cafe-bar restaurants and no souvlaki's but there is a shop serving tiropites (cheese-pies).

Bearing in mind the previous remarks in respect of the availability (or more correctly the lack of availability) of accommodation, it should come as no surprise that there are not queues of welcoming house owners swarming to beat weary travellers to the ground with offers of rooms. But we may well be able to overcome this difficulty. For a start, if arriving on the privately run Corfu to Paxos ferry, the **FB Kamelia**, a card stuck up in the craft's saloon indicates that the captain's wife has rooms to let, so make an approach prior to disembarking.

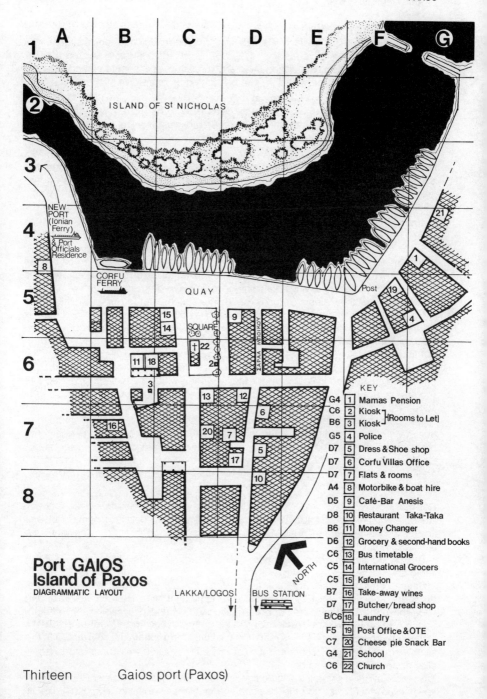

KEY

G4	1	Mamas Pension
C6	2	Kiosk }Rooms to Let]
B6	3	Kiosk
G5	4	Police
D7	5	Dress & Shoe shop
D7	6	Corfu Villas Office
D7	7	Flats & rooms
A4	8	Motorbike & boat hire
D5	9	Café-Bar Anesis
D8	10	Restaurant Taka-Taka
B6	11	Money Changer
D6	12	Grocery & second-hand books
C6	13	Bus timetable
C5	14	International Grocers
C5	15	Kafenion
B7	16	Take-away wines
D7	17	Butcher/bread shop
B/C6	18	Laundry
F5	19	Post Office & OTE
C7	20	Cheese pie Snack Bar
G4	21	School
C6	22	Church

**Port GAIOS
Island of Paxos**
DIAGRAMMATIC LAYOUT

LAKKA/LOGOS

BUS STATION

NORTH

Thirteen   Gaios port (Paxos)

The Accommodation

At the height-of-summer the lack of sufficient accommodation occasions the authorities to insist that travellers purchasing a ticket to the island must have booked a room. Naturally to facilitate this stipulation there are 'rooms for sale' prior to embarkation but naturally rather more expensive than can be located by one's own efforts.

Hotel San Giorgio (Agios Georgios)

There is really no point in giving any directions as the hotel has no rooms available, being block-booked by a dinghy sailing outfit. Sited on a hillside overlooking the sea cutting, facing towards the New Quay.

Hotel Paxos Beach

Here again the Paxos Beach is tour operator booked. This Butlin chalet-inspired complex is in a most attractive situation to the south of Gaios, on the left-hand side of the Mogonisi road. The Olive-tree covered hillside, in which the buildings nestle, slopes down to the water's edge and fringes a clear, blue-water, crescent-shaped bay.

Mamas (Tmr 1.G4)

Directions: Her house is situated on the south end of the harbour quay road, in the corner of the block immediately prior to the village school (*Tmr* 21.G3/4), about a hundred metres before the town statue of an island hero. Incidentally this statue is mounted on a small plaza jutting out into the sea by the harbour southern mole. I am on intimate terms with this square, some years ago having spent a night on the unyielding stone flags. I would have written slept, but the Gaios mosquitos made sure that the night's rest was rather fitful.

Mamas (I never was able to catch her name) has clean simple rooms. The house is splendidly sited on the quayside road overlooking the south portion of the harbour, where the local fishing boats and caiques moor up. Due to the configuration of the port harbour wall, most of the town's activity can be viewed from the narrow balconies of the rooms. The bedrooms are on the first floor. Admittedly access to the excellent bathroom and shower, positioned on the ground floor, is via the family kitchen, which is usually jam-packed with somebody. But it is invidious to expect perfection and, with a double room starting at about 800 drs, it must rate as a find.

On one occasion, whilst lazing on the balcony sipping the day away, I chanced to observe a caique berth up. Tethered to the small foredeck were a family of goats. The pantomime that ensued in order to get the animals ashore was worth the room rent alone. On the same day a fisherman and his wife moored up and dragged from the hold an enormous flat fish, which many of the villagers gathered around to shout about for the next few hours, all just beneath us.

Rooms

The ports two periptero (kiosks), (*Tmr* 2.C6 and 3.B6) advertise details of rooms to let. One is at the top left-hand corner of the Main Square, the other down the street, to the right of the first kiosk (*Sbo*).

The police station (*Tmr* 4.G5) has lists of rooms but the officers are reluctant informants.

Other rooms and flats in Gaios (as well as Lakka), are available from a rather disingenuous Greek 'Mr Fixit', actually Mr ΧΡΥΣΙΚΟΠΟΥΝΟΣ. He runs the dress and shoe shop (*Tmr* 5.D7) on the left, opposite a shop with a rather noticeable sunblind, sign-written **Athena Souvenirs Greek Art**. From the quay proceed up the lane named ΣΑΡΔΑ ΜΠΟΙΚΟΥ, across the transverse road and past the **Corfu Village** office (*Tmr* 6.D7). The slightly squalid-looking accommodation (*Tmr* 7.D7) is tucked away up a short, narrow alley opposite 'Mr Fixit's' shop.

Spiros Markris, a saturnine featured young man, and his cuddly sister Georgia, both speak excellent English and run the scooter and bike hire operation (*Tmr* 8.A4) directly opposite the quay side berth of the **FB Kalemia**. They have *Rooms* available for let in

Makratika (the first village out of Gaios) starting at about 600 drs for a double room.

Dinos Tourism & Travel close by the Square can also dispense advice in respect of rooms.

The Eating Out

As explained, there are not a great number of restaurants or tavernas. The Main Square is well endowed with cafe-bars on the left (*Sbo*), including:

Anesis (*Tmr* 9.D5)
The first cafe-bar on this side. They serve reasonably priced fare including a good plate of eggs and bacon which can, after months abroad prove a welcome and nostalgic alternative to the rather bland Greek version of a French Continental breakfast.

The opposite side of the square to the *Anesis* is a men-only Kafenion (*Tmr* 15.C5).

Taka-Taka Restaurant (*Tmr* 10.D8)
Situated in a continuation of the same road as 'Mr Fixit' referred to under **The Accommodation**, but further on up towards the bus station.

A family business offering a good value, inexpensive, but rather limited menu. Father and son serve at the patio tables, the food is hot and the usual offering of stuffed tomatoes and moussaka, are complemented with fassolakia freska (green beans) if requested beforehand and providing they have been landed from Corfu. Also available are delicious, but, as is usual, expensive fish dishes, including lobster — very nice if you can afford them.

Hunger-struck travellers might try the

Snack bar (*Tmr* 20.C7)
Good value cheese pies.

THE A TO Z OF USEFUL INFORMATION
BANKS
There are no banks, only a money-change office (*Tmr* 11.B6), run by an earnest young man, round-faced and complete with steel-rimmed spectacles. He works from a counter in a dark and dusty general store situated in the small colonnaded walkway, on a street two back and parallel to the quayside. This is off to the right from the top of the Main Square and on the right, very nearly opposite one of the periptero's. The rate of exchange is a few drachmae or so below that offered by the banks.

BEACHES
It is necessary to travel south on the Mogonisi road (*See* ROUTE TWO)

BICYCLE & SCOOTER HIRE
There are a number of bicycle and scooter operators but no cars for hire. Prices are average and my favourite firm is run by the brother and sister team of Spiros and Georgia Makris, located in the bend of the north end of the main town quay (*Tmr* 8.A4). The local olive press waste, or, dross drains into the small harbour at this point with a resultant distinctive smell. Spiros will not negotiate rates, but they are an interesting pair to while away the time with and he may acquiesce to a hirer helping him repair one of the two-wheeled conveyances or a boat.

BOOKSELLERS
There is no bookseller, but the grocer to the left, from the top of the Main Square, has a selection of second-hand English books (*Tmr* 12.D6).

English newspapers are available from the kiosk in the Main Square. (*Tmr* 2.C6).

BOAT HIRE
Or more correctly, dinghy hire. A day boat suitable for four and complete with an eight

horse-power outboard motor costs from 1000 drs plus the cost of 2½ gallons of fuel. There are a number of firms letting out craft and the beauty of the Paxos and Antipaxos coastlines is so dramatic that it is well worth considering hiring a craft. In a day there is time and enough fuel to journey completely round Paxos or out to and around Antipaxos (but not both!).

As indicated Spiros, he of the scooters (*Tmr* 8.A4), is also in the dinghy hire business.

BREAD SHOPS
See **Commercial Shopping Area.**

BUSES
The bus station is on the edge of town on the main road out of Gaios reached from the right-hand side of the top of the Main Square (*Sbo*). The bus timetable is pinned to a post on the corner of the Main Square (*Tmr* B13.C6).

Bus timetable

Lakka, Logos, Gaios	0630 hrs
Gaios, Logos, Lakka	1000 hrs
Lakka - Gaios	1100 hrs
Gaios - Lakka	1245 hrs
Lakka - Gaios	1700 hrs
Gaios - Lakka	1900 hrs

COMMERCIAL SHOPPING AREA
There is no market or commercial shopping area and sad to say, even the last family bakery was knocked down some years ago to make way for development. The proprietor of the grocery/second-hand bookshop explained to me that bread is now sold on the 'German' system. I think he means that a bakery distributes to various shops. Sounds English to me and one wonders when there will only be sliced, polythene-wrapped products available?

On the corner of the Main Square and quayside road, opposite the *Anesis,* is a shop labelled 'International Grocers' and the proprietor does stock a fairly wide range of goods. (*Tmr* 14.C5).

Beyond the money-changer (*Tmr* 11.B6) and up the street, just past and opposite a pretty arch with suspended bell, is a lane on the right, off which is a cellar with draught wines for sale. (*Tmr* 16.B7).

Prior to reaching the *Taka-Taka* restaurant and on the opposite corner of the road is a butchers shop selling bread from a cabinet (*Tmr* 17.D7).

FERRY BOATS
The island is served by the larger ferry-boats of the Ionian Lines which dock at the New Port, and the locally owned, ancient ferry **FB Kamelia** that has been discussed under **Arrival by Ferry** earlier in the chapter and is a collectable!

Tickets have to be purchased on board.

Ferry-boat timetable

Day	Departure time	Ferry-boat	Port/Island of Call
Daily (except Sundays*) Duration 2½ hrs	0730 hrs	FB Kamelia	Corfu

*But note I have known the craft sail on Sundays. As advised, nay instructed elsewhere, times and frequency must be checked out.

| Tuesday | 0515 hrs | CF Kefallinia and/or CF Argostoli | Corfu |
| | 0900 hrs | | Fiscardon (Cephalonia), Sami (Cephalonia), Patras (M) |

LAUNDRY (*Tmr* 18.B/C6)
Close by the money-change office.

MEDICAL CARE
Fall ill, if you must, while on Corfu, okay!

OTE
See **Post Office.**

PETROL
The petrol station is just out of the port on the main Lakka road.

PLACES OF INTEREST
Rather like Corfu, Paxos is not over-endowed with dramatic (or for that matter, any) ancient ruins.

The Island of Ag or St Nicholas, which forms the seeming creek, channel or estuary river of Gaios harbour front, has a castle or kastro, originally built in the 14th century and restored by the French in the early 1800s.

The Island of Panagia, just beyond Ag Nicholas, is famed for the pilgrimage that takes place on the 15th August, after which festivities continue long into the night on the plateia, or Main Square of Gaios.

On the road around to the New Port, on the left, is a most impressive building erected for the British Residency and now housing the port officials.

The varied and numerous island churches are rather lovely, if simple.

The several sea caves on the west coast are set at the base of dramatically towering cliff-face which plunges into the sea in awesome fashion. The most celebrated of the caverns is perhaps Ipapanti, 'a pit-stop' for seals but large enough to be used as a natural submarine pen by the Greeks during World War Two. Other natural phenomena include the flying buttress of rock at Tripitos, the high pillar of the rock, Ortholithos, which towers some 30 m above the sea, opposite Petriti cave and lastly the triple sea-caves at Stachai.

Did you know... Aristotle Onassis is rumoured to have paid for the island roads to be tarmacadamed, in gratitude for the islanders friendliness. Is my scepticism showing or was the gesture to alleviate the threat of a tax bill or ameliorate central government revenue enquiries?

POLICE
Town (*Tmr* 4.G5)
In the same block as the Post Office, but at the rear, on the edge of a pretty little plateia.

Port
As previously described their offices are located in the architecturally prominent building that was the British Residency, north of the town on the unsurfaced road to the New Port.

POST OFFICE & OTE (*Tmr* 19.F5)
South from the Main Square, along the quay road.

TAXIS
I am reliably informed they are in existence, but I cannot recall seeing a taxi rank.

TELEPHONE NUMBERS & ADDRESSES

Police — Town	Tel. 31222
Port	Tel. 31259
Post Office	Tel. 31256
OTE	Tel. 31215
First Aid	Tel. 31466

TRAVEL AGENTS

In the past none and the town's periptero's acted as unofficial information offices for information.

In the last few years **Dinos Tourism & Travel** has been established. Next to the Main Square. Handles rooms, villas, excursions, plane and ferry tickets.

ROUTE ONE
To Lakka (8 km)

The signposting of the island's few roads is very poor. The main road from Gaios to the north Paxos coastal resort and port of Lakka runs along the elevated spine of the island with various roads running off like the bones of a fish.

The section of the road climbing out of Gaios to the village of Makratika snakes through beautifully terraced groves of Olives and dry water courses. The old and gnarled trees, still being worked, are sprinkled with ancient, grey-stoned buildings set in the shadow of the tortured, spreading branches.

There is a fine church on the roadside at Makratika. Note that the shorter, subsidiary route from Gaios to beyond Makratika is a rather more typically Greek road, winding through boulder-strewn and shelterless foothills.

From Makratika to Bogdanatika the road has been stained black over the years with the juice of fallen olives crushed beneath the tyres of passing donkeys and vehicles.

The part of the route connecting Bogdanatika and Fountana breaks out of the Olive groves into Cypress tree and boulder strewn hills. Beyond Foutana the road plunges back into Olive groves.

Keep an eye open for the turning off to the left, leading to Boikatika village and ending up at the church of Ag Apostoli which is situated on a knoll, to the right of a shady farmyard. The naive, crude simplicity of the church is attractive. From the graveyard planted with Yew trees and complete with water cistern, there is a stunning view of the towering chalky cliffs of Erimitis. Well worth the dusty, stony, trip.

Reference to the water cistern reminds me to point out that these storage tanks abound, indicating the paucity of drinking water on Paxos. The fact that they are usually locked (which used to be a most unusual occurrence in Greece), emphasises the value of their contents.

At Fountana, a road to the right leads to

LOGOS (about 6 km from Gaios Port)

A small, very pretty but rather 'gushy holiday villa' port, with a number of agreeable cafe-bars and tavernas spread around the quay road. On the left-hand side of the harbour (*Fsw*), is an industrial building with a tall, smoking chimney on the shore of a small stony beach. To see how the place used to be, sneak a look around the far right-hand seawards corner of the quay. There is a baker and grocer.

Back on the main Gaios to Lakka road, from the village of Magazia the route which strikes out to Mastoratika is at quite a height following, as it does, the raised, rocky backbone of the island with the countryside falling away on each side.

From Magazia, a left-hand turning winds off and round to rejoin the main Lakka road via the village of Manesatika, Ipapanti church and several back gardens on a distinctly 'Z' class road or 'C' class donkey track. The enchanted down-hill journey passes through tree-covered hillsides interspersed with many large, old and dilapidated houses, finally combining with the main road, lower down on the Lakka valley plain. The interesting twin domed church of Ipapanti, and its accompanying belfry, is Byzantine and contains some relics.

Beyond Mastoratika the route diverges on its final approach to Lakka port. From the right-hand road a lovely country lane drops down to the port of Logos.

Descending on to the outskirts of Lakka, on either route, and the surroundings become depressingly dirty and ramshackle, which squalor spreads out into the lower Olive-grove covered foothills.

LAKKA (about 8 km from Gaios Port)
The northern port and village of Paxos. The very pleasant harbour bay is almost totally enclosed by a circular promontory and the narrowness of the mouth, or entrance of the port is emphasized by a stone mole built out from the right hillside (*Fsw*). The rather dusty village is still attractive, even if it is 'holiday villa' country.

A pleasant shingle beach with sandy bottom, a number of cafe-bars, tavernas and shops complete a very pleasant ambience. There are other beaches to left and right.

English is well spoken and understood due to the presence of a scattering of English expatriates domiciled here.

THE ACCOMMODATION & EATING OUT
The Accommodation
Apart from our man, Mr **ΧΡΥΣΙΚΟΠΟΥΝΟΣ**, who has accommodation (*See* Gaios) there are rooms to let at

The Pension 'Lefkothea'   Tel. 31807
Mine host, John F Grammatikos (a famous island surname), has a truly RAF flying officer, handlebar moustache, is very chatty and speaks excellent English. His establishment is near to the seafront and may be as good as he would have one believe.

Rates are negotiable from 800 drs per day for a double room.

The Eating Out
Undistinguished

ROUTE TWO
Gaios Port to Mogonisi island (3 km)
South from Gaios, a surfaced road pleasantly 'corniches' along the coastline, past the aforementioned *Hotel Paxos Beach*, finally petering out alongside a small, dirty and pebbly strip of sea-shore. Here are chocked up a number of caiques, in various states of disrepair. Once having weaved around these, there are some pleasantly shelving, flat slabs of rock on which to sunbathe and/or off which to swim. By sidling along the hillside and tripping over a causeway of rocks between the mainland, access is made to

THE ISLAND OF MOGONISI (3 km from Gaios Port)
A pretty yacht anchorage, with a small, sandy strip of beach surmounted by a large beach bar and restaurant stretching up the hillside. Although fairly crowded and on the Gaios excursion trip-boat schedule, it is a very pleasant location at which to while away a day, swimming, sunbathing, drinking and eating. The bay is buzzing with activity, as there is water-skiing as well as sailboat and dinghy hire, giving the place a leisure-centre feel.

There is a lovely, blue sea-water cave on the west of Mogonisi island off which, and separated by a channel, wide and deep enough for a yacht to cruise through, is the

ISLAND OF KALTSIONISSI
On the islet is a small, isolated hermit's chapel built beside the water's edge.

PAXOS ISLAND EXCURSION TO:
ANTIPAXOS (Antipaxoi, Andipaxi)

The 2 km straits between the southern end of Paxos and Antipaxos can be crossed by a small boat in 15 to 20 minutes. In the main, the rocky coastline of the island is split up by narrow strips of rocky, pebbly or sandy beaches. As on Paxos, the east coast consists of comparatively gentle hillsides encircling a series of bays, whilst the west coastline is much more dramatic with towering cliff-faces plunging into the deeps of the Ionian sea. Down the east coast, beyond the headland of Gremos, there are a number of lovely, isolated bays starting with Vrikes.

The second, main bay is that of Voutoumi. This is absolutely beautiful, perhaps one of the loveliest in Greece, with a clean, golden sand beach and seabed and clear, clear water. There is a rather battered, thatched-roof beach-hut, with a faded, crudely painted sign, **Water Ski School Olympic Instruction**, but this business appears to be dormant. The problem with this bay and its seemingly splendid isolation is that passenger boats from Gaios Port make this a day-trip. To avoid the excursionists, arrive early, leave late, or run on down the coast to the other bays.

Prior to reaching Ormos Agrapidias, there are two lovely bays with a sandy sea-floor but round pebble foreshores. Ormos Agrapidias is the very small harbour of Antipaxos with a low, rocky mole, six or so fishing boats that moor here and a track up to the interior.

Towards the south end of the island, stony Ormos Skidi gives access, via a winding track, to the very pretty lighthouse and dwelling complete with, surprise, surprise, an ornamental garden. Rounding the furthermost part of the island, in the channel created by the outlying islands of Bourdoubou and Daskalia, is rather awe-inspiring and reminiscent of Lands End in calm seas. The water is absolutely clear and the outlines of the great shelving slabs of rock down below that form the sea-bottom can be seen with frightening clarity.

Around the corner of the southern-most point there is a small stony bay and, a few minutes further on, a large pebble sand cove between the headland of Sazakiniko and Kontazi.

Perhaps almost the last of the western seaboard backdrops says it all. Three pebbly coves have been scoured and eroded out, over the millenium, between the headlands of Alikes and Rodovani. A lofty, mountainous islet, set in this incredibly dramatic scene, soars skywards with seagulls wheeling and screaming in their endless aerial rough and tumble.

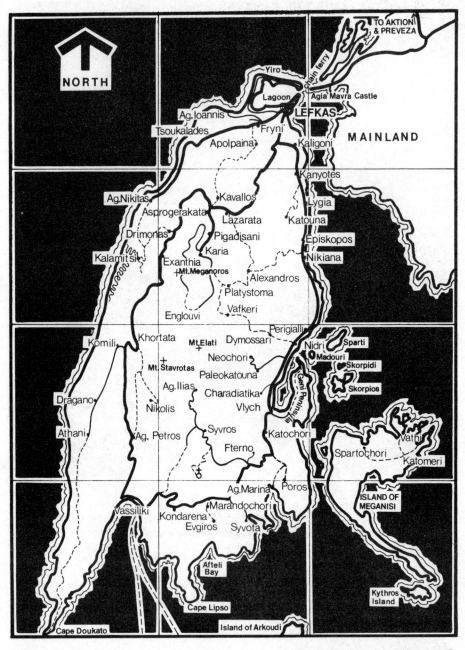

Island of **LEFKAS**

Fourteen   Lefkas island map

14 Lefkas (Lefkada, Levkas)
Ionian Islands   *****

FIRST IMPRESSIONS
Tin reinforced wooden buildings; mountainous countryside; womens brown dresses; French spoken; quintessential, unspoilt Greek island; pork meals.

SPECIALITIES
Marinated fried fish salad or savaro; salami; rice pudding.

RELIGIOUS HOLIDAYS & FESTIVALS
include: 30th May — Service followed by dancing and feasting, Faneromeni Monastery (Fryni); 11-12th August — two day festival in honour of St Spiridon, Karia; August — Music and folk dance festival*.

* See **Places of Interest, A to Z, Lefkas Town.**

VITAL STATISTICS
Tel. prefix 0645. The island is 32 km long, up to 12¾ km wide with an approximate area of 295 sq km. The population numbers some 25,000 of which total up to 7,000 live in Lefkas Town.

HISTORY
Historically and mythologically the island of Lefkas has a lot going for it. The old cutting separating the island from the mainland was a man-made channel excavated in the fifth century BC and deepened in the nineteenth century AD. A Mr Dorpfeld, a German archaeologist, rushed about excitedly at the turn of the 1900s loudly proclaiming that Lefkas was in fact the ancient Ithaca of Homeric connections. On the road between Lefkas Town and Nidri there is the site of one of his digs.

At the southern most tip of the island, the Cape of Doukato, the mythological poetess Sappho, spurned in love, is reputed to have thrown herself over the edge with the resultant 'dashing' death at the cliff bottom. Certainly during the period of Apollo worship, socially unacceptable types were sacrificed by 'urging them' to imitate lemmings. Callow Roman youth are supposed to have developed the art a stage further, a sort of historical hand-gliding, by jumping over the edge with birds feathers strapped to them. Survivors were plucked (oh no) from the 'hoggin' by craft standing off. Perhaps they were sponsored!

GENERAL
The island was left out of the first edition of **GROCs Candid Guide to the Ionian** for the (hair-splitting?) reason that Lefkas is arguably not an island at all added to which, until recently, access from the other Ionian islands was almost impossible. The hardening up of the Vassiliki to Fiscardon (Cephalonia), Kioni and Vathi (Ithaca) caique ferry-boat connections; the ability to fly between Athens and Preveza airport and the efficient bus service between Athens and Lefkas has persuaded me to correct the omission.

Despite the discreet presence of villa holiday-makers at Lefkas Town, Nidri and Vassiliki this remains a fascinatingly Greek island that has an almost unique quality amongst its genre.

LEFKAS: capital & main port
Vaguely reminiscent of Cowes on the Isle of Wight with a resident fleet of charter yachts. Certainly a town of immense charm and infinite interest. There are a number of basic types

of house architecture and building materials — stone; stone with timber overhanging the first storey; timber frame with brick infill and timber plated with tin plate, and or galvanised corrugated iron. The toy-town look to the place owes much to a long history of earthquakes culminating in the big shake up of 1948. Other little oddities include the town clocks mounted on skeletal iron frameworks (similar to the water windmills of Crete); the open gully drains and the brown dress of the women. The quay area is disporportionately massive stretching as it does from the bridge by the lagoon all the way round the eastern seaward periphery of the town. A number of private yachts moor up, bow or stern to, close by the small town park.

ARRIVAL BY AIR
There are flights from Athens to Preveza from whence a ferry can be taken to Aktion and then a bus on to Lefkas. *See* **The Lefkas Connection, Chapter Ten** for further details of these airline, ferry and local bus timetables.

ARRIVAL BY BUS
A regular service from Athens and Agrinio. The last kilometre or two of the approach road to the island skims the sea edge with a long sliver of land offshore creating a large, shallow lagoon. Solitary locals ply their punts, poling about the flat water's surface laying and tending their nets. This spectacle is best observed early morning with gentle mists filtering up and wreathing the elongated island and fishermen in ethereal wraps.

Drawing nearer one fort is passed and then another, Agia Mavra, close by the 20-25 m canal which has to be crossed on one of the two parallel chain-ferrys that ply backwards and forwards across the narrow channel. The journey is free — yes, free.

Agia Mavra castle derives its name from a chapel built within the walls by the wife of the Venetian who constructed the original structure. The ownership of the fort mirrors the islands history for the last 700 years. The Turks and Venetians swopped 'the real estate' over a period of 500 years followed by French ownership (1797-8), Russians for the next nine years, the French again for four years and the British between 1811 and 1864.

The direct route bridges the shallows to Lefkas Town on a causeway whilst another road loops around the large rectangular lagoon to the right, past a sparse, shingly beach, some forlorn windmills and then back through marshy surrounds into the Town. The latter section of this road is used to dump the town's rubbish for backfilling and is, not unnaturally, rather mosquito ridden.

ARRIVAL BY FERRY-BOAT
Apart from indeterminate, possibly mythical and certainly irregular calls by the scheduled ferry-boats at the very height of season, the only reliable connection is by a privately operated caique service that operates during the summer months in and out of Vassiliki to Fiscardon (Cephalonia), Koni and Vathi (Ithaca). *See* **Vassiliki** for further details and **The Lefkas Connection, Chapter 10** in respect of mainland ferry-boat timetables.

THE ACCOMMODATION & EATING OUT
The Accommodation
At the peak or apex of the town, behind the small park close by the bridge, there are, side by side, the *Hotel Lefkas* and *Nicros* and, to the left, the *Hotel Xenia*. They are not inexpensive!

Hotel Nicros (*Tmr* 1.C2) (Class B) Ag Mavra   Tel. 24132
Directions: As above.
   Pricey at 1800 drs for a double en suite (of course).

Hotel Lefkas (*Tmr* 2.C2) (Class B) 2 Panagou   Tel. 23916
All as for the Nicros but doubles from 2300 drs.

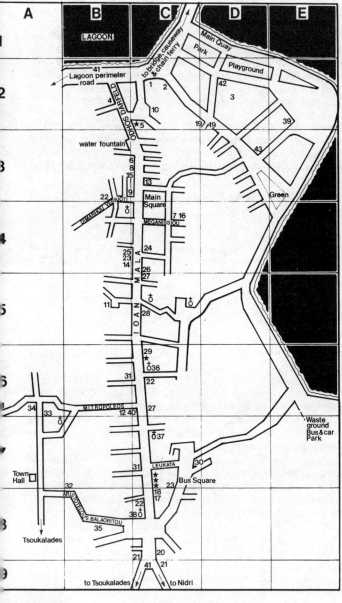

1	Hotel Nicros	C2
2	Hotel Lefkas	C2
3	Hotel Xenia	D2
4	Hotel Byzantio	B2
5	Hotel Santa Mavra	C2
6	Hotel Nº 40	B/C3
7	Hotel Patras	C4
8	Café Sunset Nº 2	B/C3
9	Peters Ouzerie	B/C3
10	Pete's Taverna	C2
11	Lighthouse Taverna	B5
12	Taverna Romantica	B6
13	Macdonuts	C3
14	Souvlaki stall	B4
15	Airline Office	B/C3
16	National Bank of Greece	C4
17	Ionian & Popular Bank	C8
18	Post Office	C7/8
19	Scooter hire	
20	Car hire	C8
21	Petrol Stations	
22	Bread shops	
23	Bus terminus	C7/8
24	Supermarket	C4
25	Bulk drink shop	B/C4
26	Fish shop	C4
27	Yoguterias	
28	Chicken Butcher	C5
29	Gaz Shop	C6
30	Laundry/Dry Cleaner	C/D7
31	Pharmacies	
32	Hospital	B7
33	Tourist Police	A6
34	OTE	A6
35	Scooter repair	B8
36	Pantokrator Cathedral	C6
37	Eisodion Theotokou Church	C7
38	Ag Minos Church	C8
39	Port Police	E2
40	Town Police	B/C6
41	Taxi ranks	
42	Dana Travel	D2
43	Yacht repair	D3
Ô	Church	
★	Periptero	

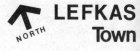

LEFKAS
Town

Fifteen   Lefkas Town plan

Hotel Xenia (*Tmr* 3.D2) (Class B)   Tel. 24762
Doubles from 1800 drs.

At the other end of the standards and prices spectrum and perhaps more in line with the usual recommendations espoused in the Candid Guides are the

Hotel Byzantio (Vyzantion) (*Tmr* 4.B2) (Class E) 10 Odhos Darfeld   Tel. 22629
Directions: On the right of the commencement of the long, High Street that slowly snakes through the town.

Simple, clean, with doubles sharing a bathroom costing from 800 drs per day.

Hotel Santa Mavra (*Tmr* 5.C2) (Class C) Odhos Darfeld/2 Sp Vianta   Tel. 22342
Directions: A few yards on up the High Street, on the left, edging a small square some 150 m from the quay waterfront.

A pleasant hotel, well situated, with doubles sharing a bathroom costing from 1100 drs.

Perhaps the most delightfully traditional Greek hostelry, not only on Lefkas but perhaps in the whole of the Ionian, is the

Hotel No 40 (*Tmr* 6.B/C3) (Class Unknown), Ioan Mala (the High Street)
Directions: Beyond the turning to the *Hotel Santa Mavra*, past a ships chandler and roadside water fountain on the right (*Sbo*), round the bend in the road and on the right. The faded, descriptive word hotel is only just discernible but the blue enamel plate proclaiming the number is shiny and fairly new.

The narrative in respect of the hotel and its amenities is perhaps best left to Richard Evetts, who has, as acknowledged in the preliminaries, helped out in the updating of this second edition.

"After entering the poorly lit interior we carefully climbed the worn, lino clad stairs to the reception office, scarcely daring to breath lest the place should fall down about our ears.

Sitting behind the massive, old fashioned desk in the tiny office was a little old lady clad from head to toe in black who must have seen her eightieth birthday several years earlier. Like most little old Greek ladies, she spoke no other language than Greek. After several minutes of unrewarding mime and gesticulations she rose from her chair, shuffled out on to the landing and shrieked in a high pitched scream up the stairs. What followed could have done justice to a scene from a Greek version of the *Goon Show*, for after a few seconds, the old lady's cry was answered by a faint voice, reminiscent of *Henry Crun*. For several seconds, the aged proprietress and the voice carried on a shouted, wavering conversation at the end of which, from somewhere high up in the building, the sound of slow, halting steps could be heard on the creaking floorboards. After a good five minutes, the owner of the *Henry Crun* voice hove into view on the stairs. He too was dressed in black but quite immaculately with white shirt, black tie and waistcoat with watch chain. He slowly negotiated the last of the steps with the aid of a silver topped malacca cane. On entering the office, he solemnly shook our hands and in wavery tones demanded 'Parlez-vous Francaise'? Fortunately we did, albeit 'un petit peu'. In fact, even if we didn't, I think we would have been tempted to claim that we did, for to have disappointed the old boy, after what must have been a major expedition down several flights of stairs, would have been extremely unkind. He turned out to be the proprietress's brother who had worked in France for a number of years. In halting French he explained that they did have a room which would cost 300 drs each a night plus a further 50 drs if we used the shower. Fearing the worst we asked to inspect 'La chambre', before committing ourselves. In fact, if one ignored the peeling paintwork, worn lino, and aged furnishings, the room was not too bad. At least it was clean, faced away from the High Street and became our base for the next few days."

Hotel Patras (*Tmr* 7.C4) (Class E) 1 Meganissiou   Tel. 22359
Directions: On the Main Square, over the National Bank of Greece.
   As for other E class establishments, with a double room, sharing a bathroom, costing 925 drs per night.

As a last shot *See* **OTE, A to Z** where, *en passant*, there is mention of **Rooms** to rent over a scooter repair business on Odhos Aristotelous Balaoritou (*Tmr* 35.B8).

The Eating Out
Unfortunately the resident flotilla yachts push up prices in the tavernas and restaurants within 'yellow-wellie' walking distance of the waterfront. On the other hand the quality of the offerings reflects these higher charges.

Sunset No 2 Cafe (*Tmr* 8.B/C3) Ioan Mala (the High Street)
Directions: Beyond and almost alongside *Hotel No 40.*
   Simple grills and toasted sandwiches. An ideal spot for a snack and more especially a cooked breakfast. Eggs and bacon plus coffee and toast costs just 140 drs per head.

Peter's Ouzerie (*Tmr* 9.B/C3) Ioan Mala
Directions: Opposite the large Main Square on the High St.
   'Free Information' and a friendly breakfast.

Pete's Taverna (*Tmr* 10.C2) Odhos Darfeld
Directions: Across the small square from the *Hotel Santa Mavra.*
   The proprietor (Pete, surprise, surprise) was a butcher in Australia for several years and, not surprisingly, takes a pride in his meats which are undeniably delicious. Arrive early especially at the height of the season because the flotilla sailing fraternity tend to block-book the establishment. Tarasomalata, pork chops, tomato salad, chips, retsina and Greek coffee for two — 1200 drs. Expensive but very good.

Light House Taverna (*Tmr* 11.B5)
Directions: Off the High Street, down an alley almost opposite the church with a distinctive skeletal clock-tower.
   A delightful restaurant/taverna with a comfortable indoors and a most attractive flower bedecked courtyard. Steve, who runs the establishment with the help of his pretty wife, worked in Washington, USA for many years as a house painter and decorator and his erstwhile skills are evidence in the decoration of the establishment. The vegetables and dairy products used in the preparation of the dishes are from the family farm on the island which perhaps helps in the creation of the superb food. A colleague is of the opinion that it was here that he was served the best moussaka he had ever tasted. Moussaka, Greek salad, retsina and Greek coffee for two cost 900 drs. (You can always tell a Richard tested taverna, he inevitably has Greek coffee with his meal — middle class reactionary).
   The wall-hung paintings (where else) are pleasant and Steve in his capacity as artist is justifiably proud of his creations.

Taverna Romantica (*Tmr* 12.B6)
Directions: Further on up the High Street (Ioan Mala), and off to the right by the Police station, along Odhos Mitropoleos and on the left. 'Green Garden (behind)'.
   Almost all comments as for the *Light House Taverna.*

Macdonuts (*Tmr* 13.C3)
Directions: To the quay side of the main town square. A 'slow-food' cafe (well possibly fast-food by Greek standards) which sells plastic (tasting) hamburgers and cardboard (tasting) chips, I don't know why Richard lowers the tone of the Guide by drawing our attention to such rubbish but he justifies its inclusion by saying ". . . but its cheap and the kids (he means children, he's from the 1960s) love it". Just look at the name *Macdonuts* —dear, dear me.

The traditional Greek fast-food joints are well represented with a number of souvlaki stalls, one half-way along the High Street on the right (*Tmr* 14.B4) and another great looking, very 'local' cafe-bar serving up shish-kebabs is sited on the left side beyond the 'Oven-Pie' bakery (*Tmr* 22.C6). There is a 'greasy' cafe on the 'Bus Square' (*Tmr* 23.C7/8).

THE A TO Z OF USEFUL INFORMATION

AIRLINE OFFICES (*Tmr* 15.B/C3)
On the right (*Sbo*), prior to the Main Sq.

BANKS
National Bank of Greece (*Tmr* 16.C4)
Located on the edge of the Main Sq. Above and over the bank is the *Hotel Patras*. The bank counter-clerk is very nearly polite, very unusual for Greece but note that the commission charges are high at 100 drs. They change personal cheques backed by a Eurocard.
Ionian and Popular Bank (*Tmr* 17.C8)
Further up the High St, next door to the Post Office.

BEACHES
The only town beach (dusty, fine shingle sand) is that to the seaward side of the lagoon perimeter road and is best at the southern end where the road bends eastwards, back towards the causeway (GROC Rating 7/10).

BICYCLE, SCOOTER & CAR HIRE
Two or three scooter outfits near the quay, two blocks back, (*Tmr* 19.D2; 19.C/D2). There is a car hire firm **Rent a Car** (*Tmr* 20.C8) at the top, far end of the High St on the square where the road forks to Nidri and Tsoukalades.

BOOKSELLERS
A couple of shops spaced out on the left-hand side of the High Street. An interesting Lefkas quirk is that newspapers are sold from handcarts. *See* **Yacht Repairs, A to Z.**

BREAD SHOPS
A number including a splendid example down the narrow lane of Dimarhou Verrioti (*Tmr* 22.B3) as well as a baker on the left of the High St (*Tmr* 22.C6), who also 'Ovens Pies', and another further along, on the other side of the road (*Tmr* 22.C8).

BUSES
Although the Athens bus usually drops passengers at the quay end of the High St, the squalid dusty, gravelly irregular square that forms the terminus is round to the left of the top end of the main street (*Tmr* 23.C7/8). Buses certainly must be boarded here. The large waiting room encompasses all those unforgettable qualities of a Greek bus terminal that include chaos, an air of expectancy, a cacophony of sounds, the shambles of a floor area 'mined' with suitcases, cardboard boxes (tied with string), a litter of assorted back-packs amongst and around which are bundles of black costumed Greek ladies, nose-picking men and a seemingly uncontrollable horde of well dressed, young children. The snacks counter desultorily serves up odds and ends of food as a Greek cannot approach the portals of a transport system without compulsively eating. Perhaps it is a form of masticatory supplication.

Bus Timetables
Mainland:
Lefkas to Athens (100 Kifissou St)
Daily   0830, 0930, 1230 hrs
Return journey
Daily   0700, 1330, 2100 hrs
One-way fare 1220 drs, duration 7 hrs.

Lefkas Town to Aktion
Daily   0715, 0900, 1100, 1515 hrs

Island destinations:
Lefkas Town to Vassiliki via Ag Petros (south inland)
Daily   0600, 1100, 1345 hrs

Lefkas Town to Athani (south-west coast)
Daily   0530, 1340 hrs

Lefkas Town to Syvros (centre south inland)
Daily   0550, 1340 hrs

Lefkas Town to Ag Ilias (centre south inland)
Daily   0500, 1340 hrs

Lefkas Town to Fterno via Katochori, Poros (south inland)
Daily   0600, 1315 hrs

Lefkas Town to Charadiatika (south-east coast)
Daily   0700, 1340 hrs

Lefkas Town to Vlycho via Lygia, Nidri (south-east coast)
Daily   0600, 0700, 1030, 1230, 1315, 1345 hrs

Lefkas Town to Katouna (east coast)
Daily   0730, 1205 hrs

Lefkas Town to Englouvi (centre inland)
Daily   0630, 1515 hrs

Lefkas Town to Karia (centre north inland)
Daily   0710, 1000, 1205, 1315, 1345, 1515, 1700 hrs

Lefkas Town to Vafkeri (centre inland)
Daily   0515, 1515 hrs

Lefkas Town to Kalamitsi (west coast)
Daily   0515, 1430 hrs

Lefkas Town to Ag Nikitas (north-west coast)
Daily   0645, 1415 hrs

Lefkas Town to Tsoukalades (north-west coast)
Daily   0800, 1315 hrs

Please note the above are 'out of height-of-season' schedules.

CHEMISTS
See **Medical Care.**

COMMERCIAL SHOPPING AREAS
No central area but Lefkas is very well equipped with numerous shops, some of which are excellent, including a well-stocked supermarket (*Tmr* 24.C4), almost opposite which is a 'bulk' drink shop (*Tmr* 25.B/C4), most unusually a fish shop (*Tmr* 26.C4), several yoguterias (*Tmr* 27.C4/5 & C6) and there are several butchers, including one who specialises in chickens (*Tmr* 28.C5). Unusual services must encompass the *GAZ* shop (*Tmr* 29.C6) and next door the senior citizen carrying out 'on the spot' shoe repairs. Further on up the High St is a general store opposite Leukata Lane (*Tmr* C7). The Bus Sq (*Tmr* 23.C7/8) has a selection of shops.

FERRY-BOATS
Rumours persist that Lefkas is, at the height of the season, included on the main Ionian islands schedules but these fabrications should be discounted. Goodness only knows why the island is not incorporated in the timetables, perhaps the residents prefer the comparative gentility of the flotilla sailing chaps to that of hordes of backpackers.

  There are height-of-season caique connections from the southern fishing boat port of Vassiliki to Fiscardon (Cephalonia), Kioni and Vathi, both on Ithaca island. Small landing craft type ferries make the connection between Nidri and Meganisi island.

HOSPITAL
See **Medical Care.**

LAUNDRY/DRY CLEANER (*Tmr* 30.C/D7)
Tucked into the apex of two angled streets off the Bus Sq.

MEDICAL CARE
Chemists & Pharmacies
Two spaced out on the right hand side of the High St (*Tmr* 31.B/C6 & B/C7).
Hospital (*Tmr* 32.A/B7/8)
From the lower or south end main street square (*Tmr* B/C8) turn right (*Sbo*) and keep to the right on Odhos Aristotelous Balaoritou. The hospital is on the right immediately after the kink in the road has straightened. Alternatively it is possible to turn along Odhos Mitropoleos and keep left.

NTOG
None but the Tourist police (*Tmr* 33.A6) ably double up.

OPENING HOURS
Usual times and days unless stated otherwise.

OTE (*Tmr* 34.A6)
Right off the High St either along Odhos Mitropoleos or Aristotelous Balaoritou St. Incidentally, before the bend in this road, on the left, is a Vespa Scooter service establishment (*Tmr* 35.B8) over which there are **Rooms** to rent.
    A modern building to the north of the Town Hall in a very dusty, modern part of the town. Open daily, 0600 - 2300 hrs.

PETROL
Several on the square at the parting of the ways to the south end of the town (*Tmr* 21.C8 & C9) and another on round past the OTE office (*Tmr* 21.A6).

PHARMACIES
See **Medical Care.**

PLACES OF INTEREST
Ag Mavra Castle
See **Arrival by Bus.**
Cathedrals and Churches
Pantokrator Cathedral (*Tmr* 36.C6)
Built in 1684 but subject, as most older Lefkas buildings, to constant reconstruction due to earthquake damage over the years.
Church of Eisodion Theotokou (*Tmr* 37.C7)
Cream and white with railings fencing off the front.
Church of Ag Minos (*Tmr* 38.C8)
Prior to earthquake damage a very fine church but now most noticeable for the water mill, angle-iron, meccano-like clock tower to one side.
Museums
Town
Combined with the Public Library off to the right of the High St.
Archaeological
On the left of the road out of town towards Fryni village.
Folklore
Close by the Town Hall (*Tmr* A7).

Annual Festival

Once a year, in August, the island hosts an international festival of drama, folk-dance, singing and speech which attracts entries from as many as 16 countries. They perform nightly in Lefkas Town, tour the island villages as well as partaking in a parade of boats that circles the island headed by a reconstruction of a Greek warship of the Hellenistic/ Roman period.

POLICE

Port (*Tmr* 39.E2)
Located where would be expected, close by the main quay.

Tourist (*Tmr* 33.A6)
Rather inconveniently, for the traveller that is, almost at the far end of the town on the same road as the OTE office. Perhaps the idea is that prospective enquirers should blunt the edge before arriving at their door.

Town (*Tmr* 40.B/C6)
On the right of the High St on the corner of Odhos Mitropoleos. Proud possessors of a car which cruises up and down the 'main drag'. The local chaps remind me rather of *Ernie Kovacs* doing his impersonation of a South American chief of police — all sunglasses and shining teeth. On my last but one visit my efforts to complete the town plan at first intrigued and then increasingly infuriated these guardians of law and order. They took to following me, one in the prowl car, his 'pardner' on the side walk — I didn't much fancy the thought provoking manner in which their hands seemed all too easily to stray to their hip-slung revolvers. The patrol car is, when not in use, neatly parked up opposite their first floor office.

POST OFFICE (*Tmr* 18.C7/8)

On the left, almost at the far end of the High Street, close to the Ionian and Popular Bank.

TAXIS (*Tmr* 41)

The main rank is on the junction of the causeway approach road and the start of the High St, Odhos Darfeld (*Tmr* 41.B2). Taxis also park up both sides of the Main Sq (*Tmr* C3/4) and there is another rank at the far, far end of the High St by the fork in the road (*Tmr* C8/9).

TRAVEL AGENTS

Dana Travel (*Tmr* 42.D2) Tel. 23629.
Behind the park on which *Andreas Cafe* is situated.
   In addition there is (or should it be are with a name this long)

'Yioannoulatos', Lefkas Travel
On the right of the High St (*Tmr* 15.B/C3).

YACHT REPAIR

Before leaving the subject of Lefkas Town a couple of very pleasant English lads were running a contract Yacht Service business (*Tmr* 43.D3) behind and in the same block as the Port police. Apart from an informal English book-swop scheme they also help out with friendly advice, especially if you own a yacht looking for an Ionian berth! I hope they prosper.

(CIRCULAR) ROUTE
To Vassiliki via Nidri, Poros & back to Lefkas Town via
Ag Petros & Tsoukalades (80 km)

From the square, at the top or south end of the High Street, proceed along the main left-hand fork. This road proceeds inland through straggling, cultivated and Olive-groved land.

Beyond Kaligoni village some of Herr Dorpfeld's diggings of Ancient Lefkas hove into view, on the right, lurking in a low, dark, tree-shaded grass meadow. Apart from the abundance of remains, including large cut and unworked stone blocks, there is, off to the left, a track down to the Alikes or saltings. The sea channel from Lefkas Town appears confusing which is not surprising considering the amount of ajdustments carried out over the centuries by the various world powers during their suzerainty. Topping an islet in the channel are the unusual remains of a Russian built fort, a relic of their short occupation.

LYGIA (6 km from Lefkas Town)

A seaside hamlet with two small shingly beaches (GROC Rating 6/10), a caique harbour and rooms to let.

A kilometre or so on the **Disco Why Not** is on the right. There are a number of small shingly beaches between Lygia and Perigialli.

After some 8 km, at Episkopos there is *International Camping Beach.* The coast hugging road from here through Nikiana, to Perigialli passes by an abundance of private houses with *Rooms* for let, ranging broadly in price from 750 - 900 drs for a double room.

Beyond Perigialli, offshore of which is the islet of Heloni, the build-up commences to

NIDRI (Nydri) (17 km from Lefkas Town)

The beautiful situation of this attractive fishing port would have ensured its continued popularity without the rise in villa holiday tourism. *Cricketers Holidays* have for many years specialised in bringing the discerning to the delights of Lefkas island and there are an abundance of *Rooms* and bungalows to rent.

Apart from the location of the small port and its ability to service the satellite islands of Sparti, Madouri, Skorpidi, Skorpios and Meganisi there is always the hint, the suggestion, the innuendo that it is from Nidri that inter-island connections are made with the islands of Cephalonia and Ithaca, but there would be, wouldn't there.

To seawards or east the various inshore islands are speckled about with the bulk of the mainland in the middle-distance and the beautiful fjord-like bay of Vlycho cutting into the island to the south, the eroded land forming a thick, crooked, mountain finger.

The long straight High Street has almost everything a visitor might want including supplies of petrol, fish, fruit and vegetables. There is a **Hardware store** and **Ships Chandlers**, a **Market-Super** (sic), a **Poster-Office** (sic), a pharmacy, 2 recommended bakers as well as Kafeneions, restaurants, a *Macdonuts* and, at the far end, **Disco Alexander**. It may be something to do with the air but at one or two shops in Nidri ladies will have to check their chastity belts. It is rumoured, only rumoured you understand that the octogenarian baker adjacent to *Macdonuts* displays amorous intentions and a certain grocer (on the left on the way in from Lefkas Town) is extremely enthusiastic!

Parallel to the High Street is the very pleasant, long, caique waterfront and promenade, with two small quays jutting into the bay. The shop and tavernas which line the opposite side of the road to the quay shut the waterfront off from the main road, access being through two narrow alleys, in addition to lanes at each end. On a corner with the main road there is a travel office run by the willing Mr George Kourtis. He speaks excellent English and will assist in locating rooms, hiring mechanical transport as well as boat trips and fishing boat excursions. To the left hand (*Fsw*) there is a pleasant, small, sandy shingle beach (GROC Rating 6/10). The quay front has the occasional green, top loading garbage bins with handwritten signs rightly urging disposers of rubbish to '**Dispose Garbage Inside**'. On the right is *Nick the Greeks*, a taverna with some celebrity value due to the owner, Nick's association with the Onassis clan in the good old days of Aristotle. Faded photos around the bar record various moments of this super-stardom. Certainly the comradeship would appear to have been beneficial to Nick as he is the proud possessor of a large, modern, imposing fast motor cruiser emblazoned with his name.

The Onassis family still own the highly guarded and adjacent island of Skorpios. The most intriguing of the islands must surely be tree-covered Madouri on the shore of which, facing Nidri, is an imposing Palladian fronted building set in apparently close-cut green lawns. It was built for and/or by the poet Aristotle Valaoritis.

There is a boat yard at each end of the waterfront and the Meganisi island landing craft type ferries are berthed up to the right.

An unsignposted inland road from Nidri, set in luxurious, green tree'd countryside, becomes a track but does lead to the Dymossari Gorge and waterfall.

EXCURSION TO MEGANISI ISLAND

Throughout the day the Nidri ferries make the worthwhile trip to the green, beautiful and unspoiled island with its three quaint villages of Vathi, Katomeri and Spartochori — all of which have **Rooms** to let. But stay overnight, don't just make a day-trip.

From Nidri southwards the views are stunning. The inland sea or more truthfully, the Bay of Vlycho is backed by the mountainous Geni peninsula whilst, to the right of the road, a steep mountain range is topped off by the 1150 m high Mt Elati which dominates the inland perspective.

VLYCHO (20 km from Lefkas Town)

The village lies to one side, alongside the bottom of the bay, and possesses an extremely elongated one-way road system. In contrast to the main body of the bay which is beautiful, this end is not particularly attractive, resembling a Pine tree edged, stagnant lake.

From Vlycho a left side turning runs out around the edge of the bay forking right to the bold campsite of *Dessimi Beach*, above a small shingle beach (GROC Rating 6/10). The left fork climbs the spine of the hilly headland of the peninsula, the unsurfaced track initially ducking and weaving on its winding way towards the churches of Apostoloi and Kryiaki. The lane breaks out of the heavy tree shield of the lower slopes to the more patchily covered hilltop from whence there are enchanting views of the bay on the one side, and the in-shore islands on the other.

The road to Vlycho proceeds through Katochori village to a fork. The left-hand track curves off to

POROS (27 km from Lefkas Town)

A mellow, provincial village, with lovely roofs edging narrow, winding lanes between the crowded houses, the whole set on the mountainside surrounded by groves of mature Olive trees.

The beach of Poros, or more correctly Ag Marina, skirts the Bay of Rouda, and is reached down a long, winding road off to the right of the village road. A very pleasant, broad, quite steeply shelving sand and shingle beach (GROC Rating 7/10) tucked into the side of the splendid bay. Perhaps the most unusual aspect is the skilfully designed, concrete bungalow holiday complex, the most obtrusive feature of which is the sign advertising its presence. The campsite of *Poros Beach* is tucked away behind the beach.

Back at the main road and proceeding towards Vassiliki, after some 5 km a turning off wanders down to the bay and hamlet of

SYVOTA (33 km from Lefkas Town)

A beautiful, rather fairy-tale fishing inlet with grass growing down to the dark water's edge. I avoid the word port as the location is not large or deep enough although there are usually a few yachts moored up in the sound. The waterfront is a shingly, sweeping sward with no beach. The headland contrives to give the impression that the bay is almost totally enclosed.

There are two tavernas, one to the left overlooking the harbour and the other to the right, alongside the fishing boat quay. The latter establishment consistently serves up good quality meals apart from which nothing can detract from the setting. The proprietor's sole knowledge of English is limited to "no problem" and "OK". These comments are made with varying vocal inflections accompanied by suitably appropriate facial expressions and much hand waving. This method of communication quite explicitly imparts his comments on the weather, the view, his food, his wife and family and the world in general — so who needs to learn Greek!

Both tavernas either have or can arrange accommodation from about 700 drs a night for two.

Incidentally, the German archaeologist Dorpfeld believed that it was at Syvota that Odysseus came ashore after his fifteen year sea voyage. Just where he made his landfall is hard to say; it certainly wasn't on the beach marked on the map for despite much rock climbing around the bay it is difficult to find even a smidgeon of sand or shingle. Nevertheless, Syvota must rate as one of the most attractive villages on Lefkas, and an ideal setting from an away-from-it-all holiday.

Certain cartographers sketch a road to the coast between the villages of Marandochori and Kondarena but this is a naughty, naughty red-herring. It is also common to indicate two beaches between the bays of Syvota and Afteli Bay but they are only accessible from the sea.

From the Syvota turning the road winds through several 'standard' island villages to the most unusual

VASSILIKI (36 km from Lefkas Town)
A lovely, relaxed fishing village community to one side of a very large bay, the village being centred along the right angled, tree-lined quay and main pier.

The main road skirts the village dropping down the hill from Kondarena village forking right to cross the agricultural valley plain. The route to the village quay is left at the junction formed by the main road and the dusty 'High Street'. A lane parallel to the main street turns sharply by a car park compound, yes, a sign-posted 'bomb-site' car-park, and spills out on to the waterfront to the right (*Fsw*) of the High St junction with the quayside.

The first building in the High St, on the right, is the newish and expensive

Hotel Lefkatos
Appears to be tour-operator, block-booked. The hotel is the centre for the **Club Vasiliki** surf boarding school and 'club' hours are 0930 - 1030 and 1930 - 2030 hrs, daily. The hotel notice board is a useful source of local information including the following:-

Bus timetable
Vassiliki, Nidri to Lefkas Town
Daily   0730, 1415, 1500 hrs
Return journey
Daily   0600, 1100, 1345, 2030* hrs
One-way fare to Lefkas Town 100 drs.
*I know this is an extra to the list under Lefkas Town but that is (I'm sure) a winter schedule.

Taxi fares
to Nidri   500 - 700 drs
to Lefkas Town   900 - 1200 drs

The hotel exchanges currency daily between 1800 - 2000 hrs except Sundays but charges a comparatively hefty commission.

Opposite the *Hotel Lefkatos* is a **'Rent a Motor Scooter'** business and further on along the High St, on the right, are *Rooms* to rent, a very provincial general store and haberdashery shop, a ships store, several 'Popular Art' shops, and a butcher. The last section of the street contains a shoe shop, two general shops and lastly, on the right, on the corner with the quay, the Post Office. To the right is the Port police office, side by side with the Post Office, alongside which is *Pizza Lefkas.*

Opposite the Post Office, two cafe-bars edge the street corner. The social life of the village centres around these, a kafeneion and the *Taverna Ionian* both on the main quay corner. The taverna serves up a limited but reasonably priced menu.

Over the intersection, a baker is to the left, in a small, ramshackle square, to the side of the very pretty, tree-lined down-leg of the quay wall. Halfway towards the pier head a fountain is fed by a constantly gushing stream of mountain water. This left-hand quay promenade has various shops, restaurants and **Rooms** to rent. The sea-front wall continues on, turning sharply left at the fenced off, tree planted memorial at the bottom of the pier. On the land side are *Let Independence Rooms,* and the *Restaurant Miramare.* The road goes on around another small cove ending in a rocky mole. This stretch of hillside constantly burbles and rustles with the sound of rushing streams tumbling down the cliff-face.

The waterfront is fully utilised by the local fishing boats and the large pleasant beach (GROC Rating 7/10) lays back and well to the right (*Fsw*), beyond the village.

Ferry-boat timetable
From Vassiliki there is the oft referred to local caique passenger service:-

Day	Ports/islands of Call
Sunday	Kioni & Vathi (Ithaca)
Monday	(Spilia, Papanikoli), Skorpios island
Tuesday	(Farodoukato), Fiscardon (Cephalonia), Sami (Cephalonia)
Wednesday	Kioni & Vathi (Ithaca)
Thursday	(Spilia, Papanikoli), Skorpios island, Madouri island, Syvota
Friday	(Farodoukato), Fiscardon (Cephalonia), Sami (Cephalonia)

Driving west out of the port, towards the far end of the large bay, there are several discos, a petrol station and some **Rooms** to rent. At the far end of the beach there is the windsurf school centre of operations.

The road climbs steeply out of the bay through the hill-hugging village of

AG PETROS (37 km from Lefkas Town)
Complete with a supermarket, narrow roads and taxis,
and on to

KHORTATA (27 km from Lefkas Town)
On this side of the island the women not only wear a brown garb but, as in days of yore, carry large loads balanced on their heads. I have also observed, a little further on up the coast, two donkeys in tandem pulling a very simple wooden dagger plough to turn the unyielding stony soil.

The views in this area are really most dramatic with the central island mountains ranging north-south and the shimmering blue Ionian Sea stretching away to the left.

Detour to CAPE DOUKATO (46 km from Lefkas Town)
Immediately prior to Khortata, a turning off to the left via Komili village rockets along all the way to the southernmost tip of Lefkas island. On this exciting and never uninteresting route, to the right, beyond Athani is one glorious beach (GROC Rating 8/10) with a 'dead' bus on the foreshore and a small strip of vineyard and ancient terracing struggling up the towering hillsides. On the other hand there is another well signposted beach, the road to which runs out about 100 m up the cliff-face on the loose chalk surface of a blind corner!

The Cape from which Sappho and others performed their desperate leap should be visited despite the long, rocky drive over the stony, unmetalled surface. The track finally opens out on to an attractive almost circular, heavily cultivated, saucer-shaped depression with the lighthouse to the far right. From here, on a clear day... it is pleasant to watch the inter-island ferries plough past on their way to the islands of Cephalonia and Ithaca, easily discernible in the middle distance.

Back on the circular route from Khortata the road progresses to

EXANTHIA (21 km from Lefkas Town)
A remarkably attractive settlement clinging to the mountainside and followed by

DRIMONAS (19 km from Lefkas Town)
A large village with the old houses nestling in a hollow. Whilst in this area it may be worth noting there is **Petrol** available at the village of Lazarata. From hereon the coastal road marked on some of the maps as surfaced, most definitely is not.

From Drymonas an unmetalled road runs off to the left to the village of

KALAMITSI (24 km from Lefkas Town)
Now, despite the ruggedness of the journey to the beach I'm about to relate, it is an excursion well worth undertaking because, like the proverbial rainbow, there is a crock of gold at the end. The steep, twisting road to Kalamitsi from Drymonas is in the process of being widened and will, eventually, be surfaced. At the time of my last visit it was in a pretty awful state, having been subjected to a fair amount of abuse by earthmoving equipment. However, there is worse to come. On entering the village a narrow unmetalled road leads off to the left, the surface of which is averagely bad. But as it descends the mountainside so it deteriorates until it becomes a boulder-strewn, deeply potholed track whose gradient in places (on the inside of the numerous hairpins) exceeds 1 in 3. This is not a drive for the faint-hearted, or, come to that, anyone with a strong will to live. Those insane or reckless enough to continue to sea level will be richly rewarded with the most magnificent beach on the whole island (GROC Rating 9/10). A long, wide shallow crescent of sand and shingle backed by towering, tree covered mountains. It is a truly idyllic spot. A word of consolation, the drive back up, whilst arduous and tricky is not quite as hair-raising since a motorised vehicle is easier to control uphill, under power.

From Kalamitsi there is another equally splendid beach, closer to the village.

Prior to attaining Ag Nikitas there is, off to the left, signposts for a rural, rustic, open-air disco and the track muddles its way on to the seashore where there is an excellent sandy beach (GROC Rating 8/10) with some facilities.

AG NIKITAS (12 km from Lefkas Town)
A very pretty, small, rather chi-chi Greek look-a-like for a Cornish fishing village with only one narrow road in, and the same narrow road out. At the entrance to the village, a steep unsurfaced track leads down to another superb sand and shingle cove (GROC Rating 8/10) whilst beyond the village is a much larger beach of sand and shingle (GROC Rating 8/10) which extends for nearly 3 km and is serviced by a number of small tavernas. This is indisputedly one of the best of the easily accessible beaches on the island. Ag Nikitas is becoming a tourist centre and there are a number of Pensions and plenty of **Rooms** available as well as the usual proliferation of restaurants, cafes and bars.

Despite the map-makers indicating otherwise, the long climb up from Ag Nikitas is on a tarmacadamed road which heads towards.

TSOUKALADES (6 km from Lefkas Town)
From this village, the road now drops steeply down to the plain surrounding Lefkas Town with unsurpassed views over the north of the island (and the adjacent mainland), and is an area rich in enchanted glades of wild flowers which include pink orchids and wild cyclamen.

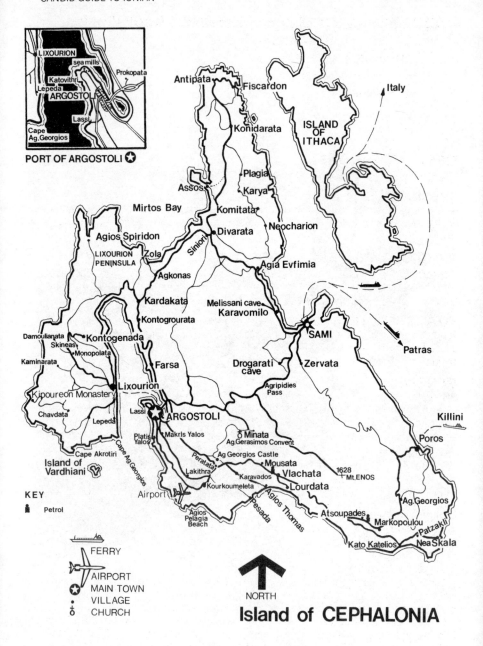

PORT OF ARGOSTOLI ✪

KEY

⛽ Petrol

🚢 FERRY

✈ AIRPORT

✪ MAIN TOWN

• VILLAGE

☦ CHURCH

NORTH

Island of CEPHALONIA

Sixteen   Cephalonia island map

15 Cephalonia (Kefalonia, Kefallinia, Kephallenia, Cefalonia)
Ionian Islands
South and west island   ******

North island   ********

FIRST IMPRESSIONS
Dramatic, mountainous scenery; prefabricated buildings; massed Cypresses.

SPECIALITIES
Lemonda; Robola wine (white and light); Monte Nero wine (red and dry); thyme-scented honey; bacaliaropitta (cod-fish pies); tserepes (spiced meat in a casserole); mandolato nougat.

RELIGIOUS HOLIDAYS & FESTIVALS
include: 17th July — Feast Day, Ag Marina, Vlachata; 15th August — Our Lady Day, Lixourion; 15th August — Assumption of the Virgin, Markopoulou; 22nd August — Our Lady of Loutra, Sami; 8th September — Feast Day of Theotokos, Poros.

VITAL STATISTICS
Tel. prefix *See* individual towns and villages. The island is 39 km long and 33 km wide with a total population of about 32,000 of which some 7,000 or so live in or around Argostoli Town.

GENERAL
Panoramically, extremely dramatic with the majority of the island taken up by mountain ranges. Despite the majestic beauty of the scenery, visitors may well have to persevere with Cephalonia to experience the inclination to stay on, a number of tourists leaving almost as soon as they arrive. There are a number of drawbacks. The main city of Argostoli (Argostolion) was unsympathetically reconstructed after the devastating earthquake of 1953; the roads that hug the edges of the hills are so mountainous that, for instance, the scooters for hire are the larger-engined models and consequently comparatively expensive and last but not least although the bus system is widespread, due to the distances involved, it is difficult to get back to the departure point on the same day.

If all the above were not enough, Cephalonia is unusual in that the main town is not the main port and the ferry-boats dock at either Poros or Sami. Argostoli's only ferry is a car and passenger boat to Lixourion, which service does save a long drive around the Kolpos or Gulf of Argostoli. There are also cruise boats running down to Zakynthos island at the height of the summer season.

Effectively the island is split into three segments — the main southern island mass; the western Lixourion peninsula and the northern island tip. Stick it out, visit the Lixourion peninsula and under no circumstances miss the northern end of the island.

One of Cephalonia's most famous citizens in recent years was the General, Prime Minister and dictator Metaxas. His eminence was firmly established on 28th October 1940, in a famous but very terse speech when he advised Mussolini 'Ochi' (No) after Mussolini had demanded the right of passage across Northern Greece for his troops. This day is now one of the country's public holidays.

That fate is fickle (or more prosaically 'There's nowt so strange as life') is no better illustrated than by the lot of a crack force of 7,000 Italian troops. After three years occupation of Cephalonia island during the Second World War, they refused to obey the orders of the German High Command. The erstwhile oppressors became the island peoples' heroes and after a week long battle against overwhelming odds, the 3,000 or so Italian soldiers who finally surrendered were murdered in a three day frenzy by the Germans. Some thirty escaped with the help of the islanders through a medieval 8 km long tunnel between Ag Georgios Castle and the lagoon at the southern end of Argostili Bay. The tunnel was subsequently destroyed by the 1953 earthquake although the Castle end of the entrance can still be seen.

POROS (Porros): port (44 km from Argostoli)
Tel. prefix 0674.
Seemingly the main reason for the existence of Poros is that it is the port for the mainland Killini to Cephalonia ferry. There is a small quay, a fishing-port community, a shingly beach to the right of the quay (*Sbo*), a collection of summer holiday homes, a few tavernas, two small hotels but few, if any, **Rooms** to let. Certainly out of season Poros closes up whilst in the summer swing everywhere is full.

Travellers who have decided not to chance their arm and stay at Poros, will find it useful to locate the green Pullman bus to Argostoli Town. This is actually the Athens to Argostoli connection, which having travelled over on the ferry, draws up on the ferry-boat square to take on more customers. The fare is 110 drs.

ARRIVAL BY AIR
The airport is situated some 14 km south of Argostoli Town on the coast close by Lakithra. An Olympic airline bus makes the connection to the capital. Cost 45 drs.
See **Argostoli Town, A to Z** for further details.

ARRIVAL BY BUS
There are some three daily connections between Athens and Argostoli.

Note that some Athens buses go via Patras (mainland) to Sami Port and on to Lixourion.

Bus timetable
Athens (Kifissou St Tel. 5129498) **to Argostoli Town (via Killini and Poros)**
Daily   0715, 0900 hrs.

Return journey
Argostoli Town to Athens (via Poros and Killini)
Daily   0700, 1130 hrs
One-way fare to Argostoli 1531 drs (plus the appropriate ferry-boat fare), duration 8 hrs.
See **Sami Port** for details of the other mainland bus connections.

ARRIVAL BY FERRY
There are three ferry-boat connections a day.

Ferry-boat timetable
Poros - Killini (M): Daily 0900, 1500, 1900 hrs.
Killini (M) - Poros: Daily 1230, 1730, 2130 hrs.
One-way fare 445 drs, duration 1½ hrs.
See **Sami Port** for other ferry-boat connections.

ROUTE ONE
Poros to Argostoli Town (44 km)
Over the hill to the north of the ferry-boat quay, the rest of Poros is laid out around the coastal part of the road. Mainly a beach resort with a supermarket, petrol pumps, cafe, restaurants and a rather scruffy, shingle beach (GROC Rating 6/10).

The road from Poros is as frightening as it is beautifully dramatic. The driver has a disturbing habit of carrying on intense conversation at a high pitched yell with a number of the passengers towards the rear of the bus. The alarming thing is that the discourse can only be executed by his facing the people involved and this whilst the bus hurtles along. The road has been sliced through dynamited rock faces, with precipitous cliff sides to the right and horrifyingly steep drops to the sea-bounded plain to the left. The fact that the scenery of Olive and Cypress-tree covered slopes is lovely, is somewhat marred by the cacophony of sound resulting from the drivers hand apparently being glued to the horn. Quite frankly, it is best, if of a nervous disposition, to take a paper bag and some boiled sweets, as the journey very much resembles a low altitude flight and all this on a road of normal Greek island inconsistency in quality, general line of construction and lack of width.

After this mountain hugging the road suddenly descends and passes through a rock bestrewn landscape. Shortly afterwards, at about Ag Georgios, the scenery changes to the 'Greek norm' of undulating hillsides peppered with flat-topped houses built amongst Olive trees, set in grass and granite rock wastelands. Here and there villages appear to have been dropped haphazardly in position. Amongst the grasses, the occasional strip of cultivated and tilled land unexpectedly appears, the raw earth contrasting starkly with the worn, scrub-covered, unyielding surroundings. Equally unexpectedly the road rushes past great areas gouged out of the hillsides, presumably for yet another prefabricated concrete filling station or house to be constructed.

MARKOPOULOU (26 km from Argostoli Town)
This village experiences a rather mysterious and strange occurrence on the 15th August. This is the Virgin Mary's day, on which the church and its environs are invaded by small, and reputedly, harmless snakes with black crosses on their heads. They are regarded as having healing powers, so much so that some pilgrims clasp them to their breasts. Well if you must, you must. Interestingly, the snakes are not seen at any other time.

It is well worth leaving the main Poros to Argostoli road at the acute junction to the west of Atsoupades in order to explore the south-east corner of the island. The little villages nestling on the south facing hillside are very pretty and well cared for, with a profusion of flowers covering the walls of the small houses. The area is predominantly agricultural and the road between Atsoupades (22 km from Argostoli Town), where **Petrol** is available, and Nea Skala is, for the most part, excellent with much road widening and re-surfacing in progress in order (sadly!) to open up the area to the delights of tourism.

KATO KATELIOS (29 km from Argostoli Town)
A seaside holiday resort village situated to one side of a large bay with an attractive sand and shingle beach (GROC Rating 8/10). Further on round the bay, to the east and rather inaccessible, are miles of golden sands as described under.

PATZAKLI (32 km from Argostoli Town)
On entering this small community there is a narrow, unmade road running off to the right. This becomes a somewhat alarming, rough, loosely surfaced donkey track which snakes down the hillside to a most spectacular, long, wide and sandy beach (GROC Rating 9/10) — undoubtedly one of the best on the island. Even in September it can be totally deserted and is devoid of any amenities (goody). A hairy drive but well worth it.

The road east from Patzakli winds dramatically down around the Cypress tree covered hillside, with views of the sea to

NEA SKALA (30 km from Argostoli Town)
A quiet seaside resort situated at the northern end of a long, wide, pebble and shingle beach fringed with Pine trees. There are several cafes and tavernas in the town and a few **Rooms** to let (a double costs from 800 to 1000 drs per day). There are the remains of a sixth century BC temple and a second century AD Roman villa with mosaics.

Returning to the main Poros to Argostoli road the drive to Argostoli Town is dominated by the cloud-capped

ENOS MOUNTAINS
The mountainside on which the road clings is a Pine tree covered massif central. It is thought that many of the Greek islands were similarly tree clad. That is prior to the massive deforestation which possibly started as long ago as the Hellenic/Greco-Roman periods (1000 BC to AD 300) and continued in fits and starts up to the fifteenth century. What timber the boat builder didn't appropriate the depredations of the goat may well have helped to ravage.

LOURDATA (19 km from Argostoli Town)
A turning off at the village of Vlachata winds down to an intensely cultivated strip of land, complete with a small stream and attractive, sandy beach (GROC Rating 8/10). Quiet, but there are signs of villa development.

Another beach, Agios Thomas (GROC Rating 7/10) on the same bay, is reached through the village of Karavados, a little further up the main road. Once again villa development is taking place here as it is further round the coast at Pesada, where the sandy beach (GROC Rating 7/10) is approached down a steep access.

PERATATA (9 km from Argostoli Town)
Extensively ruined in the 1953 earthquake (what was not?), the village's claim to fame is that it is close to part of the site of the old Venetian capital of San Giorgio. Additionally it lies in the shadow of the extensive and impressive remains of the castle of Ag Georgios (St George), towering above the village on the mountainside. Incidentally, this medieval settlement was destroyed by an earthquake in the sixteenth century.

Off to the left is the village of

MOURKOUMELETA (12 km from Argostoli Town)
Worth a visit, as it was completely rebuilt by one Vergotis, a wealthy Greek shipowner, after the 1953 earthquake. The unspectacular sandy beach of Ag Pelagia (GROC Rating 7/10) can be reached from here.

ARGOSTOLI TOWN: capital & (minor) port
Tel. prefix 0671. Argostoli is built on a thick finger of land that projects into the Gulf of Argostoli and the sea reaches well inland, giving the appearance of being a large lake, rather than an inlet. The town, which had to be rebuilt after the 1953 earthquake, is quite frankly unattractive and is laid out on a grid road pattern. Looking around Argostoli makes one realise what a splendid job the citizens of Zakynthos (Zante) island made in rebuilding their capital town.

ARRIVAL BY BUS
The Bus Station is combined with the Town Market (*Tmr* 1.C4). The building is constructed in the form of a flat 'W' on a part of the quay that juts out into the sea, on the right-hand side of the road, approaching from the south.

The main square Plateai Valianou or Metaxa (*Tmr* 2.C3 & inset), which is extensive in size and barren in appearance, has cafes and restaurants around its perimeter. It is here that one of those rather unusual, incongruous sightings that enliven each island visit might well be observed. A bewhiskered gentleman sets up shop, erecting his Victorian mobile portraiture studio on the edge of the square. It is complete with painted backdrop and an enormous, ancient plate camera. He also copies photos of loved ones with an attachment clipped on to the front of his plate camera.

After dark the square bustles with activity as tourists and locals promenade up and down, pausing for a while to drink coffee or ouzo at one of the many cafes. The citizens of Argostoli are far more liberated in respect of the moral behaviour of their young, than their

ARGOSTOLI TOWN

Seventeen   Argostoli Town & port plan (Cephalonia)

neighbours on, say, Zante where no girl under the age of 21 is permitted to walk around the town after dark, without a parental chaperone. Argostoli Town female teenagers stroll about in groups displaying the latest fashions to the delight of the young men.

The proximity of the airport has resulted in Argostoli becoming a package tourist resort. For the life of me I cannot see what attractions the town has for batches of holiday-makers requiring a swinging environment and sandy beaches, but there you go.

THE ACCOMMODATION & EATING OUT
The Accommodation

1 Metaxa St is the Esplanade or marine road and each lamp post, adjacent to the many side streets, has clamped to it a sign with the name of the hotels in that street. Apart from hotel accommodation being comparatively expensive on this island, the majority are taken over by the numerous tour companies which now offer package holidays in Argostoli. Thompson holidays, alone, operate two direct flights a week as do charter operators from other Western European countries.

Hotel Allegro (*Tmr* C4) (Class D) 2A Hoida St   Tel. 22268
Directions: Conveniently to hand. The side street is directly opposite the top or north end of the Market/Bus Station (*Tmr* 1.C4) and the hotel is on the right-hand side.

If the garrulous, English-speaking, Greek hotel-owner's accommodation was half as good as his chat then it would be an excellent establishment. As it is, the rooms are acceptable, the beds have spring mattresses, but the bathrooms leave much to be desired and for a D class hotel, it is not inexpensive with double rooms costing from 1150 drs sharing a bathroom and 1500 drs en suite.

Hotel Tourist (*Tmr* C4) (Class C) 94 1 Metaxa St   Tel. 22510
Directions: On the Esplanade road a few blocks up from the Bus Station (*Tmr* 1.C4).

Fully booked with package tourists in season but doubles start at 1125 drs sharing, in the quieter months.

Hotel Cefalonia Star (*Tmr* 5.C2) (Class C) 50 1 Metaxa St   Tel. 23180
Directions: Further on up the Esplanade, opposite the ferry berth. Over-run with Thompson holiday-makers.

When rooms are available they are expensive with en suite doubles costing from 1511 drs.

Cafe Bar (*Tmr* 6.C2) 1 Metaxa St
Directions: Next block to the *Cefalonia Star* hotel on the marine parade.

In the window there is a sign in respect of rooms to let. Run by Spiros Rouhotas, a delightful, helpful character. and probably the best value in Cephalonia, let alone Argostoli, with single rooms costing about 600 and doubles 800 drs. Get there early because by midafternoon all the rooms are taken.

Additionally the property next door has **Rooms** to rent. (Tel. 23476).

Hotel Mouikis (*Tmr* 7.C4) (Class C) 3 Vironos St   Tel. 23032
Directions: Vironos St is some 4 streets to the north of the Market. The hotel is on the junction with the first street parallel to the Esplanade.

Newly constructed and expensive with an en suite double room costing from 1511 drs and rising to 2045 drs. Again most of the rooms are taken by tour companies.

Hotel Aegli (*Tmr* 8.C3) (Class C) 3, 21st Maiou St   Tel. 22522
Directions: Left-hand side of the street on a corner, walking towards the main square, Plateia Valianou (*Tmr* 2.C3).
Doubles sharing the bathroom from 1125 drs.

Hotel Castello (*Tmr* 9.C3) (Class C) Valianou Square   Tel. 23250
Directions: Top right-hand corner of the square when approached from the Esplanade up 21st Maiou St.

Normally block booked but rooms, when available, cost from 1511 drs for a double.

Camping Site, Cephalos Beach, Argostoli   Tel. 23487
Situated some 2 km north of the town, on the coast road beyond the Sea Mills, on the far side of the Lassi peninsula.

The Eating Out
'Rex Cinema' Restaurant (*Tmr* 10.C3)
Directions: Adjacent to the **Rex Cinema**, a few yards along Georgiou B Avenue, on the left.

Perhaps the best value in town. Be warned that the choice of fare becomes limited after 2100 hrs. One tzatziki, one Greek salad, meat balls and ratatouille for two, bread and a bottle of retsina, all for 900 drs.

Along the waterfront is the

Port of Cephalos Restaurant (*Tmr* 11.C3)
Directions: As above.

Pricey and 'smart', and much frequented by British holiday-makers but serves up extremely good food. A shrimp salad (150 drs), Greek salad (110 drs), spaghetti bolognese (160 drs), lasagne (250 drs), moussaka (210 drs), fillet steak (400 drs), amstel beer for 60 drs, nescafe at 35 drs and a bottle of demestika 95 drs.

North along the front from the *Cephalos Restaurant,* beyond the *Hotel Cefalonia Star,* is the aforementioned

Little Greek Cafe (*Tmr* 6.C2)
Directions: As above.
Offering simple snack meals at reasonable prices.

The restaurants around the Main Sq tend to be expensive and packed with tourists or are the two synonymous? One of the better and quieter establishments is the

Kanaria Restaurant (*Tmr* 12.C3)
Directions: Situated on the road running off the top left-hand side of the square, approaching up Odhos 21 Maiou.

Cephalonia Pie (veal and rice with garlic and pimentoes), Greek salad, a small bottle of retsina, fresh melon and Greek coffee costs some 650 drs per head.

Another recommended Main Square eating house is the

Kefalos Restaurant (*Tmr* 13.C3)
Directions: Named after the First King of Cephalonia and on the left-hand side of the square, on the corner of Diadohou Konstantinou St, facing the side of the Government building.

The head waiter, Terry, spent 20 years in Australia running a fish and chip shop. Meat balls, ratatouille, ½ bottle demestika, an ouzo and coffee for 475 drs.

THE A TO Z OF USEFUL INFORMATION
AIRLINE OFFICE (*Tmr* 14.C4)
Between the market and ferry-boat quays, along Odhos R Vergoti, off I Metaxa (behind the Ionian & Popular Bank and *Hotel Tourist*).

Airline timetable
From Athens to Cephalonia
Up to 22nd June
Monday, Wednesday, Sunday   0700 hrs, non stop
    duration 45 mins
Tuesday, Thursday, Saturday   0700 hrs, one stop
    duration 1 hr 45 mins

| Friday | 1240 hrs, non stop |
| Sunday | 0910 hrs, non stop |

From 23rd June

Daily except Friday	0730 hrs, non stop
Thursday, Saturday	1045 hrs, non stop
Friday	1240 hrs, non stop
One-way fare 2390 drs	

Return journey
Up to 22nd June

Monday, Wednesday, Sunday	0825 hrs, one stop
Tuesday, Thursday, Saturday	0925 hrs, non stop
Friday	1405 hrs, one stop
Sunday	1035 hrs, non stop

From 23rd June

Daily except Friday	0855 hrs, non stop
Thursday, Saturday	1210 hrs, non stop
Friday	1405 hrs, non stop

From Cephalonia to Zakynthos
Only up to 22nd June

| Monday, Wednesday, Sunday | 0825 hrs |
| Friday | 1405 hrs |

One-way fare 700 drs, duration 20 mins

Return journey

| Tuesday, Thursday, Saturday | 0825 hrs |

BANKS

The **Agricultural** (*Tmr* 15.C5) and **National** (*Tmr* 16.C5) are located in the first street back and parallel to the Esplanade, adjacent to the Market Sq. The **Ionian & Popular Bank** (*Tmr* 17.C4) is north of the Market, next to the *Hotel Tourist*, on the Esplanade. Normal weekday hours.

BEACHES
There is a microscopic beach, created by a change of direction in the sea wall, beyond the ferry-boat quay, and there is a roped-off, swimming area, again to the north of the quay.

For more spacious recreation, it is necessary to make the 3 km journey on the airport road to the beaches of Makris Yalos and/or Platis Yalos. Leave town by turning up Odhos Vironos from the Esplanade in the region of the Market or why not catch a bus? The service runs between the middle of June and third week of September.

Argostoli Town to Makris/Platis Yalos:
0900, 1000, 1100, 1130, 1230, 1300, 1330, 1400, 1430, 1500, 1715, 1815 hrs.
Return journey
Makris/Platis Yalos to Argostoli Town:
0945, 1015, 1045, 1115, 1145, 1215, 1245, 1315, 1345, 1415, 1445, 1530, 1650, 1730, 1830 hrs.

BICYCLE, SCOOTER & CAR HIRE
Cephalonia does not lend itself to great bicycle rides, unless you are in strict training for mountain sections of the **Tour de France.** Scooter hire costs between 800 - 1000 drs and usually only the larger-engined versions are available, due to the taxing nature of the terrain. The *laissez-faire* attitude of the hire operators has a lot to do with their being spoiled by the steady stream of compliant package tourists.* There are two hire offices on Diadhohou Konstantinou St, just off the Plateia Valianou (leaving the imposing block of various government offices to the right). Both are run by rather cocky, smoothly dressed young men.

BOOKSELLERS
None.

BREAD SHOPS
There is a very good bread shop opposite the Market (*Tmr* 1.C4) across I Metaxa St, another on Vandorou St (*Tmr* C4/5) and a third, on Hoida St leading up from the Market towards Odhos Diadhohou Konstantinou.

BUSES
The main Bus Station (*Tmr* 1.C4) shares the dusty, scrubby forefront of the Market building.

Bus timetable
Argostoli Town to Athens, 100 Kifissou St.   Tel. 5129498
Daily   0715, 0900 hrs
Return journey
Daily   0715, 0900 hrs
One-way fare 1515 drs (plus ferry-boat fare), duration 8 hrs.

Argostoli Town to Nea Skala
Daily   0945, 1400 hrs
Return journey
Daily   0610, 1700 hrs

Argostoli Town to Sami Port
Daily   0745, 1200, 1300, 1445 hrs.
Return journey
Daily   0730, 0815, 1730 hrs
One-way fare 70 drs, duration ¾ hrs
*Connects with the ferry-boat and Patras-Athens through-bus.

Argostoli Town to Assos
Daily   1400 hrs

*Authors note: This indicates that Richard was unable to beat the blighters down using his well known and rather underhand technique of ostentatiously wandering from one to another scooter firm and haggling. Not very British.

Return journey
Daily   0630 hrs
Note no buses on Sundays/holidays

Argostoli Town to Fiscardon
Daily   0930, 1400 hrs

Return journey
Daily   0630, 1700 hrs

Argostoli Town to Ag Gerasimos Convent (Peratata)
Daily   0930, 1200, 1400, 1930 hrs
Sundays/holidays   0815, 1300 hrs

Return journey
Daily   0640, 1000, 1230, 1630 hrs
Sundays/holidays   0640, 1030 hrs

Argostoli Town to Poros Port
Daily   1315,* 1400 hrs
Sundays/holidays   1000, 1845 hrs

Return journey
Daily   0715 hrs
Sundays/holidays   0610, 1700 hrs
*Connects with the ferry-boat and Killini-Athens through-bus

Argostoli Town to Kourkoumelata (Irinna Hotel)
Daily   0720, 1000, 1230, 1400, 1930 hrs
Sundays/holidays   0630, 1230, 1930 hrs

Return journey
Daily   0645, 0745, 1030, 1300, 1430, 1630, 1950 hrs
Sundays/holidays   0700, 1630, 1950 hrs

To Makris & Platis Yalos
See **Beaches, A to Z.**

Argostoli Town to Assos via Aeonos, Drogarati, Sami, Melissani, Agia Evfimia.
Sundays ONLY: (3rd week of June to 3rd week of September)
                              0830 hrs

Return journey
                              1700 hrs

NB. Where the bus timetables look a little lop-sided it must be remembered that the driver stays overnight at some destinations.

CHEMISTS
See **Medical Care.**

COMMERCIAL SHOPPING AREA (*Tmr* 1.C4)
The main market is assembled in a rather messy, dirty building on the quay juttingout into the marine front and laid out in the shape of a flat W. The forecourt is shared with the bus company, who use it as the terminus. Shops line the Esplanade opposite the Market.

FERRY-BOATS
Only a small car ferry to and from Lixourion, from the ferry-boat quay (*Tmr* 3.C/D2) north of the Market.

   Note that the main ferry-boat port is Sami but travellers can buy their tickets from the office adjacent to the *Port of Cephalos Restaurant* (*Tmr* 11.C3) on I Metaxa St.

Ferry-boat timetable
The schedule starts from Argostoli at about 0630 hrs and the last boat docks at 2200 hrs, leaving every one and a half hours. The one-way journey takes half an hour and costs 75 drs, whilst the charge for scooters is 25 drs. Boats are not so frequent on Sundays when the last return boat ties up at 2100 hrs — don't miss it, it's a long walk!

HOSPITAL
See **Medical Care.**

MEDICAL CARE
Chemists & Pharmacies
Plentiful with a number grouped in the area of the Market (*Tmr* 1.C4) including one across the road and others in the main streets west of the Esplanade.

Hospital (*Tmr* 20.C6)
South along the Esplanade, turning right up Odhos Devossetou, opposite the arched lagoon bridge, and off to the left, after some six or seven blocks.

NTOG (*Tmr* 18.C3)
To the side and in the shadow of the referred to 'Acropolis' styled government building. A small office, which houses an English-speaking, lucid and most helpful lady. Unfortunately the office is only open weekdays for comparatively limited hours, 0800-1500 hrs. There is an island information office in the Bus/Market complex (*Tmr* 1.C4).

OPENING HOURS
Traditional days and times as set out in Chapter 7.

OTE (*Tmr* 19.C3)
Across G. Vergotoi St from the curiously elongated and narrowing block that contains various municipal offices. These include, from the Main Square end, the Town Hall, the Police administration and Archaeological museum.

PETROL (*Tmr* C4/5)
There are two petrol pumps at the causeway end of I Metaxa promenade to the south of the Market, on the opposite side of the Esplanade.

PHARMACIES
See **Medical Care.**

PLACES OF INTEREST
Sea Mills
The repaired remains of the rather unique Sea Mills are about one kilometre north of the town, at the top end of the Lassi peninsula (on which Argostoli Town stands). They were originally built in the nineteenth century at the instigation of an Englishman, to exploit the phenomenon of an underground river of sea-water, coursing inland. A team of scientists recently established that the water reappears the other side of the island at Melissani, above Sami Port. The oft-referred to 1953 earthquake probably altered the levels as the flood has slowed to a trickle.

Half a kilometre further leads to the pretty Doric-styled lighthouse at the headland tip of the peninsula.

Ruins of ancient walls of Krani
South from Argostoli and across the multiple arched bridge, spanning the inlet of sea, leads past a minor road branching off to the right which circumscribes the enclosed lagoon. Halfway around this road, and a track makes off up the hill advancing to whence part of the terraced walls can be viewed. Fine, if you get pleasure from these sometimes indistinct and nebulous lumps and bumps! The remains relate to the fourth century BC, and were part of a large defensive system.

Incidentally, the road left below, circles around to rejoin the main Argostoli road further south of the Town.

British Cemetery
Over the above mentioned bridge and on the right.

In the Town are the:

Archaeological Museum (*Tmr* 21.C3)
Along Diadhohou Konstantinou St, on the right from the Main Square and the last of the narrowing municipal building.

Cultural & Historical Museum (*Tmr* 22.C3)
Sited in the Public Library and containing a number of local interest exhibits including English memorabilia and photographs of the earthquake devasted Argostoli Town.

POLICE
Tourist
Across from the cruise liner quay (*Tmr* 4.D2/3).

Port/Customs
On the cruise liner quay (*Tmr* 4.D2/3).

POST OFFICE (*Tmr* 23.C4)
On Diadhohou Konstantinou, between Vironos and Hoida Sts.

TAXIS
Two main ranks, one on the main or Valianou Sq (*Tmr* 2.C3), the other down by the Bus Station Terminus (*Tmr* 1.C4). They also line up on the quay to meet the Lixourion ferries.

TELEPHONE NUMBERS & ADDRESSES
Police Station	Tel. 22200
Port Police	Tel. 22224
Hospital	Tel. 22434
Olympic Airways	Tel. 22808
Taxi Rank: main square	Tel. 28505

TRAVEL AGENTS
A number on R. Vergoti and 21st Maiou Sts.

ROUTE TWO
To Lixourion (½ hour by ferry, 32 km by road)
The town is across the Gulf of Argostoli and is most easily and effortlessly reached by ferry-boat.

The road route involves taking the Assos road from Argostoli and turning off left at Kardakata, down into the peninsula of Paliki, more popularly known as Lixourion Peninsula. The main road around to the peninsula is very good, having been recently re-surfaced but the inland roads despite being widened and re-surfaced are, in places, still rather rough and care should be exercised.

The cultivated terrain of the peninsula does not represent much of a visual treat.

LIXOURION (Lixouri): port
Tel. prefix 0671.
A sleepy little town which provides a pleasant alternative to the clamour of Argostoli. Lixourion is divided by a river which discharges into the sea just beyond the harbour wall.

Turning right on leaving the ferry-boat landing point (*Tmr* 2.C3) and walking up towards the local fishing boat quay, leads the traveller to the Town Square (*Tmr* 3.B3) around the edge of which are grouped a number of cafe-bars and a couple of banks. Most of the small provisions shops are located in the streets running off and across the tip of the square.

THE ACCOMMODATION & EATING OUT
The Accommodation
Few *Rooms* available in the town apart from the three hotels.

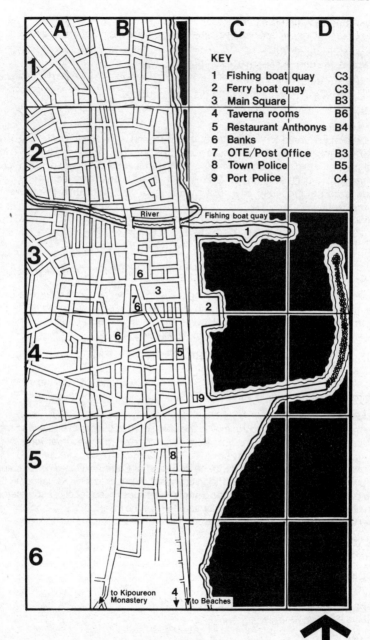

KEY

1	Fishing boat quay	C3
2	Ferry boat quay	C3
3	Main Square	B3
4	Taverna rooms	B6
5	Restaurant Anthonys	B4
6	Banks	
7	OTE/Post Office	B3
8	Town Police	B5
9	Port Police	C4

NORTH

Eighteen
Lixiourion Town & port plan (Cephalonia)

LIXOURION

Hotel Summery (Class C)   Tel. 91771
Singles from 1200 drs and doubles from 1500 drs.

Hotel Ionios Agra (Class D)   Tel. 91241
Singles from 1000 drs and doubles from 1200 drs.

Hotel Horopoula (Class E)   Tel. 91245
800 drs for a single room and 1100 drs for a double.

A pleasant alternative is

'Taverna Rooms'
    Directions: Situated on the road to south of the town. On leaving the ferry-boat quay (*Tmr* 2.C3), turn left and follow the quayside road round the harbour bearing right and then left past the Port police building (*Tmr* 9.C4). The road follows the coast passing the *Hotel Summery* on the left. After about 1½ kms the Taverna is on the right, standing in its own gardens and approached over an unmade track. *See* **Anthonys Restaurant, The Eating Out.**
    Single rooms from 700 drs and double rooms from 1000 drs.

The Eating Out
There are several cafes and tavernas spaced out around the Main Square but possibly one of the most reasonable and pleasant establishments is

Anthony's Restaurant (*Tmr* 5.B4)
Situated across from the quay, almost opposite the ferry-boat dock. Tony is a delightful character and speaks excellent English. Ever helpful, he'll phone ahead to the *Taverna Rooms* and check the availability of rooms thus saving potential clients a long, tedious and wasted walk if there should be none available.

THE A TO Z OF USEFUL INFORMATION
BANKS (*Tmr* 6)
Two situated at the top end of the Main Square (*Tmr* 3.B3) and a third in the street running behind the square leading south (*Tmr* 6.B4).

BEACHES
None in the town itself but by following the coast road to the south and taking the small track off to the left, beyond the path leading to the referred to *Taverna Rooms*, leads to several pleasant, narrow, sandy coves (GROC Rating 7/10).
    Following the above path around the headland of Cape Ag Georgios and along the cliffs, advances to one of the most magnificent, sandy beaches (GROC Rating 9/10) in the whole of the Ionian islands. Set in the Bay of Akrotiri, unspoiled, totally uncommercialised with not a cafe-bar in sight and virtually deserted. It is the ideal place to picnic and spend a quiet day. Walking time, approximately 1 hour.

BICYCLE & SCOOTER HIRE
None noted, even on the last visit.

BOOKSELLERS
None.

BREADSHOPS
In the street behind the Main Square.

BUSES
Terminus on the quayside.

Bus timetable
Lixourion Town to Athens, 100 Kifissou St.
Daily   0830 hrs

190

Return journey
Daily   0830 hrs
See **Arrival By Bus, Sami Port** for further details.
Lixourion Town to Kontogenada
Daily   0645, 1045, 1315, 1830 hrs

Return journey
Daily   0710, 1115, 1530, 1900 hrs
Lixourion Town to Kaminarata and Damoulianata
Daily   0645, 1045, 1315 hrs

Return journey
Daily   0710, 1115, 1430 hrs
Lixiourion Town to Skineas
Daily   0710, 1045, 1315, 1830 hrs

Return journey
Daily   0745, 1130, 1345, 1915 hrs
Lixourion Town to Chavdata
Daily   0645, 1045, 1315, 1830 hrs

Return journey
Daily   0710, 1115, 1530, 1900 hrs
Note there are NO buses on Sundays or holidays.

CHEMISTS
See **Commercial Shopping Area.**

COMMERCIAL SHOPPING AREA
All the shops are in the streets off, behind and around the Main Square (*Tmr* 3.B3).

FERRY-BOATS
To and from Argostoli Town only and arrive and depart from the quay within the harbour wall (*Tmr* 2.C3/4). Tickets, both passenger and vehicle, are purchased on the boat.

OTE (and Post Office) (*Tmr* 7.B3)
In the street that runs behind and parallel to the far side of the Main Square (*Sbo*).

PHARMACY
See **Commercial Shopping Area.**

PLACES OF INTEREST
On the west side of the peninsula from Lixourion is the Monastery of Kipoureon in magnificent surroundings, and still, unusually, the possessor of guest cells.

Many of the village churches on the peninsula, which were unaffected by the 1953 earthquake, have magnificent altar screens.

The pretty village of Ag Spiridon, at the northern end of the peninsula, is also worthy of a visit. The scenery, and the drive is beautiful, not unlike Dartmoor in places, but the road is very bad in parts with deep potholes. Alas the beach (GROC Rating 3/10), which is approached down a very steep track below the village, though sandy and in a beautiful setting is heavily polluted with sea-borne rubbish.

POLICE
Town (*Tmr* 8.B5)
On the outskirts of the town, on the right-hand side of the coast road, heading south.

Port (*Tmr* 9.C4)
At the left-hand end of the ferry-boat quay.

POST OFFICE (*Tmr* 7.B3)
With the OTE, in the street behind the Main Square.

TAXIS
Ranks on the left (*Sbo*) of the Main Square (*Tmr* 3.B3).

ROUTE THREE
To Sami Port (25 km)
The journey between Argostoli Town and Sami is truly dramatic (as are most journeys on this mountainous island), the route climbing the central mountain range through the Pass of Agrapidies. The road surface is, on the whole, good but here and there rock-falls create potholes which can unseat the unwary.

SAMI: main port (25 kms from Argostoli Town)
Tel. prefix 0647.
This uninteresting, small, main port of Cephalonia is rather dusty in appearance. It is on the other hand set in a lovely bay, with a finger pier jutting poetically into the deep blue sea with the dark, mountainous bulk of Ithaca island lowering in the distance. Maybe the bland appearance is due to the fact that it is amongst these Ionian towns that had to be rebuilt (with British help) after the devastating 1953 earthquake.

The road system is a simple flattened circle. On approaching the village there is a petrol station on the left-hand side, followed by a large domed church in the process of being built. (You would think there were enough churches scattered about).

ARRIVAL BY BUS
Comments as for Poros but Sami connects to Athens via the mainland port of Patras.

ARRIVAL BY FERRY
The ferry-boats dock at the far end of the main quay street (*Tmr* 1.B/C1/2).

THE ACCOMMODATION & EATING OUT
The Accommodation
The Hotel Ionian (*Tmr* 2.D2) (Class C) 5 Horofylakis   Tel. 22035
Directions: Almost straight ahead from the ferry-boat quay.

Clean and more reasonably priced than similar hotels in Argostoli Town, with double rooms from 1000 drs.

The Hotel Kyma (*Tmr* 3.C3/4) (Class D) Plateia Kyprou   Tel. 22064
Directions: On the High Street/Main Square.

As for the Hotel Ionian but double room prices start at 880 drs.

There are a number of **Rooms** to let for which it is best to enquire at the *Waterfront Cafe-bar* (*Tmr* 4.C2).

Caravomilos Beach Camping   Tel. 22480
Directions: Some 900 m, west round the curving bay, leads to the well organised site.
English is spoken and charges include laundry facilities.

The Eating Out
The 'Waterfront' Cafe-bar (*Tmr* 4.C2)
Directions: On the waterfront road.

Caters for nearly everyone's requirements. Perhaps its most important function is that it is within 'eyeball' distance of the various bus marshalling points and the ferry-boat quay. The cafe is a source of widely differing opinions! Incidentally the quay front has a number of other cafe-bars but none so conveniently located.

THE A TO Z OF USEFUL INFORMATION
BANKS
Two — one (*Tmr* 5.C3) across from the quayside, on the corner of the side road from the

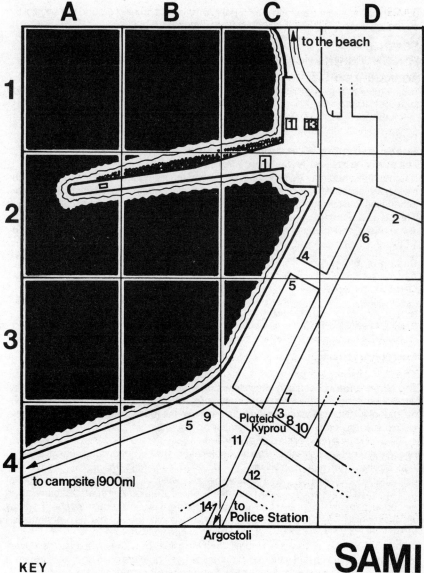

to the beach

to campsite (900m)

Plateid
Kyprou

to
Police Station

Argostoli

SAMI

NORTH

KEY

1	Ferry boat docks	B/C1/2		8	General Store	C4
2	Hotel Ionion	D2		9	Ferry Office	B4
3	Hotel Kyma	C4		10	O.T.E.	C4
4	Café-bar Waterfront	C2		11	Petrol	C4
5	Bank			12	Pharmacy	C4
6	Bookshop	D2		13	Port Police	C1
7	Butcher	C3		14	Post Office	B4

Nineteen   Sami port plan (Cephalonia)

bus turn-round and the second (*Tmr* 5.B4) is on the road running around the edge of the bay to the west.

BEACHES
Unspectacular, pebbly foreshore (GROC Rating 6/10) to the right of the port (*Fsw*).

BOOKSHOP (*Tmr* 6.D2)
At the northern (ferry-boat) end of the street parallel and one block back from the quayside road.

BUSES
The mainland Athens buses are ferried over from Patras and proceed on to Lixourion. For Athens to Argostoli buses *See* **Poros Port.**

Although advice may be asked of one person regarding the matter of bus times and routes, a 'committee' will form almost immediately with much gesticulation. The information must be treble checked, as always, when about to embark on a bus journey in Greece.

The buses tend to turn round and 'terminus' in the area of the *Waterfront Cafe-bar* (*Tmr* 4.C2).

Bus timetable
Athens (Kifissou St) **to Lixourion via Patras and Sami Ports**
Daily   0830 hrs

Return journey
Daily   0830 hrs
One-way fare 1583 drs (plus the ferry-boat cost), duration 8 hrs.

Local buses include:
Sami Port to Fiscardon
Daily at 1330 hrs.

Should the driver not seem to know where he is going this should not be treated as an unfavourable sign as this journey is of a most interesting nature. The initial foray is in the manner of a false start, meandering from Sami into the foothills and back to Sami again, only to start the 'proper' journey, in earnest, an hour later.

The driver has a mind of his own and seems to stop off here and there to make the odd phone call (perhaps he is calling up his bookmaker). The bus follows the coastal route via Agia Evfimia, to the mountain village of Divarata. To really fool travellers everybody has to disembark here into a conveniently placed taverna. The owners seem rather overwhelmed by the whole thing, speak no English, but are quite prepared to carry out an elaborate pantomime in an effort to gratify foreign travellers requirements. The toilet situated behind the building appears to drain away despite the fact that it is not connected to any pipes. Goodness knows what happens when it fills up.

The connecting bus arrives at Divarata from Argostoli Town and completes the journey to Fiscardon, at the cost of a further 50 drs, takes three quarters of an hour and departs a few metres up the road from the taverna. *See* **Argostoli** for further details.

BUTCHERS (*Tmr* 7.C3)
Adjacent to the *Hotel Kyma*.

CHEMISTS
See **Pharmacies.**

COMMERCIAL SHOPPING AREA
None but a reasonable selection of shops including a butcher and, the other side of the *Hotel Kyma*, a general store (*Tmr* 8.C4) that sells fruit and vegetables.

FERRY-BOATS

Cephalonia's ferry-boats represent all the magnificent uncertainty of the system. Certain ferries can be vouched for, others cannot. There is the occasional 'rumour' and 'printed lies' involving a ferry-boat connecting Fiscardon, Sami and Ithaca to Lefkas twice weekly from 1st July to 15th September. Frankly I am of the opinion that the Lefkas connection is on a 'may be' basis — may be once upon a time... The inter-island ferries berth up in the harbour at the western end of the quayside road (*Tmr* 1.C1).

NOTE: There is a new year-round, daily service operating between Karavomilo, 3 km up the coast from Sami, or from Ag Evfimia(!) and Astakos on the Greek mainland which also connects with Ithaca.

Ferry-boat timetables
Karavomilo/Ag Evfimia to Astakos (M)
Daily   0900, 1800 hrs

Return
Daily   1400, 2030 hrs
One-way fare 490 drs, duration 3½ hrs.
Note the first boat either way also calls at Vathi (Ithaca)

Inter-island and mainland ferries

Day	Departure time	Ferry-boat	Ports/Islands of call
Daily	0900 hrs	CF Argostoli and/or CF Kefallinia	Patras (M)

One-way fare 850 drs, duration 3½ hrs

Day	Departure time	Ferry-boat	Ports/Islands of call
Daily	1700 hrs		Ithaca
Daily	1800 hrs		Ithaca
Monday	2330 hrs		Fiscardon (Cephalonia), Paxos, Corfu
Tuesday	1330 hrs		Patras (M)
Friday	0300 hrs		Ithaca, Corfu
Friday	0615 hrs		Patras (M)

FERRY-BOAT TICKET OFFICES

The **Ionian Lines** office (*Tmr* 9.B4), at the southern end of the quayside, is a mine of information. Well, the lady who runs it is most helpful but when questioned closely about the possibility of a Lefkas ferry, her ability to communicate in English becomes seriously impaired! Tickets for the island connections can be purchased on the quay, prior to boarding.

OTE (*Tmr* 10.C4)
On the corner of the street behind the *Hotel Kyma.*

PETROL
Two stations on the Argostoli road out of Sami, one on the right near the Main Square (*Tmr* 11.C4), the other just beyond the church (that is being newly constructed).

PHARMACIES (*Tmr* 12.C4)
One to the left of the Sami to Argostoli road beyond the Main Square.

PLACES OF INTEREST
Not a lot! Well not quite...
   Behind the town are the remains of a Roman building and its mosaic.
   The surrounding hills have sections of ancient walls that were once part of the defences of a much older city but they are best seen outlined against the skyline from approaching ferry-boats.
   Two caves are worthy of a visit. The one,

Limni Melissani
Three kilometres along the Sami to Ag Evfimia road at the village of Karavomilo. The large, dark, water-filled, stalactite dotted caves are approached via a small lake in a small boat accompanied by a guide. It is here that the sea-waters that used to power the Argostoli Sea Mills emerges after the long underground journey across the island's width. Entrance fee including the boat trip costs about 100 drs.

The other is

Spileon Drogarati
Four kilometres along the Sami to Argostoli road. A very large cave hung with stalactites, and the cavern floor growing stalagmites. Admission costs 50 drs.

POLICE
Town
On the Sami to Argostoli road, 200 m from the Main Square (*Tmr* C4).

Port (*Tmr* 13.C1)
Located on the harbour square.

Note there are no Tourist Police.

POST OFFICE (*Tmr* 14.B4)
On the turning that branches off the Sami to Argostoli road, 50 m from Plateia Kyprou.

TELEPHONE NUMBERS & ADDRESSES
Hospital	Tel. 21240
Port Office	Tel. 21231
Customs	Tel. 21344
Police	Tel. 21208
Taxi stand	Tel. 22308

EXCURSION TO AGIA EVFIMIA (10 km)
North from Sami port, the road edges the large elongated Bay of Sami passing, after 3 kilometres.

KARAVOMILO
Once only noteworthy for the admittedly outstanding Limni Melissani Cave (*See* **Places of Interest, Sami**) but now a ferry-boat departure point. Well is it or do the ferries dock at Agia Evfimia? *See* **Ferry-Boats, Sami Port.**

AG EVFIMIA
A lovely fishing port complete with a small harbour prettily situated around the waters edge. Prior to the 1953 earthquake, Ag Evfimia was once-upon-a-time the main eastern coast port.

Well provided with a grocery, baker, small Post Office combined OTE, taverna, a few rooms and the C class *Hotel Pylaros* (Tel. 61210) with doubles sharing the bathroom starting from 1100 drs.

From Ag Evfimia the road progresses over the neck of the island to Divarata (*See* **Buses, Sami Port**).

ROUTE FOUR
To Fiscardon via Divarata & Assos (50 km)
From Argostoli Town head south along the harbour road and across the causeway from whence the road starts to climb. The road to Sami Port bears off to the right whilst the Fiscardon road swings northwards, hugging the mountainside. At each bend, the views of the Gulf of Argostoli and Livadi Bay become more and more dramatic — truly a magnificent drive.

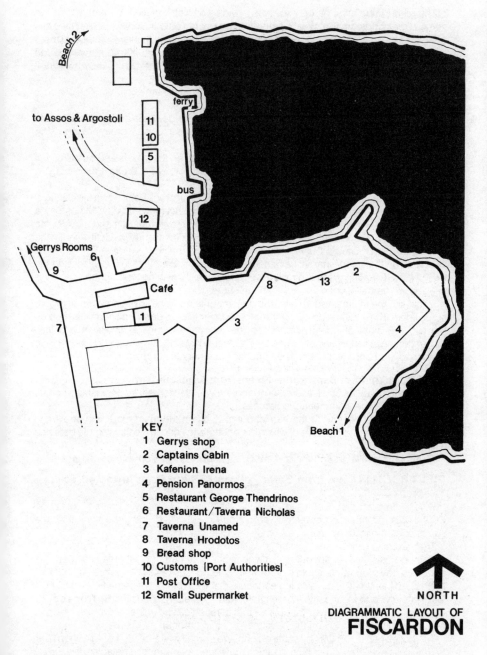

The road for the most part is excellent — wide and well metalled. Here and there, on some of the bends, small rock-falls cause the occasional obstruction and the surface has been broken up by the passage of heavy traffic over the fallen stones. The route passes through the pretty village of Farsa (11 km from Argostoli Town) and Kontogrourata (17 km from Argostoli Town) before reaching Kardakata (19 km from Argostoli Town) where it crosses the top of the western Lixourion peninsula.

At the village of Agkonas a track drops down to the small hamlet of Zola. The beach is pretty but polluted (GROC Rating 3/10).

Shortly after reaching the north-west coast, the road swings inland and joins the Sami to Fiscardon road at Siniori (31 km from Argostoli). Both here and at the pretty neighbouring village of Divarata there are **Rooms** to let.

One feels that Divarata's modern day eminence rests on the inter-island buses use of the village as a terminus and staging post — a sort of Greek **Wells Fargo** staging post.

Beyond Divarata the road rejoins the coast but pause and look back down the cliff-face. One of the most beautiful views in the Ionian islands breaks forth into view. Mirtos Bay, a wide, dazzling white crescent of fine shingle, flanked by towering cliffs and a sea of the deepest blue, patchworked with aquamarine — breathtaking and idyllic. Until recently, the bay was heavily polluted but not any more. The rather hair-raising drive from Divarata village down the steep, sharply hairpinned, loose surfaced track (1 in 3 in places) to the beach (GROC Rating 9/10) is amply rewarding since, if anything, the rugged scenery is even more dramatic when viewed from the shore.

Back on the main road again and the mountain scenery becomes even more sensational. The rock wall on the right seems awfully close as does the enormous drop on the left. The sight of goats perched on the rocky cliff-niches at eye-level is a little disconcerting at first, especially when they suddenly leap off, seemingly into the wild blue yonder, to land and nimbly perch on impossible pinnacles of rock.

ASSOS (24 km from Sami Port & 36 km from Argostoli Town)
Dramatically beautiful. The tear droplet of land, the Venetian fortressed peninsula, appears to float on the blue shimmering Ionian sea.

Buses do not descend to the hamlet but stop off on the main road high above the narrow neck of land either side of which are anchorages and tiny white shingle beaches (GROC Rating 8/10).

Rooms are available and there is the B Class *Myrtos Pension* with six rooms.

FISCARDON (41 km from Sami Port and 53 km from Argostoli Town)
Tel. prefix 0674.
Disappointment may well have been the emotion accompanying part of a stay on Cephalonia but the line between Divarata and Ag Evfimia, dividing the north from the south, once crossed, opens up a completely different world.

The Cornish 'look alike' fishing village of Fiscardon surely completes the metamorphosis. It is a captivating, working, small boat harbour, set on a sea inlet. This ends in a bay around the south side of which the houses of the village are laid out in a haphazard fashion. The devastating earthquake of 1953 did not damage Fiscardon, thus leaving the village in its early and delightful form, some say not unlike **St Tropez** of 30 years ago. The port is used by the flotilla yacht companies and at the height of the season becomes rather crowded on the days they put into harbour.

The buses pull up on the tiny square alongside a small white-painted village shop (*Tmr* 1). This sells everything from pins to beach mats, food, drinks and vegetables. It is run by 'Gerry', one of the village's most informative men and he and his brothers operate, amongst other enterprises, the village shop, a fishing caique and have **Rooms** to let. Do not be put off by his somewhat long haired, introverted air, he is a praiseworthy chap and could not be more helpful.

In a village of characters surely the extroverted 'Tassou' must be outstanding. He and his Rhodesian-born, English-speaking, Greek wife, runs the splendid *Captains Cabin* quayside taverna (*Tmr* 2). Oh! by the way, Tassou reads the **Sunday Times** every week to keep abreast of events. Can you imagine asking the local newsagent to drop the **Athens Weekly** in amongst the other Sundays? One other word of warning, do not mention Cyprus. A sore subject this.

THE ACCOMMODATION & EATING OUT
The Accommodation
Rooms
Directions: Ask '**Gerry**' at the village shop (*Tmr* 1), if his accommodation is available. For directions, *See* **Bread Shops** and why not? Try '**Tassou**' at the *Captains Cabin* (*Tmr* 2), or '**Irena**' at the Kafenion (*Tmr* 3) beside the square, across from Gerry's.

Average rates work out at 600 drs for a single and 1000 drs for a double room.

Pension Panormos (*Tmr* 4) (Class B)   Tel. 51340
Directions: Around the corner, beyond the *Captains Cabin* taverna.

Often block-booked so no-go for the casual stay but advertises double rooms from 1200 drs.

The Eating Out
Restaurant George Thendrinos (*Tmr* 5)
Directions: On the left as the village is entered.

The fish is expensive (where is it not?), otherwise average fare at average prices. The 'colourful' owner is reputed to have lost his hand whilst fishing with dynamite. Sounds a dangerous sport to me.

Nicholas Restaurant/Taverna (*Tmr* 6)
Directions: Turn right by the cavernous, very Greek supermarket store (*Tmr* 12), down the dusty side lane, and the restaurant is at the far end of the dead-end alley. Often a 1930s motor car is parked alongside.

The restaurant is in a high-ceilinged building with a walled courtyard garden at the rear. The excellent food includes pizzas and barbecued dishes. Fish pie for two, stuffed tomatoes for one, one Greek salad, one portion of chips, a large bottle of retsina for 637 drs. A lunch time snack of a large plate of whitebait (well sardines really), bread and ½ carafe of local wine 230 drs.

Taverna 'Unnamed' (*Tmr* 7)
Behind '**Gerry's**' shop. A very Greek taverna with the usual offerings and tables set out across the dusty street.

Hrodotos Taverna (*Tmr* 8)
On the way around the quayside beyond *Irena's Kafenion.*

The owner, Mr Hrodotos, is an engaging gold-toothed man who doubles up as the village taxi driver and specialises in lobster dishes (if you can afford them). Perhaps his driving is on a par with his cooking but let's hope not, for his passengers sake. . . (think about it).

Captains Cabin (*Tmr* 2)
Tassou serves up an excellent breakfast of scrambled eggs, toast and butter and fruit juice, at one of the pavement tables under the giant awning. Seated here, his clientele can idly watch the sea sparkle and the shimmering water reflect the outlines of the gently bobbing fishing boats. . . and the scrambled eggs are good too!

Splendid company with a man who one feels is not only larger than life, but is, rather incongruously, a resident of sleepy Fiscardon. He personifies that elusive character that newspaper editors occasionally demand their travel reporter to go and search out. You know. . . 'go find a Zorba, it'll make good copy'.

THE A TO Z OF USEFUL INFORMATION

BANKS

None, but most of the aforementioned village worthies will effect a transaction.

BEACHES

In the environs of Fiscardon are two small beaches in beautiful settings (GROC Rating 6/10).

Beach 1: Reached by walking on, around past the Captains Cabin (*Tmr* 2), all the way to the end of the road, where there is a small bay with Olive trees growing down to the clear blue water's edge. The fairly long trek is enlivened initially by the various villas scattered along the dusty walk, the beautiful view of the sea-channel between Cephalonia and Ithaca and lastly, wonderment that in such a magnificent setting, a philistine could have constructed the now apparently abandoned stone crushing plant on the tree covered hillside.

Beach 2: Attained by climbing out of the village up the approach road, turning off down a wide, bulldozed and scraped track and then scrambling down to the left, to a bay scalloped out by the sea from the rocky coastline. The seashore consists of large rounded pebbles set in sand in surroundings of Olive trees and scrub-covered land. The large, almost horizontal slabs edging the cove are ideal to sunbathe on after a swim in the azure sea.

BREAD SHOP (*Tmr* 9)

The bakery is rather difficult to locate and it is easy to walk past it but over the low door frame is an indistinct sign, APTOMOIEION. From the quayside walk beyond Gerry's shop leaving the large, shabby village square to the left. Another track converges and the pair rapidly narrow down swinging right, on the corner of which is the baker. Incidentally, this lane leads on to one of Gerry's houses, wherein he has some very pleasant rooms to let.

BUSES

As detailed under Argostoli Town. The bus 'overnights' on a concrete ramp specially constructed for the purpose, almost opposite *Restaurant George Thendrinos* (*Tmr* 5).

I am not sure, but I think the bus departs to scour the foothills for locals and then returns again before finally departing for Argostoli Town.

CUSTOMS HOUSE (*Tmr* 10)

Beyond *George Thendrinos*' restaurant.

FERRY-BOATS

A new, local trip boat service started up in 1984 connecting Vassiliki (Lefkas) with Sami (Ithaca) and Fiscardon twice a week during the height-of-the-season. (*See* **Vassiliki, Lefkas Chapter 14** for more detailed information). Certainly the once shallow harbour has been dredged to allow deeper draught vessels to enter the bay.

The service certainly makes life a lot easier for the traveller since local boatmen charge about 500 drs a head to ferry clients from Fiscardon port to Stavros on Ithaca. Enquire at Gerry's or Irena's for details of this *ad hoc* arrangement.

The scheduled inter-island ferry-boats 'pull-up' in the mouth of the entrance to Fiscardon's sea inlet, collecting and delivering passengers to a local boat owners craft. The system under which this is organised is a complete mystery and what method of Greek bush telegraph transmits the information from the shipping line to Fiscardon defies imagination. I know we have put a man on the moon but even contemplating the technical difficulties of making the above arrangements. . .!

PLACES OF INTEREST

On the headland opposite the village there are the ruins of a possibly Norman church and a very pretty lighthouse. It is postulated that the name Fiscardon derives from a Norman knight, one Robert Guiscard, who died on his ship in the harbour whilst capturing the town from the Turks.

POST OFFICE (*Tmr* 11)
At the entrance to the village, beyond *George Thendrinos'* restaurant.

SHOPPING (*Tmr* 12 and 13)
Being a busy little port and a flotilla stopover, it is not surprising that there are a number of supermarkets, although this is a misnomer as they tend to resemble dingy, Dickensian warehouses. There is one large establishment (*Tmr* 12) across the side street from *George Thendrinos'*. The other (*Tmr* 13) is almost alongside the *Captains Cabin,* whilst **Gerry's** village shop (*Tmr* 1) in the centre of the village, will supply nearly everything a traveller requires.

Almost every morning a fruit and vegetable van pulls up on the square.

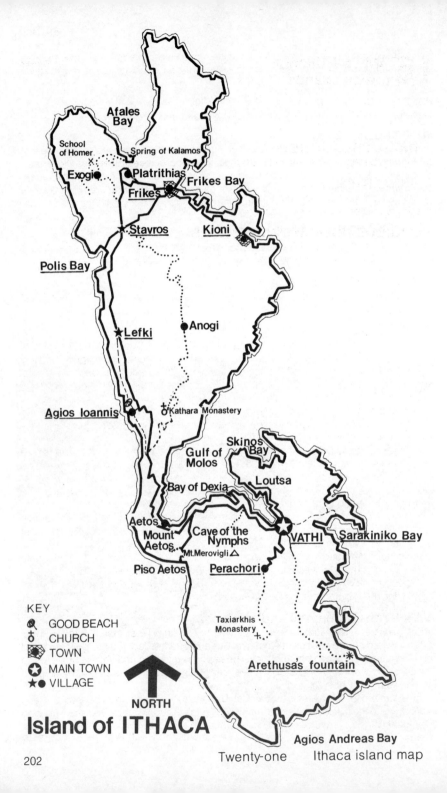

Afales
Bay

School
of Homer   Spring of Kalamos
          X
Exogi●   ●Platrithias
              Frikes Bay
          Frikes

★ Stavros   Kioni

Polis Bay

★ Lefki   ●Anogi

Agios Ioannis   ✝ Kathara Monastery
              o

              Skinos
              Bay
          Gulf of
          Molos   Loutsa

          Bay of Dexia

Aetos   Cave of the
Mount   Nymphs   ☆ VATHI   Sarakiniko Bay
Aetos   Mt.Merovigli △
Piso Aetos   Perachori ●

          Taxiarkhis
          Monastery
              ✝

              Arethusa's fountain   ＊

KEY
Ⓐ GOOD BEACH
✝ CHURCH
▦ TOWN
✪ MAIN TOWN
★● VILLAGE

NORTH

Island of ITHACA

Twenty-one   Ithaca island map

Agios Andreas Bay

16 Ithaca (Ithaki)
Ionian Islands
*****

FIRST IMPRESSIONS
Mellifluous sheep bells; Martello towers; fjord-like indents; Greek men bearing roses.

SPECIALITIES
Homer; ravani (sweet cake made up of honey, sugar and semolina); a lamb dish, casserole cooked; local wine; ginger beer.

RELIGIOUS HOLIDAYS & FESTIVALS
include: Apart from the traditional holidays, 22nd August to 15th September — theatre festival, Vathi; 6th September — feast day, Monastery of Kathara.

VITAL STATISTICS
Tel. prefix 0674. The island is 29 km long, up to 6½ km wide with a total population of 6,500 of which the capital, Vathi houses about 2,500. ·

GENERAL
Ithaca, one of the smallest islands in the Ionian chain, has a 'village' feel about it, with few concessions to the holiday-maker although the local inhabitants are delightful, friendly and helpful. It also claims to be the home of the hero of the Homeric legends, Odysseus, and there is an annual seminar every summer that attracts students of Homer from all over the world.

Prior to the blasting of the road system into a coherent, if limited, layout, much island travel was by caique and some vestiges remain in the occasional boat trips from various fishing villages to and from Vathi (Ithaki), the capital.

A rather singular island in that despite its drawbacks, or more accurately the lack of concessions to the twentieth century traveller, visitors will invariably be left with very fond memories of their visit and more especially struck by the warmth of the islanders. To the North, the few villages have a surprising number of English or rather, Colonial speaking natives, who are only too pleased to engage in long and detailed conversation, answering any enquiries and regaling listeners with details of their overseas travels. I write Colonial which will be understood by those right-minded 'Brits' who do not consider that the US of A ever left the Empire's glorious fold. It is surprising how many young men leave Ithaca to go seafaring, or live and work in America or Australia, returning to their native island to take up the reins of the family agricultural holding or retire to build their dream home.

Although a landing might be made at Stavros, or more accurately, Polis Bay, of which more later, it is almost certain that the traveller will dock at

VATHI (Ithaci): capital and main port
The town is set in a beautiful, deeply indented bay which opens out in front of the ferry-boats' onward progress, once the mountainous and barren headland has been rounded and the narrow approach channel cleft. The setting is romantic and Vathi is built around the bottom end of the 'U' shaped or horse-shoe bay, on a narrow coastal plain, hemmed in by a low range of hills.

In appearance the town is not unlike Dartmouth in Devon, the houses clinging impossibly to the hillside with steps, more steps and even more steps. The smell of wood smoke pervades everywhere and chickens scratch around in the dirt at the side of the roads.

The occasional cartographer, (not my own) perpetrates a few little inaccuracies here and there on some of the maps. For instance the Stadium could be moved in an eastwards direction a few hundred yards and for that matter Frikes, a north-eastern fishing port, is positioned inland. Perhaps the rate of coastal silting has increased dramatically.

Two other items of note are the rather pleasant pedal-operated litter bins and, lo and behold, a public toilet block to one side of the Customs House. Incidentally, the litter bins are very rarely emptied. They are there, but would the average holiday-maker ever dream of using one? Certainly a Greek wouldn't!

Vathi is also one of those places where an alarm clock is quite superfluous for, being essentially a rural community, roosters abound and commence their clamorous dawn chorus at around 0400 hrs.

ARRIVAL BY FERRY

From the ferry-boat quay the main part of the Town is to the left (*Sbo*), at the bottom of the bay. The ferries do not moor up alongside the Main Square, instead they casually tie up alongside the narrow marine parade road (*Tmr* 1.B2/3), incongruously towering over the road and adjacent houses. The reverberations of the ferry's siren echoing over the Sound as it enters the harbour bay is guaranteed to send a shiver of anticipation down the backbone of even the most blasé travellers.

The ferries are not met by the traditional swarm of room-offering islanders. Immediately after disembarking, as a traveller heads along the waterfront road, there is a Tourist Information office (*Tmr* 2.B3) which will give assistance regarding **Rooms**. The few owners of hostelries who do attend a ferry-boat's arrival, loiter quietly in the background, near the information office, thoroughly vetting everybody prior to making any approach.

Vathi 'dies' on Sunday and, for that matter, there is not much activity any afternoon.

THE ACCOMMODATION & EATING OUT
The Accommodation

Not a lot! What is available, is quickly taken as Vathi lacks an abundance of hotels and pensions.

Hotel Aktaeon (*Tmr* 3.B3) (Class E) Georgiou Gratsou St   Tel. 32387
Directions: Conveniently situated adjacent to the ferry-boat quay, on the Esplanade road.

Run by an agreeable Scandinavian looking Greek, who speaks excellent English. The rooms are very clean and pleasant with a single room costing from 600 drs and doubles from 880 drs.

Hotel Mendor (*Tmr* 4.D4) (Class B) Georgiou Dracouli/Paralia Sts   Tel. 32433
Directions: Quite a long haul from the ferry berth. It is necessary to turn left off the boat, following the quayside road around past the Town Hall and the Customs House, cut across the Main Square (keeping to the sea wall), on along the Esplanade to where the bay bears left again, and the hotel is across the road.

A rather up-market, very pleasant hotel but it is only open during the summer months and is largely booked by tour companies. Rooms when available are comparatively expensive with prices ranging from 1800 drs for a double room sharing the bathroom facilities and 2800 drs en suite.

Hotel Odysseys (*Tmr* 5.A1) (Class B)   Tel. 32381
Directions: On the Esplanade road, north-west beyond the ferry-boat quay, almost directly opposite Lazareto Island.

Confusingly also known as *Pension Vathy* the establishment only opens during the summer months. Clean and tidy with single rooms from 796 drs and double rooms from 1250 drs.

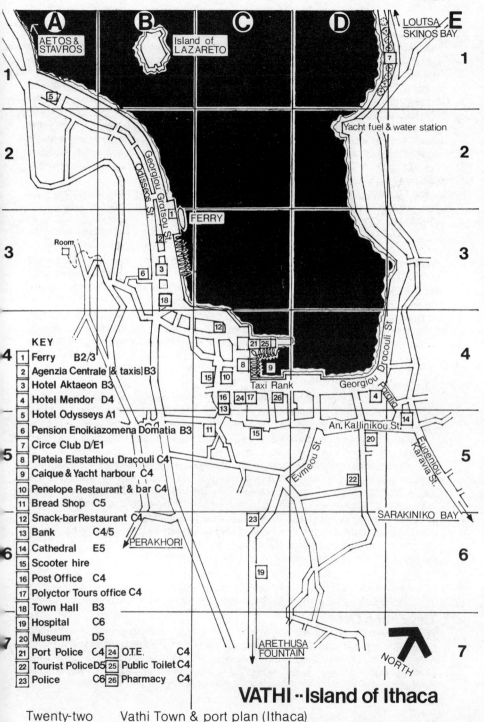

LOUTSA
SKINOS BAY

A   B   C   D   E

AETOS &
STAVROS

Island of
LAZARETO

1

Yacht fuel & water station

2

Room

Georgiou Gratsou St.

Odisseos St.

FERRY

3

Ferry

KEY

4

1	Ferry	B2/3
2	Agenzia Centrale [& taxis] B3
3	Hotel Aktaeon	B3
4	Hotel Mendor	D4
5	Hotel Odysseys	A1
6	Pension Enoikiazomena Domatia B3
7	Circe Club	D/E1
8	Plateia Elastathiou Draçouli C4
9	Caique & Yacht harbour C4
10	Penelope Restaurant & bar C4
11	Bread Shop	C5
12	Snack-bar Restaurant C4
13	Bank	C4/5
14	Cathedral	E5
15	Scooter hire
16	Post Office	C4
17	Polyctor Tours office C4
18	Town Hall	B3
19	Hospital	C6
20	Museum	D5
21	Port Police	C4	24	O.T.E.	C4
22	Tourist Police D5	25	Public Toilet C4
23	Police	C6	26	Pharmacy	C4

Taxi Rank

Georgiou Draçouli St.

Paralia

An. Kallinikou St.

Eugeniou
Karavia St.

Evmeou St.

PERAKHORI

SARAKINIKO BAY

ARETHUSA
FOUNTAIN

NORTH

VATHI ·· Island of Ithaca

Pension Enoikiazomena Domatia (*Tmr* 6.B3) ΝΟΣΤΟΥ (Alleyway) off Odisseos St
Directions: From the ferry-boat berth, keep left and turn right up the narrow lane alongside
the Town Hall (*Tmr* 18.B3). This leads into Odisseos St, which runs parallel to Georgiou
Gratsou, the Esplanade road. Turn right and after 20 yards there is a narrow, upward-
sloping, stepped alley on the left. The pension is half-way up on the right.

Papa George and his wife run a very friendly Greek provincial pension. The rooms and
furnishings are aged, colonial Victorian in character, but clean and well equipped. The
shared bathroom shower is very hot, almost too hot, but who's complaining. Plumbers
should note the installation of the shower drain pipe, which simply pokes out through the
wall of the bathroom and from which the shower waste water just pours — who wants a
drain? Access to some bedrooms is via an ante-room wherein a local may be asleep on
the sofa (at any time of day or night). The house and garden are bedecked with flowering
climbers.

The household washing machine resembles a 1950 American car, crossed with an
early juke-box — all chrome and knobs. Incidentally, it was also not plumbed in, just
draining off into another patch of the garden.

A double room for 800 drs, after some negotiation. The later in the day you arrive the
smaller the base from which to haggle over the price.

As advised, there is not a superabundance of rooms and on my first visit to Ithaca some
years ago we only found Papa George's due to an American Greek lady observing our
plight, ringing up and sending us in tow with her rather reluctant daughter as a guide.

Circe Club (*Tmr* 7.D/E1)
As a fall back, the verandah of this club appears to offer those who have not located a bed
somewhere to rest their head. I presume that to qualify for this dubious facility, one must
participate, in part at least, in the evening entertainment of the club. If you must . . . from the
ferry proceed left on the quay road all the way around the flattened horseshoe bay. The
club is located some way up alongside the shorefront, in a tree-lined grove.

Village Rooms
A number of houses on the hillside behind the *Pension Enoikiazomena Domatia* (*Tmr*
6.B3) have rooms to rent. The aforementioned Tourist Information office (*Tmr* 2.B3) near
the ferry berth will give directions.

Rooms range from the very basic — bed, chair, small table, stone floor with tiny cotton
mat and use of a primitive cold water shower costing some 500 drs a night to near luxury
apartments annexed to existing houses. This latter accommodation is well furnished with
2 or 3 beds, easy chairs, dining table, bedside lights and modern en suite bathrooms with
ample hot water costing from 800 drs per night. The building has, as likely as not, been
financed by a husband, son or relative, working abroad or in the Merchant Navy. Curiously
enough the owners often still live in primitive conditions themselves with for instance the
cooking being done over an open fire in the garden. In fact the majority of the household
chores — washing, meal preparation, and sewing are all undertaken in the open air, whilst
the chickens and roosters wander in and out of the house!

The Eating Out

Yes! well there you go. There is very little choice but that to hand is good and reasonably
priced. The main square, Plateia Elstathiou Dracouli (*Tmr* 8.C4) is edged by a row of
pavement cafes across the road from the caique and yacht harbour (*Tmr* 9.C4). One or two
of these establishments serve limited menus including cheese pies and toasted
sandwiches.

On the first floor and centrally located in this row is

The Penelope Restaurant and Bar (*Tmr* 10.C4)
Directions: The bar is on the ground floor with the restaurant up a flight of steps, to one side.

Ben and his family appear to be in a perpetual state of nervous exhaustion and near hysteria. Ten out of ten for effort and entertainment. The menu is varied and the food good, but if you think it takes time to be served, just wait till you try to pay the bill. . .

A meal for two of Green beans, squid, lamb chop with spaghetti, bread and retsina cost 800 drs. Good news, but do arrive early, as the whole performance, from ordering to settling up, takes an extremely long time. Surprisingly for an ex merchant-seaman, Ben's English is very limited.

Taverna
Directions: Located at the end of the street in which the Bread Shop (*Tmr* 11.C5) is situated.

An excellent establishment selling marvellous charcoal cooked chops and delicious souvlaki. It has an attractive garden at the rear but for atmosphere it is best to eat inside since the place is a meeting place for local 'characters'.

It is here that a lucky patron might for instance meet a former leading Tenor with the Welsh National Opera. He was taken as a child from Ithaca to Cardiff by his parents, only returning to his birthplace to retire a few years ago.

It appears that one evening, he and three of his Greek cronies joined Richard and a New Zealand companion for a monumental feast of souvlaki's, Greek salad and fried potato all washed down with numerous bottles of retsina. The meal was something of a marathon since as dishes and bottles emptied, others appeared to take their place. I am advised that they finally staggered out into the night, deliriously happy with life, well fed and extremely content (sounds faintly disgusting to me). The pleasure was augmented by the fact that the meal had cost just 1400 drs — for six!

Snack-bar Restaurant (*Tmr* 12.C4)
Recently opened, on the quay road between the Customs House and the Town Hall.

Offers simple fare including excellent eggs and bacon at 100 drs which includes bread and DIY tea (cup + tea bag, hottish water and jug of tinned milk).

See **Beaches A to Z,** for details of restaurants and beach bars on the Loutsa side of the bay.

THE A TO Z OF USEFUL INFORMATION
BANK (*Tmr* 13.C4/5)
One (once two) off the bottom corner of the Main Square, close by the OTE office (*Tmr* 24.C4).

BEACHES
Apart from the long out-of-town hikes, the far side of the bay (from the town) has a narrow, tree-lined, shingle beach (GROC Rating 6/10) stretching from the yacht fuel and water station right around that part of the headland named Loutsa. The whole of this length is very pleasantly shaded by the unusually large and assorted trees and 'enjoys' a scattering of good-value restaurants and beach bars serving a wide range of food and drinks.

Typical of the genre is an excellent restaurant, on the right, beyond the *Circe Club* (*Tmr* 7.D/E 1). The prices are more expensive than in the port with a meal for two costing 1600 drs but the food is very good, the setting and atmosphere convivial. At those prices it would have to be. . . !

At Loutsa, which is just below some antique gun emplacements (a historic **Guns of Navarone**?), there is a small bay and unbelievably a couple of Greek lads who clean up the small beach. This is to make their very small beach bar more attractive to the punters but surely does merit a mention.

There are also two shingle beaches (GROC Rating 6/10) on Skinos Bay, approached by taking the unmade road leading up over the hill from the Loutsa road. However, a number of well-heeled Greeks from the mainland have commenced building villas along the seafront which has narrowed even further the already slim foreshore.

Possibly the nomination for the best beach, not just local to Vathi Town but on the entire island, lies directly to the east of the town and can be easily reached on foot by taking the road behind the Cathedral (*Tmr* 14.E5) that runs out to Sarakiniko Bay. (*See* **Excursions**).

BICYCLE & SCOOTER HIRE
There are three main establishments hiring scooters and bikes in the warren of streets behind the Main Square (*Tmr* 15.B/C4) (caique and yacht harbour behind one) and another on Odhos An Kallinikou (*Tmr* 15.C5) but no car hire firm.

A large moped costs around 600 drs a day and a larger scooter about 900 drs. It is debatable if it is worth hiring any form of locomotion due to the comparatively small size of the island, the few roads, the mountainous terrain and the excellent and reasonably priced taxi service.

Hirers making the journey from one end of the island to the other by scooter should be cautious. Whilst the main Vathi Town to Kioni road has been extensively widened and re-surfaced in the last 2 years, and is excellent by general standards, the surface on some of the sharper bends has suffered as a result of rock falls. A scooter and its occupants could all but disappear without trace into some of the resultant potholes. Great care should also be taken when negotiating the section between Aetos and Lefki in high winds, since sudden gusts can push a machine and rider precariously close to the unguarded edge and precipitous drop! You have been warned!

BOOKSELLER
The closest to a specialised vendor is a shop just off the bottom left-hand corner of the Main Square, almost opposite the Post Office (*Tmr* 16.C4).

BREAD SHOP (*Tmr* 11.C5)
Once again, off the bottom left-hand corner of the Main Square, past the Post Office and half-right leads to an excellent bread shop, on the left, in the corner of the junction.

BUSES
Pull up on the Main Square (*Tmr* 8.C4). The service is subject to delays caused by the 'transport modules' breaking down, often for weeks on end. One machines misfortune means that the taxi drivers are exultant and busy.

Bus timetables
Vathi Town-Lefki-Stavros-Platrithias-Frikes-Kioni
Daily   0600, 0900 hrs

Kioni-Vathi Town-Perachori
Daily   1000 hrs

Vathi Town and Kioni
Daily   1300 hrs

Return journey
Daily   1600 hrs

CHEMISTS
See **Medical Care.**

COMMERCIAL SHOPPING AREA
There is no specific market area but most of the shops are on or close by the Main Square. Ithaca is one of those islands where closing times are strictly adhered to and shops cannot be expected to be open 'out of hours' or on Sunday.

FERRY-BOATS

The ferry-boat system for Ithaca is tied into that of Cephalonia.

During the high season there is a local caique service connecting Ithaca, Cephalonia and Lefkas. For details *See* **Vassiliki, Lefkas, Chapter 14.**

Another useful service, started up in the last few years is the 'Astakos connection'. This daily ferry-boat trip links Astakos on the mainland (*See* **Chapter 10**), Vathi Town and Cephalonia (*See* **Chapter 15**).

Ferry-boat timetable

Day	Departure time	Ferry-boat	Ports/Island of call
Daily	0700 hrs		Sami (Cephalonia), Patras (M).

One-way fare to Patras 850 drs.

Friday	0430 hrs		Corfu.
Friday	0445 hrs		Sami (Cephalonia), Patras (M).
Every other day	0215 hrs 1345 hrs		Paxos, Corfu. Sami (Cephalonia), Patras (M).

Astakos (M) to Vathi Town (Ithaca), Karavomilo/Ag Evfimia (Cephalonia)
Daily   1400 hrs
Return
Daily   1100 hrs*
One-way fare 363 drs, duration 1¾ hrs
*Departs from Cephalonia for Vathi Town @ 0900 hrs.

FERRY-BOAT TICKET OFFICES

Agenzia Centrale, (*Tmr* 2.B3) Georgiou Gratsou

Shares an office with a Tourist Information office, the town side of the ferry-boat quay. It is run by a Greek 'character' with good English, the staff are very helpful and the office 'opens up' for ferry-boat arrivals.

Polyctor Tours, (*Tmr* 17.C4) Plateia Elstathiou Dracouli

South end of the Main Square, alongside the OTE office. The Greek manager/owner is a snappy dresser, wearing white ducks, but despite his excellent English is not as helpful as he might be. In fact he appears rather disinterested and gives every indication of being easily bored by detailed and persistent enquiries which, with the complexity and dubious nature of the ferry-boat schedules, are very necessary. He does own a smart motor boat which takes up quite a lot of his time!

There is a third agency in the block almost adjacent to the Town Hall (*Tmr* 18.B3) where a very attractive young Greek lady, who speaks reasonable English, is generally very helpful.

HOSPITAL
See **Medical Care.**

MEDICAL CARE

Chemists & Pharmacies (*Tmr* 26.C4)

Situated in the parade of shops, across from the quay, on the flattened part of the 'U' of the horseshoe bay.

Hospital (*Tmr* 19.C6)

On Evmeou St, which leads south in an arc from the centre of the bottom of the horseshoe shaped bay.

NTOG

This is in the Town Hall building (*Tmr* 18.B3). Unusually its value is limited to making available a handful of leaflets laid out on a small table inside the door.

OPENING HOURS
Strictly traditional.

OTE (*Tmr* 24.C4)
On the bottom left-hand side of the Main Square.

PLACES OF INTEREST
Archaeological Museum (*Tmr* 20.D5)
Odhos An Kallinikou, which is parallel to the quayside road and one back. It has been closed for some 18 months whilst being refurbished.
The Cathedral (*Tmr* 14.E5)
Turn right away from the bay, beyond the *Hotel Mendor* (*Tmr* 4.D/E4) and on Eugeniou Karavia St (which leads via Old Vathi to Sarakiniko Beach).
N. Lazareto Island (*Tmr* B1)
A rather incongruous, tiny islet, set in the harbour bay. Once a prison it is floodlit at night. I have an itch that Byron is reputed to have taken a daily constitutional swim there and back whilst staying on Ithaca.

POLICE
Port (*Tmr* 21.C4)
Beside the Customs House, which is built on the jetty that juts out into the harbour to the north end of the Main Square.
Tourist (*Tmr* 22.D5)
Turn along the road leading off Odhos An Kallinikou, beside the Museum and 400 m up on the right.
Town (*Tmr* 23.C6)
On Evmeou St.

POST OFFICE (*Tmr* 16.C4)
In the street off the bottom, left-hand corner of the main square.

TELEPHONE NUMBERS & ADDRESSES
Police   Tel. 32205

TAXIS
An excellent service with sharing as the order of the day.

Several ranks including one alongside the Agencia Centrale (*Tmr* 2.B3) close by the ferry berth, and another on the quay road, in front of the chemist shop (*Tmr* C4).

Many taxi drivers park up by the cafe bars lining the Main Square and while away some of the day at one or the other of the 'watering holes'. Certainly the taxi driver from Stavros 'camps' up here.

TOILETS
A clean public lavatory (*Tmr* 25.C4) at the end of the row of offices occupied by the Customs and Port police on the north side of the main square, Plateia Elastathiou Dracouli.

TRAVEL AGENTS
See **Ferry-Boat Ticket Offices.**

EXCURSIONS TO VATHI TOWN SURROUNDS
Excursion to Sarakiniko Bay (4 km)
Leave Vathi by turning right beyond the *Hotel Mendor* (*Tmr* 4.D4), past the Cathedral and along Odhos Eugeniou Karavia on up the winding lane, which is lined with very pretty

cottages. After the church, fork left and keep left at the chapel (numbered 1052). On the summit of the hill, immediately after the chapel, bear left (not on up the mountain), start down the unmade road and follow this (past a goat track to the nearside bay), to the far, fine bay. This has been occupied by a self-supporting community of young Germans who cultivated part of the valley. The other bay is reached by scrambling over the rocks on the foreshore or cutting down the unmarked goat track halfway down the unmade road. Both are pretty but the stony foreshore of the nearside cove is rather dirty, sprinkled with tar and the clear sea has a trifling sheen of fuel on the water's surface. (GROC Rating 5/10).

A far more delightful beach — and possibly the best on the island, lies on the other side of Cape Sarakiniko. To get there proceed along the newly widened track which heads off to the left of the main track, about 500 metres before reaching the far bay as detailed above. This climbs up over the hillside before dropping steeply down to a beautiful cove with a lovely, white shingle beach (GROC Rating 8/10). The ruins of a farmhouse and a now overgrown Olive grove lie behind the beach. All in all, a very pleasant setting to while away a few hours and well worth the 30 minutes walk from Vathi Town.

Excursion to Arethusa's Fountain and Ravens Crag (5 km)
Both have strong Homeric connections and are reached by leaving Vathi Town past the Hospital (*Tmr* 19.C6) and forking left. The route is signposted, but the unsurfaced road deteriorates into a rather bad track. It is a long but delightful walk.

Excursion to Perachori Village (2 km), Palarokhora and Taxiarkhis Monastiri (Monastery) (4½ km)
After the hospital, fork right for Perachori village which has two restaurants and some rooms to let. Beyond the village, to the south, the paths wind up through the terraced Olive trees to the Monastery and the island's ancient capital, the abandoned hamlet of Palarokhora dating back to 1500 BC. The track is initially signposted, but it becomes a question of following one's nose. The actual remains are rather disappointing but the views of the harbour and Vathi Town are quite magnificent.

ROUTE ONE
To Kioni via Stavros (24 km)
The main road to the north of the island sets off, leaving the bay's edge and climbing up over a hillside. The road is very dramatic, breathtakingly beautiful and initially runs along the sea's edge of the Gulf of Molos which almost separates the north from the south of the island by its bold intrusion. The route climbs on to a spine and for a short length of the isthmus seems to tightrope between the sea on both left and right. The Gulf of Molos usually contains two or three tankers laid up and floating at anchor in the startlingly clear seas. From here the road hangs to the mountain side all the way to Stavros. But that is rather leaping ahead.

Shortly after reaching a small and shingly beach (GROC Rating 5/10), at the bottom of the Gulf, a turning to the left after 1½ km leads to

THE CAVE OF THE NYMPHS (4 km from Vathi Town)
Another 'Homeric' connection (naturally) has been made with this narrow entranced, once dim cave into which lights were installed in the Autumn of 1984. The cave is normally kept locked, except during the high season, when there is an attendant on duty during the daytime. At all other times a key can be obtained from Vathi Town Hall.

Back on the main road, almost immediately (2½ km), the route circumnavigates the small horseshoe Bay of Dexia, which is believed to be that of **Phorkys**, where Odysseus was landed by the Phoenicians. Whatever, the sea of the bay is beautifully clear.

Prior to reaching the narrow neck of land connecting north and south to the island, there is a turning off to the left leading to

MOUNT AETOS & PISO AETOS (7 km from Vathi Town)

Aetos is the Greek word for 'eagle' and Ithaca is host to eagles as a nesting bird. On the side of Mount Aetos are the remains of an ancient city and below, to the south-west side of the mountain, the road leads down to the tiny, one-time port of Piso Aetos. Just off to the right is a narrow path to a small, shingle beach (GROC Rating 6/10).

Back on the main road to Stavros, a side turning to the left leads to the village of

AGIOS IOANNIS (11 km from Vathi Town)

From whence a short ramble descends to a series of shingly beaches and a further track proceeds in a loop back on to the main road at Lefki.

Almost immediately after the first turning to Agios Ioannis, a secondary road takes off to the right. This circuitously wanders around the sympathetically rebuilt Monastery of Kathara, with a wide arc of splendid views, on through the village of Anogi and rejoins the main road in the village of Stavros. However this is a walking route since the track is too steep for a scooter.

Back on the main road, the sprawling and extensively rebuilt village of Lefki (14 km from Vathi Town) is the only settlement prior to reaching

STAVROS (17 km from Vathi Town)

The village is really a wide main street with a small top section in the shape of a T. The main square is formed by the area in the way of the junction of the two roads. It has a church on one side and a rather ugly, sprawling, but extremely friendly taverna on the other side, the tables of which are strewn around part of the square. The rustic taverna has some simple, 'provincial' **Rooms** available. So long as you have a drink or two, bags and back-packs may be left in the taverna owner's care which saves lugging baggage about all day.

Just beyond the church, and on the same side, there is a small cafe where it is possible to enjoy an enormous bowl of delicious home-made vegetable soup served with hunks of fresh bread, slices of raw onion and a dish of olives — all for 120 drs. This is a true artisans cafe where the 'locals' break their day. The atmosphere is that of rural Devon and it is not impossible to imagine the little, grey haired lady who serves, appearing with a jug or two of cider!

The inhabitants emanate a welcoming and good-humoured ambience, but the village cannot be termed pretty. In fact it is a rather curious place with a small and pathetic public garden on the wall of which a mural has been painted. Some of the once earthquake-shattered dwellings have been rebuilt as ugly, concrete boxes, one of which, as if to confirm its unattractiveness, is painted a lurid green. There are the usual shops and, perhaps not surprisingly considering the number of the citizens who have lived and worked in Australia or America, a few English signs and notices in the neighbourhood. These include **Grocery** shop, two 40 gallon drums on the Polis Bay quay neatly labelled **Rubbish** and **The White House** in nearby Frikes.

Hard by the church, a path leads up into the hillsides, whereon are some ruins, a Martello tower and a magnificent view of the mountain range opposite, on the very top of which some demented fellows of yore built an indefinable and ancient structure.

If the bus is not functioning, an excellent taxi service runs to Vathi Town at least once a day.

Any or all enquiries will be volubly answered at the aforementioned taverna, which is conveniently sited at the top of the twisting and very steep road, up from

POLIS BAY (18¼ km from Vathi Town)

Apart from the interest of its inevitable Homeric connections, a supposedly sunken city and an erstwhile cave to the north of the bay, the quay and its finger pier are used by a small fleet of fishing benzinas and caiques. It may well be that a traveller will use the *ad hoc* caique and trip-boat service between here and Fiscardon on Cephalonia. The beach is shingly and unremarkable (GROC Rating 5/10).

From Stavros there is a choice of route to Frikes port. The high road leads to the village of Exogi and on to the impressive ruins of the School of Homer, a popular place of pilgrimage during the summer months, and the path to which is well trodden. Nearby is the Spring of Kalamos below which lies a simple, shingle beach (GROC Rating 6/10).

The low road makes for a very pleasant walk down the well cultivated and tree filled valley to the village and surprisingly extensive port of

FRIKES (19½ km from Vathi Town)

The walk can be enlivened by conversing with the occasional elderly Greek gentleman passed on the way down the valley. One who stopped for a chat (carried out in perfect Australian), had left Ithaca when he was 12 to live in the southern hemisphere for 62 years, only returning home when his parents died. Incidentally, the property settlement with his four brothers was made on the 'different length of straw' method. I imaging many a Greek family would prefer this sudden death but marvellously simple method of settling an inheritance compared to the usual tortuous state of affairs resulting for the antiquated inheritance laws. The all too evident, once solid but crumbling ruins located in prime positions, substantiate the enormous complexities of Greek property law.

The pretty village of Frikes spreads up the valley from a small square with the sea framed by the surrounding hillsides. The foreshore spreads out and the larger part of the village is to the left. Centre stage are some welcoming cafe tables belonging to the taverna across the road. This port has been 'breached' by a villa holiday company and, although very polite, leisure activities now include outboard engined dinghies for hire and a Sailing Centre. Very Greek!

The coast road wanders around a bluff to the right, past the substantial port quay and, once around the headland, the snake-like, hill-hugging route borders the sea. There are steps down from the roadside to some little white pebbled coves (GROC Rating 6/10). Beyond a cleanish, but barren, small horseshoe cove, a very large bay comes into view after rounding a truncated Martello tower as does the upper part of Kioni village. Surprisingly, the road and the hillside are rather unattractive, being stony and bare of any vegetation.

KIONI (24 km from Vathi Town)

The oldest and most attractive part of Kioni is set up on the hilltop shared with the now defunct windmills. They overlook the port and the village snakes down the hillside, to the water's edge. There are rooms to let, a baker, a general store and, naturally, several tavernas and a Kafenion. The reasonable communications with the rest of the island ensure that Kioni is a very pleasant resort for a stopover despite (depending of course on one's viewpoint) having been discovered by a Villa Company. It must be stressed this is a less intrusive form of invasion than most other outbreaks of organised tourism.

There are two very small beaches to the right and to the left, backed by a graveyard, there is a pleasant, if small, pebble beach (GROC Rating 7/10).

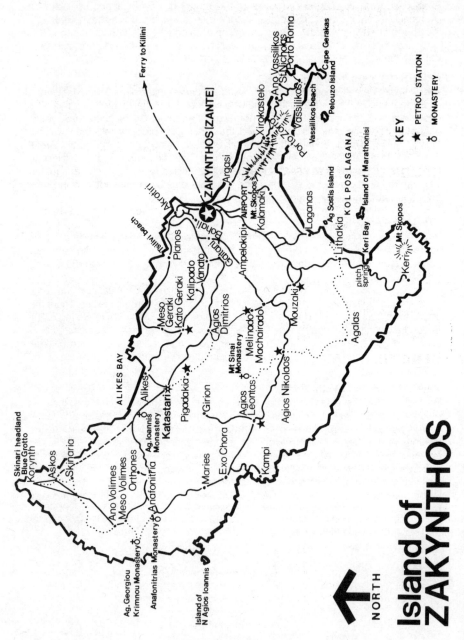

Twenty-three   Zakynthos island map

17 Zakynthos (Zante, Zakinthos) Ionian Islands

FIRST IMPRESSIONS
English country lanes and fertile plains; snakes; motor bikes; friendly people; dramatic views.

SPECIALITIES
Mandolato nougat; pasteli — a sesame and honey biscuit; perfumes.

RELIGIOUS HOLIDAYS & FESTIVALS
include: (The whole) Easter weekend, Zakynthos Town; 24th August and 17th December — Feast of St Dionysios, Zakynthos Town.

VITAL STATISTICS
Tel. prefix 0695. The island is about 27 km wide, and 38 km long with some 31,000 residents, of which 9,500 live in Zakynthos Town.

HISTORY
The islands name dates back to Homer, the Venetians coining the alternative Zante. Unusually the island was not occupied by the Turks, apart from a few years in the 1480s, the Venetians almost hanging on until the British assumed overall responsibility, between 1809 - 1864. The islands great artistic traditions were reinforced by Cretans fleeing the Turkish invasion of their island in 1669.

GENERAL
Overall, possibly one of the most attractive of the Ionian chain. The splendid mix of countryside, beaches, sympathetic rebuilding after the earthquake of 1953 and lack of (as yet) outright tour-operator exploitation, combine to make this a delightful island.

It is geographically divided by a mountainous range, running from the north-west to the south-east corners. The diagonal west coast, which runs parallel to the spine of the hills, descends very steeply into the sea. Almost all the rest of the island is a large fertile plain. The roads and countryside of Zakynthos are, in the main, very lovely and rather reminiscent of England, with hedgerowed fields, orchards of trees (even if they are Olives, Cypresses, Orange trees and Pines), tree-topped hills, green-clad slopes and winding lanes.

When planning any journey bear in mind that a number of roads shown on some of the official maps are only in the cartographer's mind. I stress that the maps in this volume do not repeat the referred-to errors.

The people of Zakynthos are extremely friendly and welcoming which helps make this lovely island a great joy to visit.

My mention of snakes under **First Impressions** should possibly be quantified, more especially as a lady reader contacted me last year to expand on the subject. Certainly in the remote countryside they are more noticeable than on the other Ionian islands but I can assure readers that any snakes encountered are more interested in getting out of the way than hanging around. On the other hand care should be taken when sitting down on country lane stone walls.

ZAKYNTHOS: capital and main port
Very extensively damaged by the 1953 earthquake, the citizens preferred reconstruction

to take place along the lines of the previous municipality, rather than have a grid and modular layout imposed on them. To realise how sympathetically much of this has been carried out, we need only compare the rebuilt Zakynthos Town with Argostoli (Cephalonia). Certainly the town has an air of vigorous commerce and prosperity.

Much of the old-town feel of the back streets, which throb with activity late into the evening, has been kept with the architecturally attractive, colonnaded arcade style retained. In contrast the harbour road of Lombardou, as well as Plateia Solomou, Vassileos Georgiou B and Plateia Ag Markou all at the north end of the town, have benefited from a spacious, imaginative, if rather disconnected redevelopment.

The official town maps are often inaccurate, as are the island roads which are not, repeat not as shown. The town maps usually show various areas as open space that have now been built on and very little of the harbour promenade is not developed.

ARRIVAL BY AIR
The airport is located close by Ampelokipi, some 7 km from Zakynthos Town.

Over the years the facility has been extended and by 1985 the work necessary to extend the runway to take the larger jumbo jets should be (unfortunately) complete. The old days of 2 or 3 internal flights a week has been overtaken by progress(!) and now there is not only a daily connection with Athens but several international charter flights every 24 hours.

ARRIVAL BY BUS
The Athens bus arrives via the mainland port of Killini (*See* **Chapter 10**).

ARRIVAL BY FERRY
One of the reasons for the lack of mass tourist exploitation of the island is that Zakynthos is not the easiest of the islands to reach by ferry-boat, unlike say Corfu or Cephalonia. In fact the island can only be reached from the rather fly-blown, scruffy little Killini on the Peloponnese mainland.

The ferries moor up stern-on to the main marine parade, Lombardou or Strata Marine (*Tmr* 1.B/C3/4). The town stretches out to left and right in a narrow coastal strip with the main squares, municipal and official buildings to the right as is the harbour finger quay.

THE ACCOMMODATION & EATING OUT
The Accommodation
Plenty of rooms 'offered' on arrival at between 600 - 700 drs per night. Unusually for a port of this size there are only two quayside hotels for late arrivals.

Strada Marina Hotel (*Tmr* 3.B3) (Class B) 14 Lombardou   Tel. 22761
Directions: Just to the right facing the town. Pricey with a low season double room costing from 1500 drs.

Hotel Aegli (*Tmr* 3.B3) (Class C) 1 Anast Loutzi/12 Lombardou   Tel. 28317
Directions: On the corner of the two streets, at the far end of the block in which the *Hotel Strada* is located.
A double room en suite costs from 1350 drs.

Xenia Hotel (*Tmr* 4.B/C3) (Class B) 60 Dionissiou Roma   Tel. 22232
Directions: From the ferry-boat quay turn right along the Esplanade road, past the finger pier, across Plateia Solomou and on the left.
Not inexpensive with a low season double room costing about 1800 drs.

As is always the case, or almost always, the further from the quay front, the more reasonably priced accommodation becomes.

Striking out from the harbour, preferably up Dalvani St, leads to the main street of Alex Roma. To the right on the opposite side of the road is the

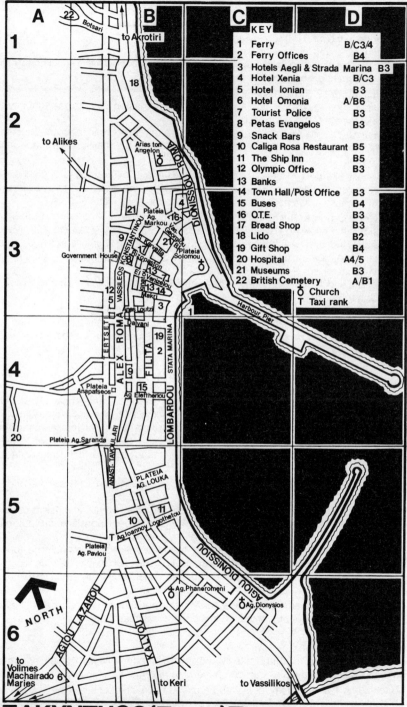

KEY

1	Ferry	B/C3/4
2	Ferry Offices	B4
3	Hotels Aegli & Strada Marina	B3
4	Hotel Xenia	B/C3
5	Hotel Ionian	B3
6	Hotel Omonia	A/B6
7	Tourist Police	B3
8	Petas Evangelos	B3
9	Snack Bars	
10	Caliga Rosa Restaurant	B5
11	The Ship Inn	B5
12	Olympic Office	B3
13	Banks	
14	Town Hall/Post Office	B3
15	Buses	B4
16	O.T.E.	B3
17	Bread Shop	B3
18	Lido	B2
19	Gift Shop	B4
20	Hospital	A4/5
21	Museums	B3
22	British Cemetery	A/B1

Ŏ Church
T Taxi rank

ZAKYNTHOS (Zante) Town

Twenty-four   Zakynthos Town & port plan

Hotel Ionian (*Tmr* 5.B3) (Class D) 18 Alex Roma   Tel. 22511
Directions: As above.
   The owners would appear to own the art and craft shop below this small hotel, which offers accommodation from 960 drs for a double room.
Village Room 12 Rizospaston
Directions: North towards Plateia Ag Markou and Rizospaston St is off to the right, beyond the Government House (*Tmr* 23.B3).
   The proprietor Tasis Pomonis charges 500 drs a day for a single room and welcomes guests with a coffee. A double from 600 drs. The shower/toilet facility is in a shack on the terrace roof.
South back along Alex Roma St (which becomes Anast Tavoulari St) to where the road forks at Plateia Ag Pavlou and the area encompassed by the streets of Agiou Lazarou and Kalvou contains a number of small hotels and rooms to let including:-
The Hotel Omonia (*Tmr* 6.A/B6) (Class D) 4 Xantopoulou   Tel. 22113
Directions: At Plateia Ag Pavlou fork right and proceed up Agiou Lazarou. This street is moderately industrial with houses knocked in warehouses, a flour mill, and innumerable scooter, motorbike and car repair shops. Turn left down the slightly uneven Xantopoulou St and the hotel is half-way down on the right.
   Christina and Xenoy Zhnoy run a very clean, pleasant establishment charging 1200 for a double room.
   Note that the Tourist police officer, who speaks excellent English and whose office (*Tmr* 7.B3) appears to only open between 0830/1030 and 1200 hrs, has a list of **Rooms** (and buses), and admits he prefers to advise females, so remember to send the girls. *See* **Police, A to Z.**

The Eating Out
Strangely wanting are 'middle-of-the-road' tavernas and restaurants. There are two rather smart restaurants on the edge of Plateia Ag Markou, with menus in neon-lit display cabinets, enough said. To compensate for this, there are a number of excellent snack-bars doing a roaring trade, as well as the to-be-expected cafe-bars, and, at the Town Hall (*Tmr* 14.B3) end of the marine front, a number of restaurants serving everything from coffee to a full-blown meal.
   An acceptable restaurant is
Petas Evangelos (*Tmr* 8.B3)
Directions: Situated at the northern end of Alex Roma Street (which changes its name for some inexplicable reason at this point to 21st May or Vassileos Konstantinou(!), take your choice), on the right-hand side prior to the Plateia Ag Markou.
   The head waiter, Denis, hurtles around the tables like a whirlwind. The food is comparatively expensive but good. A taramosalata, pork kebab, Greek salad, bread, ½ bottle Demestica and coffee costs about 600 drs for one. Denis is also a source of helpful information.
Still proceeding towards the Plateia Ag Markou and on the left-hand side, beyond Government House, is one of the recommended, reasonably priced
Snackbar's (*Tmr* 9.B3)
Directions: As above.
   Serving souvlakis, a range of take-away Greek snacks and a limited menu. Bench seats and wooden-topped tables outside on the wide pavement.
Back along the very pretty, quaint and arcaded main street of Alex Roma, away from Plateia Ag Markou, and another excellent, crowded and inexpensive snack bar is located on the left-hand side of the road.

'Chip' Snackbar (*Tmr* 9.B4)
Directions: As above.
A rare sight. An island 'chippy', but very Greek in character with a restricted menu and a selection of take-away snacks. Hardly a tourist in sight, but both snackbars are extremely well patronised by locals, which can only auger well for quality and price. Tzatziki and bread, 3 souvlaki pita with salad, coffee, ½ litre retsina costs 200 drs.

From the south end of Lombardou Esplanade turn up Ag Ioannoy Logothetou towards Plateia Ag Pavlou and on the right hand side is an excellent open air restaurant.

Caliga Rosa Restaurant (*Tmr* 10.B5)
Directions: As above.
The prices mirror those of the *Petas Evangelos* and there is live Greek music on Friday and Saturday evenings. Occasionally local talent competitions are held but Greek singing is an acquired taste at the best of times and on our last visit a young man succeeded in doing to the Greek song what Annie Bordon did to her mother! In fact, he was so bad that it was hysterically funny and even the band were forced to stop playing on a couple of occasions, they were laughing so much.

Incidentally, the food for the restaurant is prepared in a little taverna across the road and 'Mama', the proprietress, sits at a table just inside and notes down each meal order in a large black ledger— presumably to ensure that the taverna owner does not try to pull a fast one on her. The spit-roasted lamb is particularly tasty.

At the Esplanade end of Ag Ioannoy Logothetou, on the junction with the harbour road and adjacent to the Shell petrol station, is

The Ship Inn (*Tmr* 11.B5)
Directions: As above.
Run by Jiannis and his pretty English wife Leslie. Unlike most Greek island 'Pubs', this is not packed with beer swilling, inebriated tourists (the old prejudices will show through. . .) but is a delightful little bar with a friendly atmosphere and a dart board. The young couple literally built the bar themselves, converting it from a run-down cafe. Besides serving excellent drinks at reasonable prices they are an excellent source of information and helpful advice.

In and around Plateia Ag Pavlou (*Tmr* B5) there are several small souvlaki establishments offering a limited menu. All are well patronised by locals, being a bit out of the way for the average tourist, which augers well for both price and quality.

THE A TO Z OF USEFUL INFORMATION
AIRLINE OFFICE & TERMINUS (*Tmr* 12.B3)
The Olympic office is on Alex Roma, alongside the *Hotel Ionian*. The usual airport bus at 45 drs.

Aircraft timetable
Zakynthos to Athens
Up to 22nd June

Tuesday, Thursday & Saturday	0825 hrs (1 stop)
Monday, Wednesday & Sunday	0925 hrs
Friday	1505 hrs

From 23rd June

Monday, Tuesday, Wednesday & Sunday	1210 hrs
Friday	1715 hrs

One-way fare 2390 drs, duration (non-stop) 45 mins

Return journey
Up to 22nd June

Monday, Wednesday & Sunday	0700 hrs (1 stop)

| Tuesday, Thursday & Saturday | 0700 hrs |
| Friday | 1550 hrs (1 stop) |

From 23rd June

| Monday, Tuesday, Wednesday & Sunday | 1045 hrs |
| Friday | 1550 hrs |

Zakynthos to Cephalonia
Only up to 22nd June

| Tuesday, Thursday & Saturday | 0825 hrs |

One-way fare 700 drs, duration 20 minutes

Return journey
Only up to 22nd June

| Monday, Wednesday & Sunday | 0825 hrs |
| Friday | 1405 hrs |

BANKS (*Tmr* 13)
In the main, gathered together in the 'Municipal' area (*Tmr* B3), just off the Esplanade road and flanked by Plateia Solomou, Rizospaston, Makri and Ignatou Streets. In the blocks encompassed within these confines are the Town Hall, Post Office, Customs, Tourist police and Information offices.

BEACHES
The town beaches and foreshore are at the north and south end of Town. The northern end is rather drab with a stony foreshore, whilst the southern end is signposted *Zante Beach and Bungalows*, which appears promising. Forget it! The referred-to beach and bungalows are between four and six km out of town and have to be reached by passing through a dusty 'Soweto' type slum of stone bungalows bordering a boulderous sea-shore.

To the north of the town, on Dionissiou Roma, a continuation of the Esplanade road, there is a NTOG lido complex (*Tmr* 18.B2) with swimming, tennis courts and changing rooms in a setting of lawns and flower beds.

BICYCLE, SCOOTER & CAR HIRE
A number of reputable and convenient establishments trade in the area of Vassileos Georgiou B, Plateia Ag Marko and Vassileos Konstantinou St (*Tmr* B3).

Faros Rentals, (*Tmr* B3) Anas Loutzi
Well recommended and located behind the *Hotels Aegli* and *Strada*.

Scooter hire costs an average of 600 drs per day, a large moped 300 drs and a bicycle 150 drs. Car hire as elsewhere is expensive; even the cheapest vehicle — a 2CV Jeep, costs from 2,600 drs per day including local tax but do not forget the large daily damage deposit.

Although there are now more petrol stations throughout the island than a few years ago, it is still prudent to fill up a powered two wheeled conveyance when possible, especially if venturing to the northern extremities of the island. Added to this the inaccuracies of some maps, combined with running short of the necessary propulsive agent, could cause much pushing and frustration and a long walk.

BOAT HIRE
Motor boats are available for hire from the south end of the harbour. Costs range between 4,000 and 6,000 drs per day.

BOOKSELLER
No particular specialist shop, only the usual scattering of tourist postcards and guide books.

BREAD SHOPS
Bread shops, as is often the case, are a little difficult to locate but there is one 200 to

300 m beyond the *Hotel Ionian* (*Tmr* 5.B3) going south on the right-side of Odhos Alex Roma. The 'best buy' is a corner shop situated on Rizospaston St (*Tmr* 17.B3).

BUSES
A rather sparse service which definitely hides its light under a bushel, the schedules being very difficult to locate. The depot is on the junction of Filita and Ag Eleftheriou St (*Tmr* 15.B4).

Bus timetables
Local services
The following may well be incomplete, but can be taken as a guide.

Zakynthos Town to Volimes
Daily   0500, 1300, 2000 hrs

Zakynthos Town to Alikes
Daily   0730, 1200, 1600 hrs

Zakynthos Town to Agios Leontas
Daily   0500, 1400 hrs

Zakynthos Town to Machairado
Daily   0700, 1100, 1400 hrs

Zakynthos Town to Vassilikos
Daily   0700, 1400 hrs

Mainland Services
A service links Athens and Zakynthos using the Killini ferry route and there is a pick up point at Patras by the railway station.

Athens Kratinou & Kifissou Sts   Tel. 5129432
Daily   0830, 1200, 1530 hrs

Return journey
Daily   0800, 1200, 1600 hrs
One-way fare (including the ferry-boat) 1200 drs, duration 7 hrs.

Patras to Zakynthos
Daily   0915*, 1445 hrs
One-way fare 600 drs, duration 2½ hrs
*This bus connects with the 1200 ferry to Zakynthos which docks at about 1315 hrs, in plenty of time to find accommodation. The later bus necessitates a wait for the 1800 hrs ferry at Killini — and arrival at Zakynthos at around 1915 hrs when it can prove difficult to find accommodation, especially at the height of the season.

CHEMISTS
See **Medical Care.**

COMMERCIAL SHOPPING AREA
There is no particular concentration of commercial shopping or a market, more scattered clusterings of fish, vegetable and fruit stalls and shops, including those located in El Venizelou St (*Tmr* B3), Plateia Ag Saranda (*Tmr* B4/5) and Plateia Ag Pavlou (*Tmr* B5).

There is a European style supermarket on the Esplanade, most un-Greek and out of place.

A useful source of information is a young (and pretty) Greek girl, who speaks perfect Australian and works as an assistant in the large gift shop (*Tmr* 19.B4) on Lombardou Esplanade, close by the ferry-boat ticket offfice.

FERRY-BOATS
Arrive and depart from the harbour at the north end of the marine esplanade (*Tmr* 1.B/C3/ 4). Killini is the only mainland port of connection (*See* **Hydrofoils**).

Ferry-boat timetables
Mid-summer
Killini - Zakynthos
Daily   0800, 1000, 1200, 1400, 1600, 1800, 2000, 2200 hrs

Zakynthos - Killini
Daily   0600, 0800, 1000, 1200, 1400, 1600, 1800, 2000 hrs

Out of Season
Killini - Zakynthos
Daily   1030, 1430, 1800 hrs

Zakynthos - Killini
Daily   0830, 1230, 1600 hrs
One-way fare 345 drs, duration 1¼ hrs.

FERRY-BOAT TICKET OFFICES (*Tmr* 2.B4)
A small kiosk on the left side of the quay (facing north towards the ferry-boat dock) and there is a convenient taverna nearby.

HYDROFOILS (Flying Dolphins)
There used to be, during the high season, a hydrofoil service between Patras, on the mainland, and Zakynthos. It was of course commensurately more expensive than the ferry-boat, the one-way fare costing approximately 900 drs compared with about 350 drs. But whether it is still in operation is on a maybe basis, maybe it does, may be it doesn't . . .

HOSPITAL
See **Medical Care.**

LAUNDRY
Two establishments in Tertseti St.

MEDICAL CARE
Chemists & Pharmacies
Chemists need no pinpointing, as they are plentiful, especially along Odhos Alex Roma.

Hospital (*Tmr* 20.A4/5)
A large facility behind the town, on the white scarred hillside.

Incidentally the town is encircled by a hill range, pitted with great white scars, possibly as a result of landslips caused by the fifteenth century earthquake.

NTOG
None. *See* **Tourist police.**

OTE (*Tmr* 16.B3)
To the right of Vassileos Georgiou B St, walking up from Plateia Solomou. Open daily 0700 - 2400 hrs.

PETROL
There are several petrol stations on the marine Esplanade in the area of the ferry-boat quay, another on the junction of Ag Ioannoy Logothetou with the Esplanade and a station at the junction of Odhos Kalvou and Ag Lazarou on Plateia Ag Pavlou.

PHARMACY
See **Medical Care.**

PLACES OF INTEREST
Museums
One on the edge of Plateia Solomou (*Tmr* 21.B3), at the junction with Vassileos Georgiou

B. Displays of Ionian art and some splendid icons from various island churches.

The other museum (*Tmr* 21.B3) is in the next square of Plateia Ag Markou and is dedicated and named after the famous Zakynthos poet, one Dionysos Solomos. It also exhibits the works of two other famous island poets, Andreas Kalvos and Ugo Foskolo, as well as the legacies of some noble Zantiot families.

Churches and Cathedrals
A number of the town's churches are noteworthy including, at the southern end, the distinctive tower or campanile of

Agios Dionysios (Tmr C6)
It is dedicated to the patron saint of the island — whose embalmed remains can be viewed by request to the priest. It is claimed that the Saint's slippers have to be changed several times a year because he is alleged to rise from his coffin at night and walk about the island doing good works (well, yes).

Church of Phaneromeni (Tmr B6)
Nearby, and to the west is the church that was the island's finest prior to the 1953 catastrophe after which it was sympathetically rebuilt.

Kirias ton Angelon (Tmr B2)
This very pretty church is located by following Dionissiou Roma around the seafront and turning up Archiepiskopou Kokkini.

The Venetian Castle
More accurately, the remains of the old fortress reached through the village of Bohali (Bokhali) from whence there are magnificent views of the Town, much of the island, the Zante Channel and the Peloponnese.

British Cemetery (*Tmr* 22.A/B1)
As with other Ionian islands there is a British cemetery, dumbly lying witness to the years during which Great Britain administered the Ionian island protectorate. It is situated adjacent to the ruins of the Church of Agios Ioannis at the north end of the Town along Dionissiou Roma, past the Lido and up Botsari St.

POLICE
Tourist (*Tmr* 7.B3)
Customs House in the 'Municipal' area on the Esplanade, south of the harbour finger quay and Plateia Solomou. Go through the entrance arch of the building and turn to the right. *See* **Accommodation** for further notes.

POST OFFICE (*Tmr* 14.B3)
In Makri St, just off the Esplanade, in the 'Municipal' quarter, alongside the Customs and Tourist police offices.

TAXIS
Two main ranks, one between the Town Hall and the Tourist police office in El Venizelou St (*Tmr* B3) and the other on Plateia Ag Pavlou (*Tmr* B5).

TELEPHONE NUMBERS & ADDRESSES
Customs	Tel. 22322
Hospital	Tel. 22514
Taxi Rank (Plateia Ag Pavlou)	Tel. 28261
Tourist Police	Tel. 22550

TRAVEL AGENTS
A sprinkling of offices on Lombardou Esplanade. Tours include tickets for the excursion boat 'Delfini', which operates trips to the 'Blue Grotto', adjacent to the Skinari headland at the north-western tip of the island.

ROUTE ONE
To Vassilikos (15 km)
South-east from Zakynthos Town, a road leads through lovely countryside still basically unspoilt and undeveloped, via the village of

ARGASI (6.5 km from Zakynthos Town)
Subject to some villa development and two hotels which package holiday firms have taken over. There are also a couple of discos to cater for tourists. Beaches are very narrow (GROC Rating 6/10). On the hill beyond Argasi, there is a nice little taverna, just the place for an evening drink, looking out over Zakynthos.

The road commences to skirt Mt Skopos and further along the coast, through Xirokastelo, there is a turning off to

PORTO ZORRO
Sounds rather as if it should feature in a Spaghetti Western. A very steep access to a pleasant beach (GROC Rating 8/10) complete with a taverna.

Continuing through Ano Vassilikos, a turning to the left leads to the beach at

ST NICHOLAS (GROC Rating 8/10)
Fortunately(!) the inevitable taverna. Apartment development is taking place at the top of the track behind which there is a scruffy, dirty beach.

Straight on leads to Vassilikos and left to

PORTO ROMA
Here there is a nice, if a rather narrow beach (GROC Rating 7/10) and a taverna alongside the foreshore with a vine hung trellis. One kalamari, one spaghetti, two salads, 2 beers and bread costs about 600 drs.

The road on through the village of Vassilikos becomes a dusty track, but quite driveable, (with care), to the beautiful

VASSILIKOS BEACH
Golden sand (GROC Rating 9/10) set in a clean bay and possibly the best beach on Zakynthos. The taverna at the top offers free camping. Beer, coffee and drinks are dispensed from a small, wooden shack and at the south end of the beach nude bathing is the order of the day. Unfortunately pedaloes and canoe hire is creeping in and *Club Med* wanted to build a complex. Thank goodness, they were turned down by the local authorities principally because the beach is a favoured spot for sea turtles to lay their eggs at the appropriate time of year.

To the right leads to a bluff with views over the Gulf of Lagana with the small islet of N Pelouzo in the foreground, N Marathonisi island in the distant background set against a backcloth of Mt Skopos (that is the Keri Mt Skopos) and the headland it forms.

ROUTE TWO
To Keri (21 km)
Once again south-east of the Town. A turning off to the left leads to the widespread hamlet of

KALAMAKI (7 km from Zakynthos Town)
Technically at the far eastern end of Laganas beach. From the village a track leads down to an almost unfrequented beach, set in a superb, once deserted bay, but now a hotel has been completed and others are under construction. . .

Back on the main road and immediately after the Kalamaki turning, the airport is passed on the left-hand side. Well, that is it would appear to be there, although some maps detail it as some miles further on, in a swamp. Perhaps there has been some recent local movement of the earth's crust!

There is a turning off to the left, signposted for Laganas, which cuts off a small corner. Further on, another left-hand turn is the usual route leading straight and level across the fertile plain, past the occasional small thatched huts on stilts. The peasants used to rest up in these in days gone by, but now they are almost lost in amongst the fairly thickly scattered modern-day villas which line the roadside. These houses all appear to have *Rooms* for let and it would be quite possible to land at Zakynthos Town, head straight for this area and rent a room or rooms.

LAGANAS (10 km from Zakynthos Town)
The narrow, hardpacked, slate-coloured, sandy, sloping shore (GROC Rating 6/10) stretches away to the left and is covered with sunbathing tourists during daylight hours. The beach has to be used as an access or promenade road as the hotels spill right on to the edge of the foreshore. The colour of the beach tends to give the location a rather scrubbly, grubby look. To the right the bay curves quickly around to a small headland, at the end of which is the islet of N Ag Sostis.

Back on the main road, the thoroughfare winds on towards Keri. A signposted lane off to the left leads down to

ORMOS KERIOU or LAKE KERI (18 km from Zakynthos Town)
Since time immemorial, a natural phenomenon has resulted in a number of springs giving forth pitch. For many centuries fishermen caulked their craft, using these petroleum by-product.

Three kilometres on is

KERI (21 km from Zakynthos Town)
The village is situated on the most southerly headland of Zakynthos and nestles on the slopes of the 413 m mountain. This is the end of the range of hills which runs down and edges the western coastline.

A pretty village, Keri has some *Rooms* to let, a beach and a splendid church dating back to the seventeenth century. At the end of the village a rough track winds along the hillside to a lighthouse. Some maps indicate a beach here but unless you list abseiling amongst your pursuits you'll be out of luck if you want a swim, as it is only accessible by boat.

ROUTE THREE
To Planos a circular route via Kampi, Volimes, Korynth & Alikes
Take ROUTE TWO beyond the Laganas turnings as far as a signpost, off to the right to

LITHAKIA (15 km from Zakynthos Town)
Occasionally a surfaced road is inked in to Agalas village, but I deny the existence of any such form of thoroughfare — it is just a wide track.

AGALAS (19 km from Zakynthos Town)
There are some *Rooms* to let and from here the road winds on to the village of

AG NIKOLAOS (23 km from Zakynthos Town)
Again some maps make an error in showing the road between Agalas and Ag Nikolaos as surfaced. It is not, being in places nothing more than a wide donkey track, but a donkey track that meanders through lovely countryside. A main, and mercifully surfaced main, road is joined at Ag Nikolaos and **Petrol** is available.

From Ag Nikolaos via Agios Leontas (**Petrol**), the road passes through rather barren scenery to where a turning off to the left leads down and along a metalled road to the village of

KAMPI (32 km from Zakynthos Town)

From the dusty, quiet valley village of Kampi, a track winds up the hillside until it ends dramatically on the towering cliff heights, overlooking a beautiful bay, way down below. The crest is impossibly topped off with a giant concrete cross facing out to sea, and incongruously crowned by a lightning conductor.

There is a taverna set amongst Olive trees at the foot of the hill which boasts the most unusual Village **Room** on the island. It comprises a wattle hut of plaited branches measuring 2 m x 2 m and set on four stilts 2 m off the ground. The interior is taken up with a straw palliasse and access is by ladder, but what makes the 'room' quite out of the ordinary is that it is just 3 m from the cliff edge and a 160 m drop to the sea. Wonderful view but don't sleep-walk and pray there aren't any high winds during the night. Cost 400 drs per night. The local shepherd may well be found asleep behind the bar of the taverna, his shot gun and bandolier hanging from hooks beside the bar.

The main road progresses through attractive countryside and the villages of Exo Chora and Maries.

At Maries some maps show a surfaced road leading east over the hill, inland, to the village of Katastari. This road is in the mind of that particular cartographer only and lacks physical presence.

About 4 km further on is the large village of

ANAFONITRIA (40 km from Zakynthos Town)

In the vicinity are the monasteries of Anafonitrias and Ag Georgiou Krimnou. Anafonitrias Monastery, built in the fifteenth century, was extensively damaged by the 1953 earthquake, but what remains is well worth a visit.

The monastery of Ag Georgiou Krimnou can be reached from Anafonitrias, or Volimes, via a crude track along which it is just possible to manoeuvre a scooter, despite it being necessary to get off and push on occasions. The religious house, in excellent condition, is now occupied by a lone monk. It is worth taking the little path beyond the monastery out on to the headland from where there are magnificent if distant views of Cephalonia island. The fragrance of wild mint and thyme pervades everywhere in this wonderfully peaceful spot.

VOLIMES (45 km from Zakynthos Town, or 33 km by direct route)

Instead of returning to the main road at Anafonitria village, by following the continuation of the track from the monastery, it is possible to reach Meso Volimes but once again the track is in very bad condition in parts.

There is a new surfaced road from Meso Volimes to Ano Volimes, built on an extremely steep hillside, and another new, wide road to Korynth with a spur off to Askos. If desperate and a local is asked, petrol may well be made available.

On entering Korynth the turning to the right drops towards the sea. Halfway down, on the left, there is a taverna from whence operates a boat to the **Blue Grotto** during the tourist season. These natural phenomena are rather beautiful, the eroded sea caves being set in an irridescent azure sea, and they are probably worth a visit, if time allows.

The new coast road back to the junction with the old Zakynthos Town road, towards Alikes, may now be complete. The authorities are obviously planning to open up this stretch of the coast for development. Add to this the airport extensions and one can only fear the worst, that is that Zakynthos will slide down a sea of sun-oil towards Corfu's level of tourist saturation.

The drive back to Zakynthos Town from close by the village of Orthones on the old road, sweeps steeply downhill to Katastari, which is about 16 km from Zakynthos Town. On the road rounding the hillside bluff, above the large village of Katastari, a dramatic view is laid open of the great fertile plain of the north-west, heavily planted with Olive and Lemon trees, the coastline as well as panoramic views of the distant mainland. In the foreground large salt pans show up very clearly as does the seaside development of

ALIKES (16 km from Zakynthos Town)
A very pleasant beach (GROC Rating 8/10) is backed by sand dunes and a number of reasonably priced tavernas along the backshore. For example tzatzaki and bread cost 45 drs, a salad 65 drs, moussaka 165 drs, melon 60 drs, Coke 28 drs, a bottle of beer 57 drs and wine from 200 to 250 drs. A good beach for families and there are villas and **Rooms** for rent.

At Pigadakia there is a wayside **Petrol** station, as there is at Kato Geraki. From Meso Geraki a road leads towards the coast and then runs parallel to the shoreline at a distance of about half a kilometre. The area is heavily wooded so the sea is hidden.

PLANOS (7 km from Zakynthos Town)
There are plenty of **Rooms** to rent here at a cost of about 400-500 drs per night. Tracks lead down to Tsilivi Beach (GROC Rating 7/10), which is rather long and narrow but unspoilt and not a taverna in sight. In the area of the village there are three spur tracks with **Rooms** to let and that individually lead to sandy but narrow beaches.

The last has a rather unprepossessing looking inn, the *Hotel O Anethe*, at the track end.

Back on the main road, the last stretch of the road to Zakynthos Town, in the area of Akrotiri, is very lovely.

ROUTE FOUR
Inland Villages
The road system of the large plain to the west of Zakynthos Town radiates out rather like a drunken spider's web.

An excellent road advances to

MACHAIRADO (10 km from Zakynthos Town)
Here is a very interesting church with a beautiful interior, although the subject of extensive nineteenth century restoration. **Petrol** is available.

On the approach road from the direction of Mouzaki, there are fleeting glimpses of a stately home, a most unusual sight on the Greek islands. On closer inspection it appears that the 1953 earthquake substantially damaged the fabric of this once majestic dwelling and its outbuildings.

From Machairado the route west to Ag Nikolaos starts to climb the wide but hairpin bends of this spectacular drive, not unlike the Pennines or West Riding of Yorkshire.

INDEX

Artwork by Ted Spittles.
Typeset by: Barbara James, The Monitor Business Magazine.